Product Development
Performance

PRODUCT DEVELOPMENT PERFORMANCE

Strategy, Organization, and Management in the World Auto Industry

KIM B. CLARK   TAKAHIRO FUJIMOTO

HARVARD BUSINESS SCHOOL PRESS
BOSTON, MASSACHUSETTS

95   94   93   92   5   4   3   2

The recycled paper used in this publication meets the requirements of the American National
Standard for Permanence of Paper for Printed Library Materials Z39.49-1984.

Library of Congress Cataloging-in-Publication Data

Clark, Kim B.
    Product development performance: strategy, organization, and
management in the world auto industry / Kim B. Clark and Takahiro
Fujimoto.
    p.   cm.
Includes bibliographical references and index.
ISBN 0-87584-245-3 (alk. paper):
    1. Automobile industry and trade--Management. I. Fujimoto, Takahiro, 1955-   .
II. Title.
HD9710.A2C57   1991
629.2'068's--dc20   90-47967
                                                              CIP

We dedicate this book to the memory of William J. Abernathy. He started us down this path, and the quality, depth, and originality of his work on the auto industry has been our inspiration. He was our mentor, colleague, and friend. We have tried to write a book that would make him proud.

CONTENTS

PREFACE AND ACKNOWLEDGMENTS

This book is about the development of new products in a turbulent, demanding, and exciting environment: the world automobile industry. The work has taken shape over the past five years, but its roots go back even further. Our first collaborative research effort was a grueling three-week visit in the summer of 1981 to twenty-five automotive research laboratories, engineering departments, and manufacturing facilities in Japan. Working under the direction of the late Professor William Abernathy, we sought an understanding of the sources of superior performance in manufacturing quality and productivity, and of the dramatic changes in technology and competition sweeping through the industry in the early 1980s. Our field research with Professor Abernathy in Japan in 1981 played an important role in the development of the argument and evidence presented in *Industrial Renaissance,* published in 1983.

The work on *Industrial Renaissance* and subsequent field studies in Japan, Europe, and the United States convinced us of the central role that product development would play in the 1980s. The worldwide market was becoming more international and technology more diverse. Moreover, it appeared that an important part of the Japanese manufacturing advantage lay in the way products were designed and developed. These factors argued that effective development of new products was likely to be a critical dimension of competition and a source of advantage. We therefore made plans to study the effects of strategy, organization, and management on product development performance; by 1985, we had launched intensive field research.

It has been a fascinating experience. No one had ever been inside all of these companies at the same time or been granted such access to information about the inner workings of the product development process. The logistics were especially daunting: twenty companies in six countries on three continents; repeated, extensive visits; massive amounts of data. Our field work has been highly interactive. We not only developed information in the companies, but also returned to share preliminary insights and findings in presentations and discussions. Doing this would have been impossible without the cooperation of hundreds of people.

Many people from numerous disciplines and departments in the companies we studied gave of their time and experience, sharing valuable information in interviews, filling out questionnaires, and digging out old documents and reports. We promised people confidentiality, and for that reason (and because they are far too numerous) we cannot mention everyone by name, but we are grateful for their support.

Outside the companies there were several people who helped us find and interpret data. We are particularly indebted to: Shoichi Suita, Mikio Matsui, and colleagues at Mitsubishi Research Institute; Professor Koichi Shimokawa of Hosei University, who visited companies with us and generously advised us on the work; Yoshiro Ikari, freelance writer; Ryuji Fukuda and members of the Japan Association for Research on Automotive Affairs; Yu Okawa, former editor, *NAVI* magazine, and his associates.

Our research on product development evolved through a series of paper and seminar presentations, and we benefited greatly from the many comments and suggestions we received. Special thanks go to the Mitsubishi Bank Foundation for the opportunity to present a paper at the International Conference on Business Strategy and Technical Innovation in August 1987, and to Moriaki Tsuchiya, Henry Mintzberg, Michael Cusumano, Ikujiro Nonaka, and Kiyonori Sakakibara and other conference participants for their advice and encouragement. We also received comments from seminar and conference participants at The Brookings Institution, the University of Michigan, MIT, UCLA, Wharton, Northwestern, Brigham Young University, the Operations Management Association, the Strategic Management Society, the Society of Automotive Engineers, and the American Society of Mechanical Engineers.

Our colleagues at the Harvard Business School have generously helped us throughout the years of research and writing. Dean John McArthur urged us to set our sights high, invested his time and resources in opening doors for us, and provided strong and unwavering support in what turned out to be a six-year project. Jay Lorsch, director of the Division of Research, funded our work, encouraged us at every turn, and made the system work. Bob Hayes, chair of the Production and Operations Management area during much of this time, not only stimulated our thinking, but also shouldered extra administrative tasks and kept us focused on the research.

Several members of the POM area and the Science and Technology Interest Group at Harvard played a central role in the intellectual development of our work. Our biggest debt is to Steve Wheelwright, who taught courses with us, wrote cases with us, and shaped our thinking through his own work on product development. We are also grateful to Paul Lawrence for his help in linking our work to organization theory; to Bruce Chew for collaboration on one of the early papers from the project and for his assistance with empirical work; to Oscar Hauptman for helping with the conceptual framework; to Dave Garvin for his insights on concepts and measurement of total product quality; to Marco Iansiti for sharing the fieldwork; and to Earl Sasser for his help in linking product development to competition and strategy.

Both Phil Barkan of Stanford University and Jan Benson read our initial draft and offered valuable suggestions for improvement. In the field interviews, data analysis, writing, preparing, graphics, and editing we received great support from great people. Frank Dubinskas, Karen Freeze, Brandt Goldstein, and Elaine Rothman, research associates at the Harvard Business School, provided outstanding research support. John Simon, our editor, worked tirelessly and with great skill to turn our drafts into a readable manuscript. Dick Luecke, Natalie Greenberg, and many others at the Harvard Business School Press watched over us, prodded us, and made the book happen. Kathy Peterson and Rosemary Harkins kept the office focused and organized amidst all the flurry of activity. Jean Smith was responsible for the manuscript itself. She typed drafts, designed and executed graphics, handled revisions, managed the authors and the editor, found things we had lost, and did it all with consummate skill and good spirits.

Finally, we want to thank our families for their love, support, and interest ("Why do you write books, Daddy?," "Isn't it done yet?") in our work. We want to recognize especially the late Gunji (George) Fujimoto, a race car driver, mechanic, and repair shop owner in the early years of this century, and the late Takahiro Fujimoto, an entrepreneur in various auto-related businesses. They have had a decisive influence.

Product Development Performance

CHAPTER 1
PRODUCT DEVELOPMENT AND THE NEW INDUSTRIAL COMPETITION

New products have long been a source of fascination and excitement. Novel industrial artifacts displayed in the famous Crystal Palace at the Great Exhibition in London in 1851 generated great enthusiasm. Three-quarters of a century later, Henry Ford's introduction of the long-awaited Model A made front-page news as it created near riots outside dealer showrooms. Today, Gillette's Sensor razor receives extensive coverage in national papers such as *The Wall Street Journal* and *USA Today*, and even plays on the evening television news.

But though new products still evoke fascination, in the competitive environment of the early 1990s their role goes well beyond curiosity and excitement. The development of new products has become a focal point of industrial competition. For senior managers around the world, developing better products faster, more efficiently, and more effectively is at the top of the competitive agenda. Evidence is mounting that effective design and development of new products have a significant impact on cost, quality, customer satisfaction, and competitive advantage.

THE DRIVING FORCES BEHIND THE NEW INDUSTRIAL COMPETITION

The new industrial competition that focuses so heavily on product development is driven largely by three forces that have emerged over the past two decades in many industries worldwide. The emergence of intense international competition; the creation of fragmented markets populated by demanding, sophisticated customers; and diverse transforming technological change have combined to push new product development to the center of the playing field in the competitive game.

1

INTENSE INTERNATIONAL COMPETITION

The 1980s have witnessed the internationalization of many markets and industries. Though important regional and local differences persist in many industries, growing similarity in product concepts and the emergence of global product segments have paved the way for more intense competitive interaction across national boundaries. The number of players capable of and actually playing in the international arena has increased. Where competition was once among the few with a strong regional orientation, it now occurs among many more players across an international stage. Direct rivalry among products of different regional origins is observed more often as brand selection has become increasingly cosmopolitan.

International players possess similar basic skills but bring different backgrounds and experience, and thus different approaches, to the international market. With a growing number of competing brands and more capable and diverse players, it is increasingly important to counter competitor moves quickly with well-differentiated products.

FRAGMENTED MARKETS AND SOPHISTICATED CUSTOMERS

Customers have not been passive participants in the process of industrial evolution.[1] Accumulated experience has sensitized customers to subtle differences in product dimensions that go beyond technical performance and superficial design features to the degree to which a total product concept fulfills customer needs at a deeper level. For consumers the deeper fit is with lifestyle and values; for industrial customers it is with other components that make up a system or with a larger production process. The effect is to make customer expectations more holistic, complex, demanding, and diversified, and to increase opportunities for and the necessity of subtle differentiation.

This is true not only for custom-built capital equipment that has always catered to customer differences (though here the demands are greater and the criteria more valid), but also for products that have achieved a good measure of standardization in technical terms. Discerning customers for whom nuances of design and subtle physical differences in products are important create an opportunity to compete successfully through targeted, differentiated product development even in apparently mature industries.

Customers who expect something more than price and basic performance do not ignore a product's fundamentals. Good fundamentals simply become a necessary precondition for even participating in the competitive game. Here too product development has proved to be a powerful tool for improving performance. Research aimed at finding ways to improve manufacturability has led to greater understanding of the power of the design and development processes to affect manufacturing performance. Experience in a variety of industries suggests that a significant fraction (as much as 80 percent in some cases) of total product cost is established during the product engineering stage of development.[2] Product quality and reliability may be determined to a similar degree by the product engineering stage. Pressure for continual improvements in cost and quality has led to a focus on effective management of engineering design.

DIVERSIFIED AND TRANSFORMING TECHNOLOGIES

Technological change makes possible the increased differentiation demanded by more sophisticated customers. Novel technologies and new understanding of existing technologies yield a broader and deeper base of knowledge about the phenomena underlying particular applications. For example, in pharmaceuticals developments in biochemistry and molecular biology have created new processes for discovering and synthesizing proteins with potentially important therapeutic properties. At the same time, new understanding in these fields and developments in chemistry make it possible to improve the efficacy of and reduce the side effects associated with pharmaceuticals developed from traditional chemical synthesis. Deeper and broader knowledge thus creates new options for tailoring products to meet the needs of an increasingly diverse and demanding market.

Technical development has reinforced the drive for new products in another way. The growth of scientific and engineering capability worldwide has resulted in many centers of expertise in a given field. Perhaps the most dramatic example of this is the many laboratories worldwide that were immediately able to participate in research on high-temperature superconductivity when the first developments were announced in 1987. Such widespread expertise makes it much more difficult for a company to build competitive advantage solely on the basis of a unique technology. Patent issues notwithstanding, other firms often can either duplicate a technology or find alternative means to achieve similar results.

We have a new paradox: at a time when technology has never been more important, it has become more difficult (although not impossible) to build advantage around technology alone.[3] Except in very young high-tech industries, product development is no longer synonymous with technology development. Technology may be necessary, but it is generally not sufficient for new product success. Successful product development requires capabilities that extend well beyond technical skill in the R&D laboratory. Competitive advantage accrues to firms that can bring a technology into the marketplace in a product that meets customer needs efficiently and in a timely manner. Experience, illustrated by three examples from as many industries, suggests that effective product development makes a difference.

> *The VCR (video cassette recorder).* Sony launched its Betamax VCR for the mass consumer market in 1975. JVC introduced its VHS version of the VCR in 1976.[4] JVC's response was both fast and technologically distinctive. Its parent company, Matsushita, moved quickly to introduce a new product based on VHS technology. The Matsushita/JVC team eventually won the "VCR war." Though its financial performance was affected by this loss, Sony struck back with a stream of new video-related products that included a compact video camera with built-in VCR using 8-mm video cassette technology and a combined small TV and VCR (a "video walkman"). While this second VCR war continues among the Japanese producers, the main players are already preparing for the next war: the development of a digital VCR.
>
> The Dutch firm Philips, a frontrunner in VCR technology, was too slow in responding to competitors; its first VCR, comparable to Sony's Betamax, reached the market five years later. Ampex, the original innovator of the video recorder, also failed to keep up with the rapid pace of product introductions in this highly competitive market.
>
> *The single-lens reflex (SLR) camera—Canon EOS versus Minolta Alfa Series.* The Canon AE-1 had been the top seller

for nearly a decade in an SLR camera market that was fairly stable and mature in the early 1980s. Then came a new product concept: auto-focus SLR. First introduced commercially by Minolta, then a mediocre player in the SLR market, the auto-focus concept changed the industry completely, propelling Minolta past Canon and into market leadership in 1985.

Canon faced a tough choice: to develop a me-too product within one year or a well-differentiated product line with a completely different technical concept (lens-in-motor auto-focus versus Minolta's motor-in-body concept). Considering Canon's past development schedule, the latter alternative might have taken three years. Canon decided to develop a technically distinctive product within two years—a major challenge that it met through new organization and processes. Canon regained market leadership with its motor-in-lens auto-focus SLR camera, called EOS, only to lose it again as Minolta struck back quickly with an improved product. A stream of new products followed from other companies, and a see-saw game in new product introduction followed.

Jet engines for commercial aircraft. As of July 1989, 63 percent of commercial airliners used engines manufactured by Pratt and Whitney (P&W). The main strength of the long-time leader in jet engines for commercial aircraft lay in better fuel economy.[5] But for engines under construction and in backlog, the picture changes completely: General Electric engines are outselling P&W engines by a margin of 51 percent to 31 percent. Many industry observers ascribe this turnaround to efficient product development; GE responded flexibly to the recent needs of airline and aircraft companies for product variety (e.g., engines for long-body and wide-body craft) by introducing a series of modular engines that shared a basic design, so that a variety of engines with very different thrusts could be created with dramatically shorter lead time and at less cost.

In each of these examples, and in many more that we could cite, success or failure of product development has had increasingly serious effects on companies' long-term market performance. For a company with a broad product line, the isolated disappointment with a new product need not bode ill for the firm as a whole, unless that new product is targeted at a rapidly growing segment, in which case failure can have serious long-term consequences. Failure that is part of a recurring pattern across many products and market segments may significantly affect the fortunes of the firm. This is particularly true in the industrial environment of the last quarter of the twentieth century, which has been characterized by intense competition, demanding customers, and rapidly changing technology. In short, in the new industrial competition, product development matters.

THE CHALLENGE OF PRODUCT DEVELOPMENT

Effective product development is difficult. In a host of industries—including major appliances, semiconductors, televisions, VCRs, pharmaceuticals, medical instruments, industrial controls, machine tools, automobiles, lighting products, engineering workstations, printers, chemicals, advanced ceramics, hospital products, software, copiers, cameras, steel, and aluminum—we have found managers and engineers struggling with new products that are too slow to market, have failed to meet cost or performance objectives, are beset by rampant engineering changes and quality problems, or have found no market at all.[6] We have also found firms that have done extremely well. Indeed, as the examples above illustrate, product development makes a difference in the long-term competitiveness of a firm and its products. The promises associated with developing a successful new product—increased market share, new customers, lower cost, and higher quality—are exciting, but the reality of managing product development is sobering. Many firms can point to one or another product that worked well, but only a few seem to achieve excellent development performance consistently. Because doing it well matters so much, consistently successful product development holds significant competitive leverage and affords the few firms that achieve it an important advantage.

RESEARCH ON THE SOURCES OF SUPERIOR PERFORMANCE

What makes long-term success in product development so

difficult? What explains such wide differences in performance among firms in the same industry? What are the underlying principles that govern superior performance in the technical and competitive environment of the 1990s? These are the questions that motivated the research reported in this book. We offer no easy answers, no "three steps to high-performance development." Effective development cannot be achieved simply by increasing expenditures on research and development, though this may be part of the answer for some firms. Nor does it lie in finding a breakthrough technology or introducing new tools and techniques, important though these may be. Effective product development is not a question of getting the right project planning system, implementing quality function deployment (QFD), installing an advanced computer-aided design (CAD) system, or incorporating simultaneous engineering. Such practices and equipment are valuable, but not sufficient.

What seems to set apart the outstanding companies in product development—and this is a central theme of our book—is the overall pattern of consistency in their total development system, including organizational structure, technical skills, problem-solving processes, culture, and strategy. This consistency and coherence lie not only in the broad principles and architecture of the system, but also in its working-level details. Consistency in performance results from consistency in total organization and management.

The importance of consistency and detail in organization and management has implications for how we do research on product development. Above all, it means we must have depth. To gain insight into the sources of outstanding performance, we need a good comparative perspective among several companies. Finally, to understand product development in the context of the new industrial competition, we must study companies that are facing intense international competition and changing markets and technology. These requirements— the need for depth, for comparison, and for a turbulent environment— have led us to examine closely a single, global industry, one in which there are many companies in different countries developing similar products for similar markets in direct competition with one another. This focus on a single industry brings the issues of organization, management, strategy, and competition into sharp relief.

All of the data, observations, interviews, and anecdotes in this book come from the world automobile industry. In studying major development projects in twenty automobile companies worldwide over the past six years, we have tried to develop a consistent base of data that includes both measures of performance and patterns of organization and management. We have probed and checked and double-checked to ensure that we had an accurate, credible account of the development process and its performance, and we have used a variety of methods—including structured and unstructured interviews, questionnaires, and statistical analysis—to get at the sources of superior performance.

This focus on a single industry, though it gives us the power to grasp patterns of consistency in the total development system, raises questions about the generalizability of our insights and conclusions. Readers outside the automobile industry must draw implications and insights from our work indirectly by way of analogy.

LEARNING FROM THE AUTOMOBILE INDUSTRY— A FRAMEWORK FOR COMPARISON

The world automobile industry is a microcosm of the new industrial competition. In 1970, only a handful of companies competed on a global scale with products across the full range of market segments. Today the number of capable, world-scale players numbers more than twenty, and once-dominant companies like General Motors face serious competitive threats in all markets. At the same time customers have grown more discerning, sophisticated, and demanding. Though growth has slowed, the number of models has multiplied. Technology has become more complex and, especially in the United States, more diverse. Twenty years ago, the American car buyer had to look long and hard to find a model with anything but a traditional V-8 engine with rear-wheel drive. Today, the variety of engine-drive train combinations is large—4, 5, 6, 8, and 12 cylinders, multivalves, front-wheel drive, and four-wheel drive. Looking at other parts of the car, we find new technology in brakes and suspensions, engine control systems, and materials and electronics. In this environment, product development has become a focal point of competition and managerial action. Speed, efficiency, and effectiveness have become critical issues as automobile manufacturers in North America, Europe, and Japan search for new approaches to managing product development in order to be more responsive to customers and competitors.

Product development in the automobile industry has peculiar characteristics. A car is a complex, "fabricated-assembled" product, comprising a large number of components, functions, and process steps. Moreover, the product is complex from the buyer's perspective, giving rise to a number of important performance dimensions. Although the automobile has a long history and customers generally have a good deal of experience with it, buying one involves a very complicated evaluation of many criteria—some highly subjective, subtle, multi-faceted, and holistic—and all of which change over time, sometimes in unpredictable ways.

A project to develop a new car is complex and long lived; it may involve hundreds, even thousands, of people over many months. Planning and design are complicated by changing markets, long lead times, and a multiplicity of choices. Engineering complexities include the numbers of parts and components, demanding levels of cost and quality, the number of competing objectives, and inherent ambiguity in the customer's evaluation of the product.

These characteristics make the development of a new car a fascinating arena in which to study the management of product development. We are confident that much of what there is to learn is translatable to other industries. For one thing, the auto industry is so rich that it cannot help but share some basic patterns with other industries. For another, many of the frameworks we develop and the basic conceptual themes that emerge out of our work deal with general problems. Comparison with case studies and discussions with senior managers in other industries suggest that the principles reported here have broad application among firms that face the conditions of the new industrial competition. For example, many of the critical problems in developing a new car—integrating engineering and manufacturing, establishing links between technical choices and customer requirements, and establishing effective leadership—show up in the development of most "fabricated-assembled" products. Even in process-intensive industries such as steel, aluminum, and engineered plastics these problems are sufficiently general that analysis of the auto industry can provide useful insights.

No matter what the industry, the challenge is to modify and adapt insights gained from the auto study to particular circumstances. The auto study, for example, does not deal with all the important issues in the medical devices industry, one in which new product development is heavily regulated in most countries. But though the study does not deal with the issue of regulation, it does provide many useful analogies to other aspects of development in the medical devices industry.

We developed the framework sketched out in Figure 1.1 to aid in drawing analogies from and adapting principles developed in the auto study. The figure is essentially a grid that allows us to plot two dimensions of a product: (1) complexity of internal structure (i.e., number of distinct components and production steps, number of interfaces, and technological difficulty of and severity of the trade-offs among different components), and (2) complexity of user interface (i.e., number and specificity of performance criteria, importance of measurable versus subtle and equivocal dimensions, and holistic versus narrow criteria). Different combinations of internal and external complexity give rise to different issues in managing development. The framework thus helps to focus attention on similarities between new cars and other types of new products.

An automobile is composed of thousands of functionally meaningful components, each requiring many production steps. The technological sophistication of each component may be somewhat lower than that found in some high-tech products, but subtle trade-offs and tight interdependence among many components makes internal coordination of the total vehicle extremely challenging. Small size makes layout coordination for some cars quite difficult. Use of common parts across products complicates interproject coordination. The automobile thus places high on the internal complexity axis in Figure 1.1.

The automobile is also externally complex; the customer-producer interface is generally subtle and multifaceted, and a vehicle can satisfy customers in a number of ways beyond basic transportation, not all of which are clearly recognized by the customers themselves. Automobiles are generally not purchased by professional industrial buyers trained to analyze the product. Car consumers are often unable to articulate their future expectations, although they can tell which products they like when they see them. Because criteria that are identified tend to be highly subjective and emotional, involving fantasy and symbolism, they are difficult to translate into technical specifications.[7] Furthermore, because what *current* customers say about a product may obscure some important aspects of the latent needs of *future* customers, following the voice of existing customers may not

Figure 1.1   Type of Product by Complexity

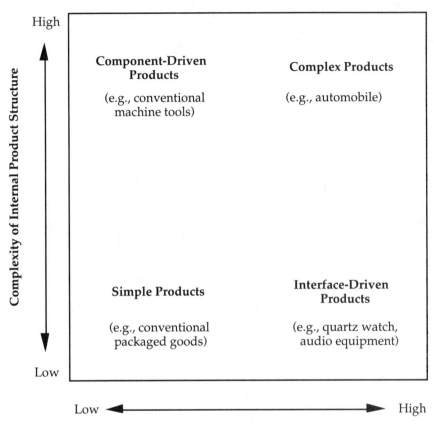

Complexity of Product-User Interface

always be a good thing. Subtle, latent, equivocal, and inarticulate market needs make the automobile's user interface highly complex.

We are thus able to establish a frame of reference with the automobile in the upper right corner of the product complexity grid. Few products exhibit the combination of complexity that automobiles do, but the more complex a product is along either dimension, the more direct the application of our findings. A very high-performance disk drive sold to makers of engineering workstations, for example, is quite complex internally but has a much less ambiguous user interface than a new car. In this case, the key lessons are likely to come out of our work on managing the integration of engineering and manufacturing, prototyping, engineering problem solving, and the organization of development—all issues that deal with internal coordination. Conversely, issues of external complexity are likely to be more central in a new, high-performance audio system for the home, which is not as complex internally but has a complex interface with the user. In this case, the auto development experience may shed light on the problem of interpreting the customer's voice and translating it into the details of the design.

ANALOGY AND INTERPRETATION

Even in areas of significant difference, insights may come through analogy and interpretation. In the disk drive case, for example, although the customer interface may be simpler, the auto study may still yield insights about the process by which the disk drive firm brings customer information into the development process. Associated adjustments for key differences are summarized below.

If a product is much simpler in internal structure. The complexity of the project mirrors the complexity of the product and the process. Complex projects that have to be completed in a relatively short time generally involve large numbers of people. For a new car, the number is often several hundred. For many other, less complex products the number is more likely to be on the order of 15 to 20. From the standpoint of development performance, the difference between large and small projects might be likened to the difference between a symphony orchestra and a double string quartet: both have the potential to create high-quality music, but patterns of specialization, coordination, communication, and conceptual leadership may be quite different. Size, therefore, may have important implications for the management of development.

A major automobile development project, for example, may require the leadership of a strong, very senior product manager, who—much like the conductor of an orchestra—possesses multiple skills, coordinates specialists, and champions product concepts. Smaller projects in other industries might bear greater similarity to a double string quartet, in which ongoing mutual adjustment and individual flexibility are more important. Leadership is important in this instance too, but it is of a different kind. In very small projects conducted by people who know each other well, leaders may emerge naturally from among team members to provide vision and direction, much as a quartet plays coherent music without a conductor, alternating leading roles among the players. The fact is that the same activities we examine in the development of a new car—designing, building prototypes, and testing—go on in smaller projects, only in a different organizational context.

In somewhat larger projects involving a less coherent or homogeneous group, in which the leader may need to have broader experience and be able to translate among different specialists, the problems of leadership and management in car development—e.g., multiple specialists, many languages, and integrating across disciplines and functions—become more directly relevant.

If the product-user interface is much simpler. One of the central problems in product development is incorporating insight about customer needs into engineering decisions. To the extent that a product is externally complex, product development planners and engineers must not only listen to current customers, but they must also interpret and articulate the latent needs of potential customers, propose new product concepts that address those needs, and perhaps eventually create new markets. They must also ensure that every detail of product design is consistent with the product concept, which is not articulated in technical terms. In short, to the extent that a product is externally complex, the task of identifying key customer needs, translating them into attractive product concepts, and realizing them in detailed product designs is challenging.

The focal point of effective product development is likely to be much different when the product-user interface is simple. In the case of certain industrial products, for example, users often have stronger and more direct influence on the product development process, particularly in the development of concepts and specifications, which professional users often can state clearly in objective terms.[8] Functional requirements for new products (and even detailed designs, in some cases) are often defined technically by such users. New product success with such customers comes from developing good contacts with them, listening to what they say, translating their needs into precise technical specifications, and ensuring that the product conforms to those specifications. Competition on cost and performance may be intense, but the rules of the development game are straightforward, and there is consensus among users and suppliers as to which performance dimensions are important and how they are measured.

Where the product-user interface is less complex and the voice of the customer much clearer, specialized market interface units, such as sales engineers or marketing staff, may effectively handle the development and communication of market information to project engineers. Direct connections between customers and core designers and engineers may not be as critical in these industries as in automobiles, but the principles that seem important in the automotive context—going after deep understanding of the customer and developing a process and engineers with a strong customer focus—are still relevant. Highly specified industrial products also rely on identifying customer requirements and translating them into design, although the process is different.

As the product-user interface becomes more complex, detailed specifications may not cover all the important dimensions of customer choice, and nuances of design and a holistic view of the customer and the product become more important. As this happens, the market-engineering interaction that is central to the auto story—direct, continuous contact between customers and engineers, strong product concepts, and explicit management of linkages with the customer by strong project leaders—becomes more central to effective management of product development.

OUTLINE OF THE BOOK

The best way to learn from the auto study is to start with a sense of the key differences between developing a new car and developing a new product in your business and look for the basic principles that deal with the challenges you face. The next step is to make direct connections, draw analogies, and adapt the principles to your situation.

We have organized the book to help in this process. Chapter 2 lays out a general conceptual framework for product development, and Chapter 3 examines the role of product development in the competitive history of the automobile industry in Japan, Europe, and North America. In Chapter 4, we look at product development performance, with particular attention to lead time, engineering productivity, and total product quality. Chapters 5–10 identify the sources of superior performance in product development and examine basic principles that seem to make a difference. We first present an overview of the development process to provide background and context for the analysis that follows. In Chapters 6–9 we look at project strategy with respect to innovation, off-the-shelf parts, and suppliers (Chapter 6), and then at organization and management (Chapters 7–9), including manufacturing capability, integrated engineering, and organization and leadership. In Chapter 10, we examine the overall patterns of consistency that seem to be critical to superior performance. Chapter 11 postulates the future of product development in the automobile industry of the 1990s.

In the final chapter we return to the issue of learning. We summarize the general principles that seem to govern high-performance product development and discuss their application in other industries. Using examples of product development in very different industries, we illustrate how practical insights derived from the auto study may inform the product development challenges faced by managers in those industries in the years ahead.

NOTES

1. See Rosenberg (1982) for "learning by using" in the case of capital goods.
2. See Soderberg (1989) and Jaikumar (1986).
3. See Clark (1989).
4. For a detailed study of the VCR industry, see Rosenbloom and Cusumano (1987).
5. "Bei Koku Enjin 90-nendai Kessen he," *Nikkei Sangyo Shimbun* ("U.S. Aircraft Engine Manufacturers Engage in a Showdown in the 90s," *Japan Economic Journal*), 20 September 1989.
6. Product development experience in many of these industries has been examined in a series of case studies conducted at the Harvard Business School. See, for example, Ampex Corporation: Product Matrix Engineering (687-002), BSA Industries—Belmont Division (689-049), Bendix Automation Group (684-035), General Electric Lighting Business Group (689-038), Sony Corporation: Workstation Division (690-031), Plus Development Corporation (A) (687-001), Ceramics Process Systems Corporation (A) (687-030), Applied Materials (688-050), Everest Computer (A) (685-085), and Chaparral Steel (Abridged) (687-045); see also, Rosenbloom and Freeze (1985).
7. See, for example, Marsh and Collet (1986), Holbrook and Hirschman (1982), Hirschman and Holbrook (1982), and Levy (1959).
8. See, for example, von Hippel (1988).

CHAPTER 2
THE FRAMEWORK:
AN INFORMATION PERSPECTIVE

Long before your customer unpacks that new laptop computer, high-speed packaging machine, or television set, and certainly long before that new car rolls off the showroom floor, the product, or some early version of it, takes shape in the mind of a designer. The designer's proposal and drawings may capture the imagination of senior management, and early models and concepts may excite potential customers, but before the factory can start pumping out the real thing, the product idea must get from the designer's mind into the hardware and software of commercial production—drawings, parts, tools, procedures, equipment, and processes. What the firm does (its product strategy) and how it does it (its management of development) will determine how the product fares in the marketplace. How the firm performs product development—its speed, efficiency, and quality of work—will determine the competitiveness of the product.

What determines performance in product development? How important are strategy and the competitive environment? What scope is there for differences in management and organization? Why are some firms so much more effective than others? These are the kinds of questions we examine in this book. But development is a complex process that involves many people and touches much of what a company does—in strategy, design, marketing, engineering, manufacturing, and customer service—and without a framework to guide us, we are liable to become lost in a welter of detail with little sense of what is important.

This chapter describes the conceptual framework we use in our research on product development. It identifies the broad competitive and organizational context in which we study product development and presents the information-processing perspective that frames our study of the development process. The chapter concludes with three themes that emerge from this perspective and carry throughout the book:

17

- The development process as a simulation of future production and consumption;
- The importance of consistency in the details of development; and
- The power of product integrity in competition.

PERFORMANCE, ORGANIZATION, AND ENVIRONMENT

We study product development in a broad context that includes performance, the competitive environment, and the internal organization of the firm. This context is summarized in Figure 2.1, which recognizes that performance in product development interacts with a firm's strategy and internal organization and is ultimately an important contributor to overall competitiveness.[1]

Performance in a development project is determined by a firm's product strategy and by its capabilities in overall process and organization. But the relationship between a firm's capabilities and its competitive environment is dynamic and rooted in its historical context. Uncertainty and diversity of the market environment over time, for example, change the role of product development in competition. To maintain and improve their performance and competitiveness, producers must adapt their organizations and management to the patterns of the environment. But it is also the case that a firm's products help to shape the market environment; the nature of the market environment changes as consumers and competitors learn from new products and services. Organizations and environments thus evolve side by side through a process of mutual adaptation.

The products we study in this book are tangible; they are things you can see, touch, and use. They are designed and constructed from physical materials, and we find out how well they perform through hands-on tests. But though it might seem natural to focus on the physical product—the material developments that support it (the parts, tools, and equipment) and its use by the customer—we have found a different perspective, one that focuses on information, to be more useful for understanding the management of development. Throughout the book we look at the development process as a total information system and identify important problems from the perspective of information processing.[2] By focusing attention on how

Figure 2.1 Performance, Organization, and Environment

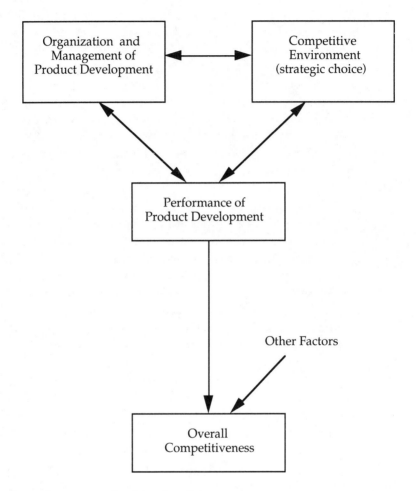

Note: Some flows are omitted for simplicity.

information is created, communicated, and used, this perspective highlights critical information linkages within the organization and between the organization and the market. In doing so, it helps to clarify the role of product development within the broader context of competition.

Linking the product to the firm and its customers is a powerful way to organize thinking and research about product development. In the model we present, a product's development, production processes, and ultimate consumption by customers are described in terms of an integrated system of information creation and transmission. In this context, product development is a process by which an organization transforms data on market opportunities and technical possibilities into information assets for commercial production. During the development process, these information assets are created, screened, stored, combined, decomposed, and transferred among various media, including human brains, paper, computer memory, software, and physical materials. Ultimately, they are articulated as detailed product and process designs stored in blueprints and computer-aided design data bases and eventually deployed in production processes on the factory floor.

Our application of the information perspective extends beyond design and engineering to other functions such as production and marketing, and to the behavior of consumers. Figure 2.2 contrasts the information view of the entire scope of business activities with the conventional view, which focuses on the flow of materials. In the latter perspective, which yields the well-known "food chain"—linking supplier, producer, distributor, and consumer—product development is a secondary or support activity.[3] A focus on the flow of information—from product development to production, marketing, consumers, and back to product development—brings product development to the fore.[4]

The impact of the information perspective does more than modify the flow diagram; it affects in a fundamental way how we think about producers and consumers. Consider consumer behavior. In the information framework, the customer consumes an experience delivered by a product rather than the physical product itself. This experience takes the form of information a customer receives about the product and its behavior in the environment in which it is used. While driving a car, for example, a customer receives a barrage of messages about the vehicle's movement from one point to another, including steering response, feel of acceleration, engine noise, wind noise, radio, squeaks from the dashboard, outside views, other cars, people watching the car, passengers talking about the car, and so forth. The customer interprets these messages and imposes meanings on them, which gives rise to a sense of satisfaction or dissatisfaction with the product experience. "Marketing" in this framework is communication at the producer-

Figure 2.2 Information Perspective versus Material Perspective

Conventional Material View

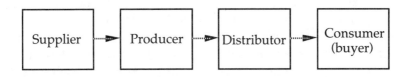

Information System View

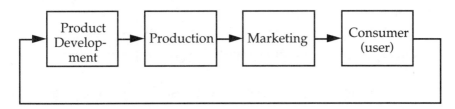

Note: Some flows are omitted for simplicity.

▶▶▶▶   Material/Commodity Flows

▶   Information Flows

consumer interface. Through media such as advertising, catalogues, sales personnel, and the product itself, marketers create and deliver messages intended to represent the product and its prices and benefits in such a way as to inform and influence the way consumers interpret the product experience.

On the production side, the information perspective focuses attention on the transmission of information from the production process deployed on the shop floor to actual products.[5] The key notion here is that by the time product development is finished, complete information about a product's design is embodied in elements of the production process (e.g., in tools, equipment, worker skills, standard operating procedures, numerical control tapes, and so forth). Production activities transfer the product design to materials that become the physical product. A set of molds for a dishwasher, for example, contains full information about the design of the tub. As plastic resin goes through the injection molding process, this information is transferred to the material, which becomes a part of the dishwasher.

In the information framework, communication with customers is the main objective of the firm—the product as a physical object is only the medium or vehicle by which the product experience and the producer's messages are delivered to customers. Product development creates value-carrying messages that production embodies in actual products and marketing delivers to target customers, who interpret and generate experiences of satisfaction or dissatisfaction from the product-embodied information. Looking at the development, production, marketing, and consumer experiences from a consistent, informational point of view enables us to see important interrelationships.

THREE THEMES IN EFFECTIVE PRODUCT DEVELOPMENT

Effective product development rests on a product design's ability to create a positive product experience. This involves a complex translation of product information from customers to engineers to production to sales and back to customers. In the chapters that follow, we use the information perspective to shed light on the strategies, management practices, and organizational capabilities that enable some firms to perform those translations quickly, efficiently, and accurately.

Three themes guide our study of product development in the information framework: development as rehearsal for future customer use, the importance of consistency in many significant details, and the power of product integrity to create competitive advantage. Each of these themes grows out of viewing development in informational terms, and each focuses attention on a set of critical issues in its management.

PRODUCT DEVELOPMENT AS A SIMULATION OF CONSUMER EXPERIENCE

The development of a new product involves creating a new design concept and building and testing prototypes. One way of interpreting what engineers do during this process is to think about how they decide whether a design is attractive. Though they follow a variety of technical specifications and established test standards, if we cut through all the formal detail, at the core of the evaluation, engineers are simulating what future customers will experience. Figure 2.3 illustrates the notion of product development as a rehearsal of future customers' product experiences. As the figure suggests, development, production, and consumption are integrated into a larger system by information flows that circulate throughout the system.

Figure 2.3 Product Development as a Simulation of Consumption

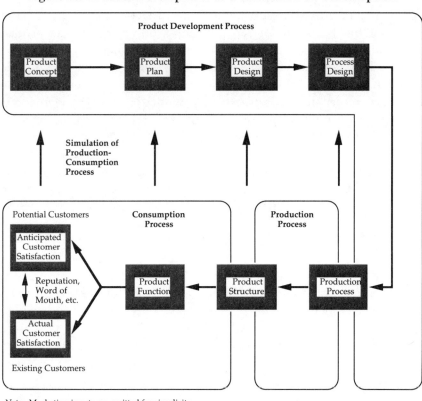

Note: Marketing inputs are omitted for simplicity.

☐ Information Created

➤ Information Creation/Transmission Process

This theme has a number of implications for the management of development. Consider, for example, the challenge facing a typical group of auto engineers and planners just starting a project in 1990. The upper half of Figure 2.3 depicts product development from 1990 to 1994—from concept creation through process engineering. The lower half of the diagram depicts factory production and the product's use in the marketplace between 1994 and 2010, assuming a six-year production period and a useful product life of ten years.

The symmetry between the upper and lower halves of this diagram is intriguing; product development appears to mirror the production and consumption processes. The product concept antici-pates future customer satisfaction, and the product plan specifies product function. Similarly, the product design represents product structure, the process design represents the production process.

This symmetry suggests that, at a detailed level, product de-velopment is essentially a simulation of production and consumption. It creates information assets that are intended to represent elements of the future consumption process. An automobile prototype, for example, stands in for the future automobile, while test drivers play the role of future customers, test tracks are designed to simulate actual road conditions, computer-aided engineering programs try to reproduce vehicle dynamics, and product planners try to anticipate customer expectations and internalize customer needs several years into the future.

How well a development group simulates target customers is critical to the effectiveness of a product development effort. It is critical to manage the linkages between development and the sources of information about future consumption—i.e., customers and the market. This is precisely why we must analyze customer behavior and product development concurrently. As customer needs and evaluation criteria change, so do effective patterns of development. We call a firm's efforts to match development activities with customer experience "external integration."[6]

When customer needs are easy to identify and articulate, internal efficiency and effectiveness may play a greater role than the ability to simulate customer experience. External simulation capabili-ties create major competitive differences among producers when market needs are unpredictable and difficult to articulate. For example, as long as customers emphasize a few unequivocal criteria such as speed, economy, power, and size, product concepts and plans can be fully described technically and effectively communicated through drawings and CAD data files. In effect, simplicity of information processing in development mirrors simplicity of information processing in customer behavior. On the other hand, when customers appreciate more subtle product characteristics such as style, expressiveness, and fit with lifestyle—characteristics that are more difficult to articulate in plans and specifications—face-to-face discussion and physical prototypes become more important as communication media.[7]

To summarize, the information framework suggests that effective product development simulates future consumer experience accurately at a detailed level. When customer choices are complex, difficult to articulate, and changing, it becomes more difficult to get an accurate simulation. But because customer requirements and expectations are difficult to forecast, and because firms rarely are able to impose their own view of what constitutes a good product, getting the simulation right is critical. Matching the development and consumer processes at a detailed level seems to be the single most important task for new product development.

CONSISTENCY OF DETAIL

The second theme that guides our work is the importance of consistency in the details of the development process.[8] We focus in particular on the way designers, engineers, and marketers frame and solve problems at the working level. This does not mean that details of problem solving can be managed independently, without consideration of the bigger picture; attention to both the whole and the parts is necessary for effective development. Just as capable conductors must attend simultaneously to overall harmony and individual sounds to produce good symphony music, effective managers must pay attention to the total development system and detailed activities at the same time in order to produce successful products.

The information system framework provides tools that are useful for detailed analysis. It enables us to look closely at the information assets that are created, connected, transferred, and modified at each step, and thereby allows us to describe and analyze detailed aspects of product development from a consistent point of view.[9] This is an information version of the process flow analysis often used in manufacturing.[10] We first identify key information assets and their creation process and the critical linkages that must be managed for overall performance; then we find ways to improve the process in terms of effective information creation and communication.

The simplified model of the product development process shown in Figure 2.4 outlines a relatively generic sequence of activities for fabricated and assembled products; this sequence has analogies in process industries such as chemicals, paper, and aluminum.* The model identifies four major development stages: concept generation, product planning, product engineering, and process engineering.[11] Although in practice the development process has many loops, parallel steps, and obscure boundaries that render it far from linear, we portray the process as sequential for purposes of description.

Information on future market needs, technical possibilities, and other conditions is merged and translated into the product concept at the concept generation stage.** Here designers and planners face the problem of creating a concept that will attract future customers. A powerful product concept is more than a set of dimensions or a list of specifications. It defines the character of the product from a customer's perspective. The product concept is essentially a projected experience, a complex message delivered by the new product in the hope of satisfying the target customers. It is most often expressed verbally, possibly with some visual aids and preliminary technical specifications.

Product planning translates the product concept into specifics for detailed product design, including styling, layout, major specifications, cost and investment targets, and technical choices. The central problem at this stage is to come up with a plan that reconciles competing objectives and requirements. Though most of the information assets created at this stage are still intangible, engineers and designers may employ physical models for styling evaluation, mockups for interior and layout evaluation, and early-stage prototypes to evaluate styling and layout and to test advanced components. Product

---

*   For purposes of this book, product development includes not only concept generation, product planning, and product engineering, but also process engineering, which creates the production process. Lawrence and Dyer (1983, Chapter 10) develop a similar diagram.

**   Basic research or advanced engineering aimed at searching for technical possibilities is generally outside the scope of the current study.

Figure 2.4 Information Asset Map

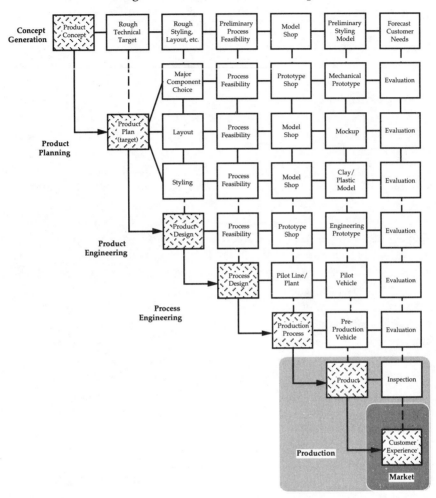

Note: Horizontal relationships represent problem-solving cycles, and vertical relationships denote
       refinement of knowledge or information assets. The map assumes that a given information asset is
       potentially connected to all other assets in the same row and same column rather than to adjacent
       information assets only. Also, the product planning row is shown with three simultaneously
       running and horizontally linked cycles related to major component choice, layout, and styling.

planning represents the first opportunity to interpret the product
concept in physical form.

Product engineering translates product planning information
into detailed product designs. Full-scale commitment to engineering
resources begins at this stage. The problem faced by product engineers

is to realize the product concept in real parts and components while satisfying business requirements (e.g., cost and investment). Product targets and constraints are first broken down into components for detailed design and stored in drawings and CAD data bases. The drawings are then converted into prototype components, which are normally embodied in representative materials without using volume production tooling. The components are assembled into engineering prototypes, which constitute the first complete physical expression of the product design. The prototypes are tested, at both the component and total vehicle levels, to ensure that the design hits the original targets and concept. Engineering drawings may be modified on the basis of test results. The design-prototype-test cycle continues until the detailed product design is officially approved.

Process engineering translates detailed product designs into process designs and ultimately into actual shop-floor production processes. Process design information created in the upstream part of this stage includes overall plant design (e.g., material flows and plant layout), hardware design (e.g., for tools, jigs, dies, and equipment), software design (e.g., part programming), and work design (e.g., standard operating procedures). Process design information is subsequently converted into the actual production factors—such as tools, equipment, numerical control tapes, and trained workers—that are deployed in volume production plants. The performance of these factors is tested at various tryouts (at the level of individual tools and equipment) and pilot runs (at the level of production lines). Design changes for both products and processes may follow.

The information map highlights critical linkages within and across the four stages of development. The vertical links show step-by-step refinement of key information assets down through the stages; the horizontal links suggest problem-solving cycles within each stage. For each problem-solving cycle, boxes to the left represent alternative solutions; boxes to the right denote evaluation results of those alternatives, and the boxes in between represent information assets that may be used in experiments or simulations to gain further knowledge. These simulations are, in a sense, rehearsals of downstream stages of the development-production-consumption system. The results of an upstream cycle (e.g., a product concept) become the goals or assumptions for the downstream cycle through the links on the diagonal.

Vertically, the process of refining or elaborating knowledge and information assets begins at the top with rough or preliminary information and ends at the bottom with final or complete outputs. For example, the information representing a physical product may emerge at the concept generation stage as small-scale styling models, evolve into life-size clay models, mechanical prototypes, or mockups representing different aspects of the vehicle at the product planning stage, and ultimately become an engineering prototype representing the total vehicle. Pilot vehicles and pre-production vehicles are subsequently developed using representative production tooling. This step-by-step process of refinement yields models that are increasingly "real," closer and closer to becoming commercial products. The vertical movement of knowledge between development stages is critical to the increasing representational integrity of these experimental tools.

Using the information map to sketch the development process underscores the importance of information integrity at detailed levels. The timing and integration of multiple information linkages may greatly affect overall lead time or productivity. The quality and strength of the horizontal links affect the speed and effectiveness of problem solving within stages. The vertical links determine the effectiveness of knowledge transfer across stages, which is reflected in how well the early stages simulate actual production and market conditions and how well the later stages implement the designs and plans developed earlier. Today's CAD technology, for example, makes it relatively easy to create line drawings that represent three-dimensional models of a part. However, simultaneously translating inarticulate customer tastes into articulate product concepts, or verbal product concepts into visual styling designs and numerical specifications remains difficult. Similarly, the timing of problem solving in critical, adjacent stages of development, such as prototyping or tool building, and the number of iterations in the design-build-test cycle may affect overall lead time and development productivity. Applying the information framework at the detailed process level can help us systematically identify the critical links for product success.

COMPETING ON PRODUCT INTEGRITY

Generally speaking, the focus of competition varies across industries and changes over time.* In a young, high-tech industry, raw performance in a few core technologies may be the focus of competition;

in a very mature industry, cost may be the primary focus of difference and advantage.[12] But in many of today's industries—including automobiles, consumer electronics and other consumer durables, medical products, computers, food, and photographic products—neither component performance nor cost is the sole driver; in these industries, product integrity has become the focus of competition. Companies in these industries cannot compete effectively on the superiority of a single technology because the technology in the product is complex and changing. In addition to occasional significant innovations, what might be called "rapid incremental innovation" in both products and processes is constantly shifting the standard of product excellence upward, making new product development a critical capability for competition.

"Product excellence" is much broader than basic functionality or technical performance. Consumers who have accumulated experience with a product and become sensitive to subtle differences in many product dimensions demand total balance of numerous product characteristics, including basic functions, aesthetics, semantics, reliability, and economy. The extent to which the totality of a product achieves this balance and attracts and satisfies customers is a measure of product integrity.

Product integrity has both internal and external dimensions. Internal integrity refers to consistency between the function and structure of a product—e.g., the parts fit well, components match and work well together, layout achieves maximum space efficiency. External integrity is a measure of how well a product's function, structure, and semantics fit the customer's objectives, values, production system, lifestyle, use pattern, and self-identity.

When the market emphasizes product integrity, effective product development must emphasize its own internal and external integrity. Organizationally, the development process achieves internal integrity mainly through cross-functional coordination within the company and with parts suppliers. Simply put, parts that work well together are produced by organizations that are closely linked and

---

* The focus of competition for our purposes refers to an aspect of a firm's product or service to which customers are sensitive and in which significant cross-company differences in capability exist. In other words, it is a high-leverage competitive dimension.

integrated. External integrity is related to the quality of customer-producer linkages. Because the product concept is a key intermediary that bridges customer needs and product designs, the process a firm uses to create a product concept and implement it in a design is particularly critical to external integrity. We hope in the chapters that follow to impart an understanding of how outstanding firms achieve internal and external integration.[13]

FOCUS ON THE AUTOMOBILE INDUSTRY

This book takes a broad-gauged approach to product development in an effort to understand both its role in competition and the managerial and organizational sources of superior performance. The framework we have sketched in this chapter seems up to the task. It allows us to examine customers, markets, and competition in terms closely linked to the way we look at the organization and management of product development. Using the information paradigm in this way focuses our attention on the critical dimensions of managerial practice and makes the connections between those practices and competitiveness transparent and direct.

The arena in which we make these connections—the world automobile industry—also seems well suited to the task. The markets are large, dynamic, and increasingly global; customer behavior is complex; the competitive environment is turbulent. Moreover, the industry contains some of the largest, most complex, and most intriguing firms in the world. In-depth analyses of product development at Daimler-Benz, Toyota, BMW, Ford, Nissan, General Motors, Honda, Peugeot, Volkswagen, and many others provide a rich source of information about contrasting approaches to organization and management. This richness—of both the managerial and competitive contexts—makes the auto industry a fruitful arena in which to examine the sources of superior performance in product development, the task to which we now turn.

NOTES

1. This model draws on contingency theory in organization studies and strategic management. For classical examples, see Lawrence and Lorsch (1967), Thompson (1967), Child (1972), Galbraith (1973), Miles and Snow (1978), and Chandler (1962). For other literature, see Scott (1987) and Miles (1980).

2. The information paradigm we use in this book has its roots in a variety of academic disciplines. The information processing framework is a standard approach in the literature on R&D management. See, for example, Marquis (1982), Allen (1977), and Freeman (1982). Frameworks that emphasize information processing have also been important paradigms in manufacturing and organization theory, as well as in studies of consumer behavior and marketing; see, for example, Galbraith (1973) and Tushman and Nadler (1978) for organization, Kottler (1984) for marketing, and Engel, Blackwell, and Kollat (1987) and Bettman (1979) for consumer behavior. However, the existing literature lacks integration *across* disciplines. Because each discipline has used the information paradigm separately to study its own problems, its potential for integrated analysis of development, production, marketing, and consumer experience has been ignored. Our information framework is thus a new application of an old paradigm. For further references to literature on the information framework, see Fujimoto (1989, Chapter 3).

3. See, for example, the value-chain concept in Porter (1985).

4. Diagrams similar to Figure 2.2 are found in Maidique and Zirger (1985) and Urban, Hauser, and Dholakia (1987, Chapter 5).

5. See also Fujimoto (1983, 1986).

6. A similar concept in organization theory is "boundary spanning," which refers to the interface between organization and environment; see, for example, Thompson (1967, pp. 19–23), Aldrich and Herker (1977, p. 219), Miles (1980, pp. 330–335), and Tushman (1977). These authors tend to emphasize passive aspects of the interface such as buffering and screening.

7. For a discussion on the relationship between equivocality of information and media selection, see Daft and Lengel (1986).

8. Burgelman and Sayles (1986) also stress the importance of consistency in the details of the development process.

9. In organization theory, some authors emphasize information creation; see, for example, Weick (1979) and Nonaka (1988a). Others emphasize information transmission (communication); see, for example, Galbraith (1973) and Tushman and Nadler (1978). Here we pay attention to both creation and transmission.

10. There has been detailed and systematic study of communication structures in R&D organizations (see Allen, 1977), but they have tended to focus on the frequency of communication and different roles in the communication network at a point in time. Here we treat the management of product development as a process which occurs over time. We thus are interested in the dynamics of information flows and communication.

11. These development stages correspond roughly to the standard description of the innovation process in the literature on the management of technology, i.e., idea generation, problem solving, and implementation. Some companies merge concept generation and product planning.
12. For patterns of competition and industrial evolution, see, for example, Abernathy (1978), Abernathy and Utterback (1978), Abernathy, Clark, and Kantrow (1983), and Clark (1985).
13. For further discussion of internal and external integration, see Fujimoto (1989).

CHAPTER 3

COMPETITION IN THE WORLD AUTO INDUSTRY

By 1990, the world automobile market had become sophisticated, international, and cosmopolitan. The hot car in Japan was a high-performance sedan designed and built in Bavaria, the BMW 3-Series. It competed in the American market with Honda's Legend sedan, a design that grew out of a joint development effort with British Leyland. American aficionados were taken with the Nissan 300 ZX, a new sports car designed in Atsugi, Japan, which competed directly with the traditional sports car segment leaders from Porsche. Germans were buying up Chrysler's front-wheel drive minivan, a product much in demand in the United States, which offered strong competition to Renault's Espace van. This pattern of direct competition among cars designed, developed, and sold on different continents—which had emerged in the low end of the world market in the late 1950s and 1960s and was beginning to characterize even the high-performance and luxury segments of the market—was a world apart from the competitive situation during the early years of the postwar era.

In 1958, Alfred Sloan, the architect of General Motors' highly successful product strategy ("a car for every purse and purpose") and justly famous management system ("centralized coordination with decentralized control") had just retired from the chairmanship after almost 40 years. The company he left behind dominated its industry. In the world's largest market, the United States, the two major competitors—Ford and Chrysler—generally followed GM's lead in matters of styling and product content. Imports were then a minor part of the market. Volkswagen was a curiosity; Nissan and Toyota engineers were busily trying to figure out why their first exports were falling apart on the Los Angeles freeway; and Honda was producing motorcycles. The U.S. market was large and fairly homogeneous. Popular cars such as the basic Chevy sold around 1.5 million units.

Their designs emphasized glitz, chrome, and power. Basic technology, such as that in the power train (engine, transmission, and drive), was well established and relatively standard.

Three driving forces have since transformed the world automobile industry.[1] One is increasingly intense, international competition. In the late 1950s, the auto industry counted four or five major world players. Today, more than twenty companies are capable of playing on a global scale. A second force is the growing fragmentation of markets. The top-selling model in the U.S. market today accounts for only about 0.4 million units compared to the 1.5 million units it sold in the late 1950s. All the major automobile markets have been characterized by an increase in number of models and a decline in volume per model. The final force is an explosion in technology. In 1970, 80 percent of all U.S. production utilized one basic power-train technology—a water-cooled, carbureted, V8 engine that was longitudinally mounted and connected to a three-speed automatic transmission and rear-wheel drive. There were only five such power-train packages in production in the entire U.S. industry in 1970. By the mid 1980s, there were 35, representing a sevenfold increase in technical diversity. Were we to add electronics, new materials, and new components, the growth would be even greater.[2]

These forces have played out in an industry that has had a decidedly regional character. Differences in geography have given rise to different product designs for different road systems (think of driving across the plains of Kansas, in the mountains of Switzerland, and around metropolitan Tokyo) and for different customers (the mass-market character of the U.S. automobile arrived much later in Europe, where cars had been a luxury item for the wealthy and driving considered a skill). During the 1960s some European producers were designing cars for sophisticated, third-generation drivers, while Japanese firms were dealing with many first-time drivers.

Players in the world auto industry come to the global arena with capabilities honed and refined in competitive battles fought on home ground. These capabilities are rooted in people, systems, and organizational processes that are changed only with time and great effort. Therefore, during a period of transition from regional to global competition such as occurred in the 1980s, we observe sharp differences in capabilities even under intense competitive pressure. These gaps in capability are likely to be focal points of competition. Therefore, to understand competitive interaction and performance in the auto industry, we need to understand the industry's historical context. To anticipate which capabilities will be critical and decisive, firms need insight into the roots of effective capability and the forces that are driving change.

We look first at regional differences in competitive and market environments, with particular attention to the role of product development. We then examine historical differences in strategic behavior between volume producers and "high-end specialists." Finally, we look briefly at the globalization of competition and its implications for regional markets and strategic groups.

REGIONAL DIFFERENCES IN COMPETITION AND BASIC MARKET STRUCTURE

Competition in the auto industry from the late 1940s until the oil crises of the 1970s evolved quite differently in Europe, Japan, and North America. Although basic product structure and use were similar, differences in relative prices, customer income levels, geography, and history gave rise to sharp differences in product concepts, consumer behavior, and overall patterns of competition. These cross-regional differences were clearly reflected not only in the product's technology, but also in its basic concept.

A product concept is a producer's message to consumers about what constitutes a good product. The concept is created initially in the minds of product planners, articulated in product planning documents and engineering drawings, and ultimately embodied in the product itself. One "reads" a product's concept or message in the product experience. Concepts evolve over time as producers learn about technology and customer needs and as customers refine their views of the product. For automobile producers, the home market has played an important role in shaping the character of product concepts. Table 3.1 compares traditional product concepts across three regions.

The product concept that dominated the U.S. market from the postwar years until the mid 1970s was the all-purpose road cruiser with a large body and engine, a variety of optional equipment, a comfortable cabin, and a soft ride. The 1972 Chevrolet Impala was such a car. It had a 122-inch wheelbase, a spacious trunk, a long front

Table 3.1 Traditional Product Concepts: United States, Europe, and Japan

Category	United States	Europe	Japan
Packaging	loose; large exterior and interior	compact; efficient use of space	compact; efficient use of space
Styling	boxy; long nose/deck; emphasis on size	round; short nose/deck; emphasis on aerodynamics and space efficiency	segment dependent; influenced by both European and U.S. styling
Engine/ Body	large, powerful engine; heavy body; slow response	small engine; light body; emphasis on fuel economy; sharp response	small engine; light body; emphasis on fuel economy; sharp response
Handling/ Ride	smooth, soft, comfortable ride	firm ride; precise control; emphasis on road feel	segment dependent
Source of Value- Added	options and features	total balance	options; many features standard equipment
Overall Image	all-purpose road cruiser; large, comfortable, powerful	a driving machine; responsive, precise, sophisticated	eclectic; depends on segment

Source: Clark and Fujimoto, "The European Model of Product Development: Challenge and Opportunity," presented at the second international policy forum, International Motor Vehicle Program, MIT, May 1988.

hood, and its 220 inches in overall length created a substantial rear overhang. Powered by a 5-liter V8 engine with great response but poor fuel economy, the car offered a soft ride, roomy interior, and extensive options. The "American Concept" was based on a package of distinctive product experiences rooted in a world of low energy prices, long-haul transportation, wide and straight roads, and a culture that appreciated "bigness." American cars were free from many of the constraints that confronted European and Japanese designers. Low energy prices made trade-offs among vehicle weight, engine power, and fuel economy less important, and the large body created space flexibility, making packaging less critical. The freedom to build "room to maneuver" into their cars allowed American producers to develop cars with less coordination among components.[3]

European products delivered a markedly different experience. Despite great variety, one could find common themes in European cars. The first-generation Volkswagen Golf, introduced in 1974, captures the "European Concept" well. The first Golf set the standard for the subcompact hatchback worldwide. The concept was clear—an "econobox" with superior handling and performance. The car achieved a high level of balance in economy, convenience, roominess, and comfort. European cars, even small cars like the Golf, were "driving machines" characterized by space and fuel efficiency, relative simplicity of options, sharp response, firm ride, precise handling, and functional sophistication. The concept was rooted in the economic, demographic, and technological context of Europe that included a long tradition of engineering excellence; high energy prices; knowledgeable and so- phisticated customers; and narrow, winding roads.

Product concepts in Japan reflected the pressures of rapid growth and economic development. Japanese producers, in catch-up mode until the 1970s, borrowed initial concepts from American and European companies. The preferences of the rapidly expanding base of customers, many of whom were encountering an automobile for the first time, were varied and unstable. The result was a variety of different models that reflected American and European heritage. Toyota's third-generation Corolla in the 1970s, for example, had the engine power, body size, and integrated packaging of a European car, along with the proliferation of options and features and the interior comfort of a much larger American car. Handling and ride in the Corolla were closer to the European concept, but other Japanese products in other segments opted for the soft, boulevard ride of American cars. In a word, the Japanese automobile product concept was eclectic.

The differences in product concept seen in Table 3.1 reflect the very different social and economic contexts in which European, American, and Japanese cars developed. Table 3.2 provides an over- view of the market and competitive environments in these three regions. Differences across regions are clear. In Japan, a larger number of competitors have battled over a smaller, more volatile domestic market. Europe has also had a large number of competitors, but the market has been less volatile. The U.S. market, a classic oligopoly led by General Motors, was intermediate in frequency of product intro- ductions and product longevity. Differences in the nature of competi- tion in these markets exerted an important influence on the character of product development. We look first at the situation in Europe.

Table 3.2 Summary of Product-Market Patterns by Region

Product-Market Pattern / Region	United States	Europe (EC)	Japan
Annual Car Sales (1985)	10.9 million	9.5 million	3.1 million
Annual Car Sales (1975)	8.3 million	7.6 million	2.7 million
Average Annual Growth of Car Sales (1975–1985)	2.8%	2.3%	1.3%
Number of Major Domestic Car Producers (1987)	4	West Germany: 6 France: 2 United Kingdom: 5 Italy: 3	9
Production Share of Top Three Car Producers (1985)	95%	West Germany: 76% France: 100% United Kingdom: 90% Italy: 100%	71%
Car Import Share (1985)	28%	16% (EC total)	2%
Average Number of Car Models (1982–1987)	28	77	55
Number of New Car Models Developed (1982–1987)	21	38	72
Average Major Model Change Interval (1982–1987)	8.1 years	12.2 years	4.6 years

Note: See the Appendix for sources and detail.

COMPETITION IN EUROPE

Europe was the birthplace of the automobile. European producers, particularly in Germany and France, were leaders in automobile production and technology when cars were still custom-made for the wealthy.[4] The tradition of European automobiles, which emphasizes variety and technical sophistication over standardization and low cost, had its origins in the late nineteenth century. Without a large, unified market, different companies in different countries have developed cars with various concepts and identities. German cars, for example, tended toward hard suspensions for better road holding, reflecting the needs of high-speed driving on winding roads. French cars generally had softer suspensions and seats in response to relatively bumpy roads. Thus, "it has been quite impossible for a single producer to dominate the European market or for a single design philosophy to prevail. At any given time, a wide range of models and national preferences protects the mass market producers from dramatic demand shifts."[5]

Strong corporate identity. Traditional patterns of competition and product differentiation in Europe are characterized in Figure 3.1, which illustrates how individual product concepts interact or cluster across companies (horizontal axis) and product segments (vertical axis). Each of the black nodes represents a product, and each of the shaded areas represents a cluster of products that share a common theme or concept. Thus a vertical clustering (i.e., similarity in concepts) implies the existence of a company-wide product identity, while a horizontal clustering suggests the existence of intense competition within a segment. Cross-company similarities in concepts indicate that consumers tend to compare these products more directly.

Figure 3.1 illustrates how significantly different historical patterns of concept clustering have been across regions. Europe, with stronger vertical clustering than either the United States or Japan, tended toward strong corporate identity or common engineering philosophies that prevailed throughout a company's entire product line. Each European company defined a good car differently and maintained that concept consistently across segments and over time.

The customer side of the European market mirrored this pattern of concept clustering. Customers established different expectations for products of different companies independent of product segment. They expected Fiat cars, for example, to possess a distinctive personality, or "Fiat-ness," that was markedly different from "VW-ness," "Mercedes-ness," or "Citroën-ness." Consequently, European consumers tended to evaluate cars less through direct comparison with other companies' products than through comparison with their expectations of products from a particular company. As long as a car lived up to their expectations, European consumers tended to remain loyal to its producer. This resulted in spirals of mutual interaction between product designs and consumer tastes. The stability and consistency of product concepts led consumers to develop sophisticated and complicated expectations of design, function, concept, and aesthetics for each model and company. This, in turn, motivated producers to refine product details to a very high degree, while maintaining conceptual continuity in order not to confuse customer expectations. The result of this mutually reinforcing process was a combination of demanding but loyal customers on the one hand, and sophisticated product designs with strong identity on the other.

Figure 3.1 Traditional Clusters of Concepts by Region

1. European Cluster of Concepts

Concept Clustering
by Companies
(corporate identity)

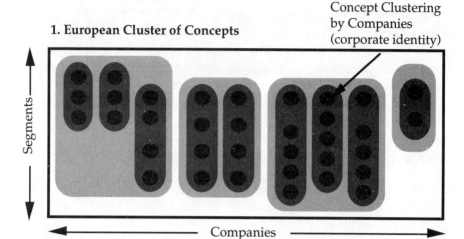

Segments

Companies

2. U.S. Cluster of Concepts

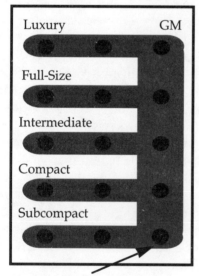

Luxury   GM

Full-Size

Intermediate

Compact

Subcompact

GM's Concept Leadership

3. Japanese Cluster of Concepts

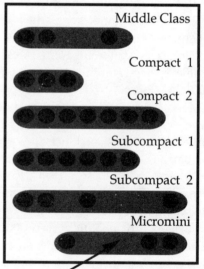

Middle Class

Compact 1

Compact 2

Subcompact 1

Subcompact 2

Micromini

Concept Clustering by Segments
(direct product rivalry)

● Individual Product Concepts

━ Clusters of Similar Concepts

━ Country Clusters

Take the example of BMW. Established in 1917 as an aircraft engine manufacturer, BMW developed its first original model, the 303, in 1933.[6] Characteristics of prewar-era BMW models are clearly in evidence in their offspring, sporty sedans with sharp handling, a smooth in-line engine, and clean styling beginning at the famous "kidney grille." One is struck by the remarkable continuity in basic concepts and design between BMWs of the 1960s and those of the 1980s. Many of the functional, mechanical, and formal characteristics of the 1962 BMW 1500—such as the well-balanced, in-line overhead camshaft engine; McPherson strut front suspension; semitrailing arm rear suspension; distinctive styling features in the grille, hood, and quarter pillars; and overall handling and ride—can be found in today's BMW models. Its basic four-model line-up, with small, medium, and large sedans and a medium coupe, has also remained unchanged.

Even stronger conceptual continuity is observed in the world's oldest automobile producer, Daimler-Benz. Today's Daimler-Benz (Mercedes) passenger cars, from luxury to compact class, are characterized by functional superiority (e.g., performance and safety at 200 km/hour), technical sophistication (e.g., multilink suspensions), high product image (e.g., status symbol), distinctiveness in styling, and so forth. Many of these characteristics—including large, high-output engines, commitment to racing and speed records, distinctive radiator grille, and high-status image based on product sophistication—were present in the 1920s or even earlier.[7]

Indirect product rivalry. Another aspect of the vertical concept clustering exhibited in Figure 3.1 is indirect product rivalry within segments. Product differentiation with strong companywide identity apparently alleviated competitive pressure to match basic functional performance with rivals. Because customers applied different expectations to different producers, products were less subject to direct comparison. As long as consumers remained loyal to a product concept, the producer did not need to match its product performance with that of others. Thus, the main challenge for a Citroën designer was not to match Renault models but to meet the expectations of Citroën customers.

The context for European product development embodied the challenge of developing a new product that maintained continuity of concept, while offering the kind of performance and value that would appeal to sophisticated, demanding European customers. What emerged were relatively long product life cycles, heavy emphasis on engineering elegance and sophistication, and continuity of design. Infrequent model changes incorporated major changes in technology and performance.

COMPETITION IN THE UNITED STATES

With the advent of Henry Ford's Model T, the United States became the clear leader in automobile production. This product introduced the U.S. market early to a mass-market-oriented, highly standardized design. Competition in the Model T era was a matter of economies of scale, production cost, stable design, and widespread dealer networks. Ford excelled at all of these. But the industry changed dramatically in the 1920s, as customers sought greater variety, comfort, and performance. General Motors (in the person of Alfred Sloan) took the basic Ford formula and added variety in styling, color, and performance. Sloan created a development and production system that pursued commonality in chassis design, change and variety in body style and color (flexible welding lines and paint shops), and a marketing policy that emphasized value and breadth of line.[8]

Sloan chose to attack Ford with a better product and somewhat higher price rather than compete on cost with a standard product. The Chevrolet, though more expensive than the Model T, offered more car, color, and a fresher style. Indeed, Sloan's strategy involved a basic redefinition of the automobile from a rural utility vehicle (the Model T) to a living room on wheels (the all-purpose road cruiser) that changed frequently (the annual styling change) to maintain a fresh look and high appeal. This new concept, which combined fashion and style in a mass-produced product, reinforced the capital-intensive nature of the business; on top of high-volume production, there were now regular, major tooling changes to produce the annually changing parts and sheet metal. By the 1930s, GM had established a dominant position in a highly concentrated U.S. auto industry. Sloan's concept and GM's dominance persisted into the postwar era and gave competition—including the role of product development—a very different character than that observed in Europe or Japan.

GM leadership. GM's leadership was evident in most aspects of the U.S. auto business. Other major Big Three U.S. auto makers offered packages that reflected GM's broad concept of product and product line built around a large car with a long hood, large trunk, powerful engine, comfortable interior, and smooth ride. But GM stood out in styling.[9] Sloan established the first (and for many years the only) design group dedicated to automotive styling. The Art and Color Section, run by the legendary Harley Earl, established leadership in the industry in two ways: (1) the group was the source of many important styling trends in the postwar era (e.g., tail fins, sculpted body sides, and heavy use of chrome), and (2) many of the designers that eventually worked for Ford and Chrysler got their start and learned the craft in Earl's group.

Though GM exerted considerable influence over automotive design, there was tactical rivalry within segments and in the creation of new categories.[10] In the 1960s, for example, Ford introduced the Fairlane, a somewhat smaller version of the standard Ford. This new class of car—the intermediate—soon drew entries from Chevrolet (the Chevelle) and Plymouth (the Belvedere). Ford's 1964 introduction of the Mustang, a small, affordable, sporty two-door coupe was followed by Chrysler's Barracuda, Chevrolet's Camaro, and Pontiac's Firebird. In both cases, tactical moves to find a niche in the market led to similar products by competitors. The result was that for any given segment or category, customers found a relatively common product concept.

A customer base willing to accept a greater degree of standardization, the small number of competitors, and GM's market leadership led to industrywide clustering of concepts within product segments in the U.S. market, while GM's product line strategy created some clustering across segments. Thus, concepts in Figure 3.1 cluster by product category (luxury, full-size, intermediate, compact, and subcompact) within an overlaid cluster around GM. Rivalry in the U.S. market was more intense than in Europe but less intense than in Japan.

Variety of form—uniformity of function. One of the central themes in product development and competition in the U.S. market has been the tension between scale economies and product variety. Manufacturing strategies were built around the notion that low cost required high volumes of standard parts at the same time that customers, though more accepting of standardization than their European cousins, wanted a degree of variety and even customization. GM's genius lay in achieving scale economies through standardization of parts and components, while offering variety in style and color and customization in the form of optional equipment.

GM's strategy fit not only the market, but also the product concept and basic technology. Until the 1970s, U.S. car designs emphasized body-on-frame construction, which allowed body development (where most styling changes occur) to be separated from power-train and chassis development, except for interfaces between the two. Moreover, because U.S. cars were large and constraints few, stylists enjoyed a measure of freedom that was limited only by the physics of bending sheet metal. In the extreme (and some designs of the late 1950s were extreme), this resulted in a tenuous relationship between form and function—body styles inspired by jet fighters and speed boats coupled to the basic V8 engine, rear drive-automatic transmission power train and chassis.

Americans were in love with the U.S. product concept—the annual styling change and the broad range of choice. It was a concept that generated huge volume and large profits. When small imports challenged that product concept, domestic producers fought back, not with highly integrated, efficient small cars, but with smaller versions of the basic large car (e.g., the Dodge Valiant).

With low gasoline prices, a spacious design envelope, and power-hungry customers, tight packaging, advanced technology, and refined vehicle performance were much less critical than in Europe. Success lay in creative body work, the use of color and chrome, and refinements to the basic technology. Consequently, designers focused on more elaborate styling while engineers pursued greater power and comfort and more profitable options within narrow areas of specialization.

COMPETITION IN JAPAN

The Japanese auto producers' rise from small, backward players to industry leaders has been a central theme in competition over the last fifteen years. Western observers tend to view these Japanese producers as aggressive exporters who have deliberately tuned their strategies and organizations to compete effectively in foreign markets. This model may tell part of the story, but it overlooks the fact that the primary competitive arena for Japanese producers has been Japanese markets. Japanese producers who do not survive in the domestic market cannot become volume exporters, and the competitive realities of the Japanese domestic market are unique. Japan has been a dynamic, complex, intense arena in which to design and develop cars.

Concept clustering around segments. The pattern of concept clustering shown for Japan in Figure 3.1 contrasts sharply with those observed for Europe and the United States. With neither a clear concept leader nor strong companywide identities, Japanese product concepts have clustered around product segments. Japanese product concepts have tended to be unstable over time, partly because Japanese auto makers were playing technical catch-up throughout the 1950s and 1960s and even in the 1970s, and partly because Japanese customers were relatively inexperienced. Moreover, the existence of many competitors in more narrowly defined segments resulted in strong intrasegment rivalry. Competitors acted quickly to match the new standards in design and performance introduced with each model. Design continuity over time or across models was much less critical than matching rivals.

Instability of concepts and designs. In commercial volume production of passenger cars, which began after World War II, Japanese car technology remained for years in catch-up mode at both the total vehicle and component levels, requiring Japanese producers to import technologies and concepts from the United States and Europe.[11] The result was a lack of conceptual continuity. Japanese products seldom had a strong identity at the company level; one did not get a sense of "Nissan-ness" in the products produced by Nissan.

Instability of customer tastes. Partly because product concepts were unstable, and partly because Japanese customers in the 1950–1970 period had relatively little experience with automobiles, customer tastes were also unstable. Unable to develop a solid idea of what constituted a good car, consumers tended to be attracted to whatever was new (new mechanisms, features, styling, standards of performance, and so forth). Customer loyalty was directed at dealers or salespeople.

The intense intrasegment rivalry that resulted from the instability of product concepts and customer tastes created a distinctive pattern of new model sales. Figure 3.2, which compares product sales in the U.S. and Japanese markets for selected Japanese models, shows larger sales fluctuations for particular models in the Japanese market.

Figure 3.2 Impact of Model Renewals on Sales: Selected Japanese Models

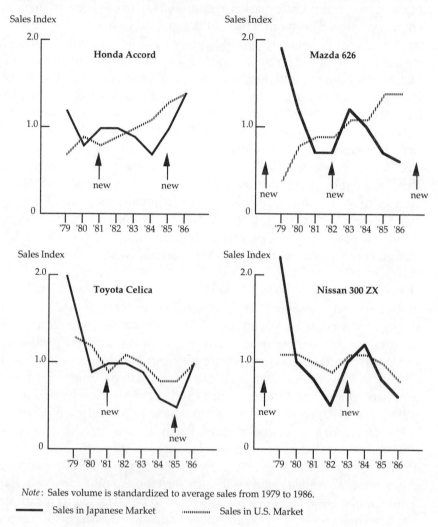

Note: Sales volume is standardized to average sales from 1979 to 1986.

——— Sales in Japanese Market   ⋯⋯⋯⋯ Sales in U.S. Market

Japanese sales jump following new model introductions and then decline quickly until the next new model. This volatility of sales at the individual model level is remarkable considering the fact that overall sales are much less variable in Japan than in the United States. New products are critical to maintaining sales performance in this environment.

Intense domestic competition. During the 1950s, the Japanese automobile market resembled those of less developed countries. Customer incomes were low, roads were underdeveloped, and products were utilitarian. Bicycles, motorcycles, three-wheelers, and commercial trucks were common, but personal car ownership was rare until the 1960s, when it expanded rapidly. Domestic unit car sales went from 100,000 in 1960 to 2.4 million in 1970 and 3.1 million in 1986. As growth in the domestic market slowed in the 1970s, competition intensified, partly as a result of the number of competitors. In 1965, eleven Japanese companies were producing cars on a mass-production basis. Nine were still competing in domestic and global markets in 1990.[12]

Intense competition was accompanied by aggressive sales force expansion and large price discounts. Although the Japanese dealer system, like the U.S. system, included franchise contracts and multiple channels, the actual pattern of sales activity was very different. The Japanese dealer system was characterized by long-term, exclusive relationships between producers and dealers, heavy reliance on door-to-door sales, diversification to after-sales service, high service quality, and low productivity (see Table 3.3). Large discounts and high trade-in values were common, and many dealerships that suffered from chronically negative profits in the early 1980s survived only by transfusions of rebates and incentives from manufacturers.[13]

Direct product rivalry. Competition in the Japanese domestic market was intense at both the individual product and producer levels. Market segments were defined narrowly, and comparisons between similar models were visible and direct.[14] The rivalry between the Nissan Bluebird and Toyota Corona—the main products of these two companies throughout the 1960s, 1970s, and 1980s—is classic. The Bluebird and Corona have competed with each other continuously in product content and sales volume since their respective introductions in 1959 and 1960.[15] Both underwent major changes every four years. Domestic sales volume see-sawed according to the success or failure of product renewals on either side (see Figure 3.3).

With a dynamic consumer market, intense competition, and direct product rivalry, the challenge for Japanese designers and product developers was clear: keep old models fresh and competitive, and develop new models where competitors are vulnerable. The firms that

Table 3.3 Comparison of U.S. and Japanese Automobile Dealership Systems

Characteristics	Japan	United States
Legal Relations	franchise contracts	franchise contracts
Implementation	flexible execution of contracts	rigid execution of contracts
Exclusivity	one dealer handles one channel with an exclusive territory	multiple-channel dealers common
Manufacturer-Owned Dealership	exist	do not exist
Stability of Relations	high (low turnover)	low (frequent dealer switches)
Goal Orientation	longer-term	shorter-term
Number of Channels in Domestic Markets	multiple (Toyota: 5; Nissan: 5; Mazda: 3; Honda: 3)	multiple (GM: 5; Ford: 3; Chrysler: 3)
Average Dealer Size	large (about 180 employees*)	small (about 30 employees**)
Showroom per Dealer	multiple (average 8 per dealer*)	mostly single-showroom operations
Main Mode of Sales	door-to-door sales (salespeople visit customers)	counter sales (customers visit showrooms)
Customer-Salesforce Relationship	long-term through after-sales services	short-term
Dealers' Diversification to Auto-Related Services	high (repair/maintenance, parts, inspection, insurance, paperwork, accident settlement)	low (some have repair shops)
Technical Ability of Salesforce	high (many salespeople have mechanics license)	low (sales specialists)
Wage System	salary and commission	commission only
After-Sales Service	wide range and high density	lower levels
Salesforce Productivity	low; little improvement from the 1970s to 1980s	high

Source: Based on Shimokawa (1981, 1985), authors' own studies, and others.

* As of 1984   ** As of 1983

Figure 3.3 Corona versus Bluebird Sales See-Saw

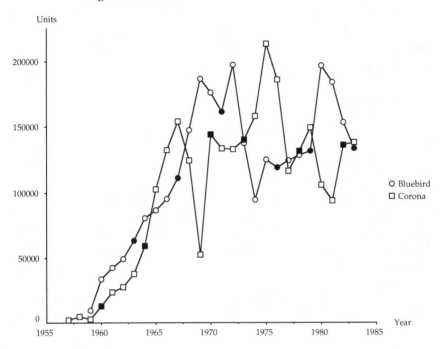

Source: Higuchi (1984).
Note: Black nodes stand for years when new models were introduced.

survived did so and did so quickly. Throughout the 1960s and 1970s, the average model-change interval was less than five years. The number of models (not minor variations, but independent platforms that shared fewer than half their parts with other models) grew from fewer than 10 in 1960 to 40 by the mid 1970s.

STRATEGIC DIFFERENCES BETWEEN VOLUME PRODUCERS AND HIGH-END SPECIALISTS

Differences in geography and national circumstance have been critical to the development of all industry participants. Differences in strategy have also been important, particularly in Europe. European firms that have chosen to focus on high-priced, high-performance, luxury products have confronted quite a different set of customers and a markedly different market environment than firms that have targeted the mass market. Patterns of competition for what we call "high-end specialists" and "volume producers" have also been different. Firms that face different markets and competition are likely to have different product development capabilities and therefore different strategies.

HISTORICAL ROOTS

The distinction between high-end specialists and volume producers has a long history. Industry observers and auto company executives seem to agree that all major U.S. and Japanese car producers are volume producers (e.g., General Motors, Ford, and Chrysler in the United States and Toyota, Nissan, Mazda, Mitsubishi, Honda, Isuzu, Daihatsu, Fuji, and Suzuki in Japan). Major European producers, on the other hand, include both volume producers (e.g., Volkswagen, PSA, Fiat, Ford of Europe, GM Europe, and Rover Group) and high-end specialists (e.g., Daimler-Benz, BMW, Audi, Porsche, Jaguar, Volvo, and Saab).

The tradition of high-end specialists is as old as the European automobile market. Classic designs from the pre-1940 era include cars from Bugatti and Delage in France; Hispano-Suiza in Spain; Isotta-Fraschini and Alfa Romeo in Italy; Daimler-Benz, Horch (later Auto Union), and Maybach (later BMW) in Germany; as well as Rolls-Royce, Bentley, and Lanchester in Great Britain. These automobiles were sophisticated not only in exterior and interior design, but also in performance—a philosophy that has been handed down to today's high-end specialists. The emphasis of these producers on high performance is evidenced by their commitment to racing activities. High-end specialists such as Mercedes, Bugatti, and Alfa Romeo were legendary in racing and sporting activities during the prewar era.

The European auto industry grew rapidly after the war. Production of motor vehicles in Western Europe rose from 1.6 million in 1950 to 6.1 million in 1960, a level almost comparable to that of North America (8.3 million in 1960). Full-fledged volume producers emerged with such "people's cars" as the Volkswagen Beetle, Citroën 2CV, Renault 4CV, Fiat 500, and Morris Minor.[16] Borrowing from the early American concept, the European volume producers created automobiles that provided basic transportation at a low price. But the advent of mass production did not eliminate the European tradition of well-crafted, high-performance vehicles. Many high-end specialists survived as independent concerns, clearly distinguished from the volume producers.

The situation in the United States was very different. The logic of volume production dominated the American market. None of the U.S. firms that specialized in high-priced luxury cars (e.g., Cadillac, Lincoln, Duesenberg, Marmon, and Packard) survived the postwar period as independent firms. Some disappeared; others merged into the Big Three. High-end products followed the GM concept; if they were continued at all, they were incorporated into the company's product line to share a significant portion of components and engineering philosophy with the volume products. American high-end models were thus managed as an extension of volume products.

A similar policy prevailed in Japan. Large, luxurious cars were treated as an integral part of the overall product line. High-end and volume products were designed and produced by the same organizations. The logic carried into advertising; the catch phrase for Toyota's high-end product, the Crown, was for many years "someday, a Crown." The message was "start with a Corolla, trade up to a Corona, and someday make it all the way to the Crown." All the while, the customer would be buying a Toyota.

Competitive behavior. The postwar competitive behavior of volume producers and high-end specialists was quite different. The contrast between the two strategic groups is summarized in Table 3.4.[17] As the table suggests, the two strategies involve different patterns in pricing, delivery, production, and product differentiation. Volume producers compete mainly in low to medium price ranges ($5,000 to $15,000 in retail price as of 1987), targeting the majority of car buyers. Sales volume, or market share, has been critical to their profitability partly because of the combination of low price and high break-even point. To minimize the opportunity cost of lost sales, volume producers try to minimize delivery lead time to customers and expand production capacity when expected sales exceed capacity. Consequently, the industry as a whole has suffered from cyclical profit fluctuations and overcapacity problems during recessions.

High-end specialists, on the other hand, compete almost exclusively in the high price ranges (typically over $20,000 as of 1987), targeting affluent car buyers. Because virtually all their products are

Table 3.4 Summary of Two Competitive Strategies in the Car Industry

Strategic Variables \ Strategic Types	Volume Producer	High-End Specialist
Regional Origin	United States/ Japan/Europe	Europe
Goal Priority	market share or sales volume	profit margin; sustaining high price
Main Price Range (in 1987 U.S. dollars)	low-middle ($5,000 - $15,000) often with discount	high (over $25,000) discount is rare
Delivery	short delivery time	long delivery time
Production Capacity	tendency to overcapacity	tendency to undercapacity
Profit Margin	less stable	more stable
Product Differentiation	differentiation by adaptation of total vehicle concept to customers' lifestyle/ image/feeling matching rivals in cost and basic performance	differentiation by high performance in well-established functional criteria (e.g., safety at extremely high speed) maintaining stability and consistency of product concept

Source: Adapted from Fujimoto (1989), Chapter 6.

designed and produced with high fixed and variable costs, sustaining a high product price is critical to profitability. Production capacity is typically and purposefully maintained at less than demand, resulting in large back orders and long delivery times. This contributes to stability of production levels and profits.

Product differentiation. The contrast between volume producers and high-end specialists is also manifested in the way they perceive markets and differentiate products. Volume producers in all three regions have shared similar differentiation strategies. Cost, of course, has been critical. Prices have varied little across competitors; profit margins (and the resulting ability to maneuver) have varied much more. Larger-scale, more efficient operations and better management of materials have been a focus of competition and a source of advantage for the firms that had an edge.

But competition has not stopped there for volume producers. They have also sought to create an edge in the product itself. Balancing functionality and economy has been a particular focus. Firms have sought to offer distinctive mixes of fuel economy (especially in Japan and Europe), acceleration, speed, braking, handling, and comfort by segment. Competition and advances in technology produced improvements in all these areas, making differentiation dependent on the ability to improve at a rate equal to or greater than one's competitors. The drive for improvement has been limited by the nature of the customer and the need to keep costs in line. Thus, exotic hardware capable of delivering an extra measure of performance has not been an attractive option in the volume market.

Compared to today's volume products, cars of the early postwar period were simple and straightforward. In retrospect, they offered ample opportunity for "featurization." Particularly in the American and Japanese markets, but also in Europe, producers sought to add convenience, comfort, and even novelty. The advantage a firm gained from bringing out a new feature, though it did not last long, prompted a steady stream of new ideas. The list includes push-button automatic transmissions, sunroofs, adjustable steering wheels, power windows, power door locks, fold-down back seats, swivel seats, heated seats, power-operated head rests, two-way tailgates, air conditioning, entertainment systems, drink holders, map pockets, and coin holders. Some of these features added value and survived; others did not and were lost.

The same has been true of aesthetics. The automobile has become a "socially significant" product; when in use, both product and buyer are on display, and appearance matters. Firms have sought to differentiate on the basis of style and fashion since the 1920s. Different tastes have prevailed in the postwar period, but in all markets a design with visual and tactile appeal has been an advantage. Car buyers have seen new kinds and colors of paint (two-tone, deep luster, metallic, clear-coat), new bodies (hatchbacks, econobox, five-door sedans), new forms (tail fins, spoilers), and new materials (vinyl, velour, leather). In a fashion-oriented market, a new design with different aesthetics offered only a transitory advantage, but the impact on sales could be substantial. Evaluating the relative importance of a new piece of technology in the 1960s, Lee Iacocca said "give 'em leather, they can smell it."

Product differentiation strategies at the high end have been very different. High-end specialists, to justify their high prices, have sought differentiation through functional superiority in established performance criteria. Image and aesthetics, though also important, are always backed by unequivocal superiority in hardware. High-end specialists emphasize total balance of basic performance (e.g., handling, road holding, stability, safety, ride, and so forth) under extreme conditions where the technical edge is obvious even to ordinary drivers.

High-end specialists tend to maintain stability and consistency of product concept across models and over time in order to protect their existing technical advantages and preserve the loyalty of existing customers. High-end specialists define the concept of excellence and impose it on customers; that is, they sell their cars only to those customers who understand their definition of product excellence. Stability of product concepts on the producer side means stability in customer expectations. Consider the following observations regarding the strategy of high-end specialists.

We have always tried to go our own way. . . . We are simply doing our best based on our own values. . . . No one knows whether our choice will be right. Even experienced engineers would have no idea on it. The answer will be known five to ten years from now.[18]

While driving at lower speeds, consumers may not be able to recognize the distinctive performance of our cars. When driving at 200 km per hour, however, a driver should be able to tell the difference in stability, road holding, active safety, and so on.[19]

We don't conduct discount sales just in order to increase production volume. In fact, we have a long waiting list of buyers, which is a desirable situation for us. We do not intend to follow the ways of Toyota, Nissan, or GM.[20]

Volume producers and high-end specialists, facing very different market segments, developed very different patterns of competitive behavior. But subsequent changes in the market, technology, and competition, first felt in the 1980s, have begun to weaken the boundaries between these strategic groups. As the 1990s open, changes in the environment affecting the character of regional markets suggest the beginning of a new era in automotive competition.

GLOBAL COMPETITION

As a result of intense competition, market fragmentation, and technological change, regional competition with some international trading at the margin is giving way to direct product-to-product competition on a global scale. Trade has expanded significantly, and truly global market segments have emerged in which basic product characteristics and concepts have converged, giving rise to strong product rivalry. Regions and strategic groups have been affected differently, but none has remained unchanged.

GLOBAL COMPETITION AND REGIONAL MARKETS

The most dramatic change in the U.S. market environment was precipitated by the double oil shocks of the 1970s. Gasoline prices have always been high in Europe and Japan. There the oil shocks added to the effects of other, longer-term but no less powerful forces. In Europe, for example, integration of the European Common Market and an increase in Japanese imports changed the pattern of competition.

The products of European volume producers who chose to compete with the Japanese became increasingly subject to direct comparison with other products, European as well as Japanese. Except in France, Italy, and Spain, the share of Japanese imports increased significantly during the late 1970s and 1980s.[21] As Japanese products approached European products in terms of product concept and level of sophistication, international rivalry intensified. Table 3.5, which

Table 3.5 Comparison of Compact Models in the European Market

Company	Model/Version	Price (Swiss franc)	Horse-power	Engine Size (cc)	Weight/ Power Ratio (kg/hp)	Acceleration (0-100 km/h in seconds)	Maximum Speed (km/h)	Fuel Economy (ECE method)
Opel	Ascona GT 2.0 i	21,225	115	1997	8.9	10.0	187	6.1/7.4/10.2
Ford of Europe	Sierra GL	21,925	101	1993	9.2	10.6	190	6.5/8.4/10.8
VW	Passat GL 2.2	23,690	115	2225	10.5	9.4	185	6.1/7.8/10.9
Renault	21 RX	21,990	110	2165	9.1	9.7	200	5.8/7.1/10.0
Peugeot	305 GTX	20,580	100	1905	10.8	9.3	182	5.8/7.6/9.2
Citroën	BX 19 TRI	21,850	104	1905	9.5	10.0	185	6.0/7.6/9.5
Fiat	Croma ie	24,950	115	1994	9.3	9.9	192	6.0/7.6/9.2
Toyota	Camry 2.0 GLi	24,490	120*	1995	9.2	9.4	190	6.4/8.8/9.8
Nissan	Bluebird 2.0 E/SGX	23,950	104	1974	10.6	n.a.	175	n.a.
Mazda	626 2.0 GLX	21,990	92	1998	9.2	n.a.	183	6.4/8.1/9.8
Honda	Accord Sedan EX 2.0	24,690	102	1954	8.6	n.a.	189	6.1/7.8/9.3
Mitsubishi	Galant 2000 GLS	21,690	90	1997	10.6	n.a.	180	7.7/8.7/12.5

Source: <u>1987 Katalog der Automobil Revue</u>, Hallwag, Switzerland.
*Net horsepower, measured according to Japanese Industrial Standards.

shows compact models offered by European and Japanese producers in the Swiss market, illustrates how basic performance and price range have become comparable across products.

As product segmentation has become more international and less company- or country-specific, the stability of the European producer-consumer relationship has weakened. European producers, facing less loyal customers, must now match cost and basic performance with rivals while adapting product concepts to consumer tastes. The competitive behavior of the European volume producers, who might maintain traditional strengths in product identity and performance, is likely to converge to fit the pattern of global volume producers.[22]

Convergence has been an important theme in the American market, where change has been more dramatic. The oil shocks of the 1970s focused American producers on improving fuel economy, initially through downsizing and later through new technology (e.g., new materials, electronics, frontwheel drive). These changes in design—which transformed the traditional American product in almost all dimensions—were accompanied by a new generation of car buyers and continuing competitive thrusts by European and Japanese firms at both ends of the American market. Thus new conditions of competition persisted even after the immediate stimulus to change, the price of oil, faded.

The shift toward product designs with higher fuel economy triggered a further shift in the focus of product competition. The international gap in fuel economy narrowed rapidly as American cars became smaller, but other gaps in product content became more apparent. Early 1980s American products designed to compete with European and Japanese products were downsized versions of the basic "American concept" (e.g., X-body by GM and K-body by Chrysler). When it became clear that customers, especially baby boomers, preferred the European concepts long dominant in the smaller-size segments, U.S. producers began to shift to more European vehicle concepts. "Until 1982," explained GM president Robert Stempel, "GM assumed that further downsizing would be necessary to be competitive. However, the market environment changed more dramatically than we expected. The focus shifted from competition in fuel economy and downsizing to competition in product concepts."[23] Like cost, manufacturing quality, and basic function, fuel economy had become a given, a requirement to play the game. Now competition focused on the product itself.

Shifts in competition in Europe and America have at least one thing in common: Japanese imports. The driving forces in the world market over the last twenty years have created an opportunity that players nurtured in the Japanese domestic market seemed well positioned to exploit. There competition was rigorous, customers were fickle and demanding, gasoline prices were higher than in the United States, and the product concepts incorporated both European and American dimensions. Furthermore, the domestic market (at least until the 1960s) was fairly well protected. On a world scale, the products were not ready for head-to-head competition with the very best, and the driving forces evident in the United States and Europe were also at work in Japan. Success at home and abroad required new capabilities.

The oil crises, government regulation, and a vigorous consumer movement pressed Japanese car producers to improve fuel economy, emission control, and safety almost simultaneously in the 1970s.[24] Japanese cars did not need a massive size-down, but the challenge was still significant. Basic automotive technology in Japan was adequate but essentially derivative, and the industry was still young and without deep technological resources. Adversity triggered a period of rapid technological progress, particularly in small engines, but when Japanese firms finally met emission and efficiency targets, other elements of performance, such as power and smoothness, deteriorated. It was not until the early 1980s that the Japanese regained a balance of emission control, fuel economy, and power.

Though Japanese firms actively precipitated international competition in America and Europe, global competition did not reach the Japanese markets until the late 1980s. Although tariffs on imports ended in 1978, rigorous government regulations on emission control and safety inspection, a domestic tax system that penalized larger cars, severe domestic competition, a complex distribution system, and lack of effective marketing efforts prevented import sales from taking off until the mid 1980s. Import sales, which had remained stagnant at 50,000 units annually (1–2 percent of the domestic car market) throughout the late 1970s and early 1980s, doubled to about 100,000 units between 1985 and 1987. In 1989, imports increased to almost 200,000 units, and some observers predicted a 10 percent market share for imports by the mid 1990s. Many of the imported products, particularly German designs, developed a strong image in the Japanese market (BMW and Mercedes cars were featured on TV programs, at high-status events, and in other venues where buyers sought to make a statement). Although more than 95 percent of 1987 imports were from Europe (about 75 percent from West Germany), there were signs that imports from American producers might find a niche in Japan (Ford's Taurus and Probe and Honda's Accord Coupe, built in the company's Ohio plant, all entered the Japanese market in 1988).

GLOBAL COMPETITION AND STRATEGIC GROUPS

In the face of the changes in markets, competitors, and technology that have transformed the industry from regional to global competition, volume producers and high-end specialists have responded quite differently. European high-end specialists have pursued an extreme version of the European strategy: strong corporate identity, engineering excellence, functional superiority, and loyal customers. With no true Japanese or American high-end specialists, the European high-end specialists have competed among themselves, where they have pursued international sales among high-performance-oriented customers.

For volume producers, the changes have been dramatic. Technology has substantially undercut the value of scale economies; profitability has come to rely more on lean, high-quality operations than on size; and market fragmentation has considerably reduced the volume for particular models. Flexibility—in product mix, in responding to competitors, and in financial strength—has become a watchword among volume producers. Today's savvy volume producer is more likely to stretch the existing system than to expand capacity. Cost remains vital, but its structure has changed. Far more important is managing indirect costs (e.g., material handling and administrative overhead) and the product and process complexity that drives them. Finally, time is of the essence. Getting to market quickly with new products has become an essential feature of competition.

The product, too, has changed for volume producers. In the mid and late 1980s, they faced customers whose needs were increasingly unpredictable, inarticulate, and holistic. These needs extended beyond basic transportation to social symbolism, self-expression, and entertainment. With rivals capable of quickly matching prices and technical performance, it was becoming increasingly difficult to sustain long-term advantage through basic technical performance (e.g., miles per gallon and acceleration) and cost. Volume producers responded by trying to differentiate their products through "total vehicle concept"—matching the vehicle as a whole and the customer's lifestyle, sensibility, use patterns, aesthetic sense, and philosophy. Basic performance and cost had to be comparable, but superiority in these traditional dimensions did not guarantee product success in the market. "In the past," explained then-president of Mazda Motor Corporation Ken-ichi Yamamoto,

> we could quantify our goals of product development by specifying numbers such as weight, cost, and engine horse-power. However, today's customers are not satisfied with such numbers any more. They are now talking about certain differences which they can sense while driving even if they cannot articulate the differences. They say that that car is different, even if its performance in braking and acceleration is exactly the same as the other cars. This is what I call the "feeling" or "sensibility."[25]

Fumio Agetsume, former product manager in charge of Corolla and other models at Toyota, observed that

> Young people are not seeking for affluence by simply owning things anymore. They want a new kind of affluence by dramatizing their lives. This means that the young car buyers do not choose their brands based on prices, qualities, and functions alone anymore. In order for a brand to become appealing to them, certain "soft" values such as "urban feeling" or "high-tech feeling" have to be added.[26]

As a result, according to president of Chrysler Corporation Robert Lutz,

> We've got to focus on the total vehicle rather than on individual components. If there's a focus on the total vehicle, you're going to find that the vehicle is greater than the sum of the parts. What's been the case sometimes—especially

with Japanese producers—is that the sum of the parts is greater than the whole. Every bit you do is somewhat noble, but when you get it all together, the vehicle doesn't quite feel as good as it should.[27]

Indications are that the traditional distinctions between these two strategic groups—the volume producers and high-end specialists—may be less sharp in the future. The success of the high-end specialists has attracted the attention of volume producers looking for profitable market niches. Rapid improvement of product design and performance by volume producers has narrowed the performance gap. Japanese producers, for example, motivated partly by unit restrictions on exports and partly by the entry of newly industrialized countries in low-price segments, began to develop high-end, high-price products, such as the Toyota Lexus, Nissan Infiniti, and Honda NSX in the late 1980s. These designs may pose a serious competitive threat to European high-end specialists such as Daimler-Benz, BMW, Porsche, and even Ferrari.

High-end specialists are not standing still. They are making major investments in new products to maintain the performance gap against new entrants to the high-end market. Many of these future models, embodying significant leaps in technology and performance, could overwhelm the volume producers, at least in the initial period following new product introduction.

Long term, the trend nevertheless seems to be toward convergence of product performance. (This reflects in part limits in improvement based on performance under extreme conditions; will cars be driven at 300 km/h on the autobahn?) Sharp product differentiation based on corporate identity and product image may linger, but unless backed by unequivocal superiority of performance, such emphasis will not be sustainable over the long term.

If, indeed, there is a convergence of strategy between high-end specialists and volume producers, competitive requirements imposed on the respective groups might change significantly. High-end specialists might have to shorten development lead time and improve development productivity in order to respond more quickly and effectively to attacks by competing products. Volume producers, on the other hand, may have to achieve greater consistency of product designs and performance across models and develop an approach to engineering that emphasizes technical sophistication and rigorous product validation.

CONCLUSION

The 1980s have been years of transition for the world auto industry. Many factors—including changes in energy prices and trade structures, the increasing influence of the baby-boom generation, the downsizing of American cars and upgrading of Japanese cars, the "Europeanization" of product concepts worldwide, and growing sophistication of customer needs—have fostered the globalization of many market segments. Competition is not only more vigorous, it is more direct. International product rivalry is now a fact of competitive life in every segment. Consumers of the late 1980s seemed ready to compare the Volkswagen Golf, Toyota Corolla, and Ford Escort in the subcompact class; the Honda Accord, Chevrolet Corsica, and Renault 21 in the compact segment; the Audi 100, Ford Taurus, and Nissan Maxima in the mid-size class; and the Lincoln Continental, Toyota Lexus, and Mercedes S-Class in the luxury category.

In the face of these changes in markets and competition, firms with different roots and different capabilities were forced to compete head to head. With effective new products a matter of survival in some cases, and a focus of competition in all cases, product development became energized and intensified.

A period such as the 1980s provides a useful window on the management of product development. If history matters, and if development capabilities cannot be refashioned overnight, then firms from different regions pursuing different strategies should perform quite differently under a new set of requirements. It should not be surprising to discover, for example, that Japanese firms learned to develop new products relatively quickly; given their home market, short lead time has been an imperative. But with comparative data on firms in other regions, we can take the analysis much further. We can begin to understand what part of the performance we observe is based on capabilities that are common to firms in a region and what part reflects distinctive capabilities of the firm. More important, perhaps, we can begin to understand the nature of the practices that lead to rapid, efficient, and effective product development. To arrive at this understanding, we need first to see firms in action and measure their performance.

NOTES

1. For further discussion of these forces and references for data, see Abernathy, Clark, and Kantrow (1983).
2. Ibid., pp. 147–149.
3. In a similar vein, Sobel (1984, p. 36) characterized the traditional American car as "atomistic" as opposed to "holistic."
4. Germany and France produced more than half the automobiles manufactured at the turn of the century; see Laux (1976) and World Motor Vehicle Data.
5. Altshuler et al. (1984, p. 195).
6. For a history of BMW, see, for example, Morozumi (1983).
7. Daimler-Benz Museum, Daimler Benz AG, 1987.
8. This story has been told a number of times. For the GM perspective, see Sloan (1963); for developments at Ford, see Nevins and Hill (1957).
9. Car design in America, with particular attention to the system developed at GM, is discussed in Armi (1988).
10. The rivalry during this period has been reviewed in White (1971).
11. For the history of technology transfer to Japanese car producers, see Cusumano (1985).
12. The Ministry of International Trade and Industry (MITI) had a long-term vision of drastically reducing the number of producers. In 1961, one of MITI's advisory committees announced a vision to "rationalize" the auto industry by limiting the number of producers to two "volume car producers," three "speciality car producers," and three "micromini producers." MITI's idea was to limit product competition within segments and obtain economies of scale so Japanese producers could survive international competition. (The Japanese auto industry was protected from foreign competition in terms of import and capital investment until the early 1970s, and imports have subsequently played an inconsequential role, accounting for only 1.7 percent of unit sales in 1985. Source: Nissan Motor Company, Automobile Industry Handbook.) MITI's vision was virtually ignored by the industry. See, for example, Oshima and Yamaoka (1987). (Japanese.)
13. Rebates and incentives in the early 1980s were financed mainly by profits from U.S. operations that combined productivity advantages, the unusually low value of the yen, and voluntary export restraints on Japanese exports to push up new car retail prices in U.S. markets. (Industry observers estimated that more than half the profits in the Japanese auto industry were generated by U.S. exports in the early 1980s, and that the total amount of rebates and incentives from manufacturers to dealers reached 300 billion yen annually. Even so, about half the dealers were

operating with negative profits. See, for example, Shimokawa [1985].) This pattern of "excessive competition" in the Japanese market continued until the late 1980s, when rapid changes in exchange rates slashed most of the profits from U.S. sales and forced Japanese producers to rely more on profits from domestic sales.

14. A commonly used industry classification in the mid 1980s included subcompact I (Nissan March), subcompact II (Toyota Tercel), subcompact III (Toyota Corolla), compact I (Nissan Stanza), compact II (Toyota Corona), compact III (Toyota Cressida), and mid size (Nissan Cedric).

15. For further details of the Bluebird-Corona competition (the "B-C War"), see Ikari (1985).

16. The basic designs of some of these models date to the prewar era.

17. For the concept of strategic groups, see Porter (1980). The sample organizations in the present study cover a majority of the companies listed here. Which companies are actually studied is not disclosed for purposes of confidentiality. For further analysis of the two strategies based on empirical data, see Fujimoto (1989, Chapter 6).

18. A marketing executive for Daimler-Benz, *NAVI*, vol. 2, no. 10 (October 1985), p. 37. (Japanese.)

19. Manager of R&D for a German high-end specialist; author's interview.

20. A marketing executive for Saab; "Yakushin Suru Hokuo Kigyo," *Nikkei Sangyo Shimbun* ("North European Companies Make Rapid Progress," *Japan Economic Journal*), 27 August 1987.

21. Market share of Japanese passenger cars in 1986 was as follows: United Kingdom, 11%; West Germany, 15%; France, 3%; Italy, 0.5%; Holland, 24%; Belgium, 21%; Luxembourg, 14%; Denmark, 36%; Ireland, 44%; Greece, 28%; Spain, 0.6%; Portugal, 10%; Sweden, 21%; Finland, 40%; Norway, 35%; Switzerland, 27%; Austria, 28%. *Source*: Nissan Motor Company, *Automobile Industry Handbook*, 1987.

22. For further details on the European model of product development, see Clark and Fujimoto (1988a).

23. From an interview by Professor Koichi Shimokawa, Hosei University. *Nikkan Jidosha Shimbun* (*Daily Automobile News*), 14 October 1987. (Re-translated from Japanese translation.)

24. Japanese emission control regulations, set mainly from 1975 to 1978, are as rigid as those of California and among the most rigid in the world.

25. "Yamamoto Ken-ichi Matsuda Shacho Kansei Keiei wo Kataru," *Nikkan Jidosha Shimbun* ("Ken-ichi Yamamoto, President of Mazda, Talks about Management by Sensibility," *Daily Automotive News*, 13 October 1987. (Yamamoto's title is as of the time of the interview.)

26. *Toyota Management* (October 1985). (Japanese.)

27. *Motor Trend* (January 1989), p. 62.

CHAPTER 4

THE PARAMETERS OF PERFORMANCE: LEAD TIME, QUALITY, AND PRODUCTIVITY

Creating new products has been central to competition since the inception of the auto industry. New cars have always attracted attention. Road races between the latest models were front-page news in the early 1900s. Ford's introduction of the new Model A in October 1927 attracted 100,000 people to Detroit showrooms and caused near riots in Cleveland and Kansas City. Alfred Sloan's annual model change at GM capitalized on the fascination with new products. Sloan made the new car introduction as much a part of the fall season as apple cider and raking leaves. Throughout the 1980s, scores of new products heretofore unrivaled in performance and reliability arrived in the market at an unprecedented pace.

Competition, new technology, and a new generation of buyers have created a turbulent environment for the world's automobile companies. In this environment the advantage goes to the firm that can offer a greater variety of new products with higher performance and greater overall appeal. American, Japanese, and European companies bring different capabilities to the market and use different approaches, but they are all seeking an edge in product development. What is outstanding performance in product development in the world auto industry as we enter the 1990s? How well have the world's automobile companies performed? And what gaps exist in performance among different companies?

These are difficult questions to answer. There are many companies, products are complex and different, and claims and counter-claims about performance circulate widely. Studying a few projects or simply interviewing people in the industry will not suffice. What is needed is hard and extensive data on specific product development projects in the major automobile companies in Europe, the United States, and Japan. We gathered such data from 29 projects in 20 companies. The rich base of information we accumulated on product development lead time, productivity, and design quality has yielded some striking insights. We found, for example, sizable gaps in lead time and engineering productivity between Japanese firms and their Western competitors. The average Japanese firm has almost double the development productivity and can develop a comparable product a year faster than the average U.S. firm. But the story is not a simple one of uniform Japanese advantage. In total product quality, some European firms have an edge, and some Japanese firms perform quite poorly. Other Japanese firms are excellent in all three dimensions.

In this chapter we summarize the basic data on project characteristics and performance. Subsequent chapters examine the forces behind the patterns we observe. What stands out in the comparisons we make here are regional differences rooted in historical experience and the effects of distinctive capabilities in particular companies. These data on performance not only provide answers to the questions posed above, but also suggest where to seek insight into the sources of outstanding product development.

QUALITY, LEAD TIME, AND PRODUCTIVITY IN THE PERFORMANCE OF PRODUCT DEVELOPMENT

When an automobile company sets out to develop a new product, its objective is to attract and satisfy a set of target customers and to do so profitably. Inasmuch as the product has a long life and the company will develop and introduce many products, satisfaction must extend over the long term. Although a company's competitiveness relative to its rivals depends on factors such as advertising, dealer quality, and delivery schedule, the competitiveness of the product—its ability to attract and satisfy customers—is critical.

Three outcomes of the product development process affect the ability of a product to attract and satisfy customers (see the Appendix for further definition). The first is what we call total product quality (TPQ)—that is, the extent to which the product satisfies customer requirements. As we use it, TPQ is affected both by objective attributes such as acceleration and fuel efficiency and subjective evaluations of aesthetics, styling, and the total driving experience. Product development affects TPQ at two levels: the level of the design, which we call design quality, and the firm's ability to produce the design, which we call conformance quality.[1] The second critical dimension of performance, lead time, is a measure of how quickly a company can move from concept to market. If we mark the beginning of a project at the launch of concept development, overall lead time is the calendar time required to define, design, and introduce the product to the market. Lead time affects both design execution and market acceptance of the design. Because planning and concept creation must occur at the front end of the project, and because the quality of these activities depends heavily on how well the project forecasts future customer needs and rival products, project lead time may affect the appeal of a product through accuracy of forecasting. For example, if lead time is six years for a product with a life of six years, product planners must forecast six to twelve years ahead. If lead time and model life are four years, the forecast must be four to eight years ahead. A two-year gap in lead time can be amplified if uncertainty is high.[2]

The converse of market acceptance is market obsolescence. Because it sets the lower limit on model-change intervals in this industry, lead time may affect the freshness of a firm's models in situations where expectations change and rivals actively seek advantage with new products. When the competitive environment is turbulent, a firm with a four-year model-change cycle has a significant advantage over a firm with a six-year cycle. Faster, however, is not always better. Excessively short lead time may cause "premature" engineering that jeopardizes the functional performance of the product. If the technologies employed in the products are so sophisticated that two years makes a difference in the level of technical excellence—and if the consumers are sophisticated enough to discern this gap—then longer lead time can be directly translated into higher product competitiveness. Therefore, optimal lead time may depend on the technology and conditions in the market.

The third dimension of development performance is productivity, the level of resources required to take the project from concept to commercial product. This includes hours worked (engineering hours), materials used for prototype construction, and any equipment and services the firm may use. Productivity has a direct though relatively small effect on unit production cost, but it also affects the number of projects a firm can complete for a given level of resources. Given the same human, material, and financial resources, the number and type of new product projects two firms will be able to complete will vary according to their levels of productivity.

A firm can use a productivity advantage in several ways. It may seek a competitive edge through more frequent product renewals, or choose comparable renewal rates but support a broader product line.[3] If markets diversify, a productivity advantage may be used to seek out and exploit opportunities in new segments and niches that open up. A highly productive development group can enable a firm not only to lower unit costs, but also to achieve a better match between diverse customer expectations and the products it puts on the market.

Figure 4.1 depicts the interaction among these three dimensions of product development performance. Specific patterns of interaction will depend on the way firms organize and manage development, on the market environment, and on company strategies. The framework in Figure 4.1 establishes a clear link between development performance

Figure 4.1 Product Development Performance

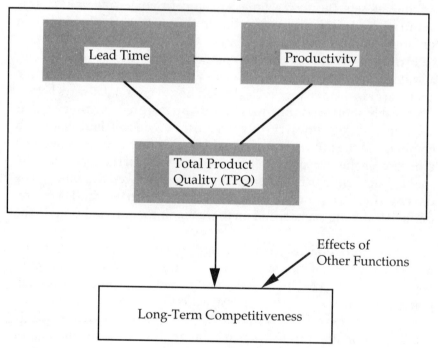

and the firm's objective in launching new products—to profitably attract and satisfy customers over the long term. The framework thus treats development performance as a reflection of a firm's longer-term capabilities.

Our first step in analyzing product development performance must be to develop measures of the three performance dimensions. We measure lead time as the time elapsed between the beginning of concept development and market introduction. Because our principal interest in productivity is in critical human resources, we use hours employed in planning and engineering to measure productivity. Whereas lead time and productivity measures are limited to the firm, total product quality is based on external evaluation of many attributes. We thus use multiple indicators to measure TPQ; these include customer evaluation of product characteristics such as ride, handling, design, and comfort, as well as customer satisfaction and product reliability surveys and changes in long-term market share. Collectively these measures enable us to identify differences across firms and regions.

Our next step is to verify the link between what we observe in specific projects and a firm's longer-term capabilities. We do this by examining the firm's product development activity over long periods of time. We develop data on frequency of model introduction, rate of product renewal, and expansion of the product line. If our evidence on performance reflects fundamental capability, we should see a strong relationship between project performance and the use of that capability in the market—more frequent new products and more rapid expansion of the product line.

The final step in our analysis is to link development performance to competitiveness. Change in market share is a critical test of a firm's success. Given our interest in the longer term, we look in particular at changes in market share over longer periods of time. The critical question is whether performance along the dimensions we have studied—lead time, productivity, and product quality—show up in the firm's competitive position.

COMPARISON OF PERFORMANCE DATA

Much has been written in the last several years about comparative performance in automobile companies. Numerous studies, using both public and private data, have analyzed cost, productivity, quality, and profitability. Most of this work has focused on manufacturing performance. Despite its central role in competition, there has been little analysis of product development. This is attributable in part to the absence of publicly available information, and in part to the inherent difficulty of measuring a complex process. Product development does not occur in one place. It cuts across many functional organizations, lasts for many months, and involves hundreds of people. Moreover, it works differently in different companies, and the objects of all this activity, the products, are themselves complex and different.

We knew that to get hard data on development performance we had to go into the field. (A description of our methods and details of data and analysis are provided in the Appendix.) We also needed an organizing framework to guide our search. Our decision to focus on major new car development projects (a major new product is one in which more than half the parts are newly designed) allowed us not only to measure performance, but also to adjust the data for differences in project characteristics. Such adjustments turned out to be very important, because the projects we studied—29 in 20 companies (three American, eight Japanese, and nine European)—were very different, ranging from large sedans to small vans and micromini cars with suggested retail prices ranging from $4,300 to more than $40,000. We first present the raw data and then adjust the data for differences in project content.

Raw data on engineering productivity, lead time, product quality, and other project characteristics are broken down by region and strategic group in Table 4.1. The average new product in our sample required 2.5 million engineering hours and 4.5 years to develop. But these averages mask wide differences in performance across regions. Japanese firms complete a project with one-third the engineering hours and two-thirds the lead time of their American and European competitors. On average, U.S. and European firms are quite similar on both measures, though high-end European firms are distinguished by long lead times.

In product quality, high-end European firms are clearly superior. Among volume producers, a slight edge in product quality goes to Japanese firms, with American and European firms very close together. Within regions there is wide variation in performance. In Japan, for example, the overall index ranges from 23 to 100, a pattern found in other regions as well. Company differences are clearly at work.

Table 4.1 Data on Product Development Performance and Project Content

	Strategic-Regional Groups / Variables	Japanese Volume Producer	U.S. Volume Producer	European Volume Producer	European High-End Specialist	Overall
	Number of Organizations	8	5	5	4	22
	Number of Projects	12	6	7	4	29
	Year of Introduction	1981–1985	1984–1987	1980–1987	1982–1986	1980–1987
Performance	Engineering Hours (millions)	av. 1.2 min. 0.4 max. 2.0	av. 3.5 min. 1.0 max. 7.0	av. 3.4 min. 2.4 max. 4.5	av. 3.4 min. 0.7 max. 6.5	av. 2.5 min. 0.4 max. 7.0
Performance	Lead Time (months)	av. 42.6 min. 35.0 max. 51.0	av. 61.9 min. 50.2 max. 77.0	av. 57.6 min. 46.0 max. 70.0	av. 71.5 min. 57.0 max. 97.0	av. 54.2 min. 35.0 max. 97.0
Performance	Total Product Quality (TPQ) Index	av. 58 min. 23 max. 100	av. 41 min. 14 max. 75	av. 41 min. 30 max. 55	av. 84 min. 70 max. 100	av. 55 min. 14 max. 100
Project Complexity	Retail Price (1987 U.S. dollars)	9,238	13,193	12,713	31,981	14,032
Project Complexity	Vehicle Size (# of projects)					
Project Complexity	micromini	3	0	0	0	3
Project Complexity	subcompact	4	0	3	0	7
Project Complexity	compact	4	1	3	1	9
Project Complexity	mid-large	1	5	1	3	10
Project Complexity	Number of Body Types	2.3	1.7	2.7	1.3	2.1
Project Complexity	Geographical Market (# of projects)					
Project Complexity	domestic only	3	3	0	0	6
Project Complexity	minor exporter	1	2	2	0	5
Project Complexity	major exporter	8	1	5	4	18
Project Scope	Off-the-Shelf Parts	18%	38%	31%	30%	27%
Project Scope	Supplier Involvement (% of parts cost)					
Project Scope	supplier proprietary (SP)	8%	3%	10%	3%	7%
Project Scope	black box (BB)	62%	16%	38%	41%	44%
Project Scope	detail-controlled (DC)	30%	81%	52%	57%	49%
Project Scope	Supplier Engineering Ratio	52%	14%	36%	31%	37%
Project Scope	Project Scope Index	57%	66%	62%	63%	61%

Notes Definitions of the variables are as follows:
Year of introduction: calendar year when the first version of the model was introduced to the market.
Engineering hours: hours spent directly on the project (excluding process engineering).
Lead time: time elapsed between start of project (concept study) and start of sales.
TPQ: constructed from various quality and market-share data (see Appendix).
Retail price: average suggested retail price of major versions of each model in 1987 U.S. dollars.
Vehicle size: authors' subjective classification based on industry practices.
Number of body types: number of significantly different bodies in terms of number of doors, side silhouette, etc.
Geographical market: "domestic only" means the model was sold only in the domestic market; "minor exporter" means that it was exported but not to any of the major markets (the United States, Europe, and Japan); "major exporter" means that it was exported to at least one of the major markets.
Off-the-shelf parts: fraction of parts common to other or previous models (measured by fraction of parts drawings).
Supplier proprietary parts: parts developed entirely by parts suppliers.
Black box parts: parts whose basic engineering is done by car makers and whose detail engineering is done by parts suppliers.
Detail-controlled parts: parts developed entirely by car producers.
Supplier engineering ratio: estimated fraction of total parts engineering hours accounted for by parts suppliers; based on interviews, it was estimated that 100% of work in supplier proprietary parts, 70% of work in black box parts, and 0% of work in detail-controlled parts was done by suppliers.
Project scope index: estimated fraction of total project workload accounted for by new parts designed in-house.

Though these performance gaps may be due to differences in organizational and managerial capability, they also reflect differences in strategic choice. Table 4.1 presents data on average retail price, number of body types, and vehicle size. The pattern we see here is consistent with traditional differences in strategy and regional markets. European high-end specialists are associated with relatively large, high-priced, sophisticated products, while American volume producers are associated with large products in the mid-price range. Both European and Japanese volume producers concentrate on smaller cars. Indeed, the Japanese sample includes three micromini cars, which accounts in part for the lower average price of the Japanese products.

With much lower prices and much smaller cars, the Japanese firms would appear to have much simpler projects, which might help explain their advantage in lead time and productivity. But the Japanese products also involve several body styles and more unique parts, factors that complicate development. Thus, though differences in complexity may reduce the advantage of the Japanese firms (and change the relative position of the high-end specialists as well), the magnitude of the adjustment is not clear. Much the same is true for differences in project scope—the fraction of total workload accounted for by new parts developed in-house—which are determined by the extent of supplier involvement and use of off-the-shelf parts. Table 4.1 shows that Japanese firms make much heavier use of suppliers in product development and have a somewhat narrower project scope. Adjusting for scope should narrow the advantage of Japanese firms.

DEVELOPMENT PRODUCTIVITY

Because they are based on "raw" data, the striking differences in productivity performance in Table 4.1 may exist simply because the firms chose to develop different kinds of cars or to conduct projects of different scope. These are interesting choices in their own right, but to gauge the importance of organizational and managerial capability, we need a better "apples-to-apples" comparison. What we are after is some sense of what productivity would look like if the firms were to carry out a similar project—the same kind of car with the same fraction of new parts, and so forth.

We attacked this problem in two ways. The engineering method adjusts the raw data based on industry rules of thumb and engineering experience (e.g., two body styles means 20 percent more work than one). Using regression analysis, the statistical method estimates the effect of differences in scope and complexity in our sample. Because the results were consistent, we present only the statistical evidence.* The analysis (described in detail in the Appendix) gives us an estimate of the engineering hours that would be required by each company to complete a standard project, in this case a $14,000 compact car (e.g., a Honda Accord or Mazda 626) with two body styles. The results are presented in Figure 4.2.

Figure 4.2 Engineering Hours Required to Develop a $14,000 Compact Car with Two Body Styles

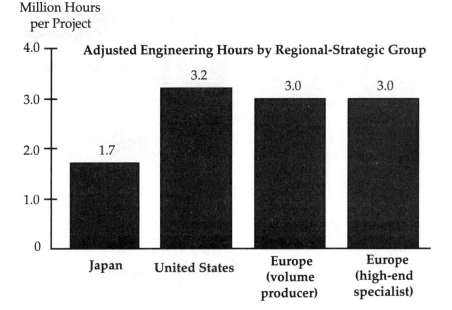

Million Hours per Project

Adjusted Engineering Hours by Regional-Strategic Group

Source: Based on regression analysis (see the Appendix for details).

Note: Adjusted engineering hours are the hours required by the average firm in each region/group to design and engineer the average vehicle in the sample.

* Spearman rank-order correlation between the result of the engineering method and the statistical method is 0.76 when the critical value of the two-tail test with 5 percent significance level is 0.42.

Taking scope and complexity into account clearly reduces the advantage of the Japanese firms. The raw data show the average Japanese volume producer with 1.2 million engineering hours; the adjusted estimate is 1.7 million. In comparison with the American projects, where the adjustment drops engineering hours by 400,000, the Japanese edge narrows from 2.3 million to 1.4 million. Similar reductions occur with the European firms. In fact, the results for Europe show that, on average, high-end specialists and volume producers achieve the same level of productivity when we control for differences in scope and complexity. In general, the advantage of the Japanese firms narrows but does not disappear. We find that scope and complexity account for about 40 percent of the original Japanese advantage. The remainder reflects regional differences in the organization and management of development.

Although the regional averages in Figure 4.2 mask differences across firms, the statistical adjustments allow us to rank the companies on the basis of productivity in completing the standard project (see Table 4.2). As might be expected, the Japanese firms are clustered in the top half of the distribution. Though most of the European and American firms are lower on the list, there is some overlap. A few of the Western firms achieved performance quite a bit above the regional average, underscoring the importance of looking at firm-specific capabilities when searching for sources of high productivity.

DEVELOPMENT LEAD TIME

Lead time is a measure of how quickly a firm can perform the many different activities that must be accomplished to advance from concept to market introduction. Because some of these activities may be pursued in parallel, lead time—unlike engineering hours—is not simply the sum of the lead times of the individual activities. It depends both on the length of the individual activities and the extent to which work is done in parallel. Though overall lead time is our primary focus, the pattern of lead times in individual activities provides important insight into the sources of lead time differences.

Figure 4.3 details regional averages in lead time by stage of development. We have found it useful to distinguish lead time in the front end of the process (where concepts are formed and plans generated) from lead time at the back end (where prototypes are built

Table 4.2   Ranking of Individual Companies in Product Development Productivity (Adjusted Engineering Hours)

Ranking	Regional Origin
1	Europe (high-end)
2	Japan
3	Japan
4	Japan
5	Japan
6	Japan
7	Japan
8	Europe (volume)
9	Japan
10	United States
11	Japan
12	Europe (volume)
13	Europe (high-end)
14	United States
15	United States
16	Europe (volume)
17	Europe (volume)
18	Europe (high-end)
19	Europe (volume)
20	United States
21	United States
22	Europe (high-end)

Source: Rankings based on regression analysis (see the Appendix for details).

and tested and the tools, equipment, and facilities are prepared for commercial production). In the diagrams the time between the beginning of concept generation and the end of product planning corresponds to planning lead time. The time between the beginning of product engineering and the start of sales is engineering lead time. We saw earlier the sizable regional differences in overall lead times. Here we find that the Japanese sample average is significantly lower than those of its American and European counterparts in both planning and

Figure 4.3 Average Project Schedule by Stages

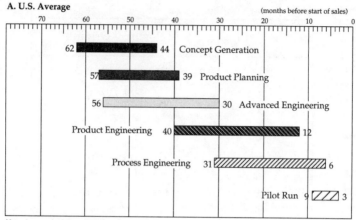

A. U.S. Average

(months before start of sales)

Note: Average lead time of 6 U.S. projects.

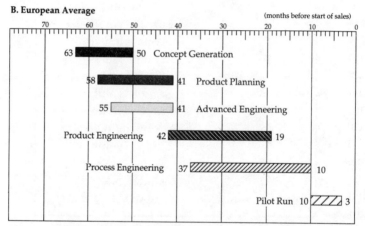

B. European Average

(months before start of sales)

Note: Average lead time of 11 European projects.

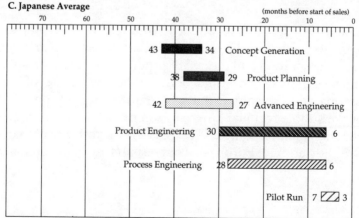

C. Japanese Average

(months before start of sales)

Note: Average lead time of 12 Japanese projects.

engineering: 14 months versus 22–23 months for planning, and 30 months versus 40–42 months for engineering. Overall patterns in the American and European projects are similar.[4]

The data on lead time by stage imply that the Japanese edge comes from both quick planning and quick engineering. But the pattern of overlap within planning and engineering suggests that the sources of the Japanese advantage in these two stages may be different. In the front end, for example, the degree of overlap between concept generation and product planning is similar across regions. What is different is the length of each stage. It appears that Japanese firms either have a less complex planning problem to begin with, or they simply execute the planning process more efficiently.

In contrast, the degree of overlap between product and process engineering appears to be decisive in differences in engineering lead time. The amount of time devoted to the product and process engineering stages differs across regions by just a few months. But Japanese firms begin and end product and process engineering at about the same time, whereas U.S. firms begin process engineering nine months later and finish it six months later than product engineering. European firms, which are fastest at product engineering, begin process engineering five months later and end it nine months later than product engineering. These patterns suggest that the source of engineering lead time differences may lie in the ability to operate effectively in parallel.

In overall lead time and lead time by stage of development, Japanese firms have a significant edge. To find out how much of this edge is a function of the scope and complexity of the project and how much might be rooted in differences in organization and management, we adjusted the raw lead time data for differences in product content and project scope using the statistical analysis described in the Appendix. The results, presented in Figure 4.4, show the difference in lead time narrowing, though a sizable gap remains. Among volume producers, we estimate that the average project in our sample would take the average Japanese firm 46 months, or about four years, and the average American and European firm about 60 months, or five years. The adjustment narrows the Japanese advantage from 18 months to about one year. Because scope and complexity account for almost a year of the original gap of 29 months for high-end specialists, the Japanese edge after adjustment is 18 months. The individual company rankings reflect these group differences in a strong clustering by region.

Figure 4.4 Lead Time Required to Develop a $14,000 Compact Car with Two Body Styles

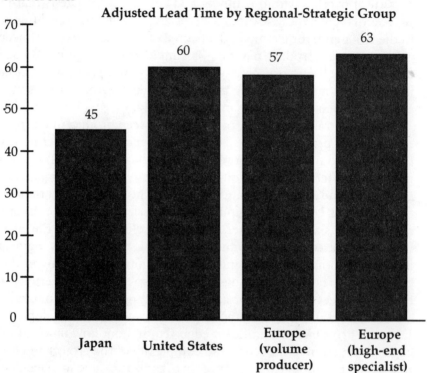

Months Before
Start of Sales

Adjusted Lead Time by Regional-Strategic Group

Japan: 45
United States: 60
Europe (volume producer): 57
Europe (high-end specialist): 63

Source: Based on regression analysis (see the Appendix for details).

Note: Adjusted lead time is the time from concept development to market introduction required by the average company in each region/group to complete the average project in the sample.

Table 4.3 presents the ranking of company lead time performance for the average project. As with the productivity analysis, there is some overlap across regions, but Japanese firms clearly dominate the top performers. Thus, rapid product development, though affected by company differences, appears to be grounded in capabilities that to an important extent are held in common by Japanese firms. This is

Table 4.3 Ranking of Individual Companies in Product Development Lead Time (Adjusted for Project Content)

Ranking	Regional Origin
1	Japan
2	Japan
3	Japan
4	Japan
5	Japan
6	Europe (volume)
7	Europe (high-end)
8	Japan
9	Japan
10	Japan
11	Europe (volume)
12	United States
13	Europe (volume)
14	United States
15	United States
16	Europe (high-end)
17	United States
18	Europe (volume)
19	Europe (high-end)
20	Europe (volume)
21	Europe (high-end)
22	United States

Source: Rankings based on regression analysis (see the Appendix for details).

consistent with the pattern of competition that has prevailed in the Japanese market; the firms that have survived have tended to develop common characteristics (see Chapter 3).

Our adjustment for the effects of scope and complexity on lead time suggests that the common capabilities critical to rapid development are in product and process engineering. Adjustments of planning and engineering lead time have quite different effects. For example, regional differences among volume producers in planning lead time are negligible after adjustment. It appears that differences in front-end lead time reflect differences in project strategy rather than differences in the way planning is organized and managed. Engineering is a different story. Project scope and complexity affect differences in engineering lead time very little; thus the Japanese edge in overall lead time for the average project must be based on differences in the effectiveness of engineering. We examine this issue in more depth in Chapter 6.

TOTAL PRODUCT QUALITY

The story told by the data on lead time and productivity is one of systematic advantage for Japanese volume producers and rough parity between American and European firms. The data on product quality tell a somewhat different tale. Returning to Table 4.1, we see that the European high-end specialists rate high in our measures of quality and that Japanese firms, though they do quite well as a whole, exhibit considerable variability. The emphasis in the mid 1980s on subtle, holistic product dimensions has made it more difficult for Japanese firms to attract customers on the basis of manufacturing-driven criteria, such as fit and finish, where they may have had a common advantage.

Figure 4.5 maps indicators of conformance quality (i.e., how well products delivered to customers conform to product design or specifications, including reliability, defects in the field, fit and finish, and durability) and design quality (i.e., the degree to which product designs match customer expectations). We also present data on customer satisfaction surveys (an indicator of total quality) and long-term changes in market share. (Detailed definitions and statistical analysis of product quality are found in the Appendix.) When a product conforms perfectly to design, design quality and total product quality are the same.

Figure 4.5 Ranking Based on Selected Indicators of Total Product Quality

Region and Strategy	Total Quality Ranking			Conformance Quality Ranking		Design Quality Ranking							Customer Base Share Change	TPQ Index
	Consumer Reports (1)	Consumer Reports (2)	J.D. Power	J.D. Power (1985)	J.D. Power (1987)	Concept	Styling	Performance	Comfort	Value for Money	Overall Rank	Value-Adjusted Overall Rank		
Japan (volume producers)	●	●	●	●	●	●	○	●	●	●	●	●	●	100
	○	●	○	●	●				○					40
	●	●	●	●	●	○	○	○	○	●	○	○	●	80
	●	●	●	●	●	●	●	●	○	●	●	●	●	100
	○	○		○	○									25
				n.a.	n.a.	○							○	23
	n.a.	n.a.	n.a.	n.a.	n.a.	○	○	○			○	○	○	58
	○	○	●		●									35
United States (volume producers)								○	●	○				15
				○	○			○	●	○				24
	○	○	○	●	○	○	●	○	○	●	●	●		75
	○	○	○	●	○	○	●	○	○	●	●	●		75
						○	○							14
Europe (volume producers)	○	○	n.a.	n.a.	n.a.	○	○	○	○	○	○	○		47
	n.a.	n.a.	n.a.	n.a.	n.a.	●	○			○	○	○		39
						○	●		●		○	○		30
	○					●	●	●	●	○	○	●		35
	○	○	●			●		●	○	○	○	○	●	55
Europe (high-end specialists)	○	○	○	○	○	●	●	●	●		●	●		70
	●	●	●			○		○	○	○	○	○	●	73
	●	○	●	○	●	●	●	●	●	●	●	●	●	93
	●	●	●	●	●	●	○	●	●	●	●	●	●	100

Notes: Entries in the map are defined as follows:

1–3 : Ranking in total quality (3 indicators), conformance quality (2 indicators), and design quality (7 indicators).

    ● = top one-third; ○ = middle one-third; none = bottom one-third

4 : Customer base share changes based on four measures of long-term market share.

    ● = increase in customer base share; none = decrease in customer base share;

    ○ = maintained share

5 : Summary index of ranking across all indicators of quality (see Appendix for details).

For further details of definition and measurement, see Fujimoto (1989, Chapter 5, Table 5.2).

What stands out in Figure 4.5 is the dominance of Japanese firms in conformance quality and the strong position of European firms in the quality of design. Only the high-end specialists and a few Japanese volume producers are strong in both dimensions. European volume producers are relatively weak in conformance quality, with

Japanese and American volume producers showing weakness in design quality. These findings are consistent with rankings from customer satisfaction surveys and with the data on changes in customer base share, which show firms with strong performance across all quality indicators increasing their market position during the 1980s.

We summarize these patterns in the last column of Figure 4.5 with an index of total product quality. The index shows a clear advantage—related to superior performance in both design and conformance quality—for the high-end specialists and some Japanese volume producers. The index also reveals significant differences across firms in total product quality.

The ranking of individual firms according to the TPQ index in Table 4.4 contrasts sharply with our earlier findings. The strong regional clustering we observed in lead time and productivity performance (especially among Japanese firms) is absent here. Firms from all regions are found at all levels of the distribution, suggesting that the relatively strong position of the Japanese firms in total product quality in Table 4.1 is a function of the outstanding performance of a few firms that have achieved both superior conformance and design quality. Less competitive firms, Japanese and otherwise, show evidence of inconsistency, being strong in conformance quality but weak in design quality, or vice versa. What appears to set the highly competitive firms apart is consistently strong performance across all dimensions of total product quality. The rankings in Table 4.4 suggest that such performance is more a matter of a firm's capabilities than of regional background.

THE LEAD TIME-PRODUCTIVITY CONNECTION

Thus far we have examined regional effects and firm capability in terms of the individual dimensions of performance (i.e., engineering hours, lead time, and total product quality). We now look at how firms perform on multiple dimensions of performance at the same time. Knowing, for example, whether firms that achieve a high level of quality are also fast and efficient—or whether there may be some important trade-offs in these dimensions—may shed light on the sources of outstanding performance.

Consider the idea that one can "buy" lead time with additional engineering resources, a common element of models of R&D man-

Table 4.4 Ranking of Individual Companies in TPQ Index

Ranking	Regional Origin	Score
1	Europe (high-end)	100
1	Japan	100
1	Japan	100
2	Europe (high-end)	93
3	Japan	80
4	United States	75
4	United States	75
5	Europe (high-end)	73
6	Europe (high-end)	70
7	Japan	58
8	Europe (volume)	55
9	Europe (volume)	47
10	Japan	40
11	Europe (volume)	39
12	Europe (volume)	35
12	Japan	35
13	Europe (volume)	30
14	Japan	25
15	United States	24
16	Japan	23
17	United States	15
18	United States	14

Source: Rankings based on data in Figure 4.5 (see the Appendix for details).

agement that often influences management practice.[5] If one adds engineers, the theory goes, one can divide up and perform in parallel tasks on the critical path, the length of which determines lead time. More engineering hours should thus mean shorter lead times, yet we have seen that on average Japanese firms have higher productivity and shorter lead times. Something else appears to be at work.

When we examine the relationship between lead time and engineering hours in Figure 4.6, which displays performance on both dimensions for each firm, we find not a negative trade-off but rather

Figure 4.6 Correlation between Lead Time and Development Productivity

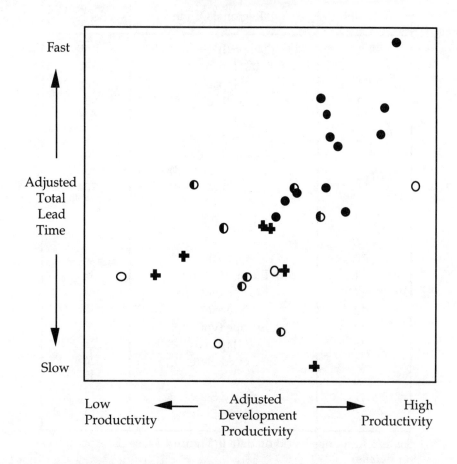

Note: The scales have been inverted so that "slow" represents a long lead time and "low productivity" represents high engineering hours.

● Japanese Producer

✚ U.S. Producer

○ European High-End Specialist

◐ European Volume Producer

a positive correlation between these dimensions, particularly for Japanese firms. Firms that are fast tend to be highly efficient; firms that are slow have low productivity. Two factors appear to be behind this relationship. One has to do with how engineers work, the other with the tight coupling of engineering activities.

A universal constant in the development projects we studied is the engineering change. In every company in every country, design changes are the rule rather than the exception, and they occupy a sizable fraction of engineering resources. Inasmuch as engineers tend to work and rework their designs as long as they are permitted to do so, a design is never complete; the engineers simply run out of time. Beyond some minimum time, lead time for a task is therefore determined by a deadline. The longer the lead time, the more engineering hours. In addition, to the extent that activities are tightly coupled, reworking a design in one area triggers rework in another. This effect is reinforced if (as is common in Japan) people are dedicated to a project. If there is not a lot of slack in the system and if people cannot move on to other projects, a delay in one area will propagate. Although lead time drives engineering hours, we should not presume that we can improve productivity simply by changing deadlines or shorten lead time simply by cutting the number of people on a project. Such actions may have that effect, but the data in Figure 4.6 also reflect the effects of skills, capabilities, and systems. The tight link between lead time and productivity among Japanese firms may reflect, for example, the capabilities that have evolved for achieving short cycle product development through tight coupling between departments and more parallel activities. Changing deadlines or cutting people may have serious consequences for product quality if these capabilities do not exist.

ADDING THE QUALITY DIMENSION

Figure 4.7 plots the TPQ index against lead time and development productivity. We find little evidence of a strong relationship between quality and productivity; firms are scattered across the diagram without apparent pattern and irrespective of region. Between strategic groups, the most competitive high-end specialists are less productive, but there is no pattern among volume producers. The same appears to be true for lead time and quality, with the exception of some interesting indications from firms with very high-quality products. For

Figure 4.7 Total Product Quality, Lead Time, and Development Productivity

Total Product Quality and Development Productivity

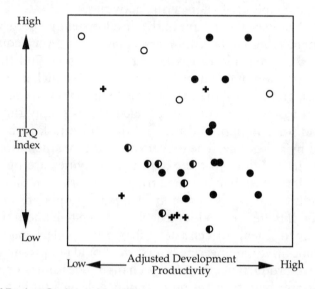

Total Product Quality and Lead Time

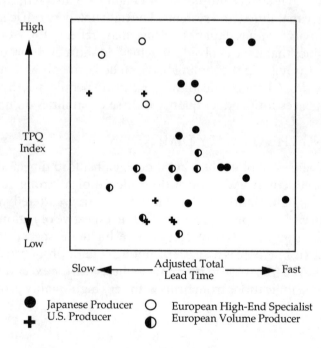

example, the two high-end specialists that rank at the top in competitiveness are relatively slow and inefficient, while competitors with lower-quality products achieve mixed results; one is fast and relatively efficient, the other average in efficiency and relatively slow. Both these latter firms fall far behind the leaders in conformance and design quality and overall customer satisfaction, implying that superior quality in the outstanding high-end firms grows out of a process that is time-consuming and expensive.

We also find a peculiar pattern in the outstanding volume producers. The two Japanese firms that achieve high levels of product quality are also fast and efficient, yet other fast and efficient Japanese firms fail to achieve the level of design quality attained by the leading firms. It appears that something particular to these companies accounts for the correlation between rapid, efficient development and outstanding design.

LINKING PERFORMANCE AND THE COMPETITIVE ENVIRONMENT

The evidence presented above is consistent with regional differences in market and competition that surfaced in the analysis in Chapter 3. Japanese firms are relatively quick and efficient in product development; European firms, particularly the high-end specialists, are strong in product content and design quality. U.S. firms, reflecting in part their transitional character in the 1980s, do not stand out in any of the dimensions of performance. On top of these regional differences, we have seen that company capability matters. Particularly in product quality, but also in other dimensions of performance, we find major differences across firms within regions, reflecting differences in fundamental capabilities that would apply to any of the projects the firms in our sample might have undertaken in the 1980s.

Table 4.5 presents data on product renewal and product-line variety that enable us to examine these differences more directly.[6] In total number of major new products introduced between 1982 and 1987, we see a dramatic difference between Japanese firms and their Western competitors. While U.S. and European firms introduced 21 and 38 new products, respectively, Japanese firms introduced 72. Such a huge difference might be attributable to Japanese firms spending a

**Table 4.5 Patterns of Product Variety and
Model Changes by Region, 1982–1987**

Pattern / Region	United States	Europe	Japan
Average Number of Car Models	28	77	55
Number of New Car Models Developed	21	38	72
Average Major Model Change Frequency (years)	8.1	12.2	4.6
Product Variety Expansion/ Product Renewal (regional average)			
Output Index	123	73	198
Expansion Index	59	12	66
Replacement Index	65	62	132

Source: See the Appendix.

great deal more money on product development or producing far more vehicles than U.S. or European firms. But such is not the case. Production levels were comparable in Japan and America, and European firms produced far more vehicles than Japanese firms, while levels of R&D spending were quite similar. Japanese firms took their edge from engineering and development productivity.

According to the data on model life, Japanese firms average less than five years between model generations, American firms eight years, and European firms more than a decade. These data highlight not only the speed of Japanese firms, but also the differences in development lead time and renewal strategy. When development of product generations is carried out sequentially (i.e., development of the subsequent generation begins only after the current generation is in the market), development lead time provides a lower bound to model life. A firm may extend the life of a model for other reasons—as seems to be the case in Europe, where model life is more than a decade—even though lead time is five to six years. In Japan, model life and lead time are very close. Japanese firms are capable of moving to market quickly and exploit that capability to achieve short model life and frequent product renewal.

These data suggest a strong link between development performance and longer-term product strategy.[7] To probe that connection further, we examine three measures of product strategy in Table 4.5. The first, the output index, is an overall measure of new product activity (specifically, a count of the number of new models introduced between 1982 and 1987 divided by the number of new models in the market in 1981). This measure is broken out into the expansion index, a measure of product-line diversity, and the replacement index, a measure of product renewal.

As might be expected, the Japanese were most active in new product introductions, but U.S. firms matched Japanese firms in product-line expansion. Because many European firms rationalized their product lines in the 1980s, relatively little expansion occurred there. In terms of product renewal, Japanese firms were far more aggressive than either American or European firms, which replaced about two-thirds of their 1981 product lines with new models. During the same period, Japanese firms replaced all their 1981 models at least once, and some twice. Thus, though U.S. firms kept pace in relative product-line expansion, productivity and lead time advantages gave Japanese firms a strong edge in model renewal.

DEVELOPMENT PERFORMANCE
AND MARKET PERFORMANCE

From the data and analysis presented thus far, it is clear that sharp differences in product development performance across firms and regions are rooted in longer-term capabilities. How and in what way do these differences in performance affect firms' competitive positions? To answer this question, we return to the framework sketched out earlier in this chapter, which established competitiveness as a matter of attracting and satisfying customers. We have some data on customer satisfaction, and attractiveness is a question of buying behavior. If superior performance in lead time, productivity, and product quality is effective in attracting customers, we should see evidence of it in the data on market share.

We examine the link between development performance and attractiveness by comparing firms' domestic market share in the 1980s (e.g., 1981–1986) with both their domestic market share in the late 1970s and over the entire 1975–1986 period (see the Appendix for details). This gives us a rough indication of underlying trends in attractiveness.

The evidence on market share gains we presented in Figure 4.5 showed that only a few companies—some European high-end specialists and a few Japanese volume producers—expanded their domestic market share in the mid 1980s. Most of the firms in our sample lost domestic share during this period. These negative shifts in domestic market position are consistent with globalization of the car market in the 1980s. For Europe and the United States in particular, globalization has been associated with an increase in imports, which has made it difficult even for average producers to maintain domestic market share. In this era of transition to a global market, a negative value for change in domestic share should not be viewed as an indicator of below-average performance; indeed, an increase in domestic share should be seen as unusually strong performance.

The data in Table 4.6 on performance in firms that have expanded market share in the 1980s underscore the strong links between competitiveness and product development performance, particularly with respect to product quality. For both high-end specialists and volume producers, these firms are at the top end of the quality distribution, their average quality index ranging from 83 to 88.7,

Table 4.6 Performance and Long-Term Market Share

Firm Categories / Performance Dimensions	Average for Firms that Gained Long-Term Market Share		Average for Firms that Lost Long-Term Market Share
	Volume	High-End	
Adjusted Engineering Hours	2,463.3	3,912.5	2,500.0
Adjusted Lead Time (months)	54.4	68.7	53.0
TPQ Index	83.8	88.7	40

Source: Calculations based on regression estimates (see the Appendix).

compared to only 40 for the sample. This close connection between customer satisfaction and product attractiveness makes sense in a product such as the modern automobile. With word-of-mouth advertising critical and customers relatively sophisticated, firms must satisfy existing customers if they are to attract new ones over the longer term.

The connection between lead time and productivity performance is less clear. Among high-end specialists, stability of market and product concepts in this market leads producers to place a premium on excellence in design and technical sophistication. Time to market and breadth of product line are much less critical, as reflected in the relative slowness and inefficiency of the outstanding high-end firms. What carries the day here is total product quality.

Among volume producers, speed and efficiency were not sufficient for market success. Japanese firms with short lead times and low engineering hours that failed to attain a high level of design quality lost market share in the 1980s. But though the fastest of these might have improved their competitive position by taking more time in development, high design quality did not guarantee expanding market share.

Some European volume producers highly regarded for the quality of their designs lost market share in the 1980s. These firms tended to be relatively slow, required far more engineering hours than the top performers, and exhibited relatively low levels of conformance quality. They achieved excellence in technical design but failed to strike a balance with manufacturability, integration, or breadth of product line.

It was balanced excellence that characterized high-performance volume producers during the 1980s. The highly competitive environment of this period forced volume producers to be fast and efficient, keep established models fresh and attractive, expand into new segments and niches, and market high-quality products. Few firms gained market share, and those that did had distinctive capabilities. Although the high performers in the volume sector were Japanese, not all Japanese firms achieved high performance. This is not simply a "Japan effect." We must look beyond common regional background to the strategies and capabilities of particular firms for insight into the sources of superior performance.

CONCLUSION

We began this chapter with questions about the nature of product development performance in the world auto industry. Our search for answers has produced clear evidence of regional differences in lead time, productivity, and product quality. We have found Japanese firms able to design and develop products a year faster than and with almost twice the development productivity of the average American or European firm. Finally, we have found that European firms, especially high-end specialists, have an advantage in design quality, while Japanese firms do very well in conformance quality, which gives them a slight edge in total product quality.

Regional differences in development performance also showed up in different product strategies during the 1980s. Japanese volume producers introduced far more new products, maintained a much shorter model life, and expanded their product lines more rapidly than their Western competitors. European high-end specialists, though they introduced far fewer products, consistently achieved superior total product quality. We have suggested that these patterns of performance are based on fundamental capabilities that firms have applied throughout the 1980s and that these capabilities make a difference in competition. Volume producers that have expanded domestic market share in the face of globalization are generally fast and efficient and market high-quality products. Outstanding high-end specialists are truly high end, marketing products with sophisticated engineering and absolute superiority in product design.

The data on performance have clarified the role of product development in competition and highlighted patterns of performance among outstanding firms. To understand the nature and sources of the capabilities that underlie superior performance, we have probed the inner workings of product development in the twenty companies in our sample. With the data to guide us and the comparative perspective afforded by our sample, we now delve into the distinctive patterns of management and engineering practice, organizational structure, and strategy that are common to superior performance.

NOTES

1. For the concept of design quality and conformance quality, see, for example, Juran, Gryna, and Bingham, Jr. (1975), Juran and Gryna (1980), and Fujimoto (1989, Chapter 5).
2. See Clark and Fujimoto (1989a).
3. See Sheriff (1988) for further discussion.
4. For further analysis of planning and engineering lead time, see Clark and Fujimoto (1988b).
5. For economic models based on the notion of time-cost trade-off, see Scherer (1966, 1984), Kamien and Schwartz (1982), and Waterson (1984).
6. See Sheriff (1988) for further analysis.
7. See Clark and Fujimoto (1989a) and Fujimoto and Sheriff (1989).

CHAPTER 5

THE PROCESS OF DEVELOPMENT: FROM CONCEPT TO MARKET

On any given day in Tokyo, Paris, or Detroit, automotive engineers are busy doing what automotive engineers do the world over—designing and developing cars. They are conducting concept studies, building clay models, testing prototypes, solving problems in pilot plants, and getting cars ready for commercial production. All have access to the latest computer systems, work with many of the same suppliers, belong to the same engineering societies, and many have attended the same schools.

Despite all this similarity, the results of these efforts are quite different, not only in concepts and designs (where we might expect differentiation), but also in the practical results of the overall development effort—the time it takes to bring the product to market, development productivity, and the quality of execution. This is what interests us. We want to identify the sources of the significant differences in product development performance documented in Chapter 4.

Before launching into detailed analysis, however, it may be useful to develop some perspective on the nature of the product development process. For readers unfamiliar with the details of developing a new automobile, a description of the way development is organized and managed will highlight the choices firms face in carrying out work and establish a context for the analytical chapters to follow. For readers familiar with automobile development, the chapter may provide a comparative perspective on the process in different companies. To these ends, this chapter presents a first-cut exploration of the *process* of product development. Using the information framework developed in Chapter 2, we identify for each of the four major development activities—concept development, product planning, product engineering, and process engineering—the information assets to be developed and the linkages that must be managed. We pay attention to differences uncovered in our research but wait until later chapters to develop an in-depth understanding of these differences and their effect on development performance.

PATTERNS OF ORGANIZATION

The information asset map presented in Chapter 2 identifies four major stages of development—concept development, product planning, product engineering, and process engineering—and the critical linkages within and across them. Though each firm we studied takes new products through these four stages, each creates and manages the linkages differently. Creating and managing these linkages effectively depends to a great extent on (1) a firm's ability to build channels of communication, (2) attitudes toward cooperation, and (3) the skill of the engineers. But how a firm organizes development, how it divides up and coordinates the work, has a decisive impact as well. In our exploration of the development process, we look first at two dimensions of organization: specialization and cross-functional integration.

SPECIALIZATION

All major car makers group engineering and planning expertise in separate subunits under functional managers (e.g., chief engineers). Though sometimes given different names, all product development organizations have standard departments organized around either car parts or development activities. Examples include body engineering, chassis engineering, power-train engineering, testing, manufacturing engineering, engineering administration, planning, styling, and advanced engineering. Each functional department and its subunits create and control an information asset that corresponds to a specific component or system and a development step. Thus the organization structure overlays the information asset map.[1]

Despite these general similarities, we do find differences across companies. In order to illustrate these differences and highlight the relationship between the development process and its organization, Figure 5.1 lays out four different organization charts rearranged according to the sequence of development activities. The stages of development are arrayed across the top, and we have identified the principal stages of involvement for each of the departments. In broad

Figure 5.1 Four Different Organizational Charts Rearranged
According to Sequence of Development Activities

(1) European High-End Specialist

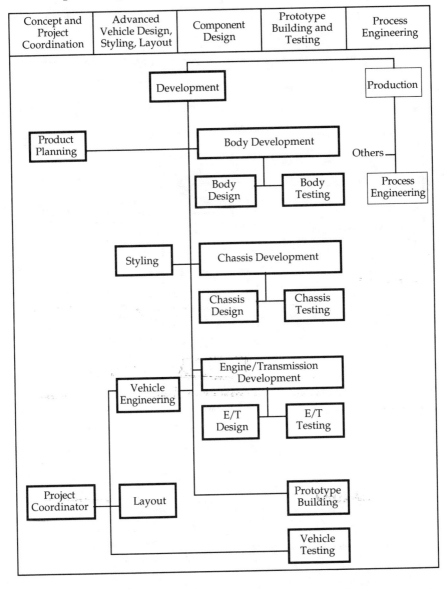

Figure 5.1 Four Different Organizational Charts Rearranged According to Sequence of Development Activities

(2) European Volume Producer

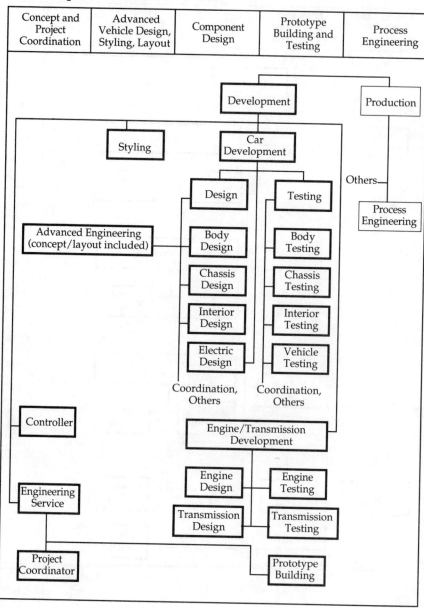

Figure 5.1 Four Different Organizational Charts Rearranged According to Sequence of Development Activities

(3) U.S. Volume Producer

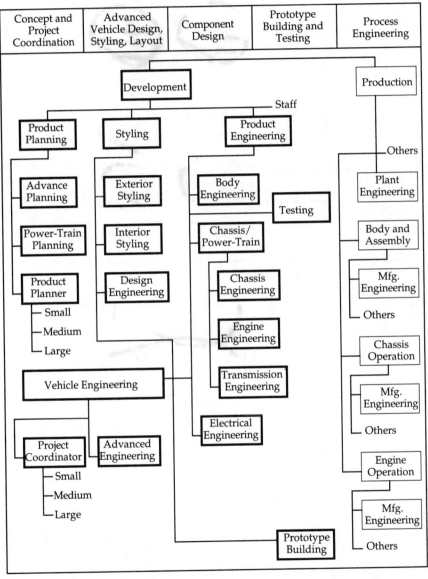

Divisions and Departments in the Development Group

Divisions and Departments outside the Development Group

Figure 5.1 Four Different Organizational Charts Rearranged
According to Sequence of Development Activities

(4) Japanese Volume Producer

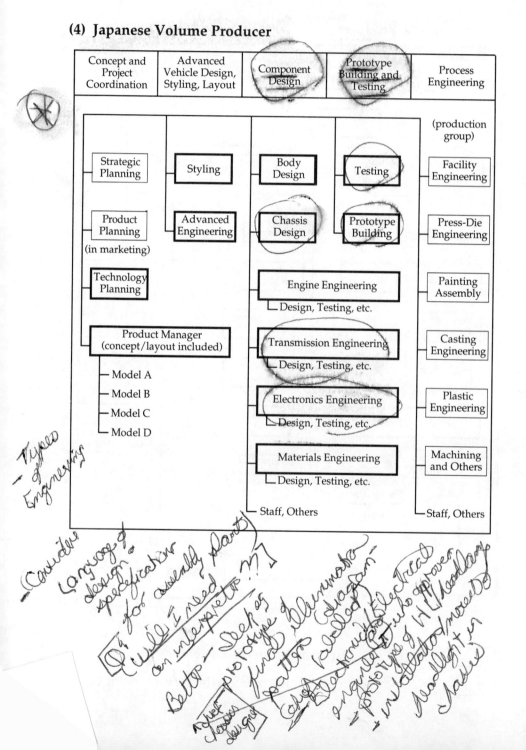

terms, these diagrams point out clear differences in structure. Larger companies, for example, tend to create more departments with narrower specialization; European companies tend to create highly rational and hierarchical structures that emphasize engineering functionalism; Japanese organization structures tend to be simpler and flatter, while those of U.S. firms are generally much more complicated, with many subunits and divisions differentiated by organizational/geographical barriers deployed in a towering hierarchy.

At the detail level, we find more subtle choices for structuring product development. Testing, for example, may either be merged into engineering design for tighter design-test linkages or remain independent in order to provide more effective checks and balances. Similarly, assigning the prototype shop to product engineering may yield faster design-build-test cycles, while assigning it to process engineering may facilitate better knowledge sharing between prototype and commercial production. Packaging (i.e., vehicle layout) may be conducted by advanced engineering, body engineering, styling, or project managers, depending on which information linkages the company emphasizes.

CROSS-FUNCTIONAL INTEGRATION

The shift from purely functional forms of organization to more integrated structures has become a trend that we find everywhere. The straightforward functional organizations of the 1960s virtually all incorporated formal mechanisms for cross-functional coordination by the late 1980s. Wherever we went, we found engineers whose principal job was to link one department (e.g., chassis engineering) with one or more related departments (e.g., body, engine, and/or production). These "liaison engineers," whose job it was to ensure that the wants of their home departments were made known and that relevant information moved back to the home department, often met in formal committees to exchange information and coordinate activities. These meetings were often supported by a department (e.g., the timing office) that tracked the schedules and coordinated activities. Multifunctional task forces and small teams organized around components or particular problems were commonplace, and most of the companies we studied had established full-time project coordinators, which we call "product managers."

over

In the face of broad similarity in structure, we must look to more subtle differences in actions, practices, attitudes, values, and skills to find aspects of organization and management that may be important in explaining differences in integration and performance. There is, for example, a certain type of integration that never surfaces in formal organization charts, yet is vital to product integrity: informal face-to-face contact between working engineers and managers. Formal structure is only a part of the overall system; our search for effective organizational patterns in product development must include detailed analysis of the way development actually works. (A more systematic analysis is conducted in Chapter 9.) Two examples illustrate the nature of the issues we must confront and the kinds of analysis we must do.

What Is a Product Manager?

Product managers are found in almost every automobile company, but their actions and attitudes can differ significantly across companies. In one European company we studied, product managers regarded themselves as neutral "coordinators" or "conflict managers." They were relatively low in rank, weak in informal power, coordinated only within the engineering group, influenced working engineers only through liaison meetings, worked on someone else's product plan, and spent most of their time at their desks doing paperwork. In contrast, in a Japanese company we studied, product managers ranked as high as chief engineers, exercised strong informal leadership, coordinated entire projects including production and marketing, influenced working engineers directly when necessary, took charge of product concepts and plans, and spent a lot of time outside the office talking with engineers, designers, testers, plant supervisors, dealers, and customers. They generally regarded themselves as product champions and internal entrepreneurs, rather than as mere coordinators. Though both jobs carried the title of product manager, the functions and the people who hold them were very different. More important, the nature and quality of the linkages they established were likely be very different.

Teams and Teamwork

Cross-functional project teams, however prevalent, do not guarantee effective development. Even good "teamwork" may not be enough. In one American company, for example, we found a very coherent "project team" with a high level of team spirit. But the team consisted only of liaison people from each department; none of the working engineers responsible for creating actual drawings and prototypes was included. The liaison team was effectively an enclave that tended to be isolated from the working engineers, who referred to the liaison members as "the team people." It took extensive clinical study to recognize that this high integration at the liaison level masked a lack of integration across the development organization.

Once we recognized that effective patterns of organization are rooted not only in formal structure and high-level integration, but also in overall patterns of behavior, culture, and informal relationships, we began to probe these latter dimensions in our field study across the entire process of product development. We present our findings beginning with upstream activities in concept development and design.

TOTAL VEHICLE CONCEPT AS A COMPETITIVE WEAPON

Development of an automobile begins with concept generation. At this stage, information on future market needs, technological possibilities, and economic feasibility is merged and translated into a product description that embodies the experiences the product will deliver to the customer. A product concept specifies how basic functions, structures, and/or messages associated with the total vehicle will attract and satisfy target customers. When products are judged on the basis of a few, well-defined, objective criteria, a product concept may be defined by a general product category and a set of specifications: "Product X, our next generation widget, will be a 500-horsepower machine with half the fuel consumption." When the product is complex and customers subjectively evaluate the total product experience, the product concept must project how the customer will experience the product as a whole; it must encompass the product's character, personality, and image.

Consider, for example, concept development for a sporty version of a subcompact car. The basic concept might be captured in two words: "pocket rocket." Fleshed out, "pocket rocket" means that the car has to be small, light, and very fast. But it also has to have quick, responsive handling and an aggressive design. While the car should sell at a premium compared to the base model, it should be affordable. And the driving experience should be fun: quick at the getaway, nimble in the turns, and very fast on the straightaways. There would, of course, be many other details in design and engineering needing definition for the product to achieve its objectives, but the basic concept of an "affordable, fun-to-drive, pocket rocket" would be critical in guiding and focusing creative ideas and decisions. Indeed, articulation of an attractive, consistent, and distinctive concept at the outset of a project is critical for market success.

But product concepts are often elusive and equivocal. When asked to relate the "concept" for a vehicle they have developed, key project participants may offer widely divergent notions about what kind of value they are delivering to the customer. Those for whom the product concept means *what the product does* will couch their description in terms of performance and technical functions. Others, for whom product concept means *what the product is*, will describe outlines of packaging, configuration, and choices of main component technologies. From others, for whom product concept is synonymous with *whom the product serves*, a description of target customers will be forthcoming. Still others, reflecting their interpretation of product concept as *what the product means to customers*, will describe basic themes reflecting the character, personality, feel, and image of the vehicle. A powerful product concept will include all these dimensions; it is a multifaceted thing. But we have found that different companies emphasize different aspects of the product concept. This emphasis, in turn, profoundly influences the character of the product. Thus concept development is critical to the competitiveness of the product. Creating an effective product concept involves effectively managing both inputs to the product concept and the process of concept creation.

MANAGING INPUTS TO THE PRODUCT CONCEPT

Effectively managing inputs to the product concept requires a subtle balance between the people charged with conceiving the product and sources of critical information and insight. Three sources of inputs seem to be central: market information, strategic plans, and advanced engineering results.

Market input. Market inputs may be obtained directly by concept creators gathering information in the market, or indirectly from specialists in the marketing group who forward to concept creators the results of market research and product clinics and feedback from dealers. Some firms use both modes of obtaining market input, but many give precedence to one. Firms that emphasize the marketing function place confidence in an organization specializing in the market interface. The marketing organization usually is well equipped with resources and expertise for formal market research, including focus groups, clinics, and detailed statistical analysis. Product planners within the marketing organization use market research to develop customer profiles and identify attractive product concepts in these terms. In markets where customers have significant experience with the product, formal methods have proven powerful in identifying customer preferences.

Firms that put responsibility for concept development in the hands of a product manager (often assisted by a product planning staff) emphasize the dynamic nature of the interaction between customer and product. While product managers may use market research as an input, they are likely to maintain their own direct contacts with existing and potential customers. They tend to see their role as "concept creator." The mission is not to look back at what has sold in the past, but to look forward to and anticipate emerging trends and to shape the future. Such a role is likely to be important where products are complex and customer preferences are dynamic.

Strategic plans. Long-range strategic plans for an entire product range, often called cycle plans, are created and revised periodically to ensure coordination of new product launch timing across projects. Resource constraints, market trends, and the availability of technologies and components are all taken into account in creating cycle plans, which typically have a ten-year horizon. Strategic plans may also include product specifications such as price range, positioning, image, engine choice, target customers, and so forth.

Like much else in concept creation, strategic planning poses a challenge of balance. Coherent strategic plans facilitate smooth and speedy conception and planning and help a product line maintain corporate identity and consistency across models, an increasingly important element of product competitiveness. At the same time, centralized strategic planning can impose excessive constraints that stifle the creativity and imagination of individual concept creators. If concept creators are demoralized and deprived of responsiveness to changing and diversified market needs, the distinctiveness and variety of products may suffer.

Thus, effective strategic planning means striking a balance between overall strategic direction and flexibility in responding to the details of competition in a specific market segment. Traditionally, many automobile firms have used cycle plans to track capacity and the timing of market introductions, but not to guide individual projects beyond that. As the environment has grown more turbulent and product lines more complex, the value of more detailed, coherent plans has increased.

Technological inputs. Technological advancements may shape the development of a product concept. Availability of a multivalve, high-performance V8 engine for a luxury car, for example, makes possible a product experience and image different than that created by a smaller V6 engine. Knowing that a technology is available is therefore likely to influence how product planners and product managers conceive a new product.

Conversely, product concepts may drive the development of technology. A concept that calls for a light but strong and rigid body, for example, may require the development of new materials and body production processes. In a market where customers are sensitive to product integrity and component technology is an integral part of the product concept, concept-driven technology development appears attractive. But concept-driven technology development is only possible when lead time for a technology is shorter than the required lead time on the product. When technology lead time is longer, as is often the case for advanced technologies, the technology needs to be already developed or be under development when work on the new product begins.

To solve the problem of long technology lead times, firms often develop technology in advance and stock it in a technology "refrigerator." To avoid a mismatch between what is in the refrigerator and what new products require, advanced development must anticipate emerging product concepts. Managing technology inputs into concept development is a problem of linking new technology to future products at both ends of advanced development—charting advanced development at the outset with an eye toward future products, and keeping product managers linked to the results of advanced engineering work.

MANAGING THE PROCESS OF CONCEPT DEVELOPMENT

Concept creation is a cognitive process associated with individuals. The challenge in concept development is to find a way to mesh individual creativity with the need for organizational consensus and support. At the level of the individual, the most important question is, "Who is in charge?" We have seen three candidates in our study:

1) Putting *specialists in a functional unit,* such as marketing or advanced engineering, in charge of concept generation for all of a company's cars. This may help ensure a consistent level of concept quality across models, but linkages with downstream functions may be weak, given that specialists tend to hand off concept proposals downstream and quit the project without much after-care.

2) Having *product planners* (usually in marketing, but sometimes in engineering) specialize in concept creation for particular models. This may be appropriate when a company needs to offer a variety of well-differentiated products to niche markets, but because the problem of weak ties to downstream remains, the result may be good product concepts realized as mediocre products that arrive too late to market.

3) Putting responsibility for concept leadership in the hands of a *product manager.* Where product managers have close links to the market, this approach may have some advantage in a turbulent environment. Further, where the product manager plays a central role in downstream activities, the linkage between concept and downstream tends to be well maintained. On the negative side, corporate identity or conceptual consistency across models may be hard to maintain with this approach.

The central challenges in the process of concept development are striking the right balance between leadership and individual creativity and fostering the wide involvement of other functions in the organization. Developing a product concept, as the information map suggests, may involve all downstream activities—product design, layout, component choice, styling, manufacturability, production constraints, cost assumptions, marketability, and so forth. Because these downstream activities affect customer satisfaction, it is desirable to involve downstream people in the concept development process (i.e., to "front-load" downstream information). However, while ignoring downstream constraints in concept development may invite disaster, broad downstream involvement can also jeopardize the coherence and distinctiveness of product concepts. Negotiations and battles among powerful functions can give rise to a series of political compromises and patchwork solutions that result in a concept without character. Many of the project leaders we interviewed argued that democracy without clear concept leadership is a prime enemy of distinctive products.

Many of the companies we studied made a choice between cross-functional involvement and concept leadership. Some companies placed responsibility for concept development in a specialized unit, often within marketing, and encouraged very little involvement by downstream functions. Others initiated cross-functional negotiations at a senior level at the outset of projects. The former approach tends to suffer from incongruity between product concept and actual product, the latter from lack of concept distinctiveness.

Other companies have combined strong concept leadership with broad involvement of downstream groups. In one company, a small group of concept creators and assistants is given about six months to establish a product concept or plan before cross-functional negotiation begins. This provides a gestation period during which the concept leader can nurture the embryo of the concept. Another company forms a cross-functional concept team that heavily involves downstream functions at the outset of a project, but installs the concept creator in a role of clear leadership over other members. Especially during the first few months of a project, clear concept leadership, together with wide involvement of other functions, appears to be an important aspect of effective concept creation.

PRODUCT PLANNING

A completed product concept must be translated into successively more concrete assumptions—including specification of cost and performance targets, component choice, styling, and layout—for detailed product engineering. This stage, which bridges product concept and product design, is often called product planning. Program approval by top management at the end of this stage triggers full-scale activities in product engineering.

Two major challenges must be met to achieve excellence in product planning. First, specifications, component choices, styling, and layout must reflect the intent of the product concept accurately. Because the product concept is effectively a statement about what customers will find attractive, matching product plans with product concept means achieving *external consistency. Internal consistency—* the compatibility of specifications, component choices, styling, and layout—is also essential. Achieving external and internal consistency simultaneously is not easy, as the following example illustrates.

Planning a Family Sedan

A leading Japanese automobile company set out to produce a distinctive family sedan. The vehicle concept included maximum space and visibility for passengers, minimum space for mechanisms, wide and low body for aesthetics, superb handling and stability, and superior economy in operation. In body styling, the designers translated the concept into an extremely low engine hood, which constrained the choice of suspension. Prevalent front suspension systems, such as the McPherson strut, were not feasible because of height. The solution, a double-wishbone type suspension system (short and superior in road holding under normal conditions) was expensive, making cost overrun an issue. In addition, the suspension system consumed space horizontally, pushing the engine room inward. There were other conflicts. Solving the trade-off between light vehicle weight (for better fuel economy) and stronger body shell rigidity (for stability) involved a complex inner body structure using thinner sheet metal, which also pushed the engine room inward. On the cabin side, the low engine hood and high visibility meant a larger glass area, which necessitated a stronger air conditioner. This, in turn, required additional engine horse power to meet the performance target. Furthermore, the long, low passenger space called for a front-wheel drive configuration with the engine near the front, creating a front-heavy weight distribution that could damage handling unless the engine was very light. A high-power, lightweight, compact engine had to be developed specifically for this model—a relatively expensive solution.

Product planning involves a complicated web of trade-offs among concept, specification, component choice, cost targets, layout, and styling. Planning a new car is like trying to solve a huge simultaneous equation system. Organizational conflicts and difficult negotiations are inevitable. In the case of the family sedan, the height of the engine hood was a major battlefield. Designers and concept leaders tried to lower the hood; engine engineers pushed it up; body engineers claimed space for structures in between. The height went up and down literally by millimeters during the battle. There were many other areas of conflict that involved component engineers, designers, product managers, testers, controllers, plant managers, die engineers, and others.

To achieve high internal and external consistency at the end of product planning, close coordination and communication among planning units—and between planning units and concept creators—are important. How a firm divides and assigns tasks may considerably influence product integrity. Three activities seem particularly critical: styling, layout, and component choice.

STYLING

Body and interior styling are normally carried out by separate design departments, typically a pool of industrial designers, modelers, technicians, and aerodynamics and ergonomics engineers. The styling process is a series of problem-solving cycles in which designers translate ideas expressed in two dimensions (e.g., sketches, renderings, and tape drawings) into three dimensions (e.g., clay or plastic models). Styling information is ultimately stored as CAD data, which is eventually used for body development.

Like other elements of product planning, design plays an important role as a bridge between the product concept and detailed engineering. In that role, effectiveness depends on links with concept development and engineering. On the concept side, customer expectations demand tight integration of design theme and technical and marketing concepts, making design an integral part of the total vehicle concept. Achieving the requisite integration is no simple matter. Organizationally, it implies intensive two-way communication between the concept creator and design unit to precisely reflect the intent of both parties from the outset of a project. When designers and concept creators interact, accuracy of concept-design communication becomes an issue. Whereas a product concept is abstract and verbal, styling is inherently visual, three-dimensional, and difficult to express in words. Because it is impossible to convey subtle nuances of a vehicle concept by written documents alone, frequent face-to-face contact between concept creators and designers is essential. Selection of appropriate keywords can be helpful, as can the creation of a short story that represents the product image (this is called image rehearsal). For their part, designers need to attend more to customer tastes, revealed or latent, than to the tastes of their superiors. In short, concept creators and designers must share a language and values despite organizational barriers to doing so.

On the engineering side, an important choice firms face in managing design is the degree of differentiation between designers and engineers. Designers are often organized into design studios, each assigned to a particular product category or make. Some regional differences are apparent. Design departments in U.S. firms, for example, tend to reflect a high degree of differentiation between engineers and designers in terms of language, attitude, clothes, and lifestyle. Engineers typically work in nondescript offices, cubicles, and laboratories, while designers are housed in artfully appointed surroundings that possess the quality of an inner sanctum. In Europe, designers and engineers work much more closely. This regional difference seems to be rooted in different traditions of automobile design. In Europe, adherence to the Bauhaus philosophy (form follows function) encouraged tighter relationships between design (form) and engineering (function); in the United States, the annual model change gave styling an independent role, and the basic body-on-frame technology made it independent from engineering design. In Japan, the design function began as a section in body engineering and is today treated like any other engineering department.

LAYOUT

Layout or packaging refers to the space distribution plan for mechanical components, body structures, luggage, and passengers. Layout and styling are as closely connected as skin and bones. Layout begins with basic component configuration (e.g., front-wheel drive) and key dimensions (e.g., wheelbase, hip point, height, and windshield angle), followed by refinement around the skeleton.

Although not as visible as styling, layout has a decisive impact on the personality of a car. A slight modification in seat and cabin layout can dramatically change a driver's impression of roominess, visibility, and driving feel. Small shifts in the engine's center of gravity relative to the front axle may alter the character of handling. Layout, a direct expression of a total vehicle concept in physical terms, is thus essential to an even greater extent than styling. This is why basic packaging precedes styling in most of the companies we studied.

When it conveys a product's primary message and philosophy, layout can have a major impact on the product's long-term fate. The success of some legendary European models—e.g., the Beetle, Citroën 2CV, and Golf—can be ascribed partly to their innovative packaging, and smart layout has been vital in developing Japanese micromini cars, which compete on an extra quarter inch of leg and head room. The major advantage of Chrysler's highly successful minivan seems to be its layout (e.g., the low cabin floor) rather than styling or performance. A vehicle can sink as well as swim on the basis of its layout; there are cases in which poor packaging, more than any other attribute, damaged a product's reputation.

Assignment of layout responsibility, particularly basic layout, is thus an important choice in organizational design. Some companies place the concept creator in charge of basic layout, an arrangement that emphasizes the concept-layout linkage. In others, particularly Japanese companies, packaging is the responsibility of the product manager. This arrangement emphasizes layout's role as a tool of intercomponent coordination. In still other companies, a section of the design department assumes responsibility for basic packaging, an arrangement that emphasizes the tight interdependence between styling and layout. Finally, layout may be carried out by a specialized engineering unit, a section in advanced engineering or body engineering, for example.

COMPONENT CHOICES

Because product technology is mostly embedded in major components, major component decisions are also choices of technologies. Decisions in three main areas—new versus existing parts, supplier versus in-house engineering, and choice of basic component technology—affect the pattern of product competitiveness through many trade-offs. Use of existing parts (i.e., common with other models or carried over from predecessor models) saves tooling and design costs and reduces the risk of reliability problems. But it may also result in suboptimal parts design from a total vehicle perspective and thereby jeopardize design quality. Similarly, use of suppliers' engineering resources, though it may enhance component design quality and lower the in-house workload for planning and engineering coordination, may also lead to deterioration of basic technical capability, and giving up core component technologies can weaken a company's bargaining position with its suppliers.

As an example of the trade-offs that must be made in component technology, consider the choice of rear suspension. Independent suspensions have become as common as the conventional rigid axle in today's cars. Among them, the semitrailing arm offers the advantage of reduced road noise and fine tuning flexibility; the lightweight McPherson strut affords superior handling but may be vertically space-consuming; and double wishbone provides the best road holding but tends to be heavy and expensive. Which suspension technology to choose depends upon the total vehicle concept, cost-performance targets, drive-train configuration, packaging, and styling. Because both component and test engineers are involved in component choice, interfunctional conflicts are common as the different groups tend to emphasize different criteria. The leadership of concept creators and the customer orientation of engineers are keys to constructive resolution of these conflicts.

The network of trade-offs and web of coordination among different aspects of a total vehicle are complex. Targets, specifications, layout, styling, and component choices must be optimized simultaneously. Auto makers are challenged to achieve total vehicle integrity—both internal and external—efficiently and quickly. Concept leadership, intensive communication, and product-customer orientation appear to be key to effectiveness at this stage.

PRODUCT ENGINEERING

When a product plan receives senior management approval (sometimes a little earlier), detailed product engineering begins. At this point a great deal of work on the product architecture already has been done. A clay model has been approved; interior mockups are complete; targets for cost and performance have been specified; the overall packaging of the vehicle has been laid out; and basic component choices have been made. It would seem that all product engineering has to do is implement the plan.

Were it that simple, the tension and pressure in product development would be greatly diminished. But it is not. What appears at first to be a well-articulated, firmly established architecture often consists of a broad (perhaps even vague) product concept; a set of evolving, sometimes loosely formulated specifications; and multiple, often conflicting targets that may be difficult to meet. The product is invariably complex and the planning process, its attention to detail notwithstanding, is unlikely to uncover all the relevant conflicts and problems in advance. To meet an objective such as "the door on the new luxury sedan should create a feeling of solidity and security when it closes" may be difficult, involving the application of technical expertise and a great deal of negotiation with engineers working on the body, electrical system, stamping, and assembly. Though planning establishes overall direction and architecture, product engineering must still confront numerous conflicts and trade-offs in local components and subsystems.

ORGANIZING PRODUCT ENGINEERING

Companies organize to meet the challenge of product engineering in similar ways. Firms base their product engineering decisions on a series of "design-build-test" cycles, the elements of which are almost uniform throughout the industry: detailed blueprints are developed for each component (and for major systems); prototype components and vehicles are built based on preliminary drawings; prototypes are tested against established targets; then tests are evaluated and designs modified as necessary. The cycle is repeated until an acceptable level of performance is achieved.

As a means of managing complexity, firms divide projects into manageable parts. At the vehicle level, firms divide up the work among in-house engineering groups, engineering contractors, and suppliers. In the in-house groups, product engineering is organized by process step and component. Design and testing are commonly split; body, chassis, and power train are usually organized into different departments. Actual departmentalization reflects relative emphasis on two principles: design-test specialization or merging of design and test into component departments.

Further specialization occurs at the working level. Individual engineers are typically assigned to an engineering step or a component. In Europe there is a dichotomy between "engineers," who have graduate engineering degrees and do only basic design, and "drafters," who are technicians and do only drafting. Specialization by process step (e.g., basic design, drafting, testing, and analysis) is common. In contrast, specialization along these lines is seldom seen in Japanese car companies, where rookie engineer-technicians (there is no clear distinction between the two) are assigned to drafting regardless of education level and gradually shift to piece-part and subassembly design over a period of years.

Narrow specialization by component, which enhances engineering expertise but makes total vehicle coordination difficult, is common in Europe and the United States. Overspecialization of component engineers in some U.S. and European companies (e.g., left rear tail light engineer) has led to difficulties in coordination, inefficiency arising out of task duplication, and lack of customer orientation and total vehicle perspective. Among high-end producers characterized by stable product concepts and component designs, narrow specialization has not interfered with total vehicle orientation, but among other European and most American companies, the trend is toward broader task assignments, reduced specialization, and greater emphasis on customer orientation among individual engineers.

Differences in departmentalization and individual task assignments and specialization are important, but more critical is the way companies perform work and implement the principle of specialization. Three aspects of product engineering—the linkage between concept development and detailed engineering, building and testing prototypes, and the management of engineering changes—illustrate the importance of implementation.

CONCEPT DEVELOPMENT AND PRODUCT ENGINEERING

Because today's sophisticated customers demand conceptual integrity down to the level of detailed component performance, subtle nuances of the total vehicle concept have to be infused into every part of the product. This calls for close ties between concept leaders and product engineers, including those involved in component design and testing. Yet close connections between concept creators and working engineers are relatively rare. Without a process or a strong product manager to make this connection, the linkage is likely to be weak. Though product managers routinely maintain contact with product engineering offices for purposes of coordination, which should facilitate communication between concept and engineering, direct contact between product managers and working engineers is uncommon. More usual is indirect contact through liaison representatives.

There are at least two ways to achieve close integration between concept and product details: through project leaders or through engineering tradition. Integration through a project leader grows out of direct intervention at the working level. On particularly critical issues such as suspension tuning, strong product managers often become directly involved in the details of design and testing. One product manager we interviewed used disagreements about component design as an opportunity to talk about his concepts with working-level engineers. This direct communication helped concept leaders in this firm maintain product integrity at a detailed level.

Concept sharing is also important in testing, particularly with respect to the marketability testers, who evaluate the total vehicle from a customer's point of view. Representativeness of testers is as important as representativeness of prototypes. "A good car cannot be developed without test engineers who can directly feel the tastes of the target users," explained the head of testing in one company. "My policy is to keep only those in the testing team for the product who can understand the product concept from the heart." In addition to maintaining market contacts and customer orientation, marketability testers must share their views on customer expectations with concept leaders.

The second mode of integration, engineering tradition, is more common among high-end specialists. Because product concepts and engineering philosophy are stable over generations and consistent across models, working engineers already share an image of their firm's products and components and the methods to achieve desired performance. This enables product integrity to be maintained without overtly emphasizing concept-engineering communication, much as a skilled orchestra with a narrow repertoire can create coherent and distinctive music with minimal participation by the conductor. Companies that require close concept-engineering linkages might be likened to an orchestra with a wide and changing repertoire that relies on a conductor's active involvement to achieve conceptual integrity in its music.

BUILDING AND TESTING PROTOTYPES

Once engineers complete detailed design, the next step in product engineering is the building and testing of prototype vehicles. Prototype construction begins with the first release of parts drawings and usually occurs in two or three "blocks"—batches of prototypes built with the same version of the design. As prototypes in the first block are completed, testing begins. Test results are fed back into design, where changes are made for introduction into the next block.

Though the building and testing of engineering prototypes is beginning to be accomplished by computer-aided engineering (CAE) simulations, the growing sophistication of customer tastes makes subtle evaluation of total product quality using physical models even more important. Speed, efficiency, and the representativeness of prototypes and their testing are essential for identifying engineering problems and improving design quality early, before engineering changes become expensive.

Common problems with prototyping recall King Richard III's experience with the nail in his horse's shoe: for want of discipline in engineering drawing release and due to late delivery of parts, the first prototypes are late and poorly crafted; for want of good, early prototypes, testing is hurried, incomplete, and unrepresentative; for want of thorough, effective testing, problems remain buried in the design. Furthermore, firms often fail to build the vertical linkages in the information map that connect the prototype shop to commercial production. Prototype parts are made by prototype parts specialists who have nothing to do with production suppliers, so potential production problems found during prototype fabrication are seldom passed from the former to the latter. Firms that fail to manage prototype production for process learning miss a golden opportunity to solve production problems early.

In the absence of prototypes that reflect design intent, without effective and thorough testing, and with weak links between prototype and commercial production, many problems in product design and production go undetected until the pilot run or even production ramp up. The result is major engineering changes late in the project that drive up the cost of engineering, delay production startup and market introduction, and lead to a flood of field quality problems, warranty claims, and recalls. The product's reputation and sales performance suffer and plant downtime rises as a consequence of fixing production problems.

There are at least two approaches to management of prototype and testing, based on very different philosophies and assumptions. One approach is to put prototype production at the center of a problem-solving cycle where it can serve not only to verify design, but also to reveal problems that might be solved before commercial production begins. This approach makes discipline and speed key to high performance. It calls for imposing discipline in drawing release and prototype procurement, completing first prototypes early, building and testing many prototypes, conducting testing early and quickly, introducing design improvements as early as possible, ensuring that prototypes reflect the design and are reasonably representative for problem detection, having production suppliers build prototype parts, facilitating communication and knowledge sharing between prototype and production, and solving major product-production problems before the start of production.

The second approach, often employed by some European high-end producers, has a perfectionist bent: build prototypes of extremely high quality and build many of them; have highly skilled testers conduct thorough testing and make drawing release contingent upon their approval; deny compromise in product performance as a solution to production problems. "Prototypes are more accurate to specifications than production models are," remarked a manager of process engineering for one high-end producer. "After the prototypes are built, prototype shop workers teach production workers how to build the car." Though it yields very high design quality, this approach may be expensive and time-consuming, making it an option only for high-end specialists.

ENGINEERING CHANGES

Engineering changes—changes to parts or drawings that have already been released—are the rule rather than the exception in product development. Some changes (e.g., those resulting from simple mistakes in drafting) are unnecessary and should be eliminated, but many are important for improving the product, and efforts to eliminate them entirely are both undesirable and unrealistic. What is more important is to better manage the content, timing, and method of changes that need to be made.

Some companies, particularly in the United States and Europe, manage the change process with an eye toward risk and cost. They construct fairly elaborate procedures involving multiple signatures and levels of approval before a change is implemented. But with a complex product and many changes, such a system may become cumbersome and inefficient as the firm adds people and structure to deal with confusion and complexity.

We found an alternative approach in some companies, particularly in Japan. The notion that Japanese auto makers do not change designs after final release of drawings is a myth; our comparative study shows that the typical Japanese project has almost as many changes as its Western counterpart. The differences in approach lie not in numbers, but in patterns and content. Procedures are less bureaucratic and oriented more toward fast implementation than toward checks and balances. In effect, this approach emphasizes early versus late, meaningful versus unnecessary, and fast versus slow. Engineers make changes earlier, when the cost of change and time pressure are still relatively low. They reduce the number of changes due to careless mistakes and poor communication so that changes that are made add value to the product. And once a change becomes necessary, engineers act on it quickly, using informal negotiation at the working level to avoid excessive paperwork.

PROCESS ENGINEERING

Design information is converted into information assets—the tools, equipment, process control software, worker skills, and standard operating procedures that will be deployed in the production process—in the process engineering stage. Process engineering generally belongs to the production group and is thus organizationally separate from product engineering (though there have been attempts to consolidate the two at the subunit or individual levels). Process engineers are usually organized by major process types—e.g., casting, machining, stamping, welding, painting, and final assembly—and are variously located at production sites, in technical centers with product engineers, or at headquarters.

Process engineering, like product engineering, is a series of design-build-test cycles. The usual progression is to develop a plan for the entire production system; develop plans for individual processes (e.g., body welding); and conduct detailed design of tools and equipment; procure or construct and install tools and equipment; try out and test tools and equipment; and conduct a pilot run.* Following the cycles of modification and improvement in product-process design, the transition to commercial production is approved (this is sometimes called "sign-off"), and commercial production (often called "Job One") begins. Start of production normally precedes start of sales by a few months in order for early production vehicles to fill distribution pipelines.

Because process engineering links the product to the factory, tensions arising out of conflicting demands for product performance and ease of manufacture often come to a head in decisions about the process. Furthermore, by the time process engineering is in full swing, the date for market introduction, which top management often

---

*   The plan for the entire production system—which includes plant assignment, outsourcing plans, aggregate-level capital investment, and work force plans—is considered part of product planning; hence, process engineering begins with the planning of individual processes.

regards as a *real* deadline, begins to loom large on the horizon. The effectiveness of process engineering thus depends as much on the ability to interact with product designers and the factory as it does on technical skills. Three themes characterize the approaches to interaction: simultaneous product and process engineering; communication and resolution of conflicts between product and process engineering; and merging of process development and volume production during ramp up.

SIMULTANEITY OF PRODUCT AND PROCESS ENGINEERING

At the working level, firms face a set of choices about the degree of simultaneity in product and process engineering. Take, for example, the process of designing, making, and assembling tail lights. Process engineering is logically downstream from product engineering; one option open to engineers is to work on the process after the design has been completed. In this sequential setup, process engineers use the finished design as input, finding ways to make the lenses and the light fixture and attach them to the body. Proceeding in sequence avoids design change confusion and allows engineers to focus on their area of specialization, but it may require a significant amount of time.

An alternative approach is to work on product and process design in parallel. Though this approach may shorten lead time, it exposes engineers to risks of confusion and inefficiency in process engineering. Starting early may get molds for the plastic lenses completed sooner but subsequent changes in the lens design may result in rework or scrappage that will increase costs and cause production delays. If rework problems are extreme, working in parallel may actually take as long as or longer than the sequential approach.

The parallel approach thus heightens the importance of coordination and communication between product and process engineering. Product engineering must comprehend implications of their designs for manufacturability, and process engineering must clarify constraints and opportunities in the process and develop a good measure of flexibility to cope with the changes inherent in the product design process. Though it can be a source of improved product quality and lower costs, emphasis on manufacturability without flexibility in the attitudes and skills of process engineers can negatively affect a product's competitiveness. Process engineers dream of product engineers who take manufacturability fully into account in the early stages of development and then freeze the design. But paraphrasing what one process engineer said of this dream: "If the voice of manufacturing dominates product design, the car may be great in the factory but a dog in the market."

PRODUCT-PROCESS COMMUNICATION AND CONFLICT RESOLUTION

Conflict between product and process engineering is an inherent part of designing and developing a new product and its production process. With multiple objectives, numerous constraints, and uncertainty about market reaction, even people with the best of intentions and motives will have differing points of view. The challenge is to avoid conflicts that stem from lack of understanding and effectively resolve those that arise. This requires continual two-way communication from the early stages of development, including early release of preliminary product design information to downstream and early feedback of production feasibility information to upstream.

Communication that makes a difference is rooted in a fundamental change in attitudes on both sides. The stereotypical product engineer is a perfectionist in product functions who changes designs for better performance as long as the schedule permits, but who hates late rework imposed by manufacturing. The stereotypical process engineer emphasizes manufacturability of product designs and hates late design changes except as they relate to manufacturability. The following comments, one from the process and one from the product side of the same company, are representative of stereotypical engineers in action.

> The design is never done. You give a body engineer more time, you get more changes. Most of the changes have to do with function or appearance. We live with them up to a point. But when we get about halfway done with the tools, we call a halt to it. We don't let any more changes in until the tool is done. Then we go back and put in the changes that really need to be made. If we didn't declare an end halfway through, we'd never get done.

We've done pretty well on the prototypes on this product, but I can guarantee you that when the product gets into the plant, we're going to see a flood of changes. Our feasibility releases are not what you would call "high-quality events." We're not getting good information early enough. The process engineers may say it's "feasible" three years before the start of production, but that doesn't always mean it's "manufacturable" at 60 jobs an hour, with real live operators on a real live assembly line.

Introducing cross-functional communication tools in such an atmosphere (which we found in many other companies as well) might easily reinforce the traditional separation of functions. For example, requiring product engineers to release preliminary information to process engineers will make design fluctuations more apparent to process engineers. If process engineers react by blaming product engineers for the changes, the product engineers will become increasingly defensive. From their perspective, early communication to process engineers only opens them to earlier attack and gives the process people opportunities to unilaterally impose design constraints in the name of manufacturability. This may reinforce a "don't-tell-them-early" attitude on the product side. On the process side, the notion that early design information, because it is likely to change, does not deserve serious consideration may reinforce a wait-and-see attitude. Attitudes of customer orientation, joint responsibility, and mutual trust on both the product and process sides seem to be the basis of a foundation for effective communication.

Effective communication is motivated by the need to produce a product that satisfies customers and launch it on time. Product-process conflicts are not resolved by abstract arguments about the benefits of communication or appeals to manufactur-ability or functionality for their own sake. Moreover, when communication is effective, conflicts do not get in the way of fast action. When product engineering releases are late, for example, process engineering starts its work anyway, initiating communication with upstream, soliciting whatever preliminary information is available, and managing the risk of subsequent changes.

In short, what seems important is the diffusion of a shared sense of competitive reality and customer orientation down to the working level. Communication is nothing more than the consequence of such a cultural change. Without it, a top-down campaign for better product-process communication may yield only a proliferation of unfocused meetings that deprives engineers of creative time and lowers their productivity.

PROCESS ENGINEERING AND VOLUME PRODUCTION

Product design and production process come together in the pilot run. Once equipment and tooling have been qualified and the process has demonstrated an acceptable level of performance, start of production is officially approved, and responsibility shifts from development to production. This sequence of activities suggests a sharp separation between development (which ends with the final pilot vehicle) and commercial production.

In reality, product development and volume production are anything but separable. Volume production constraints affect process development activities, and unsolved problems in development become production startup problems. Viewed more realistically, product development evolves gradually into commercial production. This creates a number of challenges because the logic of development and the logic of commercial production are quite different.

Consider the task of getting a new design into production. If a model is not technologically very different from its predecessor, most of the existing facilities and equipment will be carried over to the new model to reduce cost and save space, while maximizing the use of proven production lines. This creates problems in process engineering, because production of the previous model will still be going on when the pilot run for the new model starts.

In choosing where to conduct pilot production, firms have exhibited three patterns. The first is to use a separate pilot plant staffed by specialists. This has the virtue of minimizing disruptions in the production facility but may create problems if the pilot plant is not representative of the commercial factory. A second approach is to locate a pilot line next to the volume production line in the same facility. This gets the pilot work closer to the commercial operation but may create more disruptions on the volume line. The third option puts pilot production right into the volume line. To minimize disruption, companies that pursue this approach may schedule retooling for weekends and vacation periods and make production lines flexible enough to simultaneously accommodate pilot runs for the new model and existing volume production for the current model. Firms experienced in mixed-model production (i.e., producing more than one model at the same time on the same line) may thus excel at phasing in new models and phasing out predecessor models. For these firms, the transition from development to commercial production is an application of everyday production skills.

IMPLICATIONS

We have observed that technical expertise in a variety of disciplines is essential to developing an outstanding product rapidly and efficiently, but that even more important is the way expertise is applied and integrated. Firms face a variety of choices about structure, procedure, assignments, and communication. Effectiveness appears to be a function of consistency and balance in managing the critical linkages within and across the stages of development. Effective development is not a specialized task in the R&D organization, but rather a cross-functional activity that requires the best of strategy, planning, purchasing, marketing, engineering, finance, and production.

Our discussion in this chapter provides a background for more detailed analysis of the sources of superior performance in product development. To shed light on the policies and practices that lie behind outstanding performance, in subsequent chapters we take a closer look at four themes that emerged in our description of the development process.

Managing complexity. Performance in planning and engineering is determined in part by the number and difficulty of trade-offs inherent in the design and by the character of coordination requirements. Complexity—of the product and the project—appears to be an important driver of difficulty in trade-offs and problems in coordination. For example, product content (e.g., degree of innovation, features, performance objectives, and price class) influences the level of engineering effort, the nature of trade-offs, and the difficulty of sorting out interactions. Choices about supplier involvement and use of off-the-shelf parts affect how much of the work is done in-house, what constraints engineers will face, and who will have to coordinate with whom. For all these reasons, managing complexity appears to be an important issue in the performance of development.

Manufacturing capability. "Design-build-test" cycles are at the heart of the development process. The build and test portions of the cycle involve the application of manufacturing capability. Excellent performance in building tools and dies and getting the product into commercial production depends on skill in manufacturing. The hallmarks of world-class manufacturing—discipline, simplicity, and clarity of purpose—appear to be critical to effective product development.

Integrated problem solving. Product complexity and time pressure make parallel engineering essential. But effective development requires more than parallel operations; it relies on joint problem solving between upstream and downstream engineering groups. Our discussion suggests that patterns of communication, attitudes, and skills are important in fostering integration of engineering effort.

Organization and leadership. Product integrity—internal consistency in technical operation and external consistency between product experience and customer expectations—is a hallmark of high-performance development. Management direction and the organization of development appear to play critical roles in providing the integrated effort and leadership needed to achieve product integrity and move efficiently and quickly to market.

These themes do not constitute "four steps to successful product development." Rather, they are a mechanism for exploring effective management of development in greater depth. High-performance product development requires balanced excellence in many areas and coherence and integrity across the entire range of development activities. It is in the end a manifestation of the pattern of decisions and actions taken throughout the development process.

NOTE

1. For further reading on the notion that organizations overlay processes, see, for example, Thompson (1967) and Mintzberg (1970).

CHAPTER 6
PROJECT STRATEGY: MANAGING COMPLEXITY

A product begins as a concept, part of a strategy for attracting and satisfying customers. To turn a concept into a product, designers and product planners must make choices about product content. For an automobile firm, the choices pertain to trim levels, engine-body combinations, degree of innovation in the product and process, and the role of suppliers and carryover parts from predecessor models, among other things. These choices establish both *how* a firm will realize its product concept in the marketplace and *who* will undertake the necessary design and engineering work.

In the automobile industry, the choices have often been quite different even for products that compete directly. Chrysler's entry into the Ford-dominated American automobile industry of the 1920s is an example. Ford offered a simple product line with little variety ("any color as long as it's black"), did almost all its design and engineering in-house, and had given new meaning to the term vertical integration (the company owned glass plants, a steel plant, and the forests that produced the wood that went into the cars). Chrysler competed against Ford with products of greater variety and innovation and much greater reliance on suppliers. Thirty years later in the Japanese automobile market of the 1950s, we find Toyota, which developed designs and technology in-house, competing head-to-head with Nissan, which made extensive use of established British designs and technology.

Choices about product content, parts, and suppliers can also have an important influence on project performance. In product development, all roads may not lead to Rome. Decisions about innovation and variety affect product complexity; degree of supplier involvement and use of off-the-shelf parts affect the volume of engineering work to be done in-house, what we call the scope of the project. Together these choices determine the complexity of the project, which in turn influences productivity, lead time, and total product quality.

129

Because they reflect fundamental capabilities of the firm and may have a direct influence on the firm's competitive position, decisions about how and by whom product concepts will be realized are strategic in nature. Thus choices about innovation, variety, and project scope define *project strategy*.

Our analysis of project strategy and its impact on development performance begins with a summary of the patterns of choice we observed in our sample. Looking first at choices about innovation and variety, and then at supplier involvement and use of off-the-shelf parts, we see sharp differences between U.S., Japanese, and European producers, particularly in the role of suppliers. Examining the effect of these patterns on development performance, we find that greater project complexity, particularly greater project scope, though it increases lead time and engineering hours, also increases overall product quality. Ultimately we find that, like much else in product development, effective project strategy is a matter of balance in managing trade-offs.

PRODUCT VARIETY

How much variety to incorporate in a new car is a critical choice in a demanding, fragmented market. Variety in elements such as engines, trim, accessories, and color may enable a more precise match between a product and customer criteria such as budget, taste, and lifestyle. But variety comes at a price—in additional engineering hours, special tools, and possible confusion in design and production. Both the value and the cost of variety depend upon a firm's strategy and capability. With too little variety a product will not attract potential customers; with too much variety the resulting complexity may erode quality and profitability.

To understand the competitive impact of variety we have found it useful to distinguish between fundamental and peripheral variety. Major differentiation in body types (e.g., body silhouettes and numbers of doors) is fundamental variety; it requires a significant increase in engineering effort and is highly visible in the eyes of customers. Body-engine combinations and regulation-engendered features such as airbags, emission-control systems, and right side (or left side) driver's seat and steering are other examples of fundamental variety. Options such as paint color, hubcap design, upholstery, special decals, additional chrome, and vanity lights add peripheral variety because they do not affect basic vehicle design. Theoretically, given a basic body style, engine, transmission, and chassis, we can, by exhausting all possible combinations of every peripheral variety, create unique vehicles numbering in the millions.

A company can choose to pursue one kind of variety while restricting the other. Consider the traditional emphasis of U.S. firms on options variety. Planners in sales and marketing, reflecting dealers' constant requests for greater variety, continually pushed for more options. It was not uncommon for a model to have so many options that a production line could (and sometimes did) run for long periods without producing the same car twice. Taken to the extreme, variety in peripheral options adds little to sales and leads to production inefficiency and product defects. In recent years, recognizing that their Japanese competitors were deliberately restricting peripheral variety (particularly in export versions) by packaging combinations of options as standard equipment, U.S. car makers implemented so-called "variety reduction programs."

Figure 6.1, which compares average number of body types, body-engine combinations, and geographic coverage over our sample of projects, indicates that Japanese products have not offered less overall variety.* In terms of market coverage, which reflects the variety required to meet regulatory requirements and market conditions in different parts of the world, Japanese firms are much more active than their U.S. competitors and almost as broad in coverage as European firms. The data also show fundamental variety to be higher in Japanese and European projects. European firms are particularly aggressive in offering a variety of engine-body combinations. U.S. models have tended to emphasize variety in peripheral options while limiting fundamental variety. Low engine variety in U.S. models reflects the low level of activity in engine development during the 1980s, when U.S. car makers concentrated on body-chassis development.

---

*   Japanese producers tend to restrict variety in export versions while maintaining relatively high variety in domestic models. For example, it is customary for Japanese producers to develop "special versions" that are sold in small volume, for a specific period, to a local market for promotion purposes. Variety in these versions is mostly peripheral (e.g., coating, trim, seat covers, and wheels).

Figure 6.1 Average Product/Market Variety by Regions

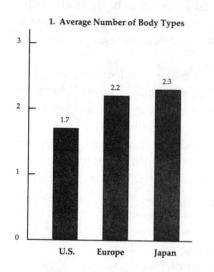

1. Average Number of Body Types

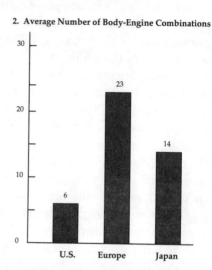

2. Average Number of Body-Engine Combinations

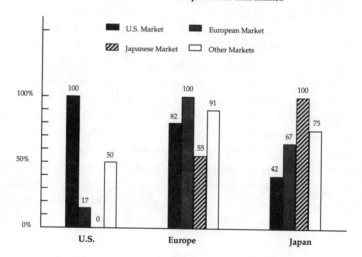

3. Average Coverage of Geographical Markets
(fraction of models in the sample sold in each market)

PRODUCT AND PROCESS INNOVATION

The degree of innovation in new component technologies and new production processes can have important ramifications. New component technologies may excite customers and contribute to increased sales. Phrases like "full-time four-wheel drive," "four-wheel steering," "16-valve," "intercooler turbo," "double-overhead cam-shaft," "electronic fuel injection," "first-in-class," often emblazoned on the car body to satisfy the owner's ego may attract young customers, some of whom may not really understand what they mean. Antilock brake systems (ABS) may attract safety-conscious customers despite their price impact. Similarly, new process technology may raise a producer's productivity and quality. But innovative processes and technologies consume time and resources; they require a significant amount of research and advanced engineering and may disturb the overall balance in product and process achieved through old technologies. Putting a pioneering technology into the market may entail a significant amount of fine-tuning and testing and, relative to "proven" technologies, may expose a firm to risks of failure in durability and reliability.

Car makers respond to these trade-offs with very different choices about where and when to innovate. Some companies immediately put whatever new technology becomes available into a new model. This strategy may generate customer enthusiasm, but without a clear vehicle concept, excessive dependence on component newness may result in a disintegrated mosaic of novelty that simply confuses customers. Other, more conservative companies refrain from introducing radically new technologies as long as a combination of existing technologies delivers acceptable performance. Daimler-Benz, for example, has been particularly conservative in commercializing new electronics technologies even though it has a huge stock of such technologies standing by.

Figure 6.2 characterizes regional patterns of innovation in terms of averages of "newness" of product and process technology. For product technology we developed two indicators. One, an internal assessment of a product's innovativeness by major component areas compared with the firm's existing models, reflects magnitude of resource commitment in the form of basic or advanced engineering. The other measures product newness against competing models. For

Figure 6.2 Innovativeness of Product/Process Technology

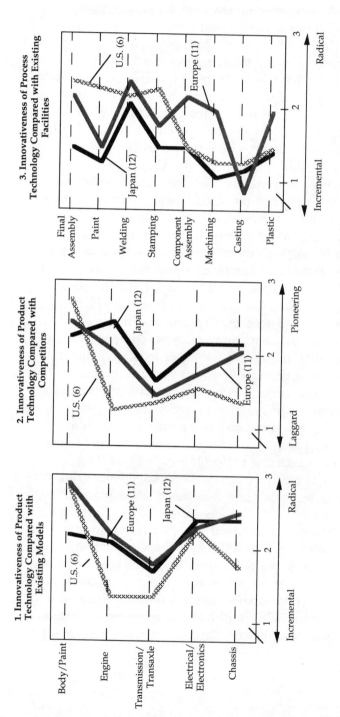

1. Innovativeness of Product Technology Compared with Existing Models

Body/Paint

Engine

Transmission/ Transaxle

Electrical/ Electronics

Chassis

U.S. (6)   Europe (11)   Japan (12)

Incremental   Radical

2. Innovativeness of Product Technology Compared with Competitors

U.S. (6)   Japan (12)   Europe (11)

Laggard   Pioneering

3. Innovativeness of Process Technology Compared with Existing Facilities

Final Assembly

Paint

Welding

Stamping

Component Assembly

Machining

Casting

Plastic

U.S. (6)   Europe (11)   Japan (12)

Incremental   Radical

Notes:
Sample size is in parenthesis.

"Chassis" includes steering, brake, and suspension as its major components.

Scores of product innovativeness index compared with existing models are defined as follows: (1) almost all drawings common to existing ones, little design work except interfaces; (2) minor change, mixture of existing subparts drawings and new ones; (3) new drawings needed down to nuts and bolts, but extensive advanced engineering not needed; (4) needed a significant amount of advanced engineering.

Scores of product innovativeness index compared with competitors are defined as follows: (1) late adopter, lagging behind rivals; (2) average industry practice, about half of rival models had already adopted concept; (3) early adoption of new concept among comparable models in industry; (4) pioneering in industry.

Scores of process innovativeness index compared with competitors are defined as follows: (1) basically no change in layout, equipment design, or tool design; (2) mostly existing layout and equipment design, but tools, jigs, and dies newly designed; (3) basic plant layout changed and newly designed equipment, tools, jigs, and dies installed; (4) revolutionary new product concept, significant amount of advanced engineering needed.

process, we used an internal assessment of newness based on a comparison with existing production processes. This reflects the magnitude of engineering resources required to bring the new process into commercial production.

In both product and process, innovation is highest in the body, followed by electrical/chassis and power train. Within this general pattern there are important regional differences. U.S. projects tend to emphasize body innovation—including commitment of substantial resources to the development of advanced systems for assembly, paint, welding, and stamping—but they lag behind in other product areas. European projects are somewhat more balanced, marked by a higher level of innovation across components and processes and greater technological leaps than either U.S. or Japanese projects. Japanese projects contrast sharply with those of rivals in terms of resources committed and newness. In both product and process technology (particularly the latter), Japanese firms attempt smaller technological jumps and tend to limit resource commitment, carrying out chassis and electronics development in existing plants using existing equipment with incremental improvements.

Despite this pattern of limited resource commitment, we find that Japanese automobiles contain more pioneering (i.e., first-in-class) technologies, particularly in engines and electronics. The strategy of Japanese producers was to keep their technological *level* slightly ahead of that of rivals through frequent but incremental product innovations. This "rapid inch-up" strategy, in which a new design tends to be a small jump from its predecessor but the rate of design renewal is relatively high, is consistent with our finding that Japanese product newness is high compared to rivals but not compared to previous Japanese models.

The "rapid inch-up" strategy of Japanese firms offers some potential advantages over the "infrequent great-leap-forward" strategy Western firms have tended to follow. Because next-generation designs use established processing concepts, Japanese firms may avoid startup confusion; moreover, regular and frequent changes of technology enable the product development organization to establish a "rhythm" of development, streamline the development process, and orient the entire organization to continual learning and improvement.

SUPPLIER INVOLVEMENT

Once a target market has been established and the level of variety and innovation have been determined, a firm must decide how and by whom the design and engineering work will be carried out. These decisions will determine project scope, meaning the fraction of total engineering effort accounted for by new engineering work (i.e., parts and coordination) done in-house. Managing project scope entails (1) dividing the development work into tasks and assigning them within or outside the project, and (2) coordinating the activities of both people in the project and outside players. Two main groups outside a project typically handle development work: other project teams within the company and other companies such as parts suppliers, engineering houses, specialists in design or prototype construction, and tool and die makers. Of the outside companies, parts suppliers are the single most important group.

Parts suppliers range from family shops with a single machine tool to diversified companies as large as automobile companies. Some are affiliated with a single car maker, while others belong to coherent groups organized around assemblers (e.g., Kyoryoku-kai in Japan). Still others are fully independent. First-tier suppliers deal directly with assemblers; lower-tier suppliers deliver piece parts to upper-tier suppliers.

As seen in Figure 6.3, Japanese, European, and U.S. firms exhibit dramatically different levels of supplier involvement. Japanese suppliers do four times more engineering work for a typical project than U.S. suppliers. European suppliers lie somewhere in between. Whereas 30 percent of the engineering work on a Toyota Camry, Nissan Maxima, or Mazda 626 has probably been done by suppliers, one can expect that almost all of the engineering work on a Chevrolet Cavalier, Buick Le Sabre, Ford Taurus, or Plymouth Caravan has been done by the manufacturer.

The differences we see in Figure 6.3 do not reflect marginal choices. They reflect suppliers with very different capabilities. Moreover, they reflect a different system of supplier relationships that includes different communication channels, contracts, and incentives. The role of suppliers in engineering and development is part of a larger pattern of supplier participation in the industry. The choices firms

Figure 6.3 Suppliers' Share of Engineering Effort

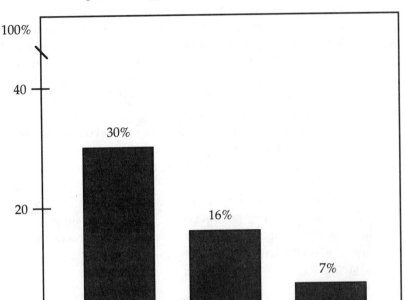

Source: See Table 6.2, column 4.

Note: Percentages represent the ratio of supplier parts engineering effort to total engineering effort. This is calculated as the product of the fraction of supplier engineering in total parts engineering and the ratio of parts engineering to total engineering effort.

make about project scope are made in the context of this larger supplier system.

THE U.S. AND JAPANESE SUPPLIER SYSTEMS

The U.S. and Japanese supplier systems stand in sharp contrast (the European system bears some similarity to the U.S. system). The traditional U.S. system is characterized by a large number of suppliers that deal directly with auto companies on the basis of short-term contracts (see the bottom panel of Figure 6.4). Except for a few highly capable firms, U.S. suppliers have little engineering capability, and because supplier-OEM relationships are treated as a zero-sum game (i.e., you win, I lose), communication and interaction occur at arm's-length and the parties behave as adversaries. Information exchange is limited to prices and data on requirements and specifications. Suppliers are effectively treated as a source of manufacturing capacity; auto companies establish requirements and play suppliers off against one another in a contest for one-year contracts.

The assumptions underlying the Japanese system are quite different (see the top panel of Figure 6.4). The Japanese supplier system has a tiered structure and emphasizes long-term relationships. A few highly capable "first-tier" suppliers provide subassembled units (e.g., instrument panels and complete seats) from parts (e.g., individual meters and pads and frames) produced by "lower-tier" suppliers.

The first-tier supplier-OEM relationship is characterized by commitment and reciprocity. Two examples illustrate differences from the U.S. system.

- In the Japanese system, costs incurred by suppliers for body dies are depreciated over the estimated cumulative production volume throughout the model life and included in the price the assembler pays for the parts. If lifetime production is less than planned, the assembler compensates the supplier for the remaining portion, thus absorbing the supplier's investment risk.

- Japanese assemblers impose demanding cost and quality targets on their suppliers. Annual or semiannual reduction of parts prices is common (assemblers assume that suppliers will improve productivity enough to maintain profitability), and suppliers are responsible for parts quality. Assemblers do little incoming inspection; suppliers pay a penalty for defective parts and the assembly costs associated with them.

Assemblers grant suppliers long-term guarantees but demand that suppliers take significant responsibility in return. Because they can create problems for assemblers in the marketplace, first-tier suppliers that fail to meet their responsibilities stand to be demoted to a lower

Figure 6.4 Typical Japanese and U.S. Supplier Systems

1. Japanese Supplier System in the 1980s

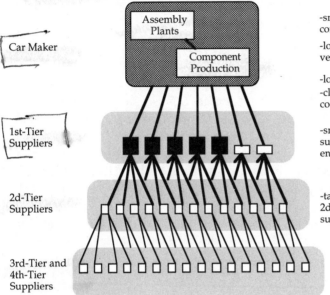

Car Maker

1st-Tier Suppliers

2d-Tier Suppliers

3rd-Tier and 4th-Tier Suppliers

-smaller in-house component operations

-lower degree of vertical integration

-long-term contracts
-close communication and coordination

-smaller number of large suppliers, mostly with engineering capability

-tall hierarchy with 2d-, 3rd-, and 4th-tier suppliers

2. Traditional U.S. Supplier System

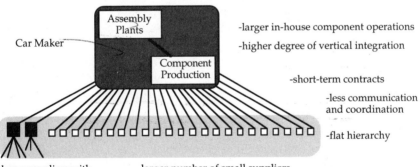

Car Maker

-larger in-house component operations

-higher degree of vertical integration

-short-term contracts

-less communication and coordination

-flat hierarchy

-large suppliers with technical capability (minority)

-larger number of small suppliers, mostly without engineering capability

Note: This diagram illustrates ideal types of supplier systems rather than reality. The size and number of suppliers in the diagram do not reflect actual data. Only one assembler is assumed in each case.

■ Car Maker   ■ Supplier with Engineering Capability
□ Supplier without Engineering Capability

tier, perhaps permanently. This mutual dependence between suppliers and assemblers motivates close coordination and communication. Contact is frequent, sharing of personnel is common, and information flows are dense (assemblers commonly acquire suppliers' cost information and possess detailed knowledge about suppliers' production processes, for example).

SUPPLIERS AND THE ENGINEERING PROCESS

Suppliers participate in the design and development of an automobile in a variety of ways. Figure 6.5 uses simplified information asset maps to illustrate typical examples of supplier involvement. Three different patterns are shown for creating information assets for a particular component: supplier proprietary parts, black box parts, and detail-controlled parts (functional and body). All yield production parts for volume production, but their implications for supplier involvement, the engineering process, and development performance are markedly different. Before reviewing data on the relative importance of these patterns, we briefly describe each pattern and the trade-offs it entails.

Supplier proprietary parts are standard products taken from concept to manufacturing by the supplier and sold to assemblers through a catalogue. In the infancy of the auto industry, the many small assemblers that built cars in extremely small volume commonly purchased generic parts from outside suppliers. An obvious merit of this approach is economy of scale: the same component design can be shared by many cars, spreading its fixed costs. Its disadvantage, from a design quality point of view, is lack of auto company control over the engineering content of the component. With tight product integrity the name of the game, fewer off-the-supplier's-shelf components fit vehicles well. Examples might include batteries and spark plugs, but even such generic items as tires and car audio equipment tend to be developed based on car makers' specifications. The data in our sample projects suggest that supplier proprietary parts account for less than 10 percent of total procurement cost, a relatively minor segment.

When developmental work is split between assembler and supplier, the result is *black box parts*. Typically an assembler generates cost/performance requirements, exterior shapes, interface details, and other basic design information based on the total vehicle planning and

Figure 6.5 Typical Information Flows with Parts Suppliers

1. Supplier Proprietary Parts

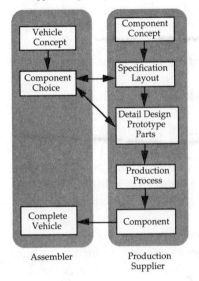

2. Black Box Parts

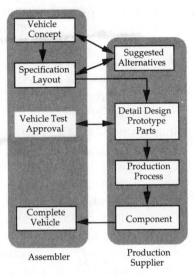

3. Detail-Controlled Parts (functional parts)

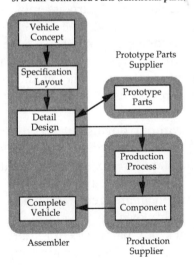

4. Detail-Controlled Parts (body parts)

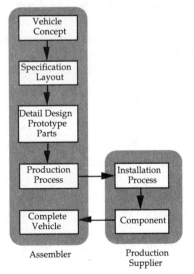

☐ Main Information Asset Created   ► Main Information Flows

layout. Functional parts and subassembly systems typically belong to this category.

In the Japanese case, requirements information is usually communicated to two or three potential suppliers that compete for the job.[1] This small group of suppliers usually does the engineering for a particular component on all the auto maker's products. This selection process, called "development competition," typically takes from six to twelve months.[2] In some cases, suppliers may not wait for inquiries from auto makers. Based on their knowledge of emerging technologies and product cycle plans, they may initiate development actions and suggestions. Once chosen, the supplier carries out detailed engineering, including drafting, prototyping, and unit testing. The car maker reviews parts drawings, tests the parts in prototype vehicles, ensures that requirements are met, and approves the design—thus the Japanese term for this arrangement, "approved drawings (Shonin-zu) system." Though the fraction of total engineering work done by suppliers varies, engineers in our study put the figure at 70 percent.

The use of black box parts enables assemblers to utilize supplier engineering expertise and manpower while maintaining control of basic design and total vehicle integrity. To the extent that a supplier accumulates expertise developing a particular type of part, assemblers may benefit from higher design quality and lower cost. The supplier's accumulation of engineering expertise becomes its competitive edge. Additionally, having one source for both prototype and production parts facilitates knowledge exchange between the two stages; it allows suppliers to detect potential production problems early and thereby improve component quality.

The black box system is not without downside risks. For example, assemblers dependent on suppliers' engineering capabilities may lose some negotiation power. Furthermore, basic design and styling ideas may leak to competitors through the supplier. Finally, losing engineering expertise in core component areas can render a car maker vulnerable in technological capability over the long term.

Effective management of the black box parts system requires careful balancing. Assemblers have to juggle long-term relationships with suppliers against the need to keep the market competitive by inviting other suppliers to participate in "development competitions." Assemblers also must balance the need to retain key component technologies (e.g., electronics) in order to effectively assess design quality while providing technical support to suppliers and controlling basic engineering for total vehicle integrity. Opting for the black box system does not mean throwing away component engineering altogether; some practitioners and researchers, in fact, distinguish between black box and gray box parts based on assembler knowledge of parts design details.

Most of the component engineering work for *detail-controlled parts*, including parts drawing, is done in-house. This concentrates detailed as well as basic engineering in the hands of the car maker. Suppliers, selected through inquiries and bids, take responsibility for process engineering and production based on blueprints provided by car makers—thus the Japanese term "provided drawings (Taiyo-zu) system." Specialized suppliers may be called upon to fabricate prototypes. In the case of body parts, some car makers also carry out process engineering and build tools and equipment, which they lend to suppliers. In this scheme, suppliers are little more than providers of production capacity.

The detail-controlled parts system is advantageous when a car maker wants to preserve detailed technological capabilities in a particular component area, tightly control component design and quality, and preserve bargaining power with respect to supplier parts prices. On the other hand, keeping all the required component engineers in-house may complicate the engineering organization and make interparts coordination within the company difficult. Moreover, detail work for numerous components can distract the in-house engineering organization from its total vehicle focus. Finally, a firm risks loss of competitiveness relative to supplier engineering units that are more focused on specific component technologies.

REGIONAL DIFFERENCES IN SUPPLIER INVOLVEMENT

All three of these patterns—proprietary, black box, and detail-controlled—were used in each of the companies we studied, but their relative importance differed markedly. On average, the breakout for the sample projects was less than 10 percent (in cost) proprietary parts, roughly 40 percent black box parts, and about 50 percent detail-controlled parts. The 1980s saw a worldwide shift toward greater supplier involvement. The popularity of black box parts, in particular, increased as many American and European auto companies followed the lead of Japanese auto makers with respect to utilizing first-tier suppliers with strong capabilities. Japanese producers have been moving away from detail-controlled toward black box parts for several decades. Western producers are making the change partly by purchasing components from Japanese black box suppliers or their overseas transplants and partly by modifying local supplier systems. This transformation has been slow, and as of the late 1980s, one still sees significant regional differences in supplier systems.

Figure 6.6, which shows regional averages of mix of parts types, tells some of the story. The average Japanese project in our sample relied heavily on black box parts, the average U.S. project on detail-controlled parts. European projects occupy a middle ground. When supplier proprietary parts are included, the average Japanese project relies on supplier engineering in roughly 70 percent of purchased parts, as compared with 20 percent in U.S. projects and 50 percent in European projects. Procurement cost as a fraction of total production cost averages about 70 percent in Japan, 70 percent in the United States (including parts from component divisions),* and 60 percent in Europe.

The consistency of patterns within regional groups for our sample seems to indicate that supplier capabilities and supplier networks are *region-specific* rather than company-specific assets.[3] Even in Japan, where most key suppliers form coherent groups around assemblers (i.e., Keiretsu), it is common for one supplier to deal with several companies at the same time.[4] The overlap of supplier networks across assemblers reflects the role of suppliers as common assets for Japanese assemblers rather than specific assets of particular auto companies.[5] Japanese auto makers' reliance on a high degree of supplier engineering involvement seems to reflect the relatively high engineering capability and effective relations that characterize Japan's supplier networks.

But effective supplier involvement, and management of black box parts systems in particular, goes beyond formal organizations and contracts. It requires consistency in daily behaviors and attitudes on the part of both assemblers and suppliers. Consider communication.

---

*   Mitsubishi Research Institute (1987), counting component divisions as part of their companies, estimates the average U.S. outside parts ratio to be 52–55 percent.

Figure 6.6 Types of Parts Produced by Suppliers

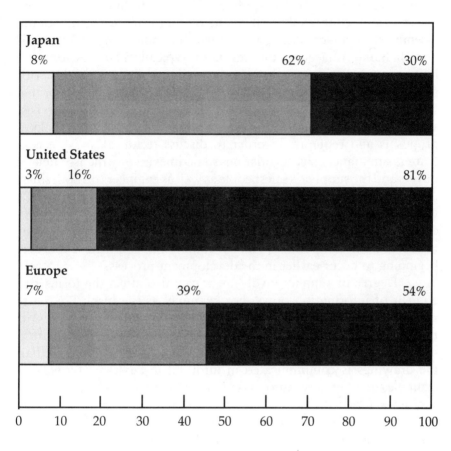

Note : Percentages shown represent fractions of total procurement cost.

Suppliers' Proprietary Parts

Black Box Parts

Detail-Controlled Parts

What we see in the more successful Japanese cases is daily contact at the working level between assembler and suppliers. Supplier engineers and sales staff continually walk in and out of the main entrance of the assembler's technical center with blueprints and component proto- types in hand. Adjacent to the entrance is typically a large negotiation room provided with many tables and chairs. Usually it is filled with people engaged in face-to-face discussions, spreading out blueprints, checking specifications, negotiating changes, examining prototypes, and so forth. Communication is two-way, with both sides making proposals and requests. In order to discuss technical and business matters simultaneously, negotiations sometimes involve the assembler's buyers and the supplier's salespeople as well as engineers on both sides. A growing number of supplier engineers, so called "guest engineers," work on assemblers' premises. Task forces or study teams involving engineers from both sides may be formed to work on the development of problematic components. Finally, communication with suppliers is beginning to occur earlier in the development process.[*]

Degree of supplier involvement can also affect the forms and content of information flows. For example, as the black box parts system comes to predominate, informal communication tends to replace formal communication. Blueprints become simpler because much of the information that would otherwise have to be specified on the drawings is communicated in informal discussions. By way of example, one Japanese auto maker that recently established an engi- neering facility in the United States found that the parts drawings it was using back in Japan lacked key information on specification and tolerance needed by U.S. parts suppliers, information known to Japanese suppliers through discussions with the auto company's engineers.

---

[*] Mitsubishi Research Institute (1987, p. 10) estimates that parts development in Japan starts three to four years prior to start of sales for major structural and engine components, and two to three years prior to start of sales for other major parts.

COMMONALITY AND CARRYOVER—
USING OFF-THE-SHELF PARTS

The strategy of using old parts and borrowing parts from other models to make a new model dates back at least to the 1920s, when GM first introduced its full-line policy with closed bodies on a mass-production basis. The industrial design group under Harley Earl was centralized to facilitate body parts commonality across GM models and hold down soaring body tooling costs. Building a car from all new, unique parts is a strategy with an even longer history. In the competitive environment of the 1980s, the issue was what mix of those strategies to employ on a particular product—how much new and unique, how much off-the-shelf. The choice could significantly impact quality of design, time to market, and engineering productivity.

Figure 6.7 shows average levels of newly designed parts (as a fraction of total number of parts) by region for the projects in our sample. On average, the data suggest that U.S. designs called for more than twice as many off-the-shelf parts as Japanese designs (38 percent versus 18 percent). European designs lie between these extremes. These sharp differences represent very different trade-offs between design flexibility and economies in tooling and high-volume production.

TRADE-OFFS ASSOCIATED WITH PARTS COMMONALITY

Using off-the-shelf parts spreads fixed R&D and manufacturing costs among different models. Moreover, reliability and durability of such parts have been substantially tested in the market already, reducing the risk of customer dissatisfaction due to design or manufacturing defects. Off-the-shelf parts also may affect lead time and engineering hours; unless common and carryover parts do not mate well with the new design, fewer engineers will be required. Existing parts that are on the critical path may well reduce time to market.

But the blessing may be mixed. When parts not specifically designed for a particular model are used, parameters and functions of the components they are used in may be suboptimized from a total vehicle perspective. In other words, the use of common parts may damage total product integrity. Excessive use of common parts, particularly exterior body parts, can also jeopardize product differentiation; the new model may become too much like an existing model.

Figure 6.7 Percentage of Parts Newly Designed

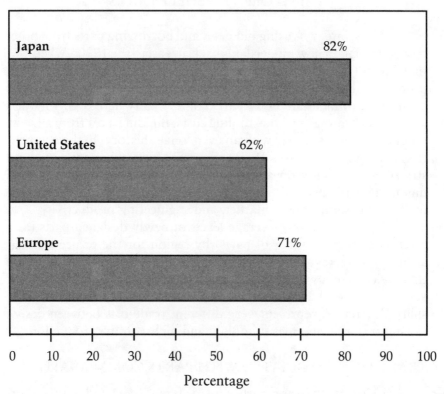

Note: Percentages indicate newly designed parts, calculated by parts count, relative to total parts in the vehicles studied.

The use of common parts has the potential to increase as well as reduce lead time and/or engineering hours. Existing component designs that impose inflexible constraints may necessitate additional engineering effort on the rest of the vehicle. Finally, a decision to use an existing component can represent a lost opportunity to introduce a new technology, which may hurt the product's competitiveness in the long run.

In our sample of major projects, about 30 percent existing parts were used. About 10 percent were carried over from predecessor models; 20 percent were common with other current models. Body parts tend to be unique to models. Engines and other "under-the-skin" functional parts are more likely to be shared with other models. This is partly because the body directly affects product differentiation, but auto makers also have improved techniques for fitting existing functional parts into new vehicle designs. Overall the trade-offs associated with parts commonality have become more difficult to make as consumer expectations with respect to product variety, integrity, and distinctiveness have increased simultaneously.

The cost impact of body-panel commonality has become particularly high with the shift to unit body structure. Because body parts are tightly integrated into chassis and other systems, major changes to the body virtually ensure major changes to the entire vehicle. The annual style change introduced by Alfred Sloan is a much more costly amenity today.

Exterior parts generally pose difficult trade-offs. In today's sophisticated market, the risk of losing styling integrity and distinctiveness is at least as great as the potential savings in tooling costs that might be realized from using common body panels. General Motors' aggressive pursuit of commonality of floor panels and other body parts as a way of holding down the enormous cost of developing a series of fuel-efficient models during the 1970s and 1980s seriously hurt its product differentiation. Other companies, particularly in the United States and Japan, have suffered from the side effects of body-panel commonality during the 1980s. However, know-how in working with common body panels to achieve differentiation has increased. Recently, in joint projects among worldwide producers, designers and engineers have succeeded in maintaining identity and distinctiveness using floor panels and body parts shared among different companies.

REGIONAL PATTERNS IN PROJECT SCOPE STRATEGY

The data on newly designed parts in Figure 6.7 suggest that Japanese firms opt for more tailored parts, whereas U.S. (and to a lesser extent European) firms seek to reduce tooling investments and limit the extent of engineering work on new designs. Both approaches are consistent with companion strategies in variety, innovation, and supplier involvement.

For U.S. and European firms, significant jumps in body innovation and required investments in body technology and processing (e.g., new paint systems, welding equipment, and flush glass) may have so

dominated capital and engineering resources in the 1980s that econo-
mizing on tooling for new parts was attractive, perhaps imperative.
Because it is implicit in the great-leap-forward strategy that a new part
is *very* new (the design of an old part may be very old, 12–15 years in
many cases), the decision to use a new part is a decision to engage in
significant new engineering work.

In contrast, in the Japanese rapid inch-up strategy the design of
each generation of parts is closely related to that of the previous
generation, and the resulting emphasis on process continuity holds the
promise of lower costs. Producing a "new" part in a Japanese company
following the rapid inch-up strategy is thus less of a stretch for both
engineers and the capital budget.

The role of suppliers also impinges upon engineering and capital
budget commitments. Faced with a choice between off-the-shelf and
new parts, a firm with a strong, involved supply base can plan to off-
load much of the new work on its suppliers. Without that base, using
new parts means committing scarce, highly valuable engineers. Off-
the-shelf parts and supplier involvement are thus alternative means to
conserve engineering resources.

The link between supplier involvement and off-the-shelf parts is
seen clearly in Figure 6.8, which compares the two main elements of
project scope: in-house engineering and new parts ratio. In addition to
plotting the variables for each project, we have used them to calculate
a summary measure of project scope—the fraction of total engineering
effort in the product accounted for by new engineering work done in-
house.[*] U.S. projects, with low supplier involvement and heavy use of
off-the-shelf parts, cluster in the upper left of the diagram. Japanese
projects, which require more engineering on average, but much less of
it done in-house, cluster in the lower right. European firms cluster in
the middle, reflecting a mixed strategy. These data suggest that supplier
involvement and parts commonality are integrated elements of a firm's
strategy for project scope, and that limits on engineering capacity and
capacity for effective internal coordination impose a limit on project
scope. Given this reality, firms must choose between using existing
parts designs and securing additional engineering resources from
outside suppliers to produce new designs. Japanese firms tend toward

---

[*]   In calculating our measure of scope, new engineering work includes new parts
       design and engineering of the total vehicle (e.g., interface design and testing of the
       complete system). See the Appendix for further details.

Figure 6.8 Project Scope Strategy by Projects and Regions

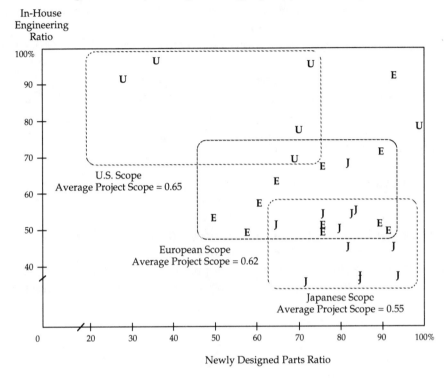

In-House
Engineering
Ratio

Newly Designed Parts Ratio

U = U.S. Project
E = European Project
J = Japanese Project

the latter, U.S. firms toward the former; European firms strike a balance.

Use of off-the-shelf parts and supplier involvement conserve in-house engineering but may have very different implications for overall development performance. Supplier engineering capabilities and tight assembler-supplier coordination enable Japanese auto makers to rely on supplier engineering without jeopardizing their edge in conformance quality and lead time-relative to their Western competitors. This, in turn, allows Japanese producers and suppliers together to devote more of their engineering resources to new component designs. A high rate of parts renewal (more new parts per project and projects done more often) is advantageous when component technologies are changing rapidly and customer expectations with respect to total vehicle integrity are rising. In the United States, where engineering work has been heavily concentrated with assemblers, the use of common parts has represented the only opportunity to limit scope.

What accounts for these sharp, cross-regional differences in project scope strategy? The efforts of individual companies certainly cannot be ignored, but historical developments have clearly played an important role. The necessity of rapidly expanding and renewing their product lines with limited engineering resources forced Japanese assemblers to rely increasingly on supplier engineering. Many first-tier Japanese suppliers responded to this situation by specializing in and rapidly accumulating engineering capabilities for certain components. Assemblers may have lost some bargaining power in the short run, but in the long run they gained the advantage of having extensive external engineering capabilities that could rapidly renew component designs. The Japanese advantage in project scope thus resulted largely from producers' long-term adaptation to historical constraints. The notion that Japanese car makers fostered suppliers' engineering capabilities based on a deliberate long-term strategy to beat their Western competitors is a myth.

IMPACT OF PROJECT STRATEGY ON PERFORMANCE

The evidence thus far suggests that world auto makers' product complexity and project scope strategies reflect trade-offs between cost, investment, and match with customer requirements. We expect that choice of strategy will have implications for the performance of product development. A more complex product reflecting more features and higher levels of performance, for example, should require more engineering hours and take longer to complete. Similarly, heavy use of suppliers should reduce engineering hours. In this chapter, we attempt to determine how great these effects are and whether there are other, less straightforward but equally important effects (e.g., the effect of project scope on design quality). In this section of the chapter, we examine the impact of project strategy on development performance. We look first at the effect of product complexity (i.e., product content, variety, and innovation) and then at the effects of supplier involvement and use of off-the-shelf parts.

PRODUCT COMPLEXITY AND DEVELOPMENT PERFORMANCE

Lines 1–3 of Table 6.1 summarize the effect of product complexity on development productivity, lead time, and total product quality using three indicators: price of product, number of body styles in the project, and degree of innovation. For variables where the evidence was strong, we have indicated the size and direction of the impact of a significant change in complexity on development performance. For example, our analysis indicates that a $10,000 change in price class—e.g., the difference between an intermediate family sedan that retails for $14,000 and a luxury car priced at $24,000—would increase engineering hours by about 30 percent. Adding a body style would increase engineering hours by 35 percent and have a moderate impact on planning lead time, but we find no evidence of an effect on total lead time. A similar lack of evidence shows up in the innovation variables. Except for the effect of body innovation on engineering lead time, where we find a consistently strong effect (i.e., 20 percent), the evidence is weak and inconclusive.

In general, product complexity has its strongest impact on engineering hours but very little effect on lead time and product quality. It appears, for example, that auto producers have developed the ability to process multiple body styles in parallel, so that adding another style has little effect on lead time. Much the same can be said of the more complex engineering implied in higher-priced vehicles. (Inasmuch as the measures we use to track quality of conformance and design are *relative to competitive vehicles*, the TPQ index has already been adjusted for differences in product content. Hence we make no further adjustments in Table 6.1.) The lack of strong effects of body and component innovation suggests that one can achieve high product quality in every price class, with single or multiple body types, with excellent but not necessarily pioneering components, and with outstanding but not necessarily breakthrough body technology. This evidence is consistent with our earlier discussion of the rapid inch-up strategy. It appears that projects that involve big jumps in technology in components or in bodies are neither necessary nor sufficient for the creation of high-quality products.

Table 6.1 The Impact of Product Content and Project Scope on Development Performance

Product Complexity and Project Scope	Dimensions of Performance				
	Engineering Hours	Lead Time			Product Quality
		Total	Planning	Engineering	
Complexity					
Increasing Price Class by $10,000	high +27%	low +7%	•	moderate +11%	N/A
Adding One Body Style	high +35%	•	moderate +15%	•	N/A
Innovation					
introduction of pioneering components	•	•	•	•	•
major changes in body process technology	•	•	•	high +19%	•
Scope					
Increasing Project Scope from 0.55 to 0.65	high +30%	low +7%	high +30%	•	high +22%

Source: Based on regression analyses in the Appendix.

• No Significant Impact

DEVELOPMENT PERFORMANCE AND PROJECT SCOPE

The logic linking choices about project scope—that is, considerations relative to supplier involvement and off-the-shelf parts—to engineering productivity is straightforward: greater use of off-the-shelf parts and more subcontracting of work to suppliers should result in a drop in internal engineering hours. Scope may also affect lead time and product quality. In fact, the data in line 4 of Table 6.1 suggest that scope has a relatively sizable effect across all three measures of performance. But we found differences in the character of the effects of project scope to be important in drawing conclusions about the longer-term competitive implications of the patterns in the evidence.

Scope and engineering hours. In the projects we studied, no strategic choice had more impact on development productivity than project scope. The impact of project scope has two sources: (1) the direct effect of reducing the workload on in-house engineering, and (2) relative productivity differences associated with differences between newly designed and off-the-shelf parts and inside versus outside engineering.

Figure 6.9 captures the direct workload issue in a block diagram using average data from our sample. The model breaks down into several blocks the total engineering workload—the amount of work that would have been necessary if all parts had been new and all jobs had been performed in-house—according to who carried out the job.* The blocks, and their average share of the total workload, include engineering of the overall vehicle (30 percent), in-house engineering of new parts (31 percent), engineering in off-the-shelf-parts (19 percent), and supplier engineering of new parts (20 percent). Our measure of project scope is the sum of the first two blocks, which in the case of the sample average is 61 percent. That is, in-house engineering of new parts accounts on average for 61 percent of the engineering workload that would have been necessary without supplier engineering and common parts, assuming efficiency of product development were the same no matter who did the work. Table 6.2 summarizes the sharp regional differences in the breakdown of total hours. U.S. projects, on

---

*   For simplicity, we assume that development productivity is identical between assemblers and suppliers and between past projects and current projects. We also assume that total engineering workload for an average project in our sample equals 1, as shown in the unit cube in the upper area of the diagram.

Figure 6.9 Estimated Breakdown of Total Engineering Workload (World Average)

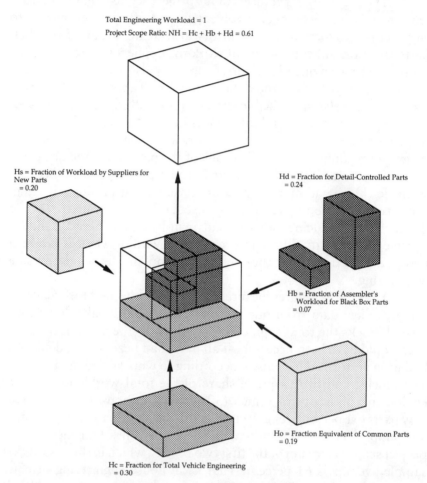

Total Engineering Workload = 1
Project Scope Ratio: NH = Hc + Hb + Hd = 0.61

Hs = Fraction of Workload by Suppliers for New Parts
= 0.20

Hd = Fraction for Detail-Controlled Parts
= 0.24

Hb = Fraction of Assembler's Workload for Black Box Parts
= 0.07

Ho = Fraction Equivalent of Common Parts
= 0.19

Hc = Fraction for Total Vehicle Engineering
= 0.30

average, are characterized by a high dependence on common (26 percent) and internally developed (36 percent) parts; Japanese projects show heavy reliance on supplier engineering (30 percent). European projects lie in-between.

Were there no differences in productivity between suppliers and auto makers, and no differences in the difficulty associated with the use of off-the-shelf and new parts, we could use the data in Table 6.2 to estimate what the average firm in each region would require to develop an average product assuming all parts were new and all work was done

Table 6.2 Breakdown of Total Engineering Workload by Region

Components of Workload / Region	Inside the Project		Outside the Project		Project Scope Index (1+2)
	Total Vehicle Development (Hc)	New Parts by Assembler (Hb + Hd)	Workload Equivalent of Common Parts (Ho)	New Parts by Suppliers (Hs)	
United States	30%	36%	26%	7%	66%
Europe	30%	32%	21%	16%	62%
Japan	30%	27%	13%	30%	57%
Average	30%	31%	19%	20%	61%

Note: For definitions of each category, see Figure 6.9.

in-house. But there are differences in productivity and difficulty. When we look at what happens in practice when scope changes, we find that shifting work outside the project has a *greater* effect than would be expected if there were no differences in productivity or difficulty.

Referring again to Table 6.1, we see that differences in scope have a sizable impact. For example, if the scope index moves from 0.65 to 0.55 (which is roughly equivalent to moving from the U.S. average to the Japanese average), engineering hours drop by about 30 percent compared to the average of 2.5 million hours per project. Because scope declines by about 15 percent when the index moves from 0.65 to 0.55, we would expect engineering hours to decline by 15 percent if suppliers were equally efficient and parts were no more difficult. The implication is that suppliers are more efficient and new parts are more difficult by a significant margin. The impact of supplier productivity appears to be particularly strong in Japan (see the Appendix for details). This is consistent with our fieldwork, which turned up evidence that long-term relationships and supplier specialization had created highly efficient supplier engineering operations in Japan. Indeed, our analysis in the Appendix shows that the impact of suppliers is largely a Japanese phenomenon, whereas the use of off-the-shelf parts has a significant impact in all regions.

Lead time and project scope. The effect of project scope on development lead time is not as straightforward as its effect on engineering hours. Suppose we move several components from internal engineering to outside suppliers; what happens to lead time for the overall project? If the components are not on the project's critical path, there will be no impact—the project will take just as long as it did before. If the components are on the critical path but the suppliers are slower or moving the work outside increases the time required for coordination, then lead time will increase. Only if suppliers can develop critical-path parts faster or the move outside simplifies coordination will moving development outside reduce lead time.

A reduction in lead time is what we find, although the size of the effect is moderate. In Table 6.1, for example, reducing scope from 0.65 to 0.55 cuts total lead time by only 7 percent, or about 4 months in a 53-month project. Probing further by breaking total lead time into lead time for planning and lead time for engineering, we find the effect of scope is quite different for each. Expanding scope—that is, developing more new parts in-house—appears to lengthen the planning process but has little effect on engineering lead time. Thus the overall lead time effect of project scope is really a planning effect.

Several implications follow from the results on lead time in Table 6.1. First, the fact that project scope has a positive influence on lead time means that companies are moving out some of the important tasks and components on the critical path of the project. The notion that car companies keep all the important activities in-house and subcontract only peripheral tasks does not fit our evidence.

Second, suppliers' engineering capability for speedy component development is in many cases as high as that of car makers. Moreover, using a supplier network for engineering does not necessarily lead to a loss of tight coordination; it appears that car producers use supplier engineering capability without sacrificing lead time for engineering execution. This is consistent with other evidence on the development of supplier capability. One of the most important criteria Japanese assemblers emphasize in supplier selection, for example, is the capability to "build in productivity" and "build in quality," which essentially means the ability to achieve cost and quality targets while flexibly responding to the continuous design changes requested by the assembler.[6] In short, doing the work in-house does not assure better execution or coordination of engineering.

Finally, our evidence indicates that narrowing project scope simplifies the coordination network and thereby reduces coordination lead time. This simplification occurs in the planning process, where the main task is intercomponent coordination, rather than in engineering, where lead time is driven by problems in coordinating across product and process engineering steps within each component area. Although conventional wisdom suggests that external linkages add constraints and complexity to such coordination problems, we find that taking components out of the internal network in fact simplifies the problem and reduces coordination time. Both off-the-shelf parts and suppliers play a role.

The basic problem in planning coordination is that parts are interdependent and developed by specialized engineering departments. Intercomponent coordination within a project involves negotiations among many engineering groups, each of which claims authority in a particular component area and equal status with the other groups. In extreme cases, everyone negotiates with everyone. Thus a change in one component tends to trigger countermeasures elsewhere, and the chain reaction of mutual adjustment makes coordination across the total vehicle time-consuming.

Taking a part off the shelf freezes its basic content and makes it nonnegotiable, which sharply reduces the number of interactions and amount of negotiation. Likewise, if suppliers have developed the capability to "build in productivity and quality" (i.e., achieve cost and quality targets while responding to the car makers' requests for changes), taking a component out of the internal network simplifies the negotiation process. In practice, suppliers do not seek their own agenda nor do they have an equal voice. Compared to internal engineers, they are more flexible, more willing to adapt to requests. Supplier capability such as that found in Japan enables assemblers to reduce the coordination problem and focus on internal issues, knowing that the suppliers will absorb the impact of internal design changes.

Project scope and total product quality. Putting work into the supplier network or using off-the-shelf parts improves engineering productivity and lead time, but not product quality. Earlier, we observed that using off-the-shelf parts and relying on suppliers could hurt total product quality if suppliers were less capable in design or the parts introduced constraints on design. That is what appears to have been going on in the projects we studied.

Table 6.1 shows that a reduction in scope hurts product quality. Changing the scope index from 0.65 to 0.55 for the average project in our sample would result in a drop in the quality index from 51 to 40 points, or about 20 percent. This implies that management of scope involves trade-offs between quality and lead time or development productivity. Where supplier relationships are strong and off-the-shelf parts are available on the critical path, reducing scope shortens lead time and reduces engineering hours, but at a cost of lower product quality. Management thus faces a two-tiered choice in decisions about scope: (1) the choice of the overall level of scope, which establishes the size of the in-house effort, and (2) the choice of composition, i.e., the mix of off-the-shelf parts and supplier involvement that will achieve the scope target. The effectiveness of these choices depends on striking the right balance between lead time, productivity, and quality, and that balance depends on which parts a firm chooses to farm out and how the choices are implemented.

The challenge is to manage supplier relationships to exploit the lead time and hours benefits while minimizing the disruption to product quality. As we have seen, this is likely to require close working relationships from the outset of a program and the conscious development of strong engineering capability in the supplier base. Similarly, effective management of off-the-shelf parts requires not only careful selection, but also attention to the need for adaptation to achieve an integrated design. Often the decision to use an existing or carryover part comes from a desire to minimize investment. But a careful focus on how the existing parts will affect product integrity may turn up opportunities to improve the design either with marginal adjustments in the carryover parts or in compensating adjustments in new parts.

SUMMARY AND IMPLICATIONS

We have found that project strategy—choices about product complexity and project scope—plays an important role in development performance, and that engineering productivity, lead time, and product quality are affected in significant ways by the choice of product content, carryover parts, and supplier involvement. More-over, differences in scope and complexity are central to explanations of regional differences in performance and thus to international competition. In particular, we find that a good part of the Japanese advantage in lead time and development productivity is rooted in differences in scope and complexity.

The relative impact of the elements of project strategy is summarized in Figure 6.10, which decomposes the lead time and hours

Figure 6.10 Decomposition of Regional Differences in Performance

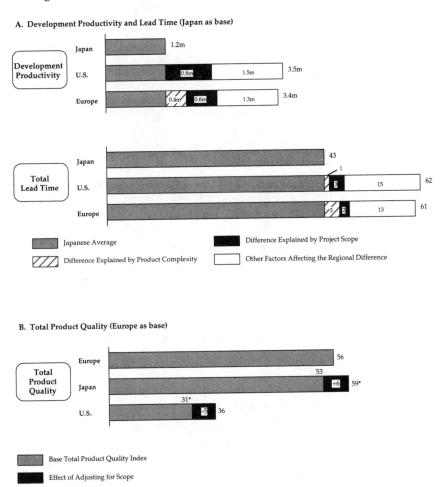

A. Development Productivity and Lead Time (Japan as base)

Development Productivity	Japan	1.2m
	U.S.	0.8m 1.5m 3.5m
	Europe	0.4m 0.6m 1.3m 3.4m

Total Lead Time	Japan	43
	U.S.	1 3 15 62
	Europe	3 2 13 61

- ▓ Japanese Average
- ▨ Difference Explained by Product Complexity
- ■ Difference Explained by Project Scope
- ☐ Other Factors Affecting the Regional Difference

B. Total Product Quality (Europe as base)

Total Product Quality	Europe	56
	Japan	53 +6 59*
	U.S.	31* -5 36

- ■ Base Total Product Quality Index
- ■ Effect of Adjusting for Scope

* Adjusted Value of TPQ

gaps between Japanese firms and their Western competitors. Panel A shows that differences in project strategy account for about 30–40 percent of the Japanese advantage in development productivity, with scope playing the most important role. The importance of project scope is particularly evident in the United States, where significant differences in the role of suppliers and parts strategy account for more than a third of the original performance gap. In Europe, scope plays an important but lesser role, accounting for about a quarter of the difference between European and Japanese firms. Here product complexity also plays a role. Whereas the products we studied in the U.S.-Japan comparison were roughly comparable in content, the European sample contains high-performance luxury cars and higher-priced family sedans. These differences in product content account for about 15 percent of the Japan-Europe gap in development productivity. Taking scope and product complexity into account reduces this gap from 2.2 million to 1.3 million hours.

The effects of project strategy on lead time are much smaller. Both scope and product content play a role, but they account for only four or five months of the 18-month gap in total lead time. The data on product quality in Panel B tell a different story. Differences in project content are reflected in the regional averages of the TPQ index, which show European and Japanese firms to be roughly comparable, both enjoying an advantage over U.S. firms. Taking project scope into account alters this picture very little; the adjustment puts Japanese firms slightly ahead of European firms, while U.S. firms fall slightly further behind. It is noteworthy, though, that differences across firms *within* a region (especially in Japan and Europe) are greater for product quality, suggesting that gaps *between* regions are not as sharp and strong as we found in the data on lead time and productivity. Company differences, as we noted in Chapter 4, play a critical role in explaining differences in total product quality. We explore these differences more directly in succeeding chapters.

The evidence in this chapter suggests that project strategy exerts "real" effects on performance and competition. Of course, some of the effects we have observed—particularly those relating to choice of target market, price level, and body types—merely put the projects on an "apples-to-apples" basis. But we have seen that comparable products that compete directly may come to market at very different times and with different levels of cost and quality, because of the choices firms make about product complexity and project scope. The following examples of common project strategies illustrate the impact such choices can have.

Project A: Great leap forward and in-house design

The product, a mid-size family sedan, is the second generation of a car introduced eight years earlier. The new generation includes significant new components and new body technology in paint and welding, but many of the underbody parts and the engine are carried over, so that only 65 percent of the parts are new. Almost all of the design and engineering work are carried out in-house.

Project B: Rapid inch-up and black box design

The product, a mid-size family sedan, is the third generation of a car introduced eight years earlier. The new generation uses improved versions of the basic components and body technology employed in the previous generation, but the level of performance is outstanding. Although adapted from previous designs, many of the parts—85 percent—for the new generation sedan are newly designed. Suppliers do much of the design and engineering work for the new parts.

These two products will compete directly, but the projects that create them are likely to perform quite differently. Our evidence suggests that project A will take longer, consume more engineering hours, and possibly achieve slightly lower quality because of all the carryover parts used and the need to begin the project much earlier than project B. The significant effort required by its new componentry may not advance performance sufficiently to create a significant edge over project B, in which the rapid inch-up strategy keeps new ideas moving frequently into the market and in which supplier capability allows the project to maintain reasonable scope even though most of the parts are new.

Differences in performance between project A and project B—in lead time, development productivity, and product quality—will be real, not functions of accounting adjustments or differences in type of product. Part of the advantage of project B will come from better management of the trade-offs inherent in choices about product complexity and scope, but much more will come from very different capabilities that underlie the project strategy.

Project strategy is clearly much more than documents or boxes moved around on charts; it is rooted in capabilities. In the case of project scope, for example, the firm doing project A can easily choose a different mix of new and carryover parts, but it cannot so easily choose to move to a much higher level of supplier involvement. Such involvement would be a disaster unless suppliers were capable and the relationships were supportive. The impact of project scope, particularly in explaining the Japanese advantage, is based on far more than a difference in the fraction of parts engineered by suppliers. Important differences in supplier capability and relationships underlie the Japanese advantage. Relationships in the Japanese system are both longer term and more like partnerships than traditional U.S. relationships, in which suppliers play little role in engineering and work at arm's-length from the car maker. The evidence presented here and interviews in Japanese firms suggest that many of these differences have to do with engineering capabilities in the supplier network and the ability of the auto firms to both nurture and capitalize on that capability; in effect, they benefit from the supplier's know-how and capture it more effectively in the design of the product and the conduct of the development process.

There is an important element of reciprocity in these relationships. Auto firms cultivate capability in their suppliers and manage the process so that that capability plays an important role. This involves investment, knowledge sharing, providing space and facilities for "guest engineers," and helping suppliers solve problems. On the supplier side, there is a commitment to build capability and a willingness to assume a critical role in the development process. Among the better suppliers, there is a focus on service that results in supplier engineers searching for new ways to meet the needs of customer designs and development processes. The better suppliers, in effect, look for opportunities to create value for their customers. This is far different than meeting specified requirements with minimum effort.

Capabilities also underlie the rapid inch-up innovation strategy. Indeed, there is something of a "virtuous circle" here. The strategy lends some advantage in lead time and engineering productivity because the engineering effort required to take the technology the next inch-up is not as great, and the work can be accomplished more quickly. But for the rapid inch-up strategy to work, the firm must be able to launch new projects frequently, and each project must be completed quickly. Moreover, the work done must be well integrated so that total product quality is high. Rapid inch-up is thus feasible if engineering productivity is high, project lead time low, and designs effective. If implemented, it helps the firm to achieve high productivity and rapid, effective development. This is the virtuous circle. Project B is thus effective because the strategy builds on and reinforces capabilities for high-performance development.

In the next three chapters we examine three sources of high-performance development—manufacturing capability, integrated problem solving, and project leadership—that play a central role in the speed, quality, and productivity of development.

NOTES

1. See Mitsubishi Research Institute (1987, p. 7).
2. Ibid., p. 11.
3. Matsui (1988, p. 124) points out that as of 1987 there were considerable performance differences between Toyota and Nissan group suppliers; the former tended to be more profitable and incur more R&D expenditures per sales than the latter. This is reflected in the performance gap between the two assemblers for the same period. The basic structure of the networks is essentially similar for both assemblers.
4. A study by Japan's Ministry of International Trade and Industry (MITI) shows that Japanese affiliated suppliers with more than 20 percent equity ownership by one auto maker supply to five auto makers on average. See Mitsubishi Research Institute (1987).
5. Nishiguchi (1987) calls the overlap pattern in Japanese supplier networks the "Alps" structure because it looks like overlapped hierarchies.
6. Mitsubishi Research Institute (1987, pp. 12–13).

CHAPTER 7

MANUFACTURING CAPABILITY: A HIDDEN SOURCE OF ADVANTAGE

Popular discussions of the development of new automobiles invariably focus on the design process and the solution of technical problems. Open up any car magazine in any country and the stories are about the early sketches, the difficult technical choices, the new bits of engineering. In Japan, in Europe, and in America the stars of these stories are the designers and engineers. Even auto company executives think of product development as the creation of intangible assets, something that goes on largely in design and engineering. But to focus only on the cognitive processes involved in development is to overlook the very real contributions made by manufacturing.

Our study of the auto industry has convinced us that the ability to make things rapidly and efficiently—to transform materials into parts, components, and assemblies—is a critical source of advantage in product development. Manufacturing capability is obviously important in commercial production. But it plays a role in the development process as well. We examine that role in this chapter. Following a general discussion of the relationship between manufacturing capability and product development performance, we look closely at three major manufacturing activities embedded in the development process: prototype fabrication, making dies for body panels, and production of pre-commercial vehicles during the pilot run and ramp-up.

BEYOND THE R&D-PRODUCTION DICHOTOMY

Standing in the body shop of an automobile factory drives home the striking differences between the very early and the very late stages of product development. Large presses rhythmically stamp out body panels from sheets of steel. Numerous robots whir and dip and weld. Transfer equipment moves and positions welded bodies with precision and regularity. Amidst this noisy, intense, regimented process, people monitor and troubleshoot, load and unload. Their performance is measured in parts per hour.

Contrast this with the high-ceilinged design studio with its large windows and bright but indirect lighting. Designers sit at large drafting boards sketching out new concepts that skilled model-shop workers downstairs render in clay, plastic, or fiberglass. Back upstairs the designers measure, study, review, and evaluate the mockups. Activity can be frantic and intense, especially before a senior management review, but no one measures sketches per hour (or anything else per hour for that matter). Performance is a matter of creativity, insight, and new ideas.

Such sharp differences in environment might suggest that management of R&D and management of manufacturing are quite different. The argument usually goes something like this: The essence of effective production management is stability, efficiency, discipline, and tight control, whereas effective R&D management requires dynamism, flexibility, creativity, and loose control. Therefore the two functions must be managed by entirely different principles. This dichotomy between research and practice stems from a traditional emphasis on the extremes of the R&D-manufacturing spectrum.

In Figure 7.1, we see at one extreme Taylor's paradigm for manufacturing management, which emphasizes repetitive conformance to a given standard through one best set of procedures. In this world, the keys to effective performance (i.e., adherence to the standard) are stability, repetitiveness, standardization, and bureaucratic control from the top down. In this paradigm, the task of changing the production system to improve its performance lies outside the production function.

The principles of effective management that govern the other end of the spectrum were developed by scholars and managers who studied laboratories conducting basic research rather than carrying out development projects aimed at immediate commercialization of a product. The keys to effective performance in this fluid world are organic structure, self-control, self-motivation, individual creativity, and ample resources. It is not surprising that we should find nothing in common between the management of a roomful of Ph.D.'s creating formulae and that of a line of blue-collar workers repetitively doing what they are told.

Figure 7.1 R&D-Production Spectrum

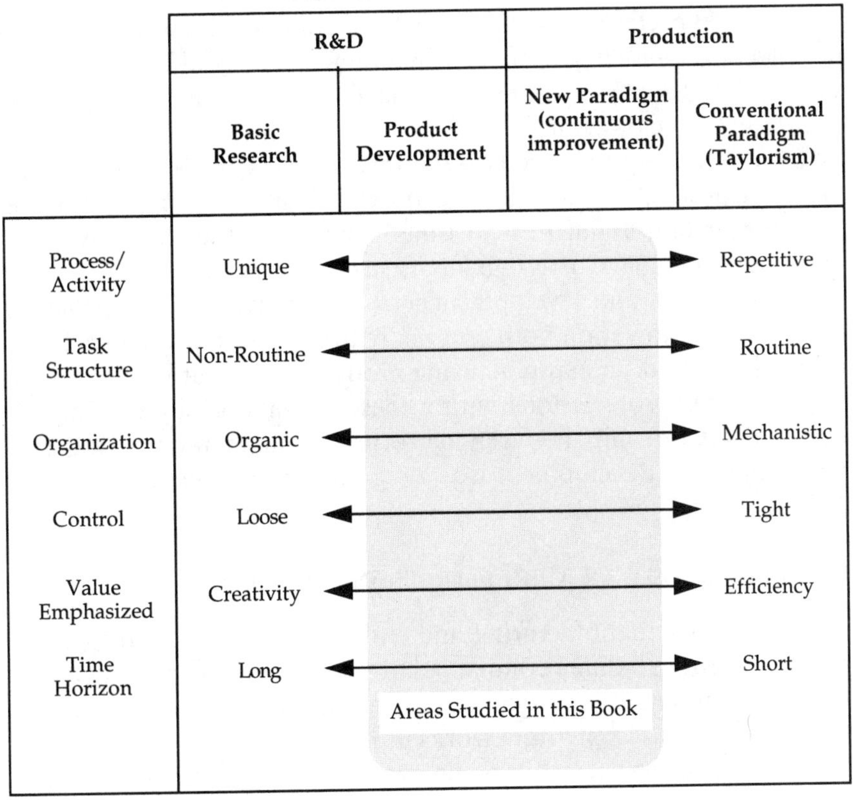

	R&D		Production	
	Basic Research	**Product Development**	**New Paradigm (continuous improvement)**	**Conventional Paradigm (Taylorism)**
Process/ Activity	Unique	←——————————→		Repetitive
Task Structure	Non-Routine	←——————————→		Routine
Organization	Organic	←——————————→		Mechanistic
Control	Loose	←——————————→		Tight
Value Emphasized	Creativity	←——————————→		Efficiency
Time Horizon	Long	←——————————→		Short

Areas Studied in this Book

These are not the realities of the world auto industry. To be effective in the 1980s and 1990s, manufacturing management has had to become quite dynamic.[1] Outstanding performance requires continuous process improvement, learning, and problem solving at the working level. These are achieved through self-renewing organizations. Process engineering is inseparable from production operations in the new manufacturing paradigm. Today's effective product development organization is characterized not only by creativity and freedom, but also by discipline and control in scheduling, resource use, and product quality. The challenge in product development is not so much unilateral pursuit of organic structure and permissive management style as a subtle balance of control and freedom, precision and flexibility, individualism and teamwork.

With the new paradigms of manufacturing and product development much closer to the center of the R&D-production spectrum, we might expect to find much more in common between effective product development and effective manufacturing. And indeed we find that high performers in manufacturing also achieve high performance in product development. The evidence is presented in Figure 7.2, in which moderately positive correlations can be seen between manufacturing productivity and product development performance (both in engineering hours and in lead time). The shaded areas show clear patterns of regional clustering. Japanese producers tend to rank higher in manufacturing and development performance, while Western players are noticeably lower on both criteria, with European producers being particularly weak in manufacturing productivity. That we do not see any significant correlations within these regional groupings implies that the relationship between performance in manufacturing and performance in development was a regional phenomenon in the mid 1980s.

DEVELOPMENT AS A PRODUCTION PROCESS

Effective manufacturing and effective development may share many elements, so that a company that is good at the former also may be good at the latter. The focus of the product development process, as our information system framework emphasizes, is the "production" of information assets. Certain principles of effective production management thus may be applicable to product development management and vice versa. Table 7.1 identifies some of the parallels we have found between the paradigm of production emerging around just-in-time (JIT) and total quality control (TQC), and the new product development paradigm identified in our study.[2] As we can see, the two paradigms share many basic characteristics, including frequent changeover; faster throughput time; reduced inventory; early feedback from downstream to upstream; rapid problem solving; simultaneous achievement of high performance, quality, speed, and efficiency; the capability to "make right things in the first place" and to handle unexpected changes; broad task assignments; and a culture that fosters continuous improvement.

Consider inventory reduction. As JIT production systems have demonstrated, reduction of work-in-process, if managed properly, can

Figure 7.2 Manufacturing Productivity and Product Development Performance

1. Manufacturing Productivity and Development Productivity

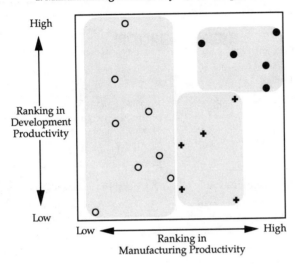

2. Manufacturing Productivity and Development Lead Time

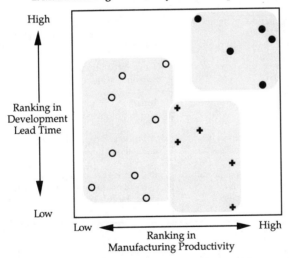

Notes: Rankings are based on data on adjusted engineering hours, adjusted lead time, and adjusted assembly hours per vehicle. Data on assembly hours are from John Krafcik of the International Motor Vehicle Program, MIT. Shaded areas indicate regional groups.

● Japan + United States ○ Europe

Table 7.1 Similarity of New Paradigms in Production and Development

Production (JIT-TQC Paradigm)	Development (New Paradigm)
Process-Flow Patterns	
- Frequent setup changes	- Frequent model changes
- Short production throughput time	- Short development lead time
- Reduction of work-in-process inventory between production steps	- Reduction of informational inventory between product development steps
- Piece-by-piece (not batch) transfer of parts from upstream to downstream	- Frequent (not batch) transmission of preliminary information from upstream to downstream
- Quick feedback of information on downstream problems	- Early feedback of information on potential downstream problems
- Quick problem solving in manufacturing	- Quick problem solving in engineering
-Upstream activities are triggered by real-time downstream demand (pull system)	- Upstream activities are motivated by downstream market introduction date
Organizational Capability	
- Simultaneous improvement in quality, delivery, and manufacturing productivity	-Simultaneous improvement in quality, lead time, and development productivity
- Capability of upstream process to produce salable products the first time	- Capability of development (i.e., upstream) to produce manufacturable products the first time
- Flexibility to changes in volume, product mix, product design, etc.	- Flexibility to changes in product design, schedule, cost target, etc.
- Broad task assignment of workers for higher productivity	- Broad task assignment of engineers for higher productivity
- Attitude and capability for continuous improvement and quick problem solving	- Attitude and capability for frequent incremental innovations
- Reduction of inventory (slack resources) forces more information flows for problem solving and improvements	- Reduction of lead time (slack resources) forces more information flows across stages for integrated problem solving

shorten production throughput time, reveal production problems earlier, and orient the entire production organization to rapid problem solving and continuous improvement.[3] In product development, a blueprint on an engineer's desk awaiting design change approval is an information buffer between development steps. Reducing such "in-process inventory" by simplifying the formal paperwork for engineering change orders, for example, may streamline the development process, speed up engineering problem solving, and improve product quality and lead time simultaneously.

Because it facilitates integrated problem solving and knowledge sharing between stages, close bilateral communication between upstream and downstream is also important in both production and product development. For example, immediate feedback from a downstream assembly worker who detects a defect can help upstream workers quickly solve the problem that created it. Similarly, in product development, continuous communication between product engineers (upstream) and process engineers (downstream) is often key to early detection of potential design problems, particularly in terms of manufacturability.

The two paradigms also share a basic philosophy of quality improvement; both emphasize "doing the right thing in the first place." In production, self-inspection and foolproof mechanisms (so called Poka-Yoke) detect assembly mistakes immediately, rather than leaving them to be detected downstream during final inspection. In development, product engineers design components to be easy to assemble initially rather than reworking designs later or leaving the plants and process engineering to deal with downstream problems.

We could cite many other instances in which principles of effective production apply to issues in product development, but the point is that companies good at fast-cycle production, to the extent that they can transfer the relevant production skills and attitudes to R&D, will likely be good at fast-cycle product development. The new paradigm prevails in both production and R&D, and companies that master it in one area tend to master it in the other.

HIDDEN MANUFACTURING ACTIVITIES IN THE DEVELOPMENT PROCESS

We have suggested that manufacturing capability matters because effective engineering builds on many of the same principles as effective production. But there is a further, more direct connection: product development encompasses a number of activities that essentially are manufacturing. This "hidden manufacturing" in product development includes prototype fabrication, the building of tools and dies, and pilot run implementation. Companies that are good at production also tend to be good at these activities.

Take, for example, prototype fabrication. Building prototypes is an obvious manufacturing activity that lies right in the middle of the development process. Prototype shops, though very different from volume production plants, are still manufacturing operations. They employ manufacturing systems that fit small-volume production—general-purpose equipment, multiskilled workers, "soft dies," manual forming and welding processes, and stationary assembly booths or very short, slow assembly lines. Runs from 50 to 100 engineering prototypes are typically assembled in two or three batches or generations, with design changes resulting from tests of one generation incorporated in the next.

Construction of tools and dies in preparation for volume production is another hidden manufacturing activity. Consider only the dies needed for body-panel stamping. A typical car body is partitioned into approximately 100–150 body panels. Each major panel may require as many as four or five dies, sometimes more if the design is complex. The number of dies produced for a project could thus range from several hundred to more than a thousand per body type. The number increases as the number of body types, stamping plants, and back-up dies increases.

The process is similar whether in-house tool shops or outside die suppliers do the work. Dies are cast or forged, machined, finished, and assembled in a job shop setting by machinists using sophisticated general-purpose equipment. Although numerical control, computer numerical control, computer-aided design, and other computer-based tools have had a major impact on die manufacturing, an excellent match between upper and lower dies generally requires precision finishing by highly skilled workers. To meet the exacting requirements of the assemblers and accommodate the many engineering changes that typically arrive in the middle of production, die making requires a substantial accumulation of technical skills and manufacturing know-how. It is a much more sophisticated and complicated process than many outsiders might imagine.

Pilot run and production startup, our last example of a manufacturing activity hidden in the development process, is much closer to volume production than prototype and die making.* A pilot run is a physical simulation or rehearsal of commercial production using production tooling. It tests the functions of the entire production system. Pilot runs are variously conducted at geographically separate pilot plants, on separate pilot lines within volume plants, or on volume production lines (the last instance might be called "preproduction"). Using an existing line provides the most realistic simulation but may disturb current production and is more difficult on production lines that utilize many special tools and equipment (e.g., body and welding lines) than on general-purpose lines (e.g., final assembly). Rarely are all the production tools for a new model ready in time for the pilot runs, which are usually carried out with a mixture of production tools, prototype tools, and hand operations. Pilot production is consequently much slower than full-scale production. Two or three runs normally precede production startup.

Production startup occurs on average three months prior to the start of sales, which allows car makers time to fill distribution pipelines. Just as in running pilots, there are different strategies for phasing in new models. Startup may be in a new plant, in which case the problem is to increase speed while debugging the line, or it may replace production of an older model either abruptly or gradually. The different approaches to ramp-up expose companies to different risks (e.g., of disrupting old model production or of late market introduction) and hence require different capabilities. How these capabilities are used in ramp-up and pilot production affects market timing, level of investment, and quality of feedback to engineering.

The popular image of new car development as an activity that goes on in design studios and on test tracks overlooks the critical manufacturing activities embedded in the development process. Because these activities, though different from commercial production in scale and configuration, nevertheless involve the manufacture of physical objects, a company characterized by excellence in manufacturing may enjoy an advantage in product development. We now look at each of these hidden manufacturing activities in turn.

---

* Some may argue that production startup is not part of the product development process, but given our definition of product development—which extends to the start of sales—we regard the startup period as the tail end of product development.

PROTOTYPE FABRICATION

At its heart, the design and development of a new automobile has traditionally been a series of "design-build-test" cycles. In recent years, significant effort has been made to improve the design process so that problems and bugs are detected early in the design stage. The development of advanced computer-aided engineering tools such as solid modeling and dynamic simulation has enhanced early detection of some problems by allowing rapid testing and analysis of designs. Evidence from several industries has shown that early detection and prevention of design problems is far more effective than waiting to discover them downstream. Given the current power of the tools and the complexity of the automobile, however, there are product characteristics that can be tested and product and process problems that can be uncovered only by building and testing a prototype.

Engineers use different kinds of prototypes to test different dimensions of vehicle design. Chassis hardware such as the suspension, brakes, steering gear, and drive train are tested on a mechanical prototype at an early stage of product engineering. A full engineering prototype—the first physical object that represents the total product in terms of structure, material, look, and function—comes later. Earlier versions such as clay models, mockups, and mechanical prototypes represent the product only partially. A clay model may look like a real car but cannot move; a mechanical prototype may be able to reproduce the ride and handling of a new model, but represents neither its exterior nor body structure. The engineering prototype provides the first opportunity to evaluate total vehicle performance.

What kind of information is generated and what kinds of problems are solved by prototypes depend on the role the prototype process plays. Prototypes can be used, for example, to provide final design verification; following extensive testing and analysis, engineers may build a prototype to ensure that the details work well together. Alternatively, the prototype may be an integral part of the design process, in which case engineers will build a less "final" prototype sooner after preliminary design and test it much differently.

PERFORMANCE IN PROTOTYPE DEVELOPMENT

Performance in prototyping—including production lead time, number and cost per unit, and quality of prototypes—will depend on the role the prototype is expected to play in development. But it will also depend on how the process is organized and managed and on the kinds of manufacturing capability that are in place. Our evidence suggests that firms perform prototyping very differently, reflecting very different approaches and capabilities.

Figure 7.3 compares regional averages of lead time to build a first engineering prototype. Lead time, defined here, consists of the drawing release period and post-release period. The release of prototype drawings to prototype shops or prototype parts suppliers one after another rather than in one shot accounts for the length of the drawing release period, which may reflect lead time for prototype parts procurement as well as for drawings. The post-release period represents the time between the release of the last drawing and completion of the first prototype.

The data show significant regional differences. Total prototype lead time in an average Japanese project is approximately six months, significantly shorter than that of the average U.S. and European project (approximately twelve and eleven months, respectively).[4] The advantage of Japanese firms seems to come from differences in both the engineering release process and in the way the prototype production process is managed. That the greatest variation occurs in the drawing release period suggests that control of parts procurement and the interaction of engineering changes and prototype production drive the difference. Our interviews revealed that in Western firms, comparatively less attention was paid to time as a critical aspect of the prototype process. U.S. firms in particular suffer from a lack of scheduling discipline at prototype parts suppliers and in engineering drawing release. Moreover, information moves less quickly between design engineering and the prototype unit in U.S. firms. When a product design changes during the prototype process in a typical Japanese company, design engineers go immediately to the prototype shop and instruct the shop technicians about the changes. They do not wait for paperwork. This contrasts sharply with the U.S. practice of subjecting design change orders to a series of formal approvals before allowing them to reach the prototype shop floor.

Figure 7.3 Lead Time for First Engineering Prototype

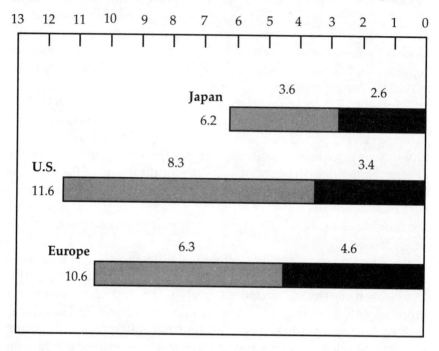

(months before first prototype completion)

Note: Numbers do not add up exactly because some respondents
        reported total prototype lead time only.

▨ Drawing Release (of first component to last component)

■ Post-Release (last drawing release to completion of first
   prototype)

When one examines the data on numbers and cost of prototypes, the European high-end specialists stand apart. Table 7.2 shows
the high-end specialists building 50 percent more prototypes at a cost
per unit twice that found in the rest of the industry. This finding is
consistent with the more extensive testing one finds in the high-end
specialists. But it also reflects very different choices about the quality
of prototypes.

Table 7.2 Characteristics and Paradigms of Prototype Fabrication

Region / Characteristics	Japan	United States	Europe (volume producer)	Europe (high-end)
Lead Time	short (6 mo.)	long (12 mo.)	long	long (11mo.)
Quantity	midrange (38/body)	midrange (34/body)	midrange (37/body)	high (54/body)
Unit Cost	midrange ($0.3 mil.)	midrange ($0.3 mil.)	mid to high ($0.3–0.5)	high ($0.6mil.)
Representativeness and Design Conformance	reasonably high representativeness and conformance	sometimes low on both dimensions	reasonably high on both dimensions	very high on both dimensions
Prototype Parts Suppliers	mostly production suppliers	mostly prototype parts specialists	mixed	mixed
Paradigm	prototype as problem detector (both product and process)	prototype as a tool for proving product design	split between master model and prove out of product design	prototype as master model

For high-end specialists, and for many European and American volume producers as well, the primary criterion for prototype evaluation has been how well the prototype conforms to design drawings. In this view, prototypes are at the center of the design-build-test cycle and are meant to help test engineers discern how well the design performs. A high-quality prototype, therefore, is one that accurately captures the design intent as expressed in drawings. High-end specialists employ skilled technicians who slowly and carefully build prototypes of very high quality. But conformance to drawings is only part of the overall quality of the prototype. From a future customer's perspective, prototype quality is measured by how well it represents what a product would be were it produced commercially. Here, too, high-end specialists excel.

The distinction between conformance quality (against design drawings) and representativeness (against commercial production) is crucial to evaluating the overall quality of the prototype. Both are important in problem solving. Testing a prototype that has been cobbled together and does not reflect design intent may cause confusion and delays and may result in missed problems. This is particularly the case in U.S. firms, where engineers we interviewed often remarked on the poor quality of the prototypes they tested.

But a prototype can also be built too well, with high conformance quality but poor representativeness. Overquality of a prototype conceals problems that will subsequently emerge at the production stage. Suppose, for example, that matching two inner body panels and achieving the required strength pose subtle design and production problems. The skilled technicians in the prototype shop may be able to make a body shell that conforms perfectly to engineering drawings by fitting the panels manually and strengthening the joints by additional welding. This same level of conformance may not be attainable on high-speed volume production lines with robots and automated jigs, and unless the technicians communicate what they have done, the discrepancy may not be discovered until production starts.

In the past, auto makers often ignored the use of prototypes to detect and solve problems in anticipation of manufacturing. Lack of communication prevented precious knowledge accumulated in the prototype shop from reaching the production plant. A similar communication gap tends to exist between prototype parts suppliers and production parts suppliers, which in the United States, as we saw in Chapter 6, are often separate companies.

Transfer and sharing of knowledge between prototype shop and production plant is particularly important in light of the differences between the two (see the information asset map—Figure 2.4—in Chapter 2). The challenge for the former is to use unrepresentative tools for prototype fabrication and still detect potential problems in mass-production. Knowledge sharing is crucial. Consider, once again, the case of body panels. Prototype body panels, once formed manually using hammers, are today made with so-called soft dies (dies made of malleable materials such as certain zinc alloys). Though this change makes the body prototype process closer to real production, important gaps remain. For example, the metal structure of sheet steel stamped slowly by soft dies differs from that of sheet steel formed by high-speed, high-power press machines. If the prototype people do not share with the plant people the knowledge that panels from soft dies are generally weaker than those from production dies, the following scenario might result. The body made by soft dies fails to pass the crash test. Product engineers, not knowing the difference between soft dies and production dies, decide to use thicker steel than would have been necessary in the production process. The result is an overweight production model.

Our evidence suggests that prototype representativeness is greatest for European high-end specialists, followed by European and Japanese volume producers. U.S. engineers frequently expressed dissatisfaction with the level of prototype representativeness, which has become a major concern of U.S. producers in recent years.

PARADIGMS OF PROTOTYPE DEVELOPMENT

Our clinical and statistical evidence reveals two contrasting paradigms of prototype development: "prototype as early problem detector" and "prototype as master model." European high-end specialists view the engineering prototype as a master to be copied by the production model. In this "master model" paradigm, no time or expense is spared in ensuring the completeness and quality of the prototype. Production models are adapted to prototypes, rather than vice versa. In short, this view of the perfect prototype and somewhat inferior production copy fits well with the strategy of high-end specialists, which emphasizes perfection of product functions uncompromised by cost and lead time.

In contrast, the "early problem detector" paradigm, followed by many Japanese car makers, regards the prototype as a tool for finding and solving design and manufacturing problems at early stages of product development. The prototype is expected to anticipate the production model to the extent that testing will reveal product and process problems. Thus the emphasis is on reasonably high quality and representativeness, not perfection. Rapid construction of many prototypes is also important because it affords more opportunities to identify and remedy problems. The early problem detector might be regarded as a "draft" of the production model, rather than the fully matured master of the master model paradigm.

Looking back at Table 7.2, we see that the characteristics of Japanese prototype development, short lead time and reasonably high quality and representativeness, are consistent with the early problem detector paradigm. Emphasis on rapid construction of prototypes and close communication between prototype shops and production facilities fosters early and accurate problem detection. In the competitive environment of the 1990s, these are critical capabilities. With shorter development lead time and highly representative prototypes, test engineers can begin prototype evaluation earlier, and more engineering changes resulting from the tests can be made in time for the development of tools and equipment, dramatically reducing the negative impact of late engineering changes on cost, time, and tooling quality. Our evidence suggests that a one-month reduction in prototype lead time results in a one-month reduction in engineering lead time. This result is consistent with the notion that building the first prototype is on engineering's critical path.

THE FUTURE OF THE PROTOTYPE

We have already noted the importance of preventing problems in design and using computer-based tools to do early testing and analysis. What do the continuing development of computer-based simulation tools and powerful graphics capabilities, as embodied in computer-aided engineering (CAE) workstations, bode for the prototype's role in problem solving and vehicle evaluation? Although auto companies invested heavily in CAE during the 1980s and major players today are equipped with at least one supercomputer and hundreds of CAD terminals for technical simulations and other developmental tasks, the importance of prototypes has not declined. As Figure 7.4 shows, the engineering prototype continues to be the primary tool of vehicle evaluation, despite enormous progress in computer technology. To some extent, this is because the factors to be evaluated have become more complicated, subtle, and holistic. Often we find computers taking over traditional tasks, allowing the human organization to expand the focus of its problem-solving activities. Because simulating problems of overall vehicle dynamics, noise, and handling is difficult for even the most sophisticated computer systems, physical prototypes are likely to remain a primary tool of engineering problem solving in the 1990s.

DIE DEVELOPMENT

Building dies for body panels accounts for both a large fraction of the total investment in a new car program and the greatest fraction of lead time in the engineering process. Consequently, outstanding

Figure 7.4 Relative Use of Prototype for Performance Testing

Noise-Vibration-Harshness Evaluation

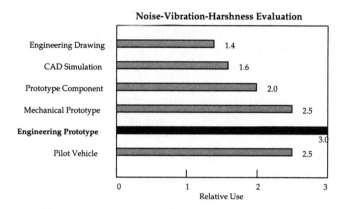

Handling Evaluation

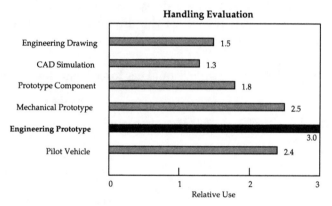

Acceleration Evaluation

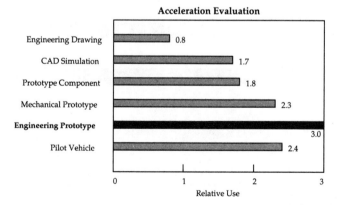

Source: Based on the questionnaire survey (see the Appendix for details).

performance in die manufacture may yield substantial advantages in overall performance.

Die development consists of four major steps: plan, design, manufacture, and tryout. It is thus itself a design-build-test cycle. We focus here on the build stage of the cycle—the cutting, finishing, and assembly that follow design and block casting. The process is generally carried out in a highly flexible manufacturing system by skilled workers using general-purpose equipment. We evaluate the performance of this process in terms of lead time and cost.

LEAD TIME

Figure 7.5 compares across regions overall lead times to design, manufacture, and test a set of dies for a body panel. Die development begins with the first release of drawings for the body panel and continues through final release of the drawings and delivery of the manufactured dies. It ends with completion of the tryout of the dies in

Figure 7.5 Lead Time for a Set of Dies for a Major Body Panel

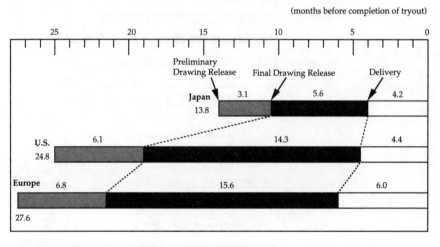

Note: Numbers do not add up exactly because some respondents reported total die lead time only.

▨ First to Final Drawing Release for Tooling Order

■ Final Drawing Release to Delivery of Die (this approximately corresponds with die manufacturing lead time)

☐ Delivery to Completion of Tryout

production. Though we see differences in lead time for each of the components of this process, the major gap between Japanese and Western producers occurs in the build phase—the period from final release to die delivery.

Why does die manufacture take 6 months in a Japanese tool and die shop and 14–16 months in U.S. and European shops? Advanced automation technology does not seem to be the answer. In fact, we found some U.S. and European producers equipped with high-tech die-making machine tools that we did not see in Japan. In any case, the time required to cut the metal is an extremely small fraction of die-making time; as is often the case in manufacturing, what we must focus on to reduce throughput time is nonoperational time (e.g., downtime, inventory time). Our interviews and direct observations suggest that the Japanese advantage in die manufacturing lead time derives from overall patterns of die production, including management of engineering changes. We defer discussion of the systemic aspects until Chapter 8. Here we focus on two factors directly related to manufacturing capability: application of JIT philosophy and integration of outside contractors.

Just-in-time in the tool and die shop. Japanese auto makers have a long history of JIT in mass-production and have disseminated much of this philosophy to their tool shops. To be sure, we did not see Kanban, Andon, U-shaped lines, or other tools typical of JIT mass-production in Japanese die shops, yet the shops seemed to be strongly influenced by the JIT philosophy. For example, in Japanese die shops we saw many fewer work-in-process dies piled up in front of die cutting machines or in finishing areas than we did in U.S. and European shops.

The seemingly streamlined operation of Japanese die shops contrasts sharply with die making in U.S. and European shops, in which a conventional job shop philosophy prevails.[5] Job shop managers oriented to maximizing utilization of expensive machine tools despite unpredictable and nonrepetitive work flows tend to pile up buffer inventories in the hope that they will absorb job scheduling uncertainty. These high levels of work-in-process inventory have the effect of lengthening throughput time.

The supplier network. Differences in the die supplier networks may explain some of the Japanese advantage in lead time. U.S. car makers have traditionally negotiated arm's-length contracts with separate companies to carry out different manufacturing steps (e.g., molding suppliers for molds, casting specialists for casting, machine shops for cutting and finishing, and jig suppliers for jigs). Such fragmentation makes it difficult to conduct die making steps in parallel and thereby compress manufacturing lead time. This contrasts with the situation in Japan, where some major die suppliers offer as a package the entire die development process, including planning, design, and die manufacture. These suppliers may subcontract part of the process, but the close, long-term relationships that prevail in the network enable them to integrate and overlap steps. Here again manufacturing capability in the supplier system contributes to higher performance in product development.

DIE COST

The cost of dies for body panels is a major element of the investment cost of developing a new model. Our field work corroborates other research that suggests that die cost accounts for half the capital investment for a new model that uses existing power trains and is produced in an existing plant.

The cost of body dies depends on the average cost of a die and the number of dies required to produce the body. Average cost and total number of dies is determined not only by die size and complexity, number of backup dies, and pattern of body-panel partition, but also by manufacturing capability as it affects two critical determinants of die cost: number of "shots" per panel and cost of engineering changes.

Shots per panel. A sheet of steel is transformed into a body panel through a series of stamping operations, each of which uses a different die (e.g., trim die, draw die, flange-up die, and pierce die) to work the metal in a particular way. The number of dies required for a given panel is determined by the number of shots required to obtain the desired shape and properties (e.g., strength). Through continuous improvement of stamping practices—including operating practices, modifications to equipment, changes in the surface quality of steel, and attention to lubricants—better Japanese shops are able to use large presses to stamp more complex dies and still achieve a high level of machine uptime and product quality. The result is that a typical Japanese body stamping plant needs only five shots (five dies and five tandem press machines) to make a complicated body panel (such as a quarter panel) that would require seven shots in a typical U.S. or European operation. A higher level of manufacturing capability—in this case process control in commercial production—can yield a significant advantage in development productivity.

Cost of an engineering change. If there were no design changes, the cost of a die set would be determined by the number of dies and the labor, materials, and capital involved in manufacturing them *once*. But despite the best efforts of body designers, prototypes almost invariably turn up problems with fit, appearance, or structural integrity that necessitate changing a die's design—sometimes several times.

In the United States, engineering changes account for 30–50 percent of the cost of a die; in Japan, such changes account for at most 20 percent. This difference is attributable to both the number of engineering changes (examined in greater depth in Chapter 8) and the cost of making the changes, both of which are lower in Japan.

The Japanese cost advantage comes not from lower wages or lower material prices, but from fundamental differences in the attitudes of designers and tool and die makers toward changes and the way changes are implemented. There seems to be in Japanese firms a tacit guideline, subscribed to by designers and tool makers alike, that the cost of engineering changes should be no higher than 10–20 percent of the initial cost of the die. In the United States, by contrast, engineering changes have been viewed as profit opportunities by tool makers. Some contracts called for the die maker to charge the auto company a predetermined fee whenever an engineering change occurred, without any guideline for overall change cost. Under other contracts, the price for changes was attended by a much higher markup than that found in the original contract price.

These differences in attitude also show up in approaches to implementation. In Japan, when a die is expected to exceed its cost target, die engineers and tool makers work to find ways to compensate in other areas. For example, the die engineers may allow deviations from the design in noncritical areas that will enable the tool maker to reduce machining and fitting time. Even more fundamentally, the emphasis in the Japanese system on direct working relationships between engineers and long-term involvement helps to reduce mistakes and rework and enables tool and die shops to handle changes with fewer transactions and less overhead. The traditional supplier relationship in the United States—arm's-length, adversarial, short term, and bureaucratic—gives rise to a more complex and expensive process because it offers less incentive to adapt and cooperate.

Once again we see the power of manufacturing capability, in particular the power of manufacturing capability in the Japanese supplier base. In both lead time and die cost, an integrated network of highly capable tool and die manufacturers creates a significant advantage for the Japanese auto makers, which organize and manage their own internal operations to capitalize on the capability of these suppliers. The effect is a die manufacturing system that in the very best firms produces dies at half the cost and in half the time compared to U.S. and European systems.

PILOT RUN AND PRODUCTION STARTUP

When engineering has signed off on the design, when prototypes have been built and tested and the production tools and dies produced, all that remains is to bring everything together to see if it works as planned. The first step is to do a pilot run—a full-scale rehearsal of the commercial production system, including parts, tools, dies, and assembly. A successful pilot run is followed by ramp-up, the startup of commercial production, which begins slowly and gradually accelerates to full production. The purpose of pilot runs and ramp-up is to find and solve problems that have gone undetected in prototype production and testing. How well and how rapidly they perform that mission can affect the success of the product.

Because they occur at the end of the product development process just prior to the start of commercial sales, pilots and ramp-up can have a critical impact on market perception and economic success.[*] Defects and poor reliability discovered during a product's introduction period can permanently destroy its reputation and image. Press and word-of-mouth reviews of a new product tend to focus on recurring defects such as squeaks and rattles, poor paint quality, and misaligned trim. To protect their product's reputation and ensure future sales, auto makers go to great lengths to ensure that only high-quality cars are introduced to the market.

---

[*]   Startup of volume production is included in the product development phase on the grounds that it normally precedes start of sales.

Auto makers face another, closely related, problem: losing sales and revenues *today*. If its engineering and manufacturing organizations cannot solve problems of productivity and quality rapidly, a firm stands to lose potential customers. Furthermore, because the investments required for the new model already are made, delays in reaching production and quality targets pushes returns further into the future. Thus, car makers need to be capable of quick and accurate problem solving and learning with reasonable cost and lead time.

PILOT RUNS IN FINAL ASSEMBLY

Final assembly is one of the most extensive yet least automated processes in modern automobile manufacturing. It typically consists of a main assembly line of a few hundred stations, complicated branches of subassembly lines, thousands of parts boxes alongside the line, and hundreds of assembly workers per shift. The challenge for the pilot run is to simulate this complex process accurately and train workers properly with minimal sacrifice in cost and schedule.

Pilot run schedules for three U.S., four Japanese, and three European development projects are shown in Figure 7.6. Black bars indicate ramp-up of commercial production. Pilot runs are differentiated according to where they are carried out: at separate pilot plants (blank bars); on separate pilot lines within volume plants (lightly shaded bars); or on volume production lines (darkly shaded bars). The figure indicates that several pilot runs tend to be conducted first on separate pilot lines or in pilot plants and later on production assembly lines.* The fraction of real production tools used, and thus the reality of the rehearsal, is greater in the later pilots. Except for the US 1 and US 3 projects, in which the plant was totally renovated for the new car pilot, existing lines with minor modifications were used to pilot the new models.

Figure 7.6 shows significant differences in the pattern of pilot runs, even within regions. Among Japanese producers, for example, the number, length, interval, and location of runs varies widely. But relative to U.S. and European projects, Japanese projects have a number of characteristics in common: pilot runs are relatively short,

---

* Pilot runs using volume production lines are often called preproduction, while pilot runs in a narrower sense refer only to the trials using separate pilot lines. In this chapter, pilot run is defined broadly to include both cases.

Figure 7.6 Schedule of Pilot Runs for Selected Projects

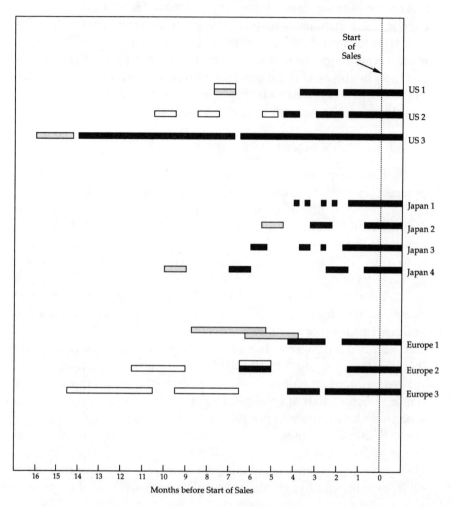

Note: US1 and US3 runs entailed major renovation of assembly line; all others entailed modification of existing assembly line.

- ☐ In a Separate Pilot Plant
- ▨ On a Separate Line Within Volume Plant
- ■ On an Existing Volume Line
- ■ Volume Production (ramp-up)

the pilot run periods are compressed, and pilots are more often carried out on production assembly lines. In general, Japanese car makers tend to be characterized by faster problem-solving cycles and more realistic (i.e., closer to commercial production) pilots. The tendency of U.S. and European firms to locate pilot production in a separate facility appears to lengthen the problem-solving cycle and complicate knowledge transfer from pilot to commercial production. None of the Japanese firms we studied operated separate pilot plants; pilot runs started in the main assembly plant, either on a small pilot line surrounded by walls or curtains for confidentiality or on the existing assembly line.

Running a pilot on a volume production line for a current model would seem to be confusing and disruptive. How do Japanese firms manage it? There are basically two alternatives. The simpler solution, to shut down commercial production for the pilot, is associated with significant production loss. The other solution is to mix current models with pilot vehicles; workers assemble new and existing models at the same station, at the same line speed, and with similar task assignments, using "empty hangers" to absorb differences in productivity. Typically, a pilot vehicle is preceded and followed by two vacant body carriers, which allows workers to spend five minutes instead of one on the unfamiliar model.

The "empty hanger" approach, being an application of mixed-model assembly, inevitably complicates work assignments and parts handling. Nevertheless, the approach reduces the opportunity cost for the pilot run by minimizing lost production for the existing model. More important, the approach involves future workers in early training in a very realistic setting, which facilitates early problem detection by the workers and their supervisors. In addition, as one Japanese process engineer pointed out to us, workers tend to get excited about a new model they see on the line and become motivated to learn more about it.

Simultaneous execution of pilot runs and commercial production on the same line, though advantageous, requires a high level of manufacturing capability—including discipline and clarity in material handling and production planning, skilled workers and supervisors, and process control that provides the flexibility needed to cope with the complexity that arises out of the mix of new and existing models. In sum, it relies on superior manufacturing capability.

RAMP-UP IN ASSEMBLY

The gradual acceleration to full-scale production is reflected in the so-called "ramp-up curve." Time to full-scale production varies from one to six months, while time to normal or targeted levels of quality and productivity varies from one month to one year. In both time to ramp-up and time to achieve performance targets, Japanese firms are much faster than their Western competitors.

Effective production ramp-up depends heavily on manufacturing capability and its fit with the choices a firm makes about the general shape of the ramp-up curve, about operating patterns such as line speed, and about the work force. The patterns we observed in final assembly startup are shown in Figure 7.7. We found regional differences in the choice of startup approach linked to differences in manufacturing capability. In terms of ramp-up, for example, U.S. and European firms favor the shut-down model (1.a). This relatively simple approach avoids mixed-model production at the risk of potentially high production and sales loss. To minimize this loss requires a steep ramp-up curve, which, unless the company possesses considerable flexibility against volume changes, may create confusion on the plant floor. Japanese firms tend to use the block (1.b) or step-by-step (1.c) approaches, which afford a smooth transition and minimize sales loss but entail complicated operations that require subtle and continuous adjustments in material handling, work assignments, and scheduling.*

The difficulty of the challenges posed by each of these strategies—in the shut-down approach of ramping-up quickly while limiting confusion and achieving high quality, and in the block or step-by-step approaches of coping with complex materials handling and scheduling while continuing to achieve quality and cost targets for new and existing models—is influenced by choices about operating patterns and work-force adjustments. Operating patterns (i.e., line speed, number of bodies on the line, and number of hours in operation) determine the rate of production. The approach to work-force adjustment determines productivity and cost during ramp-up and complexity of changes in task assignments.

---

* We did see some exceptions. For example, one of the Japanese companies, with an assembly line dedicated to a single platform, adopted the shutdown model with a very steep ramp-up curve.

Figure 7.7 Choices in Production Startup

1. Choice of Ramp-Up Curve

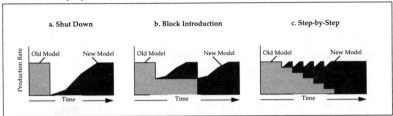

2. Choice of Operation Patterns

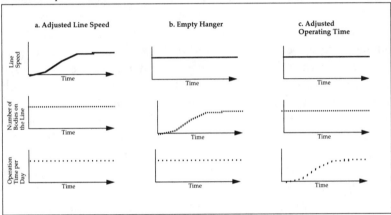

3. Choice of Work-Force Policies

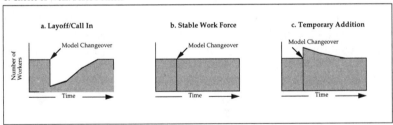

Here again we see important regional differences. Japanese firms tend to use the empty hanger model with a temporary *increase* in the work force, while U.S. and European firms usually rely on adjustments in line speed and (especially in U.S. firms) on work-force layoff and recall. In the Japanese "empty hanger-more workers" approach, line speed and operating hours are stable, but the number of cars on the line is reduced to create the empty slots. The additional workers absorb the impact of declines in productivity so that both old and new models get produced. As ramp-up proceeds, the number of empty hangers declines to zero and the extra workers are phased out. In the "line speed-recall" model favored by U.S. firms, line speeds start slow and a few additional skilled and experienced workers initially handle a broad range of tasks. As the line speed increases, new workers are brought in and tasks are reassigned. Over time, the work force is brought up to full complement and the line achieves its target speed.

The overall U.S. paradigm of "shut down-line speed-layoff/recall" attempts to resolve the conflict between learning and production by separating new and existing models and using a smaller number of more experienced and skilled workers in the early stages of ramp-up. This makes initial production less complex in terms of both material handling and work-force involvement but results in less task continuity and less stable operating conditions. The Japanese paradigm of "step-by-step-empty hanger-more workers" emphasizes continuity and stability of operating conditions and work assignments, which should give rise to an environment that supports rapid learning. The superior manufacturing capability (particularly in process control) necessitated by the added complexity associated with this paradigm tends to be characteristic of the best Japanese firms. Control over the process, together with the continuity and flexibility inherent in the Japanese paradigm, helps to minimize shop-floor confusion and enhance learning during ramp-up.

THE IMPACT OF MANUFACTURING CAPABILITY

We have seen how important outstanding manufacturing capability is to securing rapid prototype cycles, fast die development times, and effective pilot and ramp-up to volume production. But what effect does manufacturing capability have on overall development performance? Do short cycle production, deep process control, discipline in managing material flows, and an integrated supplier network result in faster time to market, fewer engineering hours, or higher quality?

We have some indication of the power of manufacturing capability in the connection between time to complete prototypes and dies and engineering lead time. On average, our analysis shows that reducing die manufacturing lead time by a month reduces engineering lead time by about three weeks. The numbers are similar for prototype lead time. In addition, we find that regional differences in die and prototype lead time account for about 4–5 months of the Japanese advantage in engineering lead time, underscoring the role prototypes and dies play in the critical path of a product development program and the impact superior performance in these critical activities has on time to market.

Manufacturing capability also has a strong effect on total product quality. It is obvious that manufacturing capability affects product quality in volume production, but here we have in mind something different. A firm that can make dies and prototypes available earlier will be able to detect more problems before pilot and ramp-up. If the firm's manufacturing organization is flexible and effective and can solve those problems quickly, ramp-up will be faster and the quality of the product at market introduction higher. To gauge the effect of manufacturing capability on the quality of design, we look at the completeness of the design at pilot and the rate of learning in pilot and ramp-up.

COMPLETENESS OF DESIGN AT PILOT

Our evidence on the quality effect begins with the comparative length of the product and process engineering stages. U.S. and Japanese projects took about the same length of time (25 months versus 22 months, respectively) to complete process engineering (see the Appendix). Given that Japanese firms complete prototypes and dies in about half the time required by U.S. and European firms, this finding is puzzling.

If Japanese firms have dies and prototypes ready so much faster, why does it take them just as long to complete process engineering? The answer lies in the completeness of the design at the time process engineering formally ends. The end of process engineering is marked by final sign-off on the design by the engineering organizations. It does not necessarily mean that all the tools and dies are complete, nor that there will be no further engineering changes. Indeed, our field work suggests that it is quite common in U.S. projects for pilot production to begin with some parts produced by prototype tools and dies. Moreover, a large number of engineering changes occur after pilot and even after ramp-up has begun.

Evidence that U.S. product and process designs are much less refined when they reach the pilot plant is found in the data on the number of prototype and pilot vehicles (see Table 7.3). Though Japanese firms vary little from other volume producers in terms of number of prototypes per body style, they make far fewer pilot vehicles. This suggests that each Japanese prototype is a more powerful problem-solving tool and that product and process designs are consequently much more complete when they reach the pilot plant.

Differences in levels of refinement also show up in the data on process engineering time. When we adjust the length of process engineering for differences in product content, scope, and engineering-manufacturing capability, we find that Japanese firms actually take *more* time in process engineering than their U.S. competitors. To engineer the process for the average car in our sample, for example, we find that the average U.S. firm would take 21 months (the average car

Table 7.3 Number of Prototypes and Pilot Vehicles

Region ⟍ Number of	Japan	U.S.	Europe Volume Producer	Europe High-End Specialist	Total
Engineering Prototypes					
total	82	44	73	61	70
per body type	38	34	37	54	39
Pilot Vehicles					
total	120	192	233	218	177
per body type	53	129	109	205	104

in the sample is less complex than the average U.S. project), while the average Japanese firm would take 27 months. In general, we find that capability for rapid prototyping and die development gives Japanese firms effectively 6–10 months of additional time for process development and refinement.

The implication is that product and process engineering in U.S. and European projects spills over into pilot and ramp-up even though the designs have been formally released. These patterns are illustrated in Figure 7.8, which plots the number of product and process problems remaining in the design (vertical axis) against the number of months

Figure 7.8 Alternative Patterns of Problem Solving: U.S. versus Japan

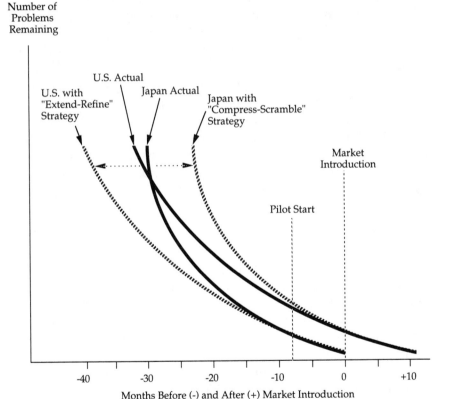

Notes: The left end of each curve corresponds with estimated start of process engineering.
It is assumed that the levels of remaining problems at the beginning of process engineering are the same.

before and after market introduction (horizontal axis). The bold lines in the center of the graph illustrate a hypothetical pattern of problem solving that is consistent with the actual data we observed—U.S. and Japanese firms both start process engineering at about the same time, but Japanese designs are more refined at pilot and market introduction. The steeper rate of problem solving observed in the Japanese case derives from more effective engineering and manufacturing capability.

The figure also illustrates alternative strategies that U.S. and Japanese firms might follow. If U.S. firms were to adopt a Japanese-style "extend-and-refine" strategy with no change in capability, they would need to begin process engineering at month 40 in order to achieve a level of refinement equivalent to the Japanese at pilot and market introduction. In contrast, Japanese firms that applied existing capabilities to a U.S.-style "compress-and-scramble" strategy could wait until month 20 to begin process engineering and still achieve a level of refinement equivalent to actual U.S. performance.

These comparisons illustrate the power of engineering and manufacturing capability. Without significant change in fundamental capability, U.S. firms are caught between the proverbial rock and a hard place; if they go after more refinement to solve quality problems, they lose on lead time. Japanese firms, on the other hand, could knock half a year off time to market without suffering any quality disadvantage. The data indicate that the average Japanese firm takes 6–10 months of additional engineering time to ensure that tools and dies are ready and the design is refined and still delivers a comparable product to market a year faster than its Western competitors.

LEARNING IN RAMP-UP

Even under the best of circumstances, startup is often a period of confusion. Productivity dives, the defect rate soars, scrap and rework mount, machines break down, lines stop, and engineers and supervisors run to fix problems. The faster the ramp-up, the more confusing things become as operational conditions and work assignments change daily.

In light of the trade-off between speed of ramp-up and level of confusion, the performance of the Japanese projects is remarkable, as shown in Figure 7.9, which compares time to reach full-scale production and average production acceleration rate throughout ramp-up.

Figure 7.9 Comparison of Assembly Ramp-Up Pace

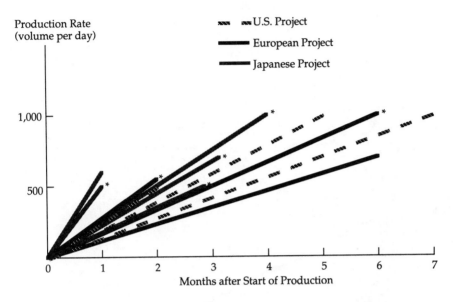

Production Rate
(volume per day)

——— ——— U.S. Project

——————— European Project

——————— Japanese Project

1,000

500

0   1   2   3   4   5   6   7

Months after Start of Production

Notes: Each line shows time to reach full-scale production horizontally and
production rate vertically; the slope of each curve is thus the rate of
production acceleration.

Asterisks indicate projects involving mixed-model assembly with old or
existing models.

Confusion in the Japanese projects, which tend to be faster, should be
greater. But the evidence on startup quality and productivity in Figures
7.10 and 7.11 tells a more complicated story. Compared to the normal
level of performance, Japanese projects suffer a sharp increase in
defects and hours per unit at the outset of ramp-up and then swiftly
achieve target performance. U.S. and European projects experience
less deviation from normal performance, but are much slower to
achieve target levels.

One reason Japanese projects start with low relative quality and
productivity seems to be simply that the normal level is high. It is now
well known that the manufacturing quality and productivity of Japanese firms has been significantly higher than that of their U.S. and
European counterparts during the 1980s.[6] Workers with broad skills

Figure 7.10 Initial Learning Curve of Assembly Productivity
(1=normal level in previous production)

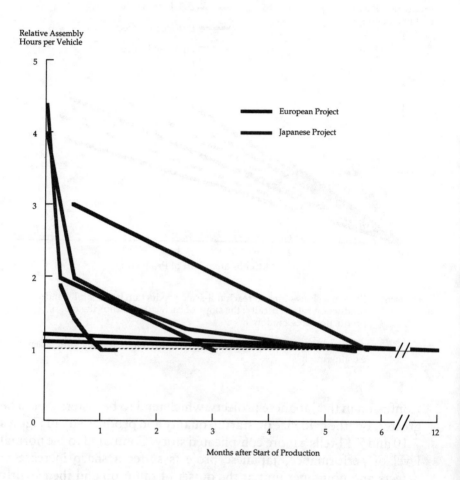

Figure 7.11 Initial Learning Curve of Defect Rate
(1=normal level in previous production)

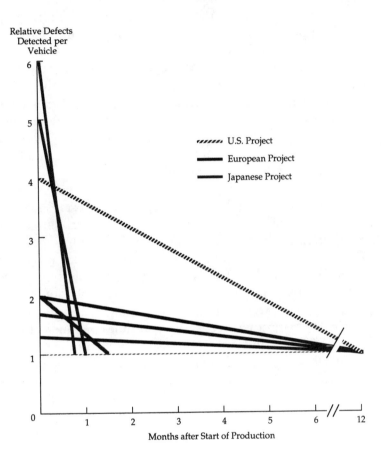

and task assignments, both in assembly sequences and in product mix, have been identified as a major factor in the Japanese advantage.[7] This implies that Japanese workers tend to require more skills and training to achieve normal productivity and that they are more subject to changes in operating conditions and job assignment. One European project we studied relied on single-skill assembly workers, who took, on average, only one or two days to achieve 80 percent of the individual productivity standard and three or four days to achieve the 100 percent level. Among Japanese producers, the average worker has multiple skills and is expected to handle more parts per cycle time (typically three instead of the usual one per minute), master jobs at more than one station (typically at two or three consecutive stations), and be able to accommodate product mix changes.

Because the skill requirement for normal operation is high, assembly productivity and quality in Japanese projects tend to be more sensitive to disruptions such as a model changeover. But despite high skill requirements and a fast ramp-up pace—both impediments to quick recovery of quality and productivity—Japanese projects return to normal fairly quickly. This is particularly true of assembly defects, with normal operation being restored in about one month.

Rapid organizational learning during ramp-up in Japanese assembly plants is rooted in effective real-time communication, continuity of the production system, exposure to the product during pilot, and skill at working-level problem solving. We noted earlier the learning value of the Japanese practice of running pilots in the assembly plant and phasing in new models. We also found that Japanese firms benefit from rapid communication. One of the better Japanese producers announces to the entire plant floor through in-house broadcasting systems information on defects and problems as soon as they are detected. For the most part, problems are solved on the shop floor, with line supervisors, rather than engineers, playing the central role. The supervisors circulate constantly, discussing problems and potential solutions with workers.

What goes on in solving ramp-up problems on the shop floor, however, is not the traditional "small-group activities" or "quality circles." As one engineer told us, "Quality circles may be OK for continuous improvement during regular production, but they are too slow for making decisions in 'war time.'" The Japanese "war time" approach—which involves experienced supervisors directing the action, deploying line workers, technicians, and engineers as needed in real time, and solving problems hour-by-hour—contrasts sharply with that of many Western producers, which employ as their main problem solvers engineers organized as a formal ramp-up team. In one U.S. manufacturer, problem solving in ramp-up was accomplished by a team of 250 engineers assigned to the plant on a temporary basis. This difference in who solves problems suggests that serious defects that require significant engineering resources are solved prior to ramp-up in Japanese projects.

CONCLUSION

We opened this chapter by contrasting the atmosphere and environment of the design studio and stamping plant, symbols of the beginning and end of product development. From that perspective, manufacturing and product development are worlds apart. But from the vantage point of the prototype shop, the tool and die maker, and the pilot plant, development and manufacturing are closely intertwined. Outstanding performance in manufacturing and product development not only share common roots, but excellence in critical manufacturing activities is also an important ingredient in the success of product development.

We have seen that rapid prototype cycles and fast die manufacturing yields advantages in overall lead time and quality of design. Effective process control in manufacturing shows up in lower die costs, in the ability to run mixed-model assembly, and in the ability to ramp-up production quickly. Getting prototypes and tools fast gives Japanese firms the opportunity to solve problems before pilot, thereby reducing engineering changes and enhancing the effectiveness of product and process design. A good part of the Japanese advantage in lead time, productivity, and quality comes from superior capability in manufacturing. This is not to say that excellent manufacturing capability in prototype building or ramp-up is found only among the Japanese. Some European and U.S. companies have excellent capability in these areas, but the evidence suggests that excellence was found more consistently in the Japanese producers during the mid to late 1980s.

The impact of manufacturing capability on development is not simply a matter of good manufacturing practice. It grows out of an integration of that capability with other skills and abilities in the organization. Being able to manufacture prototypes quickly is of little value unless product and test engineers are linked into the prototype cycle and communicate effectively. Likewise, building dies rapidly depends as much on how body engineers work with die designers as on skill in manufacturing. Thus, to comprehend more fully the role of manufacturing capability and to develop a more complete sense of the sources of high performance in development, we need to understand the nature of problem solving in development and the patterns of integration across functional groups.

NOTES

1. See, for example, Hayes, Wheelwright, and Clark (1988), Bohn and Jaikumar (1986), and Imai (1986).
2. For further details of the production paradigm, see, for example, Monden (1983), Hall (1983), and Schonberger (1982).
3. See, for example, Monden (1983), Schonberger (1982), and Hall (1983).
4. For further details of prototype lead time, see Clark and Fujimoto (1987) and Clark (1989).
5. On the issue of reforming job shop manufacturing, see, for example, Ashton and Cook (1989).
6. See, for example, Abernathy, Clark, and Kantrow (1983) and Krafcik (1988).
7. See, for example, Fujimoto (1986) and Krafcik (1988).

CHAPTER 8
INTEGRATING PROBLEM-SOLVING CYCLES

One of the central issues in the effective management of development is the linking of knowledge and information held in different departments and functions. Consider the following story from an early chapter in the history of Honda. A young engineer, fresh out of the University of Tokyo, reduced the thickness of the cylinder walls to save weight in an engine being developed for a key motorcycle race. The engine subsequently seized during the race. Later, Shoichiro Honda brought all the engineers together for a post mortem. Upon determining the problem to be the too-thin cylinder walls, Honda confronted the engineer responsible. The conversation that ensued went like this.

"Is this your work?"
"Yes."
"Why did you do this?"
"Based on my calculations, I thought it would work."
"Anyone in the factory could have told you it wouldn't! Did you ask anyone in the factory?"
"No, I did not."

The engineer was then instructed to take the offending parts and visit everyone who depended on the project (almost everyone in the factory) to apologize. The engineer made the visits and stayed with the company, eventually becoming one of Honda's most senior executives.

FINDING A FRAMEWORK

The importance of upstream-downstream links, as between the product engineers and plant engineers in the Honda story, has motivated the development of a variety of new methods and approaches to product design and process development, including concurrent engineering, design for manufacturability, and early manufacturing involvement. Each is an attempt to achieve tighter integration between upstream and downstream groups. Our study of product and process development in the auto industry has led us to search for a framework that would link alternative approaches to achieving integration.

THE PROBLEM-SOLVING CYCLE

The framework we developed builds on the problem-solving and information-processing perspective introduced in Chapter 2. It takes as its central concept the problem-solving cycle. The standard model of the problem-solving cycle (see Figure 8.1)[1] consists of at least four steps: problem recognition, generation of alternatives, evaluation, and decision making (accept or reject). Rejection of an alternative leads to a new cycle. Reiteration of cycles is essentially a learning process in which knowledge of problems and solutions increases over time. Reiteration continues until acceptable solutions are developed.

Throughout this book we have argued that product development, including product and process engineering, can be described and analyzed as a system of interconnected problem-solving cycles. All major engineering activities—including functional design, drafting, prototype construction, testing, design review, drawing release, design change, process design, tool making, pilot run, and manufacturing sign-off—are elements of a problem-solving cycle. Our framework allows us to examine the integration of problem-solving cycles at both ends of the development process, and it distinguishes between integration in the sense of the *timing* of action and integration in terms of *communication* patterns between the upstream and downstream groups.

One of the central themes that emerged from our examination of regional differences in the degree of integration and its impact on development performance is the importance of skills, attitudes, and managerial philosophy in making a particular approach to integration work effectively. Toward the end of this chapter, we examine in depth a particular upstream-downstream linkage, the design and development of body panels and associated stamping dies, to illustrate what integration means in practice and the particular skills and attitudes that are essential to achieving integrated problem-solving cycles. We found that what characterizes outstanding performance in the auto industry is not mastery of a particular technique, but a pattern of consistency in process, structure, attitude, and skill that we call *integrated problem solving*.

Figure 8.1 Problem-Solving Cycle

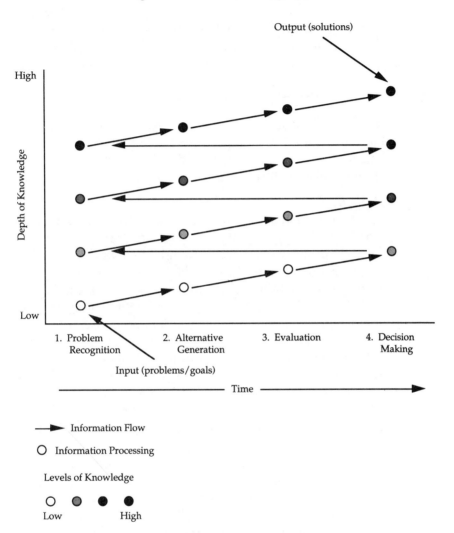

That effective integration across different functional groups and engineering disciplines is critical to successful product development is no secret. The business press is full of articles extolling the virtues of cross-functional teams, simultaneous engineering, and various methodologies for creating product designs that are easier to manufacture and better meet customer requirements. All aim at integrating effort across traditional functional boundaries. The challenge is to understand what "effective integration" means and what is required to achieve it. In some firms, integration has meant little more than rearranging the timing chart so that more work is performed in parallel. In others, it has led to acquiring new tools, learning new design methods, and changing procedures for project review and approval.

FIVE DIMENSIONS OF INTERFACE

During the 1980s, automobile firms worldwide were actively developing and trying out new approaches to cross-functional integration, particularly between product and process engineering. The variety of approaches is illustrated by the following vignettes.

Company A

Mr. G., executive vice president of R&D at Company A, had long been proud of his strong engineering disciplines. But when problem after problem with the manufacturability of new products showed up on his desk, he launched a thorough review. What he uncovered was rampant failure to communicate. Blueprints were showing up in manufacturing calling for production methods that had been discontinued a year before. (Product engineering had even signed off on the change!) Manufacturing was putting in a robotic assembly system that required redesign of parts late in the program.

Several members of the staff wanted to institute new procedures, but Mr. G. went further. Under his leadership, the company launched a program in Early Manufacturing Involvement attended by the slogan "Tear Down the Walls." The idea was to eliminate the "throw-it-over-the-wall" mentality in product and process engineering through frequent face-to-face meetings between product designers and manufacturing engineers very early in a program. In addition, Mr. G. established a new review process with manufacturing involvement at key transition points in development. And he set up a "war room" where project timetables, mockups, drawings, process layouts, and related documents were available, and where all critical meetings were held.

Company B

There was no doubt in anyone's mind that Company B was in trouble. Domestic market share had fallen for two years, and the last two new products had been delayed by last-minute engineering changes. Time to get a good product to market was longer for Company B than for Company X (its chief rival), and Company X's market share had been growing. Despite a tradition of slow and deliberate decision making, the president of Company B, Mr. F., quickly scrapped the old development system and instituted a new approach. Though Company B had long used a phase review process with early involvement of all functions, Mr. F. was convinced that the downstream groups had little influence.

"What we are going to do," he said, "is create *real* teamwork. I don't want manufacturing people going to meetings and sitting over in a corner. I don't want manufacturing just sending a 'wants' list or doing perfunctory feasibility reviews. I don't want any baton passing. Everything is too sequential. I want rugby-style teamwork, with product and process engineers working together in real time." Company B promptly dedicated teams of engineers drawn from several functions to two projects already under way.

Company C

Mr. P., senior vice president at Company C, had quickly followed up on the first report. The head of engineering had assured him it was an isolated case and that the problem had been solved. The second report, coming only two days later, had raised a red flag. But the third set off alarm bells all over the tenth floor of the headquarters building. Three newspaper articles from three different cities all about the same problem: water leaks in the brand new, high-performance sedan that Company C was counting on to expand its market position.

With Mr. P.'s personal involvement, answers came fast. The problem turned out to be a combination of design and manufacturing process. "The way they've got that sunroof designed," explained one engineer, "we just can't hold the tolerances. We've been testing and repairing them, but sometimes one that looks OK really isn't." The leak problem, added to several other problems in manufacturing, convinced Mr. P. that he had to embark on a major program in design for manufacturability, something the vice president of manufacturing had been pushing for. The program involved extensive training and the introduction of new computer-based support tools, but, more important, it required opening up lines of communication between product engineering and manufacturing.

The efforts these three companies made to deal with problems of linking functional groups illustrate the range of choices firms face. These efforts involved broad functional relationships (e.g., the engineering-manufacturing interface), but we have found it useful to focus on a single interface between problem-solving cycles in an upstream and a downstream group—the design of a part and development of a process for manufacturing it. In doing so, we have identified five dimensions of the interface that determine the nature of integration. These dimensions and their associated ranges of choice are shown in Figure 8.2.

The ends of the spectra in Figure 8.2 represent polar opposites in integration. To the left we have serial activities driven by limited communication; to the right we see parallel activities linked by rich, dense, and early communication. Adding all that lies in between, we can imagine widely varying patterns of activities across the five dimensions. Taken together, these dimensions give us a framework for describing and analyzing different approaches to integration.

Figure 8.3 uses the five dimensions to lay out an idealized example of how a company might dramatically reduce lead time by progressively moving to the right side of the spectrum on each dimension. For simplicity, we show only one upstream process (product engineering) and one downstream process (process engineering).

We begin at the top of Figure 8.3 with a pattern that is typical of traditional car development projects, particularly among Western producers: upstream and downstream processes are conducted serially, and information flow is unilateral from upstream to downstream. In practice, this plays out as product engineering releasing a complete set of product design information at the end of the product engineering

Figure 8.2 Dimensions of Integrated Problem Solving

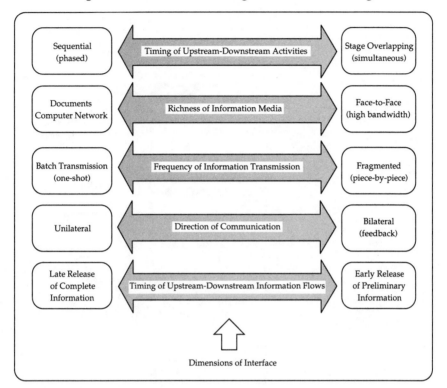

process. Process engineering commences work only after it has complete blueprints.

In theory, this pattern should reduce the risk associated with product changes. In fact, product changes, all too many of them, still occur and must be dealt with. Other potential advantages, such as straightforwardness and ease of management, are offset by distinct disadvantages. Recall that Companies A, B, and C all suffered from problems related to communication and delay. Sequential processes, in an era of rapid product change, simply take too long. Furthermore, unilateral batch transfer of information does nothing to encourage product designers to take into account manufacturability considerations, which imposes a greater problem-solving burden on downstream processes. Finally, subtle nuances in the information transmitted downstream may not be picked up, creating further problems for manufacturing.

Figure 8.3 Integrating Problem-Solving Cycles

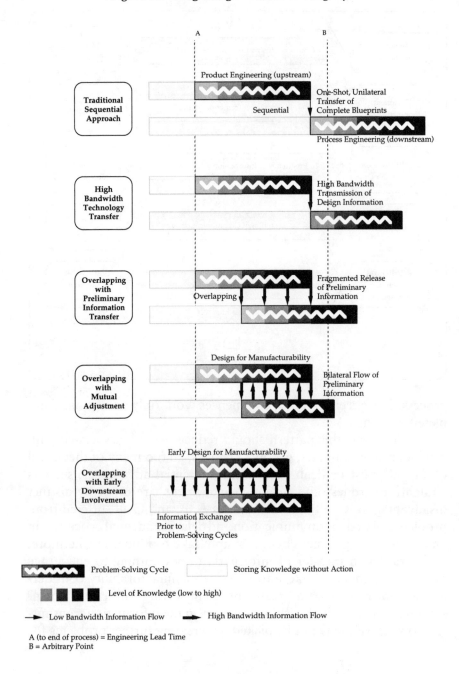

Problem-Solving Cycle   Storing Knowledge without Action

Level of Knowledge (low to high)

Low Bandwidth Information Flow   High Bandwidth Information Flow

A (to end of process) = Engineering Lead Time
B = Arbitrary Point

What happens if we improve integration on one dimension? Moving down one level in Figure 8.3, we see the consequences of enhancing the richness of the information medium. In practice, this means replacing "throwing blueprints over the wall" with face-to-face discussion, direct observation, and interaction with physical prototypes and computer-based representations.* Direct communication, an important facet of group and team work, was the objective of Mr. G.'s "war room." Even if the richer communication comes at the end of the upstream cycle, as it does in this panel, the effectiveness of the transfer may significantly reduce lead time for problem solving.

Moving down to the middle panel, we see what happens when the company increases the frequency of information transmission and introduces overlapping in engineering activity. In practice, spacing the richer information transfer out over time and releasing partial product design information as it becomes available allows upstream and downstream processes to overlap, effectively giving process engineering a flying start and further cutting lead time for problem solving. Simultaneous engineering, though appealing, is difficult to achieve. Engineers, tending to be perfectionists, are often reluctant to release work that is incomplete. The upstream group will be even less willing to release information early if the environment is hostile, with design changes triggering accusations of sloth or incompetence. If the attitude of product engineers is "I won't give you anything now because I know I'll have to change it later and I know that I'll take the blame for it," management may have to effect a fundamental change of attitude throughout the engineering organization, both upstream and downstream, a very difficult task.

---

* Electronic media are playing an increasingly important role in the product-process link. CAD-CAM data representing a complex body surface, for example, enable much more accurate transmission of body design information to die engineers than line drawings and models. This is partly because digital information (CAD-CAM), unlike analog information (drawings and models), is less subject to error accumulation through duplication (e.g., as with photocopies), and partly because CAD-CAM can eliminate some of the steps required by the traditional approach and thereby reduce the length of the communication chain. The trend in today's auto companies is for both verbal and electronic media to play increasingly important roles in product-process technology transfer; thus "high tech" and "high touch" are simultaneously emphasized for better management of the product-process interface.

In the next panel, moving from unilateral to bilateral communication creates the basis for mutual adjustment between upstream and downstream engineering. Upon receiving preliminary drawings of a body design, process engineering, for example, may feed back to product engineering information about the difficulty of manufacturing certain shapes, whereupon product engineering might make changes to the design to better utilize process capabilities. Bilateral communication is prerequisite to the efforts of Companies A, B, and C to achieve closer involvement, better designs, and teamwork. Added to simultaneous engineering and richer information flows, bilateral communication has the potential to improve problem solving by better distributing the problem-solving burden between upstream and downstream. Whether this potential is realized depends on the attitudes and philosophy that prevail in the engineering organization. If upstream is unwilling to make any concessions in product function, performance, or aesthetics for the sake of manufacturability, or if downstream always responds to new product designs with "it can't be done," bilateral communication will achieve little more than to make the adversity more direct.

When communication is not only frequent and bilateral, but also comes very early in the problem-solving cycle, we see the kind of pattern depicted in the bottom panel of Figure 8.3. When Mr. F. set out to establish his rugby-style teams, he was aiming at achieving real-time coordination between upstream and downstream. This is the essence of mutual adjustment; it enables product engineers to take into account preliminary results of process engineering problem solving in order to make products easier and less expensive to manufacture. But this adjustment begins only after downstream problem solving has begun.

The bottom panel of Figure 8.3 illustrates the consequences of early downstream involvement. Early involvement is not just getting an earlier start; it is the exchange of information and insight before the problem-solving cycles begin. In practice, process engineering "front loads" information to product engineering before it starts its work. This helps upstream to "do it right the first time" and affords downstream earlier exposure to product designs through clay models and specifications, further reducing problem-solving lead time, improving manufacturing quality, and lowering production costs.

The success of early involvement depends on the level of knowledge available prior to commencing a given problem-solving cycle. Because much of this knowledge will have originated outside the project (e.g., lessons from past development projects and results of advanced research projects), cross-project knowledge transfer—that is, the mechanisms by which a firm stores and makes available to current projects information about past engineering problems—is crucial.

Attention to these five dimensions can buy a company distinctive competitive advantage. Consider Figure 8.3 again. Engineering lead time is shown as extending from point A to the end of the process. The progressive reduction of engineering lead time as a company increases the intensity, frequency, and direction of information transfer and the simultaneity of activities and information flows is clearly evident in the patterns in the figure. Suppose that in response to market changes or attack by a competitor a company needed to introduce a product as early as point B. A company that had achieved the degree of integration represented by the bottom panel would clearly make it. A company with a level of integration characterized by the next panel, if it mounted a concerted effort, might come close. But companies with less integrated problem solving would be late to market and suffer competitive disadvantage.

STAGE OVERLAPPING AND INTENSIVE COMMUNICATION

Timing of downstream action and the intensity, frequency, and direction of information flow are closely related. But they do not always appear in effective combination. Figure 8.4 compares two patterns of integration. In the top panel, upstream and downstream engineers exchange information frequently to minimize confusion and uncertainty created by the tight interdependency between the two groups. Changes on each side are continuously updated and communicated to the other through daily contacts, meetings, product managers, and other integrating mechanisms. Now consider the bottom panel in Figure 8.4, which characterizes the introduction of simultaneous engineering with no change in batch information transmission. This may occur, for example, if top management introduces a new standard timetable that calls for simultaneity of engineering stages. Product engineers continue to throw blueprints "over the wall" to process engineers after the work is complete, while process engineers, in-

Figure 8.4 Overlapping with and without Intensive Communication

Simultaneity of
Upstream-Downstream
Activities /Intensive
Transmission of
Information

Early and Mutual Releases of
Preliminary Information
Minimize Confusion

Simultaneity of
Upstream-Downstream
Activities/Batch
Transmission of
Information

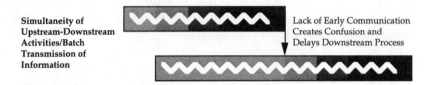

Lack of Early Communication
Creates Confusion and
Delays Downstream Process

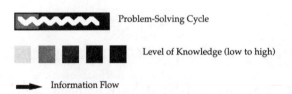

Problem-Solving Cycle

Level of Knowledge (low to high)

Information Flow

structed to do so by the new time chart, begin work earlier but blindly, without a clue from upstream. Suddenly a batch of final product design information arrives at process engineering; product-process mismatches are discovered, dies are scrapped, process designs changed, and parts reworked. The resulting confusion prolongs the latter part of the engineering process, which offsets much of the potential gain from simultaneous engineering.

Integrated problem solving is achieved only when two conditions exist: a high degree of simultaneous activity, which we call stage overlapping; and rich, frequent, bidirectional information flows, which we henceforward refer to as intensive communication. Stage overlapping without intensive upstream-downstream communication yields little of the potential advantage of integrated problem solving. In the following section, we examine more closely the two essential conditions for integrated problem solving and their effects on development performance.

STAGE OVERLAPPING

The panels in Figure 8.5, which compare average schedules of product and process engineering in the United States, Europe, and Japan, show the Japanese engineering process to be clearly more overlapped than those of its Western counterparts.[*] A simple index, the

Figure 8.5 Regional Average of Engineering Stages

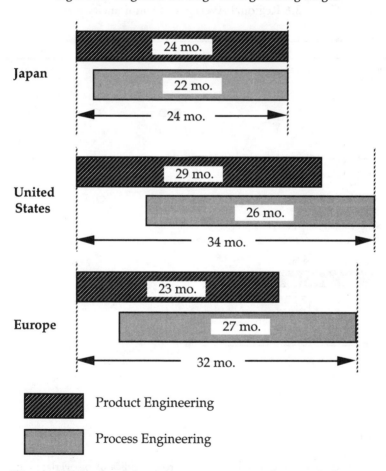

Product Engineering

Process Engineering

---

[*] Western projects do overlap engineering stages; totally sequential engineering is an ideal type that we employ here to provide conceptual insight.

simultaneity ratio (SR), which we applied to each project, serves to quantify this pattern, as shown in Figure 8.6. We calculated the simultaneity ratio as the sum of the durations of product (X) and process (Y) engineering divided by overall engineering stage length (Z). Thus, SR is 1 when the process is totally sequential (i.e., there is no overlap) and increases as the stages become overlapped, reaching 2 when they are completely parallel.[*] A statistical analysis suggests that this "Japan effect" is fairly significant even after taking account of differences in project complexity and scope.

Figure 8.6 Regional Averages of Simultaneity Ratio

Sequential ◄─────────────────────────────► Simultaneous

1.0   2.0

Note: Simultaneity Ratio = (X + Y) / Z where:

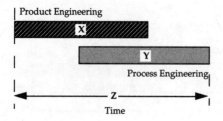

Product Engineering

X

Y

Process Engineering

Z

Time

● United States (1.58)

● Europe (1.55)

○ Japan (1.75)

[*]   The present simultaneity index is only a rough indicator of overlapping at an aggregate level; it does not capture overlapping of microlevel engineering steps within each stage.

Do differences in the simultaneity ratio affect engineering lead time? Our analysis suggests that the simultaneity ratio has a moderate to significant positive effect on the speed of development. Figure 8.7, which plots the correlation between the simultaneity ratio and engineering lead time (adjusted for project content), indicates a moderately positive correlation between engineering speed and simultaneity, and shows greater overlapping in Japanese projects relative to U.S. and European projects.

Our regression analysis estimates that, given the level of project complexity and scope, engineering lead time would be reduced by roughly one year if timing of product and process engineering were to go from totally sequential (SR = 1) to totally simultaneous (SR = 2). Much of this effect is region-specific, a finding consistent with the observation of regional differences in simultaneity ratios. As product

Figure 8.7 Simultaneity Ratio and Engineering Lead Time

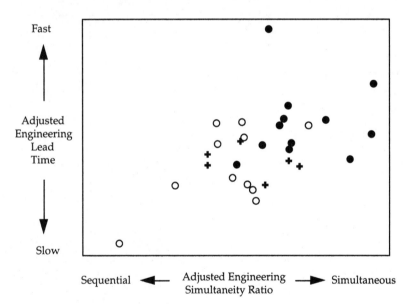

● Japan

+ U.S.

○ Europe

and process engineering are both about two years in length, going from totally sequential (which would make lead time four years) to totally simultaneous should reduce lead time by two years. It thus appears that some part of the potential impact of simultaneity on lead time is offset by coordination problems engendered by the simultaneity.

INTENSIVE COMMUNICATION

Results of extensive interviews in the companies and evidence from questionnaires about the specific projects in our sample yielded several indicators of the communication intensity between product and process engineering.[*] Regional patterns in these indicators are summarized in Table 8.1.

Table 8.1 Perceived Effectiveness of Product-Process Communication by Region

Number of Organizations

Region \ Effectiveness	Better	Inconclusive	Worse
Japan	7	1	0
United States	0	3	2
Europe	4	4	1

[*] Effectiveness of communication is difficult to measure objectively. Our approach is based on in-depth interviews with project participants, during which effectiveness of product-process communication was discussed repeatedly. On the basis of interview comments, we classified sample organizations into three categories: *better, inconclusive,* and *worse.* An organization was classified as "worse" if more than one interviewee admitted that communication was insufficient or if certain symptomatic indicators, such as late conflicts or a higher ratio of engineering change costs, were observed. Otherwise an organization was classified as "better." If the interview comments suggested that the organization was in transition toward better communication, or if mixed responses were obtained, the organization was classified as "inconclusive."

Our interviews revealed a consistent regional pattern in overall effectiveness of product-process communication. Discussions about the frequency of late conflicts due to lack of communication, data on numbers of engineering changes, and comments about overall quality and frequency of communication led us to believe that Japanese projects are characterized by more intensive and effective communication. The essence of what we discovered in Japan is summarized in this explanation by a manager of process engineering in one of the Japanese companies we studied.

> Communication between product engineering and process engineering includes both regular meetings at the manager level and informal contacts at the working level. In the latter case, design engineers voluntarily come to process engineering to show preliminary drawings. In any case, both product and process engineers are located at the same site, and communication is intensive from early stages.

In contrast, interviewees in U.S. companies were full of stories about snafus caused by poor communication, complaints by product engineers about lack of information from manufacturing and vice versa, and frequent observations about the need to improve product-process communication. Though we heard similar comments in some European companies, in others, particularly in high-end specialists, we found evidence of intensive communication within the engineering organization. Overall, we came away with an impression of intensive communication in Japanese firms and a batch style of communication in their U.S. (and to some extent European) counterparts. Evidence on several indicators suggests complexities and subtleties that shed light on the sources of effectiveness in communication between product and process engineers. Take, for example, the case of early feedback from manufacturing. Manufacturing feasibility reviews during concept development and product planning are almost standard procedure throughout the world. We find differences when we look closely at feedback in other stages and at feedback related to feasibility. In Japanese firms, for example, process engineers frequently make counterproposals to product designers. This kind of mutuality (design counterproposal) is de-emphasized by European firms, consistent with their philosophy of sequential engineering. What we see instead is emphasis on cost information, which seems to reflect the pivotal role cost estimators and controllers play in many European companies. In U.S. projects, early manufacturing feasibility reviews are often routine in character; real feedback comes much later. Noticeably less early feedback in U.S. than in Japanese projects at the concept stage becomes significant later in the product engineering stage, when a great deal of information flows back from production to engineering in Japanese projects, but very little in U.S. projects.

Overall, Japanese projects tend to exhibit more active, balanced, and continuous flows of feedback information from production, a pattern that is intriguing in light of evidence on the relative power of the process engineering organization during the engineering stage of the project. Process engineers in European and U.S. firms frequently enjoy formal veto power over product design decisions, whereas those in Japanese firms tend to have a strong but informal voice. Thus, problems in communication in U.S. companies seem not to stem from lack of *formal* authority.

In fact, it appears that the problem is absence of *informal* influence. The greater influence of Japanese process engineers on product design seems to derive from intimate communication and mutual adjustment between product and process. The stronger formal power of U.S. process engineers (e.g., in the manufacturing sign-off) ironically may hamper effective communication between upstream and downstream. Process people, with formal veto power as a final resort, may lack motivation to become involved in the design process earlier, while product engineers may hesitate to initiate early communication with process people for fear of triggering a veto. Rather than joint problem solving, this gives rise to a "we-they" relationship between product and process. A formal system of sign-off without an informal system of mutual trust and adjustment may simply impede effective implementation of integrated problem solving.

Formal integration mechanisms and systems such as task forces, liaison roles, project teams, and CAD-CAM links were found in almost all the projects we studied and are believed to be in use by most of the world's automobile companies. But the character of these mechanisms and systems shows some regional differences. Consider cross-functional teams. Whereas all of the Japanese and most of the European projects we studied utilized teams, 50 percent of U.S. projects did not. When we look at the composition of these teams, we find a paradox;

Western companies are much more likely than Japanese companies to include manufacturing people (manufacturing engineering and plant personnel) as formal members of the project team. If product-process communication is more intensive in Japanese firms than in U.S. firms, it is not because of formal involvement of production people on the project team, but because of informal ties among working engineers.

The finding that process engineers in Japanese firms seem to enjoy more intensive and effective communication with product engineers than their counterparts in U.S. firms underscores the importance of informal relationships in achieving integration, an aspect of problem solving that is evident in the way product and process conflicts are resolved. Cross-functional conflict is a focal point at which the words and actions of engineers reveal underlying attitudes about product-process relationships. We found in our field work that conflicts are the rule in all projects.

Conflict between product and process engineering centers on the manufacturing feasibility of product designs. As in other comparisons between Japanese and U.S. projects, we found differences in attitudes to be describable as "batch mode" versus "intensive mode." The following comments are illustrative of the attitudes that prevail in U.S. firms. First, a process engineering manager:

> Product engineers change designs. They don't stick to the schedule for engineering release. The major source of engineering changes is poor functional performance of the product, as opposed to manufacturability. One reason for this is that there are too many "yes men" in product engineering. They say "yes, we can do that" up front, but they don't keep their promises. Thus, problems surface too late.

And now, a styling designer in the same company:

> The major cause of engineering changes is lack of manufacturability, as opposed to function or appearance. Although we release information frequently to process engineers, they don't give us enough information back. It is too late when process engineers say, "No, we can't make that quarter panel."

The gap in perception is striking; each side faults the other for lack of communication and late engineering changes. With both sides believing the other party to be the main source of problems, constructive conflict resolution is difficult.

Process engineers in Japanese firms express a more flexible, sympathetic attitude. Two process engineering managers and a process engineer are quoted.

> In my opinion, we need to cooperate with product engineers. If we avoid risks and say no too often to product designs for manufacturability reasons, the design of the car would become more like that of a truck and would lose its marketability.

> Although we involve process engineers very early, it is not always true that the earlier the involvement the better. If we set production constraints too early in the development process, product designers may lose their spirit of challenge. After all, product appeal should get the first priority.

> Conflicts between product and process engineers seem to be solved more easily when we [process engineers] have opportunities to see the product concepts at early points. Otherwise, we tend to pursue manufacturability only. If we can see the product concept, it motivates us to think, "OK, let's make something salable," or "we don't need a car that is easy to produce but hard to sell."

These comments suggest that effective, intensive communication requires market-oriented process engineers. Emphasis on manufacturability, though key to better conformance quality, can destroy the concept or the marketability of a new product if that emphasis is excessive. The needed balance between producibility and concept/design quality seems to rely on coexistence of concept-oriented process engineers and producibility-oriented product engineers. This sharing of orientation, this ability to see the other side of an issue that is the basis for informal influence at the working level, sets apart product-process interaction in Japanese projects.

PATTERNS OF OVERLAPPING AND COMMUNICATION: THE IMPACT ON PERFORMANCE

Regional differences in simultaneity of stages and intensity of communication are plotted in Figure 8.8. We see a match between intensity and simultaneity along the diagonal, running from the lower left, where a serial process is matched to a batch mode of communication, up toward the zone of integrated problem solving, where communication is intense and problem solving runs in parallel. Points off the diagonal suffer from two kinds of problems: below the diagonal, communication patterns do not support the level of simultaneity in problem solving; above the diagonal, problem solving is less simultaneous (and thus probably slower) than communication patterns are capable of supporting. The map places Japanese car makers at the integrated problem-solving end of the optimal zone, with highly overlapped stages and intensive communication. U.S. firms are less

Figure 8.8 Stage Simultaneity and Information Transmission by Region

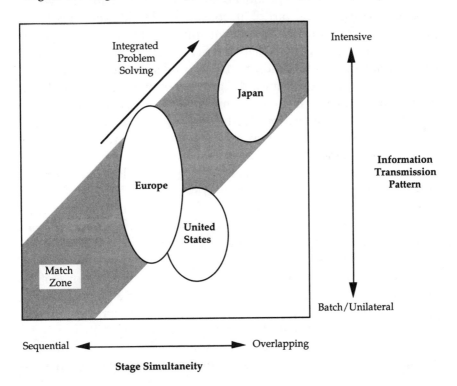

overlapped but also tend to be below the diagonal, signaling a mismatch between overlapping and communication. European firms, being more sequential in orientation but employing somewhat more intensive communication between stages, also lie in the match zone, though somewhat behind Japanese firms. (In some European companies, particularly high-end specialists, strong communication links between engineering disciplines are used to improve quality but not to support mutual adjustment or parallel activity in manufacturing.)

What impact do these patterns have on development performance? Is integrated problem solving associated with shorter lead time? Does it have any effect on productivity or quality? The impact of problem-solving patterns on lead time is direct. Effective communication between product and process engineering should enable overlapping to reduce the time required to achieve a joint solution. If integration reduces the number of unnecessary iterations and engineering changes caused by poor communication, engineering hours may also be reduced.

The effect on total product quality, however, is unclear. Where product-process linkages are tight, consumers should experience fewer product failures and conformance quality should be higher. But the effect of integration on design quality may be mixed. If linking problem-solving cycles leads to better understanding of technical constraints and opportunities, design quality may be improved. But integration may also entail compromises that sacrifice some innovative design features to enhance producibility. Further, a sequential process, though slow and expensive, may produce a very attractive design. How these effects balance out is an empirical issue.

Because integrated problem solving is a multifaceted concept and therefore difficult to measure with a single variable, we used information on nine characteristics of problem solving (e.g., high simultaneity ratio and early feedback from manufacturing) to construct an "ideal profile index" of integrated problem solving (see the Appendix for details).[2] A point was awarded each time an organization met a condition. Each organization was measured in terms of its distance from the "ideal profile" represented by nine points. Though only an approximation, we believe this index of integrated problem solving captures the essential differences across regions.

Figure 8.9 plots the problem-solving index against adjusted measures of total lead time, development productivity, and total

Figure 8.9 Integrated Problem Solving and Development Performance

A. Lead Time and Integrated Problem Solving

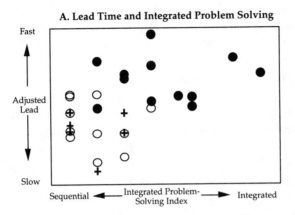

B. Development Productivity and Integrated Problem Solving

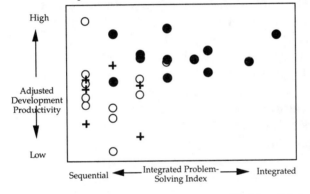

C. Total Product Quality and Integrated Problem Solving

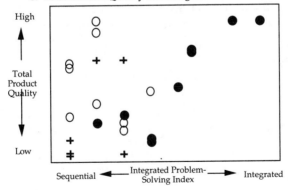

product quality. The effect on total lead time (panel A) indicates a significant positive correlation between integrated problem solving and the speed of development. Most of this relationship reflects differences *between* Japanese and Western projects. Data from Japanese projects tend to cluster toward the upper right-hand corner, with data from European and U.S. projects clustered in the lower left. The same pattern is apparent in the data on development productivity in panel B. There is little evidence of a positive relationship *within* regions. In fact, there is little difference in the degree of integration across U.S. and European projects. What we are seeing in the analysis of total adjusted lead time and adjusted productivity is a Japan effect. It appears that the degree of integration may help to explain the Japanese advantage in lead time and development productivity, but not differences within regions.

A quite different story is told by the data on quality in panel C. Here we find that integration improves performance, that integrated problem solving leads to higher overall quality. The effect is quite strong and is not regional in character. This is *not* a Japan effect; it is the impact of integration across firms. The quality effect is particularly strong in conformance quality (see the Appendix for details). It should not be surprising that the degree of integration affects measures of reliability, because better linkages between product and process design should improve manufacturability. But it also appears that some firms using a highly integrated approach to engineering have achieved excellence in both conformance and the quality of design.

Integrated problem solving thus may yield advantages across all three dimensions of performance. Linking problem-solving cycles with effective communication not only allows parallel operation resulting in improved lead time, but also reduces errors and waste that consume engineering hours and jeopardize product reliability. To reduce errors and waste without degrading quality of design requires market-oriented process engineers and producibility-oriented product engineers. When lead time is critical to competition, markets are turbulent, and customers are demanding, integrated problem solving may be essential to competitive success.

INTEGRATION IN PRACTICE: DIE DEVELOPMENT IN JAPANESE AND U.S. FIRMS

Integrated problem solving requires parallel activity and frequent and intensive bilateral communication. To be effective, such integration requires relationships that support shared understanding and responsibility and the skill and ability to capitalize on earlier, richer flows of information between upstream and downstream groups. Successful performance relies on integration at the working level. To this point, we have sketched broad patterns of problem solving based on indicators of the degree of overlapping and the intensity of communication. To deepen our understanding of the role of particular relationships and skills, we take a closer look at integration in practice at the working level; we examine the workings of a product-process interface that is critical to the successful development of a new car— the design and development of dies for body panels.[3]

Die development for body panels—a complex sequence of information processing activities that extends from clay models and line drawings to stamping dies made of steel—is a major component of process engineering. The process as carried out by a typical Japanese die maker is sketched out in Figure 8.10. Because die development is on the critical path in the product development process, shortening this step shortens overall engineering lead time. Moreover, our field studies suggest that effective reduction of die lead time relies on both overlapping of die engineering and body engineering and careful management of the informational interface between the two stages. In short, die development, in its relationship with body engineering, embraces all the essential issues associated with managing the product-process interface and integrating engineering problem-solving cycles.

We thus treat the design and development of dies as a microcosm, a manageable, compact set of activities that reflects the way engineering is done in the larger organization. We conducted a detailed clinical study of how dies were developed in each of the organizations in our sample, paying particular attention to patterns of overlapping and communication and to what seemed to be critical relationships and skills. To substantiate the implications of our findings in the microcosm, we assessed whether outstanding performers in die development were also outstanding in overall performance.

Figure 8.10 Die Development Process in a Typical Japanese Die Maker

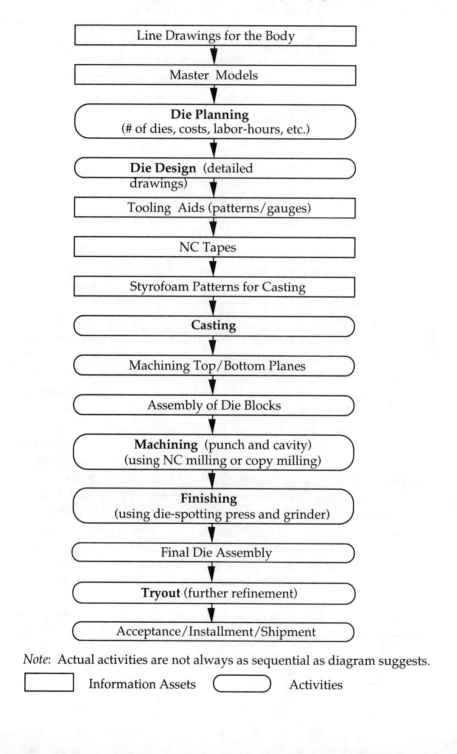

Line Drawings for the Body

Master Models

Die Planning
(# of dies, costs, labor-hours, etc.)

Die Design (detailed drawings)

Tooling Aids (patterns/gauges)

NC Tapes

Styrofoam Patterns for Casting

Casting

Machining Top/Bottom Planes

Assembly of Die Blocks

Machining (punch and cavity)
(using NC milling or copy milling)

Finishing
(using die-spotting press and grinder)

Final Die Assembly

Tryout (further refinement)

Acceptance/Installment/Shipment

Note: Actual activities are not always as sequential as diagram suggests.

☐ Information Assets   ⬭ Activities

Our study of timing and information flows in die development and body engineering combines statistical analysis and in-depth interviews. Because U.S. and Japanese projects exhibited particularly contrasting patterns (European projects were similar to U.S. projects), we focused our comparison on these two regions. Figures 8.11 and 8.12 summarize the pattern of engineering activities associated with

Figure 8.11 Timing Chart of Die Development: A Typical Japanese Case

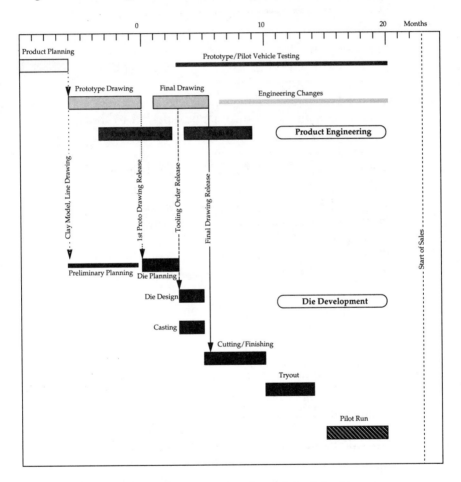

Source: Based on questionnaires (12 projects), interviews (several companies), and other data.

Notes: Assumes two runs of prototype fabrication.
Feedback information flows are omitted for graphic simplicity.
Time is measured from first prototype drawing release.

the development of a die set for a large and complex body panel (e.g., a quarter panel or door). The figures are simplified, and hypothetical time charts are constructed from data on engineering schedules, prototype lead time, die lead time, activity sequence, communication, and behavioral patterns.

Principal features of the typical Japanese process, illustrated in Figure 8.11, are summarized below.

1) The process overall is significantly faster in Japan than in the United States, partly because of manufacturing capabilities (e.g., shorter die manufacturing and prototype lead time, as discussed in Chapter 7) and partly because of significant overlapping between product engineering and die development.

2) As product engineers make progress, they release preliminary information on body design to die engineers, who incrementally step up the level of resource commitment.

3) Upon release of early information at the beginning of the body engineering stage—which includes clay models, line drawings, and digitized styling data—die engineers begin preliminary die planning.

4) Full-scale die planning gets under way when the first prototype drawing is released. Die planning includes process sequence, panel partition, number of shots per panel, and estimation of die cost and resource requirements.

5) The next milestone is a drawing release for tooling orders. This is separate from and earlier than the final engineering drawing release. Tooling order release normally triggers detailed die design and casting, the beginning of the serious commitment of resources to production. Some companies initiate die design even before completion of the first prototype.

6) Final release occurs before the last generation of engineering prototypes is complete. The die shop

is cutting dies and using milling machines at or even before final release. Die cutting is a significant point in terms of risk-taking and resource commitment; rework caused by subsequent body design changes becomes very expensive once a die is machined and finished.

7) Engineering changes continue after final release in response to prototype testing and pilot runs.

Let us now examine the contrasting features of the typical U.S. process, as illustrated in Figure 8.12.

Figure 8.12 Timing Chart of Die Development: A Typical U.S. Case

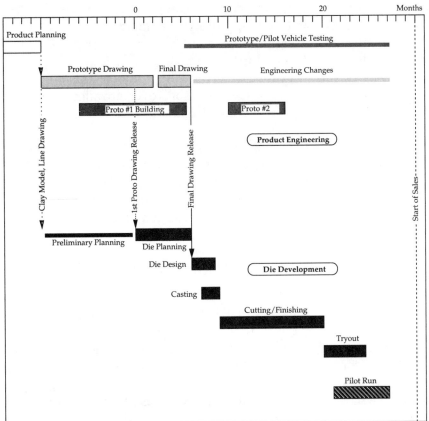

Source: Based on questionnaires (6 projects), interviews (3 companies), and other data.

Notes: Assumes two runs of prototype fabrication.
Feedback information flows are omitted for graphic simplicity.
Time is measured from first prototype drawing release.

1) The process overall takes significantly longer in the United States than in Japan.
2) Die planning begins with the first prototype drawing release, but few resource commitments are made at this time.
3) There is no formal release for tooling orders separate from final release.
4) Detailed die design begins only after final drawing release.
5) Consequently, die cutting, the critical point of resource commitment, occurs significantly later than final drawing release. Die design and die casting are less overlapped in the United States than in Japan, further delaying the start of cutting.
6) Longer lead times for prototype building and die manufacturing (discussed in Chapter 7) further lengthen die development time.
7) Because of the long cycle times in prototype and die manufacturing, die tryout spills over into pilot run, leading to overlapping at the end of the process.

The overlapping that occurs at the end of the process as practiced in the United States is not a plus for development performance. It is consistent with earlier evidence (cited in Chapter 7) that process engineering in U.S. and European projects may be too brief, leading to incomplete tooling at the pilot stage and engineering changes during ramp-up.

TWO APPROACHES TO DIE ENGINEERING: EARLY VERSUS WAIT

Figure 8.11 suggests that Japanese projects compress the die engineering cycle by quickly constructing prototypes and dies and by boldly overlapping product and process design and die construction. The sharp contrast between U.S. and Japanese patterns of overlapping is clearly in evidence in the timing of die design and cutting, major milestones of resource commitment. Japanese firms use an "early design, early cut" approach; U.S. practice is essentially "wait to design, wait to cut." That Japanese projects employ a "tooling release order" prior to final release reflects the willingness of Japanese firms to make an early start in die construction.

Because it entails making resource commitments while the body design is still subject to frequent changes, the Japanese early design, early cut approach entails significant risks of waste and duplication of resources. Even in Japanese firms, many engineering changes occur *after* final release of blueprints. At peak, hundreds of changes are ordered per month. The popular belief that Japanese firms freeze product designs early is a myth.

Behind the wait to design, wait to cut approach in U.S. projects is a desire to avoid expensive die rework and scrappage, which we would expect to be an inevitable consequence of the bold overlapping that characterizes Japanese projects. However, our study revealed a quite different reality. U.S. firms, despite their conservative approach to overlapping, were spending more on engineering changes than Japanese firms. U.S. car makers reported spending as much as 30–50 percent of original die cost on rework due to engineering changes, compared to a 10–20 percent margin allowed for engineering changes by Japanese producers.

Given these findings, effective management of overlapping is clearly much more than simply modifying the timing chart. Properly managed, the overlapping approach, even in the presence of numerous engineering changes, can simultaneously reduce lead time *and* lower the cost of engineering changes. This relies, as we have said throughout this section, on relationships and skills that facilitate intensive cross-stage communication.

A close look at the outstanding performers in die development confirms the importance of relationships and skills. As Figure 8.11 suggests, effective management of overlapped engineering problem solving results partly from early release of preliminary information from upstream and partly from downstream's efficient use of those cues to make a flying start. This process is not just a paper exercise; die engineers and tool makers act on the information they receive and make commitments before upstream work is officially complete.

A story of the development of a cast part illustrates the power and importance of close working relationships in this process. The story is true, though we have changed the names of participants. Faced with the need to get a die built and a prototype part produced for testing, Frank, a design engineer, realized that quick action was needed and bypassed formal channels; he picked up the phone and called Hans, a local tool maker. Could Hans break away for lunch and take a look at a design Frank was working on? He could and the lunch was set. Over the meal Frank showed Hans the design, and Hans made a few suggestions for changes that would make it easier to build a die and construct the part. Some of his calculations were on the back of a napkin. Hans left with the doctored design and returned a short time later (a fraction of the traditional cycle time for a die such as this) with the die built and the part produced.

This, of course, was not the first time Frank and Hans had worked together. Nor was their relationship one of arm's-length contracts and fine print. As we saw in the discussion of supplier relationships, reciprocal commitments, whether they be across firm boundaries or across departments, are an essential feature of integration. Integration here means direct, face-to-face working relationships between engineers in different departments and between die engineers and tool makers. In Japanese firms that exhibit excellent performance in die development, these people know each other and know how to work together.

But there is more to integration than good feelings and face-to-face discussion; there is also skill. Die shops in high-performing companies develop know-how and techniques for absorbing engineering changes at minimum cost by using cutting margins, build-up welding, and block replacement.* There is something of an art involved, for example, in leaving a slightly thicker cutting margin in an area of the die more likely to be affected by design changes, or in recognizing that the location of holes in a door panel change more frequently than the anticipated shape and therefore making the drawing die first and the pierce die last. In each of these situations, the key is to make subtle trade-offs between the cost and benefit of starting die making early.

Quick response to engineering changes is another important element of effective overlapping. Suppose a body engineer decides to change the design of a panel to strengthen body-shell rigidity. The high performers tend to move quickly. The body designer immediately instructs the die shop to stop cutting the die on the milling machine.

---

* When a die is made of blocks that are assembled into one piece, a change in die design may be absorbed by replacing one block.

Without paperwork or formal approval, the body designer goes directly to the die shop, discusses modifications with die engineers, checks production feasibility, and makes the agreed-upon changes on the spot. Unless the changes are major, decisions are made at the working level. Traditionally the die shop simply resumes work on the same die. Paperwork is completed after the change has been made and submitted to supervisors for approval. The cost incurred by the change is also negotiated after the fact. The attitude is "change now, negotiate later." The process resembles a line stop in a just-in-time assembly line: a problem is detected, the line stops immediately, a group of people run to the station, a decision is made and implemented on the spot, and the line resumes immediately.

In companies in which die development takes a long time and changes are expensive, the engineering change process is quite different. Consider the context in which changes occur. In extreme versions of the traditional U.S. system, tool and die makers are selected in a competitive bidding process that treats "outside" tool shops as providers of a commodity service. The relationship with the die maker is managed by the purchasing department, with communication taking place through intermediaries and drawings. The individuals who design the dies and body panels never interact directly with the people who make the dies.

From the tool maker's perspective, the relationship is with a bureaucracy. From the first moment a drawing arrives and work begins on a die, the tool maker knows that, at some time in the future, someone will call with the message to stop work on the die because a change is coming. Because they have no idea when that phone call will come, nor when the change will be approved and transmitted to the shop after work has stopped, tool makers create buffers by holding a backlog of orders and inventory of work in process.

This context creates the following scenario. When a tool maker receives notice of an impending design change, the tool shop stops working on the die, but decisions on actual die rework are made very slowly. Body engineers initiate the paperwork for engineering change requests, and those documents arrive on the desks of supervisors and chief engineers, where they may sit for days awaiting approval. Knowing that a decision in the upstream will be slow, die makers move the unfinished die to the end of the queue for the machine. Because of the need to buffer, the queue is long, adding additional waiting time when the engineering change order is finally received by the die shop.

Computerizing the engineering change process may potentially speed it up, but companies often simply embed the old process in the computer. Documents move faster from person to person, but the philosophy of multilevel approvals remains intact. Further, there is often little sense of urgency attached to engineering changes, even when the system has been computerized. As one purchasing manager involved in the process said when asked about time to implement a change, "Oh, the time is not a big problem. Everything is on the computer and moves real fast. It only takes a couple of weeks." But as comparison with the Japanese system makes clear, a couple of weeks here and there adds up. Prolonged information throughput time and lengthy queues of physical work-in-process reinforce one another to extend the engineering change process.

An in-depth look at die development generally reinforces the notion that intensive cross-functional communication is required to maximize the benefit of the overlapping approach and that working level skills and relationships are essential to such communication. Introducing overlapping without requisite changes in communication, organization, and management is more likely to reduce product quality, incur unintended schedule delays, and lower morale in the engineering organization than to improve performance.

IMPACT OF DIE DEVELOPMENT ON ENGINEERING LEAD TIME

In Chapter 7, we saw that the time to manufacture dies affects engineering lead time. Here we examine the relationship between overall die lead time and overall performance in the engineering process. Our statistical analysis (see the Appendix) suggests a significant and positive correlation between total die lead time (from prototype drawing release to tryout completion) and engineering lead time. We estimate that reducing die development lead time by one month reduces engineering lead time by about two-thirds of a month, a result consistent with our prediction that major die development is on the critical path of the engineering process.

Interestingly, shorter die lead time is *not* associated with reductions in lead time for either concept development or product planning (planning lead time is driven more by product complexity and the number of people and departments that must reach consensus about a potential design). Nevertheless, our evidence on die lead time is consistent with earlier evidence on overlapping and patterns of communication. Both in the microcosm and in our overall data, we have found integrated problem solving to be an important element of high-performance product development.

CONDITIONS FOR INTEGRATING PROBLEM SOLVING

In this chapter we have characterized integrated problem solving in engineering as a multifaceted process that combines stage overlapping and intensive cross-stage communication. We have developed a framework that treats as elements of integrated problem solving conditions for product-process integration such as simultaneous engineering, design for manufacturability, and cross-functional conflict resolution. We have argued that integrated problem solving can both speed up the engineering process and improve quality, and we have presented evidence both from our broader study and from the microcosm of die development that supports the notion that integrated problem solving is an important source of advantage in product development. Because they have faced for decades intensive competitive pressure for compressed model-change cycles and development lead time, Japanese producers have integrated their engineering cycles to a greater degree than Western producers.

Effective integration places heavy demands on the organization—in terms of communication, processes, skills, and relationships. The engineering process must link problem-solving cycles in time; patterns of communication must be "wide bandwidth" and intense; and cross-functional (and cross-firm) relationships must support early and frequent exchanges of preliminary constraints, ideas, and objectives. Because the speed and effectiveness with which problems are resolved matters, skill in using information and in operating in parallel is critical. Finally, conditions for effective integration are related to problem-solving capabilities, including the attitudes, systems, and structures that support close working relationships across traditional boundaries. We conclude this chapter by summarizing these requirements in the upstream, the downstream, and in their joint interaction.

PROBLEM SOLVING IN THE UPSTREAM

The challenge for problem solving in the upstream is to meet immediate performance objectives (e.g., getting the shape and structural rigidity of the body panel right) in a way that facilitates downstream work. We found three capabilities to be essential to this end: downstream-friendly solutions, error-free design, and quick engineering cycles.

Making upstream solutions "downstream-friendly." Effective integrated problem solving calls for the upstream group to ease the downstream workload. This entails taking downstream conditions into account up front, thereby reducing unnecessary engineering changes due to ignorance of downstream constraints and increasing the likelihood that upstream solutions will reflect downstream capabilities. Upstream engineers must develop basic knowledge about downstream constraints in order to be able to predict the consequences of their solutions. Techniques for promoting the early and continuing communication and transfer of knowledge and experience from previous projects—so essential for making upstream solutions downstream-friendly—include design for manufacturing, value engineering, failure-mode and effects analysis, and Taguchi Methods®.*

But there is more involved than making life simple for the downstream group. Ignorance of downstream constraints hampers integrated problem solving, but for product engineers to overadapt to manufacturing conditions by making excessive compromises in key features of design quality and performance can be equally harmful. Overemphasis on stamping feasibility, for example, might discourage adoption of distinctive styling. Similarly, overreliance on common parts to reduce manufacturing costs could compromise product integrity. Manufacturability must not dominate design decisions; rather, it must be carefully balanced with design quality issues in order to maximize total product quality. Thus product engineers must be capable of making subtle trade-offs between product performance, design and manufacturing quality, and cost.

Reducing meaningless changes. Engineering changes that can be avoided by early communication with downstream were mentioned above. There is another, more primitive source of unnecessary changes—

---

* For information on the principles of robust design developed by Taguchi, see Taguchi and Clausing (1990) and Ealey (1988).

careless mistakes by product engineers and technicians. These include errors of miscalculation, inconsistency between drawings and numbers, missing information, and violation of drafting rules. Internally generated errors are pure waste; effective design reviews, testing, and engineering discipline can dramatically reduce or eliminate them without any sacrifice of product cost and quality. Additionally, errors in detailed drawings may be detected earlier and more easily when engineers are cross-trained as drafters (as is done in Japan) than where there is a sharp distinction between the trades.

As it is neither possible nor desirable to eliminate engineering changes altogether, it is important to distinguish between meaningful and meaningless engineering changes. Meaningful changes improve the value of the product; eliminating them means losing opportunities for product improvement. The changes to eliminate are those caused by careless mistakes and lack of communication. *

Quick engineering cycles. Product-process disagreements are inevitable in the development of a complex product catering to demanding, sophisticated customers. A fast upstream engineering cycle contributes to integrated problem solving partly by making the upstream more responsive to downstream problems. Faster design-build-test cycles in the upstream facilitate short feedback loops and quick mutual adjustment between upstream and downstream groups. To the extent that preliminary upstream results are released earlier and more frequently, downstream may be motivated to make an earlier start.

Primacy of time is a central theme in engineering groups characterized by fast cycles. Getting things done quickly becomes a driver in the organization, even at early stages in the program. Most product development organizations feel time pressures at some stage or other in the course of development. In slow engineering groups, getting a preliminary design done in two weeks rather than four is not a big issue. In a fast organization, those two weeks are very important. As we saw in our discussion of prototype lead time, fast throughput capability—whether in building a prototype, running a test, or troubleshooting a

---

*   Such changes account for a surprisingly large fraction of the total number of engineering changes. Soderberg (1989) reports that two-thirds of the changes made in the U.S. auto and auto parts industries would have been "avoidable" with better communication and discipline.

problem—depends on manufacturing capabilities and on systems and attitudes geared to moving quickly.

PROBLEM SOLVING IN THE DOWNSTREAM

In the downstream group, the challenge is to get a flying start on development before getting complete information and without creating so many constraints that the car loses its appeal. Ability to forecast, to manage risk, and to adapt to the inevitable engineering changes is critical to success.

Forecasting upstream results. Integrated problem solving downstream means starting the problem-solving cycle before the problem is well defined. To cope with a goal (i.e., product design) that fluctuates while they are trying to achieve it, the process people must possess the ability to forecast what the upstream group is likely to do.

First, the downstream group must develop skill in finding and using clues about the upstream work. These clues, when combined with knowledge about previous patterns of upstream behavior, become the basis for downstream action. Close, regular communication and cross-participation between upstream and downstream is an important basis for developing such skills. In die development, for example, forecasting the magnitude of possible engineering changes for a given area of each die at each stage is key to deciding when to start die design, when to start machining, and so on. Intimate knowledge about past patterns of interactions between body and die engineers allows die designers to extrapolate with reasonable accuracy the final shape of a given body panel based on incomplete preliminary information.

Making time-risk trade-offs. Making a flying start based on a forecast of the final form of an upstream solution always entails risk. Downstream engineers must know how to make trade-offs between the risk of a change and the benefit of an early start. Moreover, they need to be skilled in managing the trade-off so that the early start is made in a way that reduces risk. Leaving cutting margins in sensitive locations based on assessment of the magnitude of potential body-design changes was mentioned earlier. A significant amount of know-how is involved in making such knife-edge trade-offs. Bold overlapping by downstream must be accompanied by deliberate and detailed calculation.

Quick adjustment to unexpected changes. Although forecasts of upstream behavior are important, one cannot depend on them fully; unexpected changes are almost inevitable. The downstream group thus needs to be flexible and skilled at quick diagnosis and quick remedy. When a surprise body-design change is introduced, die designers must respond to it without delay, modifying corresponding die designs and dies. Capability for short-cycle manufacturing of tools and dies, discussed in Chapter 7, is of particular importance. Short setups, short queues, reduction of throughput time, and streamlining of process flows all contribute to reducing downstream response time to a given upstream change. Quick decision making at the process engineering working level is critical.

There is also the matter of raw engineering talent. Getting tests run quickly, tools built fast, and decisions made at the working level requires particular skills, but being able to size up a situation quickly, identify a solution, and designate the appropriate test is often a matter of pure competence. Downstream organizations that are fast have many good engineers. Downstream (and upstream) groups that are slow have some very good engineers and many others that have grown accustomed to following routine procedures and looking up specifications in handbooks. Given enough time, these groups may arrive at a solution, but in integrated problem solving that time is not available.

ATTITUDES ABOUT UPSTREAM-DOWNSTREAM INTEGRATION

The last, but not least, important facilitator of cross-functional integration is attitude of both upstream and downstream personnel. Our field studies suggest that, because attitudes are pervasive and difficult to change, this informal aspect of the engineering organization might be an important source of long-term advantage for integrated problem solving.

At least three sets of attitudes are relevant in an engineering group: member attitudes about their own actions, member attitudes toward one another, and member attitudes about group goals. Integrated problem solving calls for people to be oriented to early action. People in the upstream must be disposed to release preliminary information as it becomes available. A perfectionist mentality, a dominant mindset among engineers, is not in accord with the spirit of integrated problem solving. People downstream must be willing to take risks based on their best forecast of the future. They must be comfortable in an ambiguous environment. A wait-and-see attitude, though it may minimize risk from change, is a cultural obstacle to the introduction of integrated problem solving.

A sense of mutual trust and joint responsibility is also essential to integrated problem solving. Product engineers, having worked to reduce unnecessary changes, must trust the process group's willingness and ability to cope with changes that do emerge in the course of development. Unless process engineers trust product engineers to help them overcome manufacturing difficulties, the upstream people will be unlikely to release information early.

Mutual trust hinges on mutual commitment to one another's success. Without such commitment, engineers are less likely to expose themselves to the personal risk inherent in integrated problem solving—and integrated problem solving does carry personal risk. It requires engineers, both upstream and downstream, to let colleagues in another department see much more of what really goes on. It exposes their weaknesses and their mistakes and the general limits of their ability much more than does the sequential, batch mode of operation. Without trust and commitment, the exposure inherent in early involvement and preliminary communication could encourage finger pointing and rejection of one another's proposals.

Finally, effective integration is built on shared responsibility for the results of upstream-downstream collaboration. The objective of body engineers taking an integrated problem-solving approach to the production of a body panel and its die set cannot simply be on-time delivery of a well-executed set of drawings to the die engineers. It cannot even be a body-panel design that meets styling, safety, and cost objectives. It must be high-quality, low-cost body panels that fit and join well with other panels coming off the end of the stamping line at commercial volume levels—panels that satisfy customer expectations for styling, surface finish, cost, and structural integrity, and that are available for the targeted market introduction.

This complex objective must be shared by the die engineers. But because neither group has complete control over all elements of the design and process, they must be *jointly* responsible for their *joint* output. Engineers who adopt an attitude of joint responsibility can work together constructively to resolve product-process conflicts and to strike an effective balance between time to market and design quality and manufacturability.

EFFECTIVE INTEGRATION: COMBINING THE HARD AND THE SOFT

Attitudes have a powerful effect on integration, but they are only part of the story. Effective integration requires the development of skills in short-cycle problem solving, including methods for framing problems, forecasting abilities, and tools for analysis and communication. It requires a common language and a common methodology. In effect, it means combining hard, analytical capabilities with the appropriate soft, intuitive attitudes and philosophies.

This is no mean feat. Few of the organizations we studied have successfully combined these elements. To do so requires senior managers with a strong sense of direction and a good sense of balance. Most firms go overboard in one direction; their time and energies are spent either implementing new tools or programs with insufficient attention to the soft side, or they spend their time in "off-site" meetings learning to communicate, with no thought for the necessary tools and skills. As we have emphasized throughout this book, balance is essential.

The very difficulty of achieving such balance makes integrated problem solving a source of competitive advantage. This advantage, rooted as it is in the accumulation of skill and capability and in the painstaking development of attitudes and practices, is difficult to copy quickly. Firms that successfully invest in integrated problem solving will have a significant edge. Firms that do not will find themselves a bit too slow, a bit less responsive, a bit less successful. Integrated problem solving will be a hallmark of the firms that prosper in the new industrial competition.

NOTES

1. For a generic model of problem solving, see, for example, Simon (1969).
2. See Van de Ven and Drazin (1985) and Venkatraman (1987) for the notion of an ideal profile index.
3. See Clark and Fujimoto (1987) for further discussion.

CHAPTER 9

LEADERSHIP AND ORGANIZATION: THE HEAVYWEIGHT PRODUCT MANAGER

In the early part of this century, when cars were designed and developed by a handful of engineers working under the direction of a Henry Ford, Gottlieb Daimler, or Kiichiro Toyoda, organization of the development effort was not a burning issue. Engineers possessed general skills and broad responsibility; communication was close and face-to-face; and the master architect personally guided, directed, and implemented the product concept. What mattered were skill, the group's chemistry, and the master's guidance. But it was not too many years before cars became more complex, and as they did the issue of organization became far more critical.

As problems became too complex for a few people to solve, and as growing competition demanded greater depth of expertise, the number of people involved in product development increased significantly. Ultimately automobile companies faced the classic organizational dilemma: how to apply specialized expertise and yet achieve an integrated effort. The form of the issue has changed since the 1920s, but its importance has not. How a firm organizes development and the nature of the leadership it creates influences the number of people involved, the speed of problem solving, and the quality of the solutions that emerge.

In this chapter we look closely at leadership and organization in development and their impact on performance. Leadership and organization are more than formal authority or a reflection of the official organization chart. As we have seen in Chapters 5 and 8, the attitudes, skills, and relationships that define the informal organization are critical to the character and performance of the development process. Moreover, leadership in product development is not only a matter of position and authority; it involves the practices and behaviors that exert influence over designers, engineers, marketers, and people on the shop floor and in the field.

Our look at leadership and organization will encompass informal as well as formal dimensions. Specifically we focus on those dimensions that separate the outstanding companies from the average. Because all of the companies in our sample develop automobiles, there is much about their organizations that is similar. However, the few aspects that are different seem to matter most. What we present, therefore, is not a complete analysis of the way product development is organized, but rather a probing look at three dimensions of development that are quite different across companies—the degree of specialization and of external and internal integration (see Table 9.1).[1] Degree of specialization deals with the classic issue of expertise. We divide degree of integration into two parts: internal integration, which is concerned with effective coordination within the project team, and external integration, which is concerned with matching the product to customer expectations.*

We begin by presenting a framework that defines these three dimensions of organization and links them to the information processing framework we employed in our research. We then describe four patterns of development leadership and organization that we have observed in the auto industry. These patterns include different approaches to specialization and integration in both the formal structure

Table 9.1 Three Dimensions of Product Development Organization

Organizational Dimensions	Expected Functions
Specialization	- accumulate and preserve technological expertise at the level of individual components and activities - execute individual tasks with speed and efficiency
Internal Integration	- achieve high internal integrity of total product - achieve fast product development through better task coordination
External Integration	- achieve high external integrity of total product - match product concept, product design, and customer expectations

* Because it is related to the internal consistency of the product, the integration of parts suppliers, discussed in Chapter 6, is regarded as an element of *internal* integration.

and in the informal organization and behavior of the people who manage the effort. In evaluating the impact of different organizational patterns on development performance, we find that all three dimensions—specialization and internal and external integration—affect lead time and productivity, and that external integration has a particularly strong connection to total product quality. We conclude the chapter with a brief look at changes in leadership and organization in the 1980s—and at the implications these changes hold for future performance.

PATTERNS OF ORGANIZATION

The development of a new automobile involves thousands of functional components, hundreds of complex subsystems, and several major systems. The product must achieve a level of performance that even ten years ago seemed remote. Moreover, even higher levels of performance must be regularly achieved faster and with fewer resources than previously. These challenges are not exclusive to the auto industry; competitive pressure is driving the search for better design and making organization and reorganization of product development a recurring theme in many industries.

Efforts to organize development effectively are rooted in a search for solutions to two fundamental problems. The first is how to get a product's parts and subsystems designed, built, and tested so that each element achieves a high level of functionality. In a computer, for example, this means that the processor should process rapidly, the software execute flawlessly, the hard disk read and write with speed and accuracy, the monitor display precisely, the memory remember, and the keyboard be clear and friendly. Because functionality at the component level is driven by expertise and depth of understanding, achieving it requires some degree of specialization.

From an organizational perspective, degree of specialization determines how narrowly the organization is divided into departments and other subunits, extending all the way down to the individual. Engineers, for example, may be specialized by component or subsystem, by step in the problem-solving cycle (e.g., functional design, drafting, prototyping, and testing), or by some combination thereof. A very narrow specialist might have responsibility for initial design of a small part, such as a left rear tail light. This assignment might be broadened without any change in component responsibility to include responsibility for preparing detailed drawings, supervising the building of prototypes, and conducting tests. Alternatively, the assignment might be broadened to include all external vehicle lights, but with responsibility only for their design.

The second problem facing the development organization is how to achieve product integrity. Returning to the example of the computer, this means that the software not only executes, but is well matched to the hardware and has a look and feel that fits the concept and image the product is trying to convey. Product integrity thus has an internal dimension (i.e., the parts fit and work well together) and an external dimension (i.e., the experience the product creates is consistent with customer expectations). To create a product with integrity requires a development process with integrity—activities must mesh in time and purpose.

The choices firms make about specialization and integration in product development reflect the nature of the technology, the character of the markets they serve, and the intensity of competition.[2] Consider a product built around component technologies that are technically demanding and changing rapidly. These characteristics call for a high degree of expertise, which implies specialization; and specialization, as we have learned, may make communication and coordination across functional groups more difficult and denigrate the quality of the total system.

To the extent that product performance is more than the sum of component performance or technical specifications, firms need to worry about integrity and thus about integration. The nature of that integration and the importance it plays in development will depend on the competitive environment. When markets are stable, product life cycles are long, and customers are focused on advanced component performance, a firm may emphasize functionality and commit the time and resources needed to achieve product integrity through functional organization (e.g., department heads and chief engineers hammer out problems), procedures and traditions that link functional groups, and product testing and rework. In a less stable environment characterized by relatively short life cycles, intense competition, and customers focused on the product as a system, the same firm may pursue integration through more formal and explicit mechanisms such as coordination committees, formal liaison roles for each function, project managers, matrix structures, and cross-functional teams.

In practice, these mechanisms for achieving product integrity tend to focus on *internal* integration. In the literature on organizations and in the experience of a wide range of companies, we have found coordination to be the primary objective of most project managers, committees, and liaison groups. Most are trying to get the functional groups to work together better. *External* integration has received much less explicit attention in the design of integration mechanisms. Achieving external integration—i.e., matching the product and the customer—has either been implicit in the objectives of traditional integration activities or has been made the focus of a functional group such as product planning or product testing.

If customer expectations are relatively clear and widely known, or if they are defined by component functions, external integrity may be achieved as a byproduct of achieving functionality and internal integrity. But in environments such as the automobile industry of the 1980s—in which customer expectations are changing and ambiguous, firms have achieved functional parity, and competition has shifted to the "total product experience"—external integrity is likely to be a critical dimension of competition and may need to be made explicit. To understand what is involved in organizing for external integrity, it is helpful to attend more closely to external integration.

In terms of the information processing framework developed in Chapter 2, external integration aims at achieving a match between development and consumption. If, as we believe, product development is a simulation of the consumption process, then product competitiveness depends on how well the development process simulates and internalizes that process. The objective must be to anticipate to the greatest extent possible the process of consumption as it eventually plays out in the market. External integration is thus a conscious organizational effort to enhance the external integrity of the development process by matching the philosophy and details of product design to the expectations of target customers. This entails developing a distinctive product concept that matches future customers' expectations, user environments, and lifestyles, and infusing that product concept into basic and detailed product designs and ultimately into the product.[3] To accomplish this, the product concept must be communicated to the entire engineering and manufacturing organization at each step of the product development process.

External integration is more than being "close to customers," "market-oriented," or "customer-driven." Close communication with customers must be augmented by imaginative concept creators capable of translating subtle clues of latent customer needs into visions of future products and markets. To the extent that they suppress market and product imagination, strong ties with customers and dealers (as through marketing surveys or product clinics) may even harm product competitiveness.[4] Nor is passive reaction to the market sufficient. External integration implies mutual adaptation between product and market (customer needs may influence product designs, and product attributes may influence customer needs) and mutual learning between producers and customers. In a sense customers become another department in the organization whose concerns and interests need to be integrated.

We have identified several approaches to organizing for external integration. A firm may create an explicit role for an "external integrator" and deploy people assigned to that role in each functional unit (e.g., testers in engineering or product planners in marketing). Alternatively, a firm might assign all of its external integrators to a single, specialized unit, which may be organized by product or be product-independent. Similarly, the functions of concept creation and concept realization might be assigned to different groups or consolidated under one leader. The influence, power, and strength of the external integrator, and thus the level of integration that can be achieved, vary with the different schemes.

How a firm chooses to organize for external integrity is likely to depend on the character of the markets it serves, how difficult such integrity is to achieve, and how important it is to competition. When markets are stable and customer needs well defined and focused on a set of measurable performance characteristics, external integration may be a less pressing issue in the organization of development. When customer needs are inarticulate and holistic, emphasizing total product integrity, external integration is essential because the development project requires leadership for maintaining coherence of the product concept and driving intensive communication and dissemination of equivocal customer information.

How a firm approaches external integration will also be affected by the relative importance and difficulty of achieving functionality and internal integrity. These three dimensions of organization are closely related to one another. A choice in one dimension sets up requirements and constraints in the other two. Outstanding performance is not only (and possibly not even primarily) a matter of high achievement in a particular dimension; it depends critically on the mix and balance among specialization and processes for internal and external integration. To understand how organization and leadership affect development performance in the world auto industry, we need to look closely at the overall pattern—the combination of structure and process that gives a particular organizational form its distinctive character.

FOUR MODES OF INTEGRATION

The four modes of organizing product development depicted in Figure 9.1 are ideal types meant to capture the essential features of the many different kinds of organizations we have seen in our study. Though they differ to some extent in degree of specialization, the major differences lie in the levels of internal and external integration.

In the diagram the rectangular boxes represent functional subunits, and the horizontal relations represent certain kinds of project coordination. Each functional subunit (e.g., departments in engineering, marketing, and manufacturing) is supervised by a functional manager (FM). Working engineers (or other personnel) engaged in a particular project are shown as meshed circles in the functional units. Liaison persons (L) represent these functional units. A product manager (PM) for a particular project coordinates the working engineers directly or through liaisons and is normally supported by several assistants. The dotted ovals represent the areas in which the product manager exercises strong influence. The area of influence may be limited to engineering or extend to production, marketing, and even to the market itself (through external integration). Finally, an intersection between the market and the product manager's zone of influence indicates that product managers are also in charge of concept creation (external integration) and maintain direct contact with customers.

In the traditional *functional* structure, depicted in the upper left quadrant of Figure 9.1, development is organized by functional discipline, and engineers are relatively specialized. No individual has overall responsibility for the total product. Senior functional managers (e.g., the head of body engineering) are responsible for allocating resources and the performance of their function. Coordination occurs through rules and procedures, detailed specifications, shared traditions among engineers, occasional direct contacts, and meetings.

In the *lightweight product manager* system, depicted in the upper right quadrant, the basic organization remains functional, and the level of specialization is comparable to that found in the functional mode.

Figure 9.1 Four Modes of Development Organization

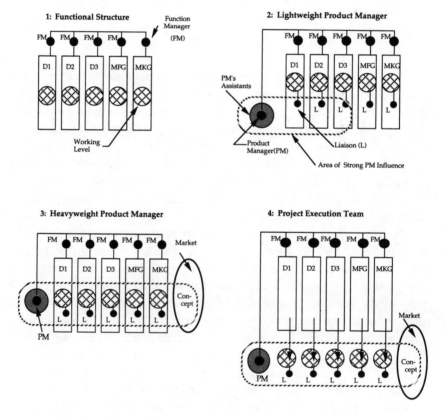

Source: Adapted from Fujimoto (1989, Chapter 8). See also Hayes, Wheelwright, and Clark (1988, Chapter 11).

Note: D1, D2, and D3 stand for functional units in development; MFG stands for manufacturing; MKG denotes marketing.

What is different is the addition of a product manager, who coordinates development activities through liaison representatives from each function. Product managers in this mode of organization are lightweights in several respects. They have no direct access to working-level people and, compared to functional managers, have less status or power in the organization. They have little influence outside of product engineering and only limited influence within it, and they have neither direct market contact nor concept responsibility. Their main purpose is to coordinate: to collect information on the status of work, to help the functional groups solve conflicts, and to facilitate achievement of overall project objectives.

The *heavyweight product manager* structure, depicted in the lower left quadrant, stands in sharp contrast to the lightweight system. Although the organization is still largely functional, there is now a product manager with broader responsibility and clout. Heavyweight product managers are usually senior in the organization, often at the same or higher rank as the heads of the functional organizations. Some of their work occurs through liaison representatives, but the liaison personnel themselves are "heavier" than in the lightweight system. In addition to working directly with the project manager, liaison people serve as local project leaders within their functional groups. The project managers, when necessary, have direct access to the working-level engineers on the project, and, though they may lack formal authority, they exercise strong direct and indirect influence across all functions and activities in the project. They are responsible not only for internal coordination, but also for product planning and concept development. The heavyweight project manager effectively functions as a general manager of the product.

Although the heavyweight system works within a functional organization, the strong product focus of the product manager may extend into the functional groups, which may organize within the function around product types. Body engineers, for example, may be grouped by type of body (e.g., large cars, small cars, and utility vehicles). Engineers still work within functional areas and may work on more than one project at a time, but they have a stronger product orientation than engineers in the purely functional or lightweight systems.

The *project execution team* structure, shown in the lower right quadrant of Figure 9.1, takes product orientation quite a bit further.

In the team setup, a heavyweight project manager works with a team of people who devote all their time to the project. This is not the same thing as a team of liaison people; people on the execution team do the work on the project. They leave their functional organization and report directly to the product manager. These individuals are not nearly as specialized as those in the functional structure, and they assume broader responsibilities in their functional tasks and as members of the team. Functional managers retain responsibility for personnel development, with local project leaders managing detailed work within functional groups. The product manager's influence on project issues may be greater in cases where people work on only one project at a time.

These idealized modes of organization range over a spectrum of approaches to internal and external integration. At one end, we have the purely functional organization with a relatively low level of integration; toward the other, we see the heavyweight product manager and project execution team, with quite high levels of integration both internally and externally.

SKILLS AND BEHAVIORS OF PRODUCT MANAGERS

What stands out in achieving these approaches to integration are sharp differences in the strength of leadership. The weight of the product manager is more a question of stature and influence than of rank or title. (One can be a lightweight with modest amounts of either.) A heavyweight product manager possesses both position and seniority, along with specific skills and experience developed while working in an organizational context that includes a structure and systems to support a strong product focus, multifunctional teams of broadly skilled people, and extensive cross-functional communication and influence. It may be difficult to tell the heavyweight from the lightweight manager by looking at an organization chart—both show up as product managers—but the two are different species at the behavioral level.

We compiled the following list of characteristics observed in outstanding heavyweight product managers in top-performing companies in the auto industry.

- Coordination responsibility in wide areas, including production and sales as well as engineering

- Coordination responsibility for the entire project period from concept to market
- Responsibility for concept creation and championing as well as cross-functional coordination
- Responsibility for specification, cost target, layout, and major component choices
- Responsibility for ensuring that the product concept is accurately translated into technical details of the vehicle
- Frequent and direct communication with designers and engineers at the working level as well as through liaisons
- Maintain direct contact with customers (PM's office conducts market research independently of marketing group)
- Possess multilingual and multidisciplined abilities in order to communicate effectively with marketers, designers, engineers, testers, plant managers, controllers, and so forth
- Role and talents in managing conflict surpass those of neutral referees or passive conflict managers; they may initiate conflicts to prevent product designs or plans from deviating from the original product concept
- Possess market imagination and the ability to forecast future customer expectations based on ambiguous and equivocal clues in the present market
- Circulate among project people and strongly advocate the product concept rather than do paperwork and conduct formal meetings
- Mostly engineers by training, they possess broad (if not deep) knowledge of total vehicle engineering and process engineering

Product managers in companies that achieve high product integrity and market success combine two roles: as internal integrators they achieve effective cross-functional coordination, and as concept champions they integrate customer insight and expectations into the details of development.

CRITERIA FOR SUCCESS IN PRODUCT MANAGEMENT

The preceding list suggests that heavyweight product managers behave differently from traditional, lightweight managers. This difference is more than a matter of doing what lightweights do but with more influence. It relies on specific approaches to an essential set of activities, as illustrated in the following examples.

Direct market contact. As external integrators, heavyweight product managers cultivate direct and continuous contact with customers. They supplement the "cooked" market information they receive from the marketing group with "raw" market information gathered directly from existing and prospective customers. Maintaining direct links between the market and the concept creation process is particularly important for today's volume producers; analysis of historical market data simply does not produce powerful product concepts. In the role of concept creator, product managers need imagination and active, holistic ways of thinking; first-hand involvement with consumers stimulates imagination more effectively than abstract market data.

That effective Japanese product managers place considerable emphasis on first-hand market data is evident in the following interview comments.

> Product managers visit dealers, go abroad, go to auto shows, and walk around trendy districts in Tokyo. Although systematic market data come from marketing, we have to confirm them by ourselves. Seeing is believing.

> We recently established a formal budget for dispatching the staff of the Product Manager Office directly to the customers.

> There is a market study team inside the Product Manager Office, which monitors the market with its own "antenna."

> Better product managers walk around the markets, get first-hand information, generate product ideas from it, and sell the ideas to marketing and engineering people.

> Market surveys, dealer feedback, and user feedback are conducted and gathered not only by marketing, but also by product managers. Marketing is short-term-oriented, while product managers are long-term-oriented.

Direct market access clearly involves more than visits to dealers and existing users; it involves assessing and projecting the wants of prospective customers. One way to do this is to take a walk in the customer's natural habitat. A concept creator might go outside to watch people walking by, observe their style, and listen to their conversation. He or she might talk with fashion designers, hair stylists, and so forth. Besides the sidewalk, places ideally suited to observation are department stores, shopping center parking lots, art museums, discotheques, and fashion districts. The manner of conducting these informal surveys and choice of location tend to be peculiar to individual concept creators.

Multilingual translator. Effective product managers must be "multilingual"; they must be fluent in the languages of customers, marketers, engineers, and designers. A heavyweight product manager who has internalized an equivocal product concept must translate it into unequivocal expressions in each of the downstream languages in order for all members of the team to understand it. A liaison from chassis engineering explains.

> A target like "sporty cars which can compete effectively in Europe" was too abstract and ambiguous for us engineers, but our product manager could always translate it for us into clear and specific targets, such as "maximum speed 250 km/h," "drag coefficient under 0.3," and so on.

Heavyweight product managers must also be able to translate the other way. During planning and prototype development, for example, they must be able to assess and communicate what engineering choices will mean for marketing and eventual customer experience. Because the translation from the language of the customer to the language of the engineer is often considered more difficult, companies with heavyweight systems tend to develop product managers whose "mother tongue" is engineering.

Direct contact with engineers. In the role of creating the product and maintaining the conceptual and technical integrity of product designs, the product manager can be likened to the conductor of an orchestra who creates coherent music with a distinctive concept.[5] As an engineering coordinator, the product manager is responsible for assuring consistency of product design and conformance to concepts and plans. Although they do not normally have formal authority over detailed designs of specific parts, product managers can influence the important details of product design through cross-functional coordination and conflict resolution. Because information on critical aspects of design flows naturally to them through daily contacts with the functional engineering departments, product managers are in the best position to review both total vehicle integrity *and* important component details. The relationship between product managers and working-level design engineers is thus a focal point of concept-design integrity.

In one Japanese company that employs the heavyweight system, it is common to see product managers talking directly with working design engineers about design details. These visits are not courtesy calls or morale-building exercises; the product manager engages the bench-level designer on the substance of the detailed design. This is not done for every detail, of course. Usually only parts and components for which the choices are particularly difficult or central to the concept are targeted for product manager intervention. Although this is clearly an internal intervention from the functional manager's point of view, it is informally accepted as a long-standing tradition. Only major design issues go up to the design section-head level or, eventually, to the head of the department.

Product managers in motion. One of the best litmus tests of the effectiveness of a product manager is the fraction of work time spent in formal meetings or doing paperwork at a desk. Lightweight product managers are largely coordinators who function much like high-level clerks. They spend a good deal of time each day reading memos, writing reports, and going to meetings. The comments of several heavyweight product managers in Japanese companies suggest the emphasis they place on getting out to see engineers, plant people, dealers, and customers.[6]

> I seldom stay around my desk. There are so many places I
> have to visit personally. Since I am asking other engineers to
> do favors for me, I shouldn't ask them to come to me; I
> should go talk to them. This job cannot be done without
> wearing out my shoes.

> I hold a brief meeting with some five assistants in the morn-
> ing on the project status. After that, I leave my desk mostly.
> It is not rare for me to go over to product engineering and
> chat with the young people there.

> I am walking around functional units for coordination and
> liaison during the daytime, asking questions, and cheering
> people on. I come back to my desk only in the evening.

At one Japanese company we visited, product managers' offices
were usually empty during the day. The product managers and their
assistants were almost always out, leaving piles of documents and
drawings on their desks.

The assumption behind "product managers in motion" is that
product concepts and product plans cannot be communicated by
written documents alone. Concept documents are incomplete information; face-to-face communication is an essential supplement. Another assumption is that product concepts tend to decay quickly in the
minds of engineers and thus need continual refreshment or reinforce-
ment. The view of concepts as inarticulate and perishable information
is expressed in the following observations by a former product manager and an assistant product manager, respectively.

> We product managers have authority to submit product
> planning documents to functional departments. However, it
> is wrong to assume that functional people will automatically
> do what we want just because we issue documents and attach
> clear explanations to them. The functional people may just
> let them sit on the desk. We have to persuade them, convince
> them, and make them think, "OK, let's try this," or "This
> looks good." Otherwise, nothing happens in engineering out
> of the documents.

There are subtle nuances, such as "taste" or "character" of the cars, to be built into designs by fine tuning that cannot be expressed completely in planning documents. Therefore, we have to interact with the engineers in order to communicate our intention accurately.

The heavyweight product manager is essentially a traveling preacher whose bible is the formal concept and planning documents. The heavyweight approach assumes that much of the content of this bible is inaccessible without supplementary "preaching."

Product manager as concept infuser. Attitudes and behaviors toward engineering conflicts are very much a function of a product manager's philosophy. The notion of "product manager as coordinator" treats the product manager simply as a facilitator, a neutral third party who helps engineers solve cross-functional conflicts. This is a role often played by the lightweight product managers frequently found in U.S. and European companies. It is also characteristic for product managers in U.S. companies to react to rather than anticipate conflicts. Because it views product managers as referees, the U.S. system tends to emphasize interpersonal skills.

A quite different notion is that of "product manager as concept guardian." Product managers in this role do more than coordinate and referee; they preserve the product concept from deterioration and infuse it into the product design throughout the engineering process. Product managers of this sort tend to view engineering conflicts as yet another opportunity to communicate product concepts to the design engineers. They may create conflicts, if that is necessary to protect or promote the product concept. This role is amplified by several product managers who play it in Japanese firms.

We tend to focus on constraints from inside the company and end up making political compromise on the products. However, the first priority should be given to what is best for the customers. Improvement of internal political situations should be considered only after that.

A car cannot become what it is meant to be unless we establish up front a philosophy of what kind of car we want. When we explain the concept to others, disagreement may come out. We then check whether we are correct, revise the

> proposal, and make compromises if necessary. The key point, however, is to show them that we made a lot of compromise on the product, while, in fact, never making any compromise on its essential parts.

> Product managers should not be mere coordinators. They should have their own philosophy and faith.

> We listen to process engineers. We listen to plant managers. But we make final decisions. Above all, we cannot make any compromise on the concept. Since the concept is the soul of the vehicle, we cannot sell it out.

For these product managers, concept clearly takes priority over coordination; they tend to regard coordination and conflict resolution as opportunities to infuse concepts into product designs. Concept and coordination are thus inseparable in their mission. As one former heavyweight described it, "Product managers are like conductors. The orchestra can create so-so music even without a baton. It is very difficult, however, to turn such music into a really good piece."

Sharing the concept with testers. Heavyweight product managers and test engineers play pivotal roles in external integration. Because both represent future customers in the development process, a shared understanding of concept and customer expectations is critical to the integrity of the product. Consequently, product managers often test-drive cars and share their experiences with test engineers. Many are capable of evaluating vehicle functions on the test track and may show up at the proving ground almost daily during critical times. A liaison in charge of chassis engineering explains how the notion of shared responsibility is realized in one Japanese company.

> Suspension fine tuning of this model is done by the concept team. Although a handling group and a ride group of the testing department are also involved, the final tuning after a certain basic level is attained is made by the whole concept team through discussions on product positioning.

Because engineering coordination naturally creates opportunities for communicating concepts to test engineers, consolidating the roles of concept creator and engineering coordinator in a heavyweight product manager enhances concept-test integrity. A product manager explains.

> When a disagreement occurs among test engineers on, say, suspension tuning, I myself would go to the proving ground as often as possible because it is a great opportunity for me to talk about my concepts to the young test engineers, with whom I do not have day-to-day contact.

To foster the close contact and mutual trust between test engineers and concept creators necessary for this process to work, one company dubbed the so-called "test planner" in charge of the product the "shadow product manager," acknowledging this person as a close partner of the product manager. The manager of a testing department captured the key issue in the following observation.

> A car is like a work of art. It boils down to human sensibility rather than theoretical reasoning. Thus the degree and quality of communication between product managers and test engineers are the keys to project success.

RECRUITING AND TRAINING PRODUCT MANAGERS

As many project participants admit, talent for effective heavyweight product management is hard to find. But, as some pioneering producers have demonstrated, it is not impossible. Product managers tend to be engineers by training. In the typical Japanese case, product managers and assistants come from a product engineering group, most often from body or chassis engineering. Engine and other component engineering and test engineering were less likely sources, and product managers from styling, marketing, and process engineering were rare.

In Japanese companies, the product manager's career track resembles an apprenticeship. The product manager's office scouts a pool of young product engineers in the engineering departments for assistants, who then work for a particular product manager. As with an apprentice, emphasis is on on-the-job training. Manager-assistant relationships tend to be long term (e.g., lasting over one generation of new model development). Assistants are typically promoted to vice product manager (e.g., section head level) and then to product manager within the same circle (i.e., in charge of the same model).*

Our interview results also suggest a relationship between personality and product type. One of the Japanese producers we studied clearly emphasized matching the character of the vehicle with the personality of the manager. For example, "fighter-type" managers tended to be assigned to sporty models that relied on distinctiveness of concept, while "gentleman-type" managers worked on family sedans for which the balancing of conflicting requirements was more crucial. Other companies emphasized the matching of a manager's technical skills and the critical performance dimensions of the product. One Japanese company, for example, assigned to a luxury coupe, for which styling was critical, a product manager who had come from styling; to a luxury sedan, for which noise reduction was more important, it assigned a manager from engine engineering. Still other Japanese companies matched product managers with target customers on the basis of age and family background, for example. Customer-manager matching was particularly appropriate when product managers were also in charge of concept creation.

PATTERNS OF ORGANIZATION AND LEADERSHIP: EMPIRICAL EVIDENCE

We found firms in the auto industry to be arrayed across the full spectrum of organization—from purely functional structures to integrated, multifunctional teams. To capture the range of differences in the sample and to gauge the impact of organization and leadership on performance, we developed a set of measures of specialization and of internal and external integration.[7] We consider these dimensions individually at first and then jointly as a way of locating organizations along the spectrum from the functional to the heavyweight system.

---

* A questionnaire given to 15 product managers in the current study revealed that average duration of product managers' assignments to a given model was about 4.5 years: 4 years in Japan (7 samples); 4 years in the United States (4 samples); and 6 years in Europe (4 samples). Duration tended to be longer with early adopters of the product manager system.

SPECIALIZATION AND INTERNAL AND EXTERNAL INTEGRATION

Our measure of specialization is the number of long-term participants in the project. The degree of specialization at the departmental level, as noted in Chapter 5, is similar across firms. What is different is the range of task assignments for individual engineers. A rough indicator of individual specialization is the number of people who participate (even if only part time) in a project on a long-term basis. Inasmuch as an individual's tasks are more or less specialized in automotive development, the number of long-term project participants would seem to reflect the extent to which the project is divided into specialized tasks.

The strength of the product manager is the basis for our measure of the level of internal and external integration. Our interviews and questionnaires yielded fifteen indicators of the role and influence of the product manager in development. Indicators that deal with engineering coordination (e.g., relative influence in manufacturing) are used to measure the level of internal integration; indicators that deal with concept development and links to markets (e.g., the role of product manager in concept development) are used to measure the level of external integration.[*]

Differences in the regional averages of our measures of specialization and integration, presented in Figure 9.2, are striking. U.S. projects tend to be characterized by a highly specialized engineering organization with a moderately high level of internal integration. All of the U.S. projects we studied had project managers who devoted considerable effort to coordinating large numbers of engineers who had fairly narrow assignments. It was not uncommon, for example, for an engineer to be responsible for the design of a small portion of a component system, such as the latch of a door. To achieve effective designs with such detailed specialization requires a high level of integration, mostly, as the data suggest, directed at internal coordination. External integration in U.S. projects was extremely low, with product managers having little involvement in concept development and little direct interaction with customers.

---

[*]   These indicators are essentially the "ideal profile indices" that were discussed in Chapter 8.

Product managers in European firms tended to be somewhat more involved with customers, though the levels in Figure 9.2 are not very high. Internal integration was also low, and specialization was almost at the U.S. level. The implication is that European product managers exercise less influence over functional organizations that have relatively specialized engineers. Whether one looks at volume producers or high-end specialists, European projects were more functionally oriented than the U.S. or Japanese projects.

Figure 9.2 Indices of Specialization and Internal and External Integration by Region and Strategy

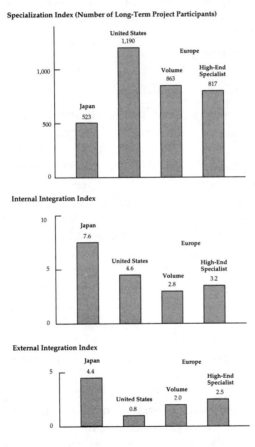

Notes: In the specialization index, the number of participants is adjusted for project content (price, body types, and project scope). A standard project is assumed: Retail price = $14,032.00; body types = 2.3; project scope = 0.612.

Definition and calculation of the indices of external and internal integration, which have been calculated at the organization level (8 in Japan, 5 in the U.S., and 9 in Europe), are contained in the Appendix.

The data for Japanese projects suggest much lower levels of specialization and much higher levels of both internal and external integration. Task assignments among Japanese engineers tend to be broader both in breadth of activities (e.g., an engineer does design and testing) and in range of components (e.g., an engineer does not only the door latch, but the entire door lock mechanism). This combination of specialization and integration is distinctive. Theoretically, an organization that is less specialized has less *need* for coordination and thus requires less integration to achieve a given level of performance. Because their coordination problems were somewhat simpler, Japanese product managers could have matched U.S. or European levels of performance with *less* effort in integration, but our data suggest that their efforts in integration were actually far greater. This ought to lead to even higher levels of consistency and coordination, and thus to a higher level of performance.

MODES OF ORGANIZATION

The particular pattern of specialization and integration in the development process defines the mode of the development organization. Earlier we identified four ideal types, ranging from the purely functional, highly specialized organization to the multifunctional, highly integrated team. To use the data presented in Figure 9.2 to map organizations into these modes, we need to make two adjustments to our idealized types. First, because few organizations have a purely team structure, we have grouped companies with teams with those with heavyweight product managers. Second, we have split the lightweight category into two groups: organizations in which product managers coordinate activity within engineering but have only moderate influence there and little elsewhere (a true lightweight system), and organizations in which the influence of product managers lies between that of the true lightweight and the heavyweight product manager (the "middleweight" and "light-heavyweight" systems). The results are presented in Table 9.2.

Most of the companies we studied fall into the lightweight and middleweight categories. Purely functional and true heavyweight systems are rare. Only three European organizations were purely functional, having no product manager and achieving coordination

Table 9.2 Types of Development Organization by Region and Strategy

(number of organizations)

Strategy / Region	Heavyweight Project Manager	Light-Heavy Project Manager	Middleweight Project Manager	Lightweight Project Manager	Functional Structure	Total
Japan	2	1	3	2	0	8
United States	0	0	1	4	0	5
Europe	0	0	2	5	2	9
Volume Producer	0	0	1	3	1	5
High-End Specialist	0	0	1	2	1	4
Total	2	1	6	11	2	22

Note: See Fujimoto (1989, Chapter 8) for further details.

through functional departments, and only two Japanese companies had product managers who were true heavyweights.

These patterns are consistent with the history of competition and traditions of engineering and design that were discussed in Chapter 3. The sharpest contrast is between high-end European producers and Japanese volume producers. The high-end specialists' traditional emphasis on functionality is reflected in the strength of the functional organizations. The strength of the product manager system in Japanese firms, particularly in internal integration, reflects the greater emphasis on rapid development and design for manufacturability in the Japanese domestic market. Though U.S. and European volume producers have adopted product manager systems, functional orientation has remained strong and the product managers consequently tend to be lightweights.

ORGANIZATION AND PERFORMANCE

To attract and satisfy customers in the 1980s, cars had to possess superior fit and finish, be reliable, and deliver a total driving experience that matched driver expectations. In short, cars had to achieve a high level of product integrity. But they also had to achieve a high level of functionality. A high level of performance was expected in acceleration, fuel efficiency, ride, noise, handling, braking, and steering. Meeting customer demands for functionality requires depth of expertise and thus some measure of specialization.

But customer satisfaction depends on product integrity as well as functionality. To satisfy customer demand, therefore, is to achieve the right balance between specialization and integration. Yet in the successful development organization of the 1980s, integration weighs heavier in the balance. We develop evidence for this assertion in the scatter diagrams presented in Figure 9.3, which capture the relationships between development performance and our measures of spe-

Figure 9.3 Specialization, Integration, and Development Performance

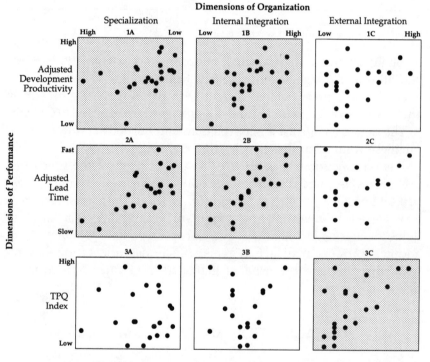

Note: In panels 3B and 3C one Japanese company was dropped from the current analysis because the process and organization patterns measured did not represent the overall profile of the company, but rather a special project in which the company tried to overhaul its traditional product development system.

Spearman rank order coefficient is significant at 5% level.

Spearman rank order coefficient is not significant at 5% or 10% level.

cialization and integration. Each diagram is associated with one of the three performance dimensions (measured along the vertical), and one of the three organization dimensions (measured along the horizontal). Thus the top row presents results for development productivity measured against specialization (1A) and internal (1B) and external integration (1C). Patterns in the data indicate the direction of the relationship (positive, negative, or neutral), while shading indicates its strength (dark represents very strong, and light denotes very weak).

Looking first at lead time and productivity, we find both to be associated with specialization and degree of internal integration. Consider diagram 2B, which relates lead time and internal integration. The data suggest a positive relationship between integration and speed of development. Where integration is high, development is fast; where integration is low, development is slow. The shading of the diagram indicates that the relationship is strong statistically. A similar pattern appears in the relationship between internal integration and development productivity in diagram 1B.

The role of internal integration is consistent with previous evidence on manufacturing capability and problem solving in engineering. Inasmuch as lead time is driven by critical path activities such as tooling, in which coordination affects speed, it makes sense that efforts to integrate across functions would pay off in shorter development cycles. Further we have seen that productivity is driven by problems created by poor coordination (e.g., many design iterations arising from engineering changes caused by poor communication, and slow decision making resulting from inconsistent functional goals and little shared understanding of priorities). A project with a strong focus on internal integration should have fewer problems of this kind (for a given level of complexity) and thus should achieve higher productivity.

The evidence on specialization suggests that many firms may have taken the division of labor too far. Consider the evidence on lead time. The data in diagram 2A of Figure 9.3 show that development is fast where specialization is low and slow where specialization is high. But specialization should have a U-shaped relationship with performance. Too little specialization finds individuals overloaded and insufficiently focused to solve problems well; too much specialization leads to problems of coordination that result in poor designs, delays, and rework. We would thus expect superior performance to be associated with a moderate level of specialization. Instead we find that high-performance organizations in our sample have low levels of specialization and highly specialized firms have low performance. Thus none of the firms in our sample, even those with low levels of specialization, are underspecialized. Many of the low performers, mostly U.S. and European firms, are so highly specialized that the sheer number of people involved in their programs creates problems of coordination. Nor does the high specialization we see in these organizations necessarily translate into superior product performance. In fact, in diagram 3A we find high- and low-quality performance at almost all levels of specialization.

External integration, in contrast, is closely associated with total product quality (3C), but not with lead time (2C) or productivity (1C). This pattern is consistent with the focus of our measure of external integration—i.e., the effort of product managers to link design with customer experience and expectations. To draw the comparison between external and internal integration more sharply, we have reproduced diagrams 3B and 3C in Figure 9.4 with regional data. The right panel suggests that the effect of external integration is particularly pronounced in Japan. This strong connection between external integration and quality is striking in light of the relatively weak effect of internal integration. In the left panel, Japanese firms with *below*-average quality rankings score *above* average on internal integration. The evidence on external integration is thus a finding not merely on integration, but on the efforts of the product manager to infuse the product concept and the customer's voice into the development process.

The regional data in Figure 9.4 suggest a different pattern for European high-end specialists. These firms achieve high total quality with a relatively low level of external integration. The data reflect the very different pressures that confronted high-end specialists in the 1980s. Traditionally, extremely demanding functionality was the main criterion of success for these firms; they experienced little pressure for short model cycles or wider product variety. Faced with relatively stable markets, high-end specialists could rely on strong functional organizations guided by traditional concepts of engineering excellence. There was not much of a role for strong product managers because a dominant engineering and design tradition lent the necessary coherence and consistency to the work of engineering specialists.

Figure 9.4 Internal and External Integration and Total Product Quality

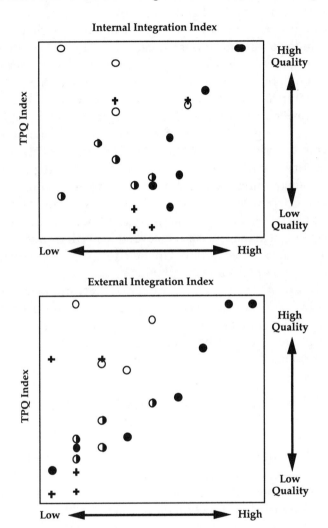

Note: One Japanese company was dropped from the current analysis because the process and organization patterns measured, rather than representing the overall profile of the company, represented a special project in which the company tried to overhaul its traditional product development system.

● Japanese Producer ✚ U.S. Producer

◐ European Volume Producer ○ European High-End Specialist

Whether or not this approach will be effective in the 1990s (a question we return to in Chapter 11) is uncertain.

Figure 9.5 draws together evidence in this chapter using our overall index of organizational integration. This index summarizes the degree of specialization and patterns of internal and external integration, ranging from the purely functional structure (highly specialized, low integration) on the left to the heavyweight product manager system (lower specialization, highly integrated) on the right. Patterns in the data in Figure 9.5 underscore the importance of integration in achieving superior performance. Low performers generally lack integration; firms with strong internal and external integration generally achieve outstanding results. However, the relationships are not exact. The very different circumstances of high-end specialists were acknowledged earlier, but even volume producers occasionally spawn lightweight product managers who achieve solid results in a *single* dimension of performance. Indeed, some Japanese firms that employ the middleweight system are both fast and efficient.

But firms that achieve superior performance on all three dimensions employ heavyweight systems. Their product managers are architects and builders, concept champions, and effective coordinators who apply their efforts at integration in a context of relatively low specialization.

ORGANIZATIONAL CHANGES FOR HIGHER PERFORMANCE

The patterns we have seen in this chapter represent a snapshot in time. Across the industry, we have seen relatively strong regional effects. In Europe, where markets have been more stable and competition has focused on functionality, functionally structured high-end specialists have performed well. On the other side of the planet, Japanese volume producers, for whom markets have been more dynamic and competition more intense, have evolved organizational structures and processes that support short lead times and promote efficient engineering. Some firms in Japan have taken integration a step further by explicitly linking customers to design. If organizational integration is central to rapid, efficient, high-quality development—if it is not an aberration of the data or the sample—it ought to show up

Figure 9.5 Mode of Organization and Development Performance

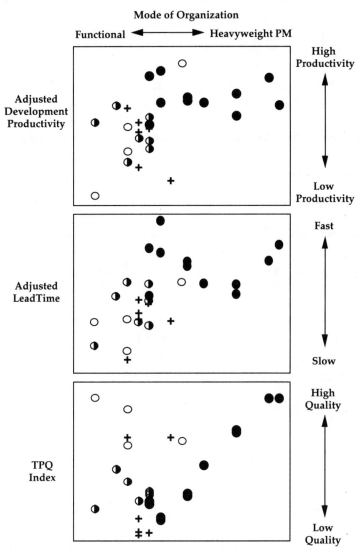

Note: One Japanese company was dropped from the current analysis because the process and organization patterns measured, rather than representing the overall profile of the company, represented a special project in which the company tried to overhaul its traditional product development system.

● Japanese Producer   + U.S. Producer

◐ European Volume Producer   ○ European High-End Specialist over time as firms respond to markets that have become increasingly dynamic and competitive. Two things should be in evidence. First, as the auto industry becomes increasingly dynamic and competitive, we should see an evolution toward heavier systems of integration. Second, within specific companies we should see improvements in performance after adoption of heavier approaches to product management. A before-after comparison should reveal improvements in lead time, productivity, and quality as internal and external integration are strengthened. A look at changes over time should yield some insight into the challenges that face firms moving to heavier systems.

THE EVOLUTION OF ORGANIZATION: 1976–1987

Figure 9.6 summarizes the history of organizational change in the 22 organizations in our sample between 1976 and 1987. The results generally agree with the predicted patterns of long-term adaptation. A trend from a purely functional to some type of product manager system was clearly observed worldwide. For companies with product manager systems, the trend appears to have been from lighter to heavier product managers. The figure also reveals regional time lags. Most Japanese companies had adopted a product manager structure by the late 1970s. By the mid 1980s, a few had already established relatively heavy product manager systems. Others were shifting from middleweight to heavyweight systems during the same period. In the United States and Europe, the shift from functional forms to lightweight systems occurred mostly after 1980. As of the mid 1980s, only a few U.S. and European companies had progressed from lightweight to middleweight structures.*

These regional time lags, which seem to reflect the historical differences in domestic competition described earlier, may have precipitated an international transfer of organizational ideas during the adaptation process that resulted from the growing pressures of global competition. In exporting the pattern of competition along with their product exports to U.S. and European markets, Japanese producers may also have exported the organizational ideas for competing effectively in the new environment. Some of the U.S. and European car producers in our sample have in recent years conducted extensive in-house studies

---

* Some of the U.S. and European companies interviewed hinted at plans to shift toward stronger product manager systems in the 1980s.

Figure 9.6 Trends of Organizational Change in 22 Organizations, 1976-1987

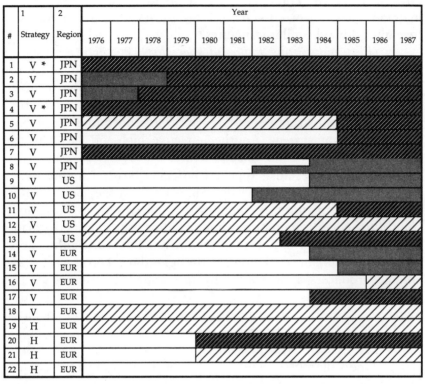

#	1 Strategy	2 Region	Year 1976	1977	1978	1979	1980	1981	1982	1983	1984	1985	1986	1987
1	V *	JPN												
2	V	JPN												
3	V	JPN												
4	V *	JPN												
5	V	JPN												
6	V	JPN												
7	V	JPN												
8	V	JPN												
9	V	US												
10	V	US												
11	V	US												
12	V	US												
13	V	US												
14	V	EUR												
15	V	EUR												
16	V	EUR												
17	V	EUR												
18	V	EUR												
19	H	EUR												
20	H	EUR												
21	H	EUR												
22	H	EUR												

Notes: Company names were disguised.
   V = volume producer; H = high-end specialist; JPN = Japan; US = U.S.A.; EUR = Western Europe.
   An asterisk denotes an organization employing a heavyweight product manager as of 1987.

"Engineering coordination" means coordination within engineering function only.
"Overall coordination" means coordination of production and marketing as well as of engineering.

Product manager, at a minimum, is responsible for overall coordination and product planning.

Product manager is responsible for overall coordination, or is responsible for engineering coordination and product planning.

Product manager is responsible for engineering coordination only.

Product manager does not exist.

of the organizational patterns of seemingly effective Japanese competitors. Dynamic organizational changes thus may have occurred partly through the international learning process.

Relatively effective volume producers tend also to be early adopters of highly integrative structures. Research has shown that it normally takes a long time for a company to master the management of highly integrative organizations, and the longer history of trial and error in these early adopters would obviously have helped them maintain their organizational advantages even after other companies formally adopted similar structures.[8]

The trend among high-end specialists. Perceiving increasing competitive pressures, even high-end specialists have moved toward product manager systems, albeit with little consistency. One relatively effective high-end specialist that attempted to adopt a fairly strong product manager structure in the early 1980s ended up shifting back to a lightweight system. Another effective high-end specialist has maintained a purely functional structure.

High-end specialists appear to be facing a crucial organizational design choice that may well be determined by how they predict future patterns of competition. A company that believes it can maintain its competitive edge through strong differentiation in product performance and stable customers may opt to maintain a functional or semifunctional structure. A company responding to the upgrading of product mixes by volume producers and to intensifying competition among existing high-end specialists is more likely to shift to a stronger product manager structure.[*] Strategic-organizational changes among these producers are likely to be seen in the early 1990s.

The effect of heavyweight product management: the case of Nissan. One of the most striking examples of organizational achievement of high integration has been Nissan. Viewed by many Japanese observers in 1985 as an ailing giant, Nissan in 1990 is recognized as a revitalized company. Company and product images recovered rapidly, and the turnaround story has been a popular topic in Japanese business journals since 1988.[9]

What is that story? Many—insiders and outsiders—point to fundamental changes of culture and organization, particularly in product development. The number-two auto company in Japan, Nissan was associated with advanced technology in the domestic market. But its technological prowess was a trap. Nissan continued to rely heavily on its component technology to attract and satisfy customers who were increasingly looking for product integrity.

[*] As of 1989, some Japanese companies (e.g., Toyota and Nissan) had concrete plans to introduce high-end models that might compete directly with the top products of high-end specialists. A similar tendency was observed among some European volume producers.

New Nissan products in the early 1980s, though fully loaded with novel component technologies and high-performance gadgets, somehow lacked a coherent and distinctive message. Rated performance in the catalogue was impressive, but product concepts tended to be confusing, styling was conservative, and layout was old. The entire product line possessed neither consistent identity nor clear differentiation. This weakness in product integrity—together with a weaker dealer network, historic labor problems, and lower productivity compared with Toyota—all hurt Nissan's market performance during the mid 1980s.[10] The crisis culminated in 1986, when the company reported its first biannual operating loss in more than 30 years. Domestic market share, once over 30 percent, was close to 20 percent and still dropping.

Product development played a leading role in Nissan's efforts at greater organizational integration, which began in the mid 1980s. Nissan's product manager system had remained lightweight until the late 1970s. Nissan product managers were traditionally coordinators within the engineering function.[11] In the early 1980s, product managers played a somewhat greater role in planning and interfunctional coordination, but external integration (concept creation) continued to be problematic. Product managers did not have clear leadership in the very early phase of product development when the product concept is still embryonic. They tended to react to sales and top management with compromises rather than take leadership in formulating a clear concept. Lacking significant direct contact with customers, they tended to be caretakers of obscure vehicle concepts (e.g., me-too styling, excessive engine variety, lack of intermodel differentiation) driven by short-term competitive pressures. Finally, levels of communication and coordination between engineering and production at Nissan were low for a Japanese company, which sometimes caused problems of design manufacturability.

Efforts to change Nissan's organization and culture began around 1985, as engineers and managers in product development sought a new development process and a new image in the minds of customers. Spurred by a sense of crisis, early informal changes focused on a new attitude toward innovation in product concepts and increased customer orientation among middle managers and working-level engineers.

With the encouragement and support of new CEO Yutaka Kume, more formal changes followed. Managers in product development created a task force to investigate current problems at the working level and make proposals. Consensus slowly emerged for a more integrated development organization, a stronger concept creation function, and an open and customer-oriented culture. Major organizational changes implemented in 1986 and 1987 included the creation of three product management departments. Each specialized in a group of products that shared a basic product concept and combined empowered product managers and marketing planning. The new system established product managers as external integrators who infused future customer expectations into product details. Structural changes were accompanied by efforts to change the attitudes of middle and top managers, and sales was reorganized to emphasize interproduct coordination and customer orientation.

Market results began to improve. Products changed first. Critics generally agree that Nissan models after late 1987 are characterized by distinctive vehicle concepts, a clear focus on the target market, cleaner interior-exterior styling, and a better fit between the technology and character of the vehicle. The Nissan Cedric, Bluebird, 240SX, Maxima, and 300ZX have brought the company into strong competition with Toyota and Honda for leadership in vehicle concept and styling in the Japanese domestic market.

Nissan changed in many of the ways we have discussed in this chapter. It emphasized stronger internal-external integration, intense information exchange, the primacy of the concept creation function, and a focus on product integrity. The result, a major improvement in the distinctiveness and appeal of Nissan's products, played a critical role in Nissan's recovery and clearly illustrates how organizational change can influence market performance.

THE CHALLENGE OF IMPLEMENTATION

Putting into practice the concepts and ideas outlined in this chapter is a challenging task. The organization of product development has a long tradition in many companies. It is deeply embedded in the way a company works. Changing it touches much of what a company does and thus requires sustained commitment from senior management. Moving from a functional or lightweight system to a heavyweight product manager structure is not a once-and-for-all event, but rather a journey whose theme is continuous improvement.

Companies that embarked on this journey during the 1980s have taken two paths. Some have introduced elements of a new system in an evolutionary, step-by-step fashion, incurring relatively mild organizational change at each step. A typical pattern involves shifting from a functional structure to a very light product manager system by creating integrator roles only within product engineering. The responsibility and influence of product managers then is expanded to include new tasks such as product planning or product-process coordination. Further steps include raising the rank of product managers, bringing in as product managers people with strong reputations, and assigning one instead of a few models per manager in order to focus their attention and expand their influence. Resistance by traditional functional units, particularly those of larger producers with a strong tradition of functionalism, appears to have been a major impetus for taking this tack.

Other companies, particularly smaller players, have taken a faster, more direct route to heavyweight product management. One small Japanese company jumped from a traditional functional form to a very strong product manager system with the introduction of a major new model. Based on consensus within the company that this project was critical—that it might well determine the future of the company as a whole—an unusually heavy product manager organization was created as a special project. An executive vice president with many years of development experience was appointed product manager, and department heads from engineering, production, and planning became liaisons and project leaders within their functional groups. With these changes, management sent a clear signal that the company in its traditional functional form could not survive.

The project yielded a fairly significant market success, a product that is today regarded as a turnaround effort for a company that had not had an effective car development project in years. In the wake of this project, the company established a product manager office for more regular projects. In effect, what the company had learned in the special project became a model case for subsequent changes in the product development organization.

The approach a company takes to changing its development organization and the speed with which it moves will depend on its position and the competitive threat it faces. But successful efforts seem to share several common themes. Three seem particularly crucial.

A unifying driver. Just as engineers need a vision of the overall product to guide their efforts in developing a new car, the people involved in changing the development organization need a vision, an objective that captures their imagination. Where changes have taken hold and worked, senior managers have linked the need for a new organization to competition and the drive for tangible advantage in the marketplace.

The quest for faster development lead time has been a particularly powerful driver of this effort during the 1980s. Lead time is not an end in itself, but its pursuit leads people to do things that improve the system overall. In this respect, lead time is like inventory in a JIT manufacturing system; of itself, a low level of work in-process inventory has some effect, but going after the root causes of excess inventory brings about powerful system changes.

Companies that have focused on improving lead time and succeeded have generally emphasized changes in internal integration. Product integrity is often what drives them to higher performance. This, as we noted earlier, is more than being market-driven or customer-oriented. There must be a drive to create products that fire the imagination, that surprise and delight the customer. Managed well, this driver gives the implementation of a heavyweight system energy and focus.

New blood. The most successful of the many efforts we have seen to change the product development organization have been led by new people. Some of these people are new to the company, but most come out of the organization. The latter are new in that they bring a different approach; they may have been viewed as mavericks in the old organization, and they see the world differently; they are not more of the same. A company cannot change everyone, but it can create new leaders, and it can empower people who are tuned in to the new direction the company needs to take.

In addition to finding people who have the skills and attitudes to be heavyweight product managers and team leaders now, successful companies work to develop such people for the future. Recognizing that their old systems for career development, training, and promotion will not generate all the talent and experience they need, they establish—concurrently with the new structure for current projects—an apprenticeship system or other method for identifying and developing future leaders.

Tenacity. Moving to a heavier product manager structure is a discovery process. Consider, for example, the task of creating effective teamwork in the following situation. Company A establishes a strong product manager and project liaisons within the functional groups. The project liaisons form a core team and meet with the product manager regularly. This group develops a camaraderie and works well together. But the working-level engineers don't feel part of the team. A perceptible barrier begins to grow between the "team" and the people doing the work. Company A has discovered that a change in structure is important but not sufficient. To create a true team, more change is needed, particularly in the behavior of the functional team leader.

The journey to heavyweight product management is hard, surprisingly so to many. Those who succeed do so because they have tenacity; they don't give up. The really outstanding companies realize that the journey never ends, only projects end. The challenge is to learn from experience and continually improve. Most companies rarely learn from their product development projects. In company after company, we have seen the same problems crop up over and over in project after project. At the end of every project, there is pressure to get on to the next. The few companies that work at continual improvement achieve a significant edge. Movement to a more effective development organization could be the basis for instilling an ethic of continuous improvement and, with tenacity, could yield a significant advantage in the marketplace.

SUMMARY AND IMPLICATIONS

Historical trends in organizational design changes, as evidenced in the experience of Nissan and other firms in the 1980s, support the notion that a strong product manager structure is an important element in high-performance product development among volume producers. These trends are likely to continue. Our interviews with senior managers at volume producers worldwide revealed a widespread intention to strengthen the role of product managers.* Mass-market-oriented producers are recognizing that a heavyweight product manager system that consolidates the roles of strong internal and external integrators for higher total system integrity can be a highly effective organizational form for coping with intensifying global competition.

Though the direction of change in the organization of development seems clear, the degree of convergence around a full-blown heavyweight product manager system will depend on the competitive and market environment. If all markets come to resemble the Japanese domestic market—with its short life cycles, seesaw battles for segment leadership, proliferation of product variety, and strong emphasis on product integrity—firms without a heavyweight structure will suffer competitive disadvantage. This seems to be the case in the U.S. market.

In the European market, the situation might be different. If European markets continue to emphasize functionality, longer life cycles, and strong customer loyalty, a middleweight structure may be adequate. The old functional or lightweight approach has been doomed by new competitive pressures from the Japanese and some measure of globalization in the market. Though the heavyweight system might yield somewhat better performance, its advantage over the middleweight system would not be as compelling in the European market. This would be particularly true for large European firms, in which inertia around the functional structure may be significant. For such firms, moving to a middleweight system would yield many of the advantages of a heavyweight system without incurring the full cost. If, however, European markets were to become more dynamic, our evidence suggests that heavier product managers would be essential to competitive success.

It seems clear that the 1990s will see firms throughout the industry moving to heavier product managers. The path they follow will depend on the patterns of competition and customer demand that emerge over the next decade. Effective product development in the 1990s will require organizations with much higher levels of integration

---

*   Most, however, hesitated to go as far as a "project execution team" structure. Their main concern was loss of expertise by dispersing specialized engineers to different projects on a full-time basis. They generally preferred more regular product manager systems in which one working engineer is allowed to work for more than one project.

than were characteristic of those in place through much of the postwar era. It will also require leaders with product imagination and conceptual vision. To the extent that the 1990s are dynamic and highly competitive, the hallmark of the outstanding organization will be a cohesive team of skilled individuals working under the leadership of a concept champion and a strong integrator to realize a distinctive product concept that attracts, satisfies, and even delights the customer.

NOTES

1. For the issue of R&D organizations and management in general, see, for example, Marquis (1969), Rothwell et al. (1974), Freeman (1982), Rubenstein et al. (1976), Maidique and Zirger (1984), Allen (1977), Von Hippel (1988), Utterback (1974), Van de Ven (1986), Roberts (1988), Kanter (1988), Morton (1971), Imai et al. (1985), Galbraith (1982), Gobeli and Ruelius (1985), McDonough and Leifer (1986), Rosenbloom (1985), Perrow (1967), and Burns and Stalker (1961).
2. For general discussions along this line, see Lawrence and Lorsch (1967), Thompson (1967), Galbraith (1973), and Davis and Lawrence (1977). For the issue of coordination and specialization in R&D organizations, see Allen and Hauptman (1987), Katz and Allen (1985), Marquis and Straight (1965), Keller (1986), and Larson and Gobeli (1988).
3. The notion of "infusion" is adopted from Dumas and Mintzberg (1989).
4. The limits of systematic marketing research and product clinics is discussed in Rosenbloom and Abernathy (1982), Lorenz (1986), Johannson and Nonaka (1987), and Shapiro (1988).
5. For a discussion of the manager as conductor, see Drucker (1954, pp. 341–342), Sayles (1964, p. 164), and Mintzberg (1989, p. 20). In the case of product managers, see Ikari (1982b).
6. This behavioral pattern seems to be a version of "management by walking about." See Peters and Waterman (1982, Chapter 5).
7. See also Fujimoto (1989, Chapter 8) for measurement of integration.
8. Davis and Lawrence (1977), p. 129.
9. See Yoshiro Ikari, *Nissan Ishiki Daikakume (Great Cultural Revolution of Nissan)*, Diamond, Tokyo (1987, Japanese); Masaharu Shibata, *Nani ga Nissan Jidosha wo Kaetanoka (What Changed Nissan?)*, PHP, Tokyo (1988, Japanese). The account that follows draws on this literature as well as interviews with managers and engineers at Nissan.
10. For a historical comparison of Nissan and Toyota, see Cusumano (1985).
11. For a history of Nissan's product development organization, see Ikari (1981, 1985).

CHAPTER 10
EFFECTIVE DEVELOPMENT PATTERNS: THE PARTS AND THE WHOLE

In the technical centers and engineering laboratories of almost every automobile company in the world, there is something called the "tear-down" laboratory. It is a place in which skilled engineers systematically disassemble new models of rival producers. Engineers in the tear-down lab go over each part and component of a particularly interesting new model in fine detail, looking for new technology, new engineering designs, new methods of processing. When they are through, the engineers know a lot about the technical details of the bits and pieces of the car. But tearing down a car and examining it piece by piece does not reveal its essence. Understanding individual components is important, but what gives a car its character and makes it attractive to customers is the way the pieces work together to create a distinctive driving experience. To comprehend the car as a whole, one needs to understand how rival engineers have balanced and tuned the elements to one another to achieve product integrity.

Much the same is true of product development processes. One can tear them down, as we have done, and try to identify the important elements. In this sense, the previous chapters are our tear-down laboratory. In each we identify critical dimensions of management practice that characterize high-performance companies. But throughout we emphasize that the key to high-performance in product development is overall consistency across many important details. It is the *pattern*, not a single critical factor, that makes the difference.

In this chapter, we step back from the details of product development to consider overall consistency in its organization and management. We believe that only an organization with coherent functions and consistent capabilities across the full range of development activities—in short, an organization with high integrity—can develop a product with high integrity. If this is true, a product should reflect the organization and the development process that created it.

After reviewing and attempting to synthesize the patterns that seem to characterize high-performance development, we examine empirical evidence that suggests that overall consistency does matter. We do this first for volume producers and then for high-end specialists.

PATTERNS OF HIGH-PERFORMING VOLUME PRODUCERS

The competitive environment of the 1980s was a turbulent one for volume producers. Advantage lay in product differentiation and product integrity (total vehicle concept). Markets were diverse, customer needs evolved rapidly, and competition took on the character of a game in basic performance and component technologies.* Volume producers faced demanding requirements:

- A need to identify and translate into appropriate total vehicle concepts and engineering designs diversified, changing, and inarticulate customer expectations.
- A need to match rival products in balancing cost and basic performance.
- Short lead times to support quick responses to competing products and better forecasting of customer expectations.
- High development productivity to generate greater product variety from a given pool of R&D funds while maintaining cost competitiveness in product development.

PRODUCT STRATEGY AND ORGANIZATIONAL AND MANAGEMENT RESPONSES

Effective volume producers mounted both strategic and organizational/management responses to these challenges. In project strategy, high-performing volume producers adopted measures aimed at

---

* For purposes of discussion, we ignore here differences in regional markets in the 1980s. We assume that volume producers face more or less similar task requirements across regions as a result of the global convergence of the competitive environment in recent years.

keeping the product line fresh and varied without exploding project complexity (see Chapter 6). These measures include:

Rapid inch-up—quick product renewals, each making a relatively small jump in innovation (cumulative effects of rapid incremental changes can be quite large over time).

Fundamental product variety—maintenance or expansion of fundamental variety in basic structure and packaging rather than in peripheral variations or options (this strategy responds to diversified customer needs without incurring the costs of excessive variety and without confusing customers).

Constrained project scope through supplier involvement—reducing project complexity, primarily through supplier involvement in engineering, to reduce lead time and engineering hours while renewing a large fraction of parts and technologies (this strategy avoids undesirable side effects associated with excessive use of common parts).

For management and organization, integral, short-cycle development has come to be the paradigm of effective volume producers. This paradigm is rooted in an intertwined physical/informational system with quick problem-solving cycles, intense information exchange, and high internal/external integration. Specific characteristics include:

Integrated product-process linkage—integrated problem-solving cycles in product-process engineering enables effective volume producers to reduce lead time without incurring expensive engineering rework or jeopardizing product quality (these linkages are supported by the integrative structures, skills, and attitudes discussed in Chapter 8).

Integrated customer-concept-product linkage—a heavyweight product manager system and broad task assignments for engineers tighten the critical information linkages among customers, concept, development, and engineering (external and internal integration is facilitated by effective engineering/manufacturing processes, as discussed in Chapter 9).

Integrated supplier linkage—intensive and early (or ongoing) communication with a relatively small number of first-tier parts suppliers effectively reduces late engineering changes, speeds the prototype parts procurement cycle, and improves vehicle-component integration (supplier capability for flexible and short-cycle engineering/manufacturing is an integral part of the total development system, as explained in Chapter 6).

Flexible, short-cycle manufacturing capability—just-in-time and total quality control principles emphasizing short throughput time, flexibility, quick problem detection, and continuous improvement are applied to prototyping, tooling, production startup, and engineering drawing changes (see Chapter 7).

Figure 10.1 summarizes the information flows and problem-solving cycles in the product development process of high-performing volume producers. Shaded areas distinguish the players; large boxes represent major stages of product development, such as product planning, product engineering, and process engineering. Each stage is a series of problem-solving cycles upon completion of which final output is approved and released to the next stage.

High performance in this system is driven by consistency in the overall pattern. The system features direct information flows from the market to a decentralized concept generation unit. Concept creation is thus proactive and draws on market insight and imagination. Subsequent development involves continual elaboration of concepts through early and intensive communication between concept generation, product planning, engineering, manufacturing, and suppliers. Problem-solving cycles are overlapped, and problems are resolved quickly within each stage to facilitate rapid response to continuously changing inputs. Critical assets such as tools and prototypes are produced quickly.

The key insight imparted by Figure 10.1 is that just as a single missing connection in an integrated circuit can destroy its function, weakness in a critical link of the development system may significantly impair overall performance. Such weakness cannot be fully offset by strength in other parts of the system.

Figure 10.1 Product Development System
of High-Performing Volume Producers

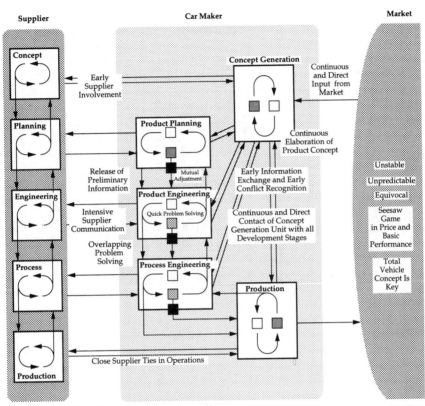

Note: Information flow prior to actions is omitted for simplicity.
□ Alternatives ▣ Evaluation ■ Final Approval ➞ Information Flow for Actions

REAL PERFORMANCE AND THE IDEAL PRODUCT
DEVELOPMENT STRUCTURE

The product development system in Figure 10.1 is an ideal. The closer a firm comes to matching this ideal, the faster, more efficient, and higher quality its product development should be. This, at least, is the theory. To test it we compared data on several indicators that represent this system with actual development performance. Table 10.1 summarizes the results of this comparison for a representative set of firms. For ease of presentation, we have grouped the indicators and ranked firms on each.

Table 10.1 Overall Consistency of Selected Product Development Organizations

		High Performer		Better Quality		Low Quality 1 (high efficiency)		Low Quality 2 (overall low performance)			High-Quality High-End Specialist	
Case		#1	#2	#3	#4	#5	#6	#7	#8	#9	#10	#11
Region/Strategy		Japan	Japan	U.S.	Japan	Japan	Japan	U.S.	U.S.	Europe	High-End	High-End
Rank in Performance	Lead Time	●	●	○	◎	●	●	◎	◎	○	○	○
	Productivity	◐	●	○	◐	●	●	○	◎	◎	○	○
	Total Product Quality	●	●	●	●	○	○	○	○	○	●	●
Rank in Organization and Management — Project Strategy	Rapid Inch-Up (model renewals)	●	●	○	●	●	○	◎	○	○	○	◎
	Rapid Variety Proliferation	●	●	○	◎	○	●	◎	●	○	◎	○
	Supplier Involvement	◎	◎	○	●	○	●	○	○	◎	○	◎
Patterns of Organization	Integration Index	●	●	●	●	◎	◎	○	○	○	○	◎
	High Engineering Overlap	●	●	●	○	●	◎	◎	○	○	○	◎
	Broad Task Assignment	●	-	-	◎	●	●	-	◎	○	○	-
Manufacturing Capability	Short-Cycle Prototyping	●	●	○	●	●	○	⊛	○	○	○	○
	Short-Cycle Die Manufacturing	●	●	○	◎	●	●	○	○	○	◎	○
	High Assembly Productivity	●	●	●	●	○	-	⊛	⊛	○	○	-

Note: Based on the ranking of 22 development organizations. For definitions of the indicators, see the Appendix.

● top 1/3   ◐ borderline between top and middle 1/3   ◎ middle 1/3   ○ bottom 1/3 – not available

The indicators include measures of performance, organization, and management. The latter two are further broken down into project strategy, patterns of organization, and manufacturing capability. Most of these indicators are adopted from previous chapters, so we explain them only briefly here.

Performance. Our standard performance measures—adjusted engineering hours, adjusted lead time, and total product quality index—were the basis for performance ranking (see Chapter 4). All data were aggregated at the organization level.

Project strategy. Project strategy (discussed in Chapter 6) includes innovativeness, product variety, and project scope. Although no direct indicators for innovativeness were available at the organization level, Sheriff's (1988) project renewal index is a reasonable surrogate for the existence of a rapid inch-up strategy, given evidence that a company is not lagging behind the technological progress of the industry. Similarly, Sheriff's product proliferation index seems to be a

good indicator of a company's commitment to expansion of fundamental product variety. Finally, the supplier involvement ratio (discussed in Chapter 6) seems to represent a distinctive project scope
strategy that emphasizes heavy involvement of capable suppliers in
development.

Patterns of organization. Here we used measures (taken directly
from Chapter 9) of both the role and influence of the product manager
in achieving internal and external integration, together with evidence
of the existence of other mechanisms for integration (e.g., the use of
task forces). The number of longer-term participants, adjusted for
product content, indicates the breadth of task assignment at the
individual level.

Manufacturing capability. To represent an organization's short-
cycle manufacturing capability (as discussed in Chapter 7), we used
prototype and die manufacturing lead time, which measure quickness
of hidden manufacturing activities in development. Data on assembly
productivity, drawn from Krafcik's (1988) extensive study, reflect the
company's general capability in commercial production.

Sample organizations were classified according to patterns of
strategy and performance. Categories included high performer (top
rank in all criteria); better quality (second best in TPQ); medium
quality (middle range in TPQ); low quality 1 (fast, efficient, but low
quality); low quality 2 (low TPQ, no strong point in other criteria);
high-quality high-end specialist (presented as a point of reference).
Companies in the middle range of quality were omitted because they
showed no common pattern except lack of consistency.

High performer (cases 1 and 2). Only two volume producers,
both Japanese, ranked in (or, in one instance, very near) the top one-
third on all three performance measures. These companies also demonstrated remarkable consistency in organization and management,
ranking in the top one-third on all indicators except supplier involvement. No other organization exhibited this level of consistency.

Better quality (cases 3 and 4). Organizations in this group (one
Japanese and one U.S.) ranked almost as high as the top group in
product quality but exhibited less consistent performance, particularly
in lead time. Case 3, for example, ranks low in performance in lead time
and productivity. In organization and management, these companies
were strong in most criteria, including internal integration, but the few

weak points that surfaced lowered consistency relative to the high performers.

Low quality 1 (cases 5 and 6). This group includes some Japanese companies that suffer from low product quality despite strength in lead time and development productivity. These companies score high in some areas of organization and management, much lower in external integration, and somewhere in the middle on other measures of cross-functional integration.

Low quality 2 (cases 7–9). Companies in this group score low on all performance criteria, particularly quality, and they consistently rank in the middle to low ranges in organization and management.

High-quality high-end specialist (cases 10 and 11). The better-performing high-end specialists rank low in lead time, productivity, and many of the organization and management indicators, but quite high in total quality performance. This very different pattern suggests that the high-end specialists were playing a quite different game than the volume producers during the 1980s.

The patterns at the ends of the performance spectrum are quite clear: high performers consistently conform closely to the ideal pattern depicted in Figure 10.1; low performers consistently deviate from it. Patterns in the middle range are less clear, although weakness in external integration seems to be a hallmark of low performance in product quality. Middle-range performers also lack consistency in engineering integration and organization of development. Indeed, when we look across indicators of integration (e.g., problem solving in engineering, leadership, and organization), consistency seems to have a strong connection with overall performance: high performers are highly integrated; low performers are relatively unintegrated; and firms in the middle are only moderately integrated.

With the seeming importance of overall integration, its link to development performance warrants more careful examination. To this end we constructed an integration index based on 29 indicators from the following four categories:

1) Power and responsibility of the product manager in external integration (concept creation);

2) Power and responsibility of the product manager in internal integration (project coordination);

3) Quick, flexible, integrated engineering cycles; and

4) Internal integration mechanisms other than product managers.

The index, constructed by totaling affirmative responses from the questionnaires and interviews across all variables, is essentially a profile consistency indicator that reflects closeness to the pattern we predicted to be effective among volume producers in the 1980s—a development system with dense and flexible information networks, intensive communication, short-cycle problem solving, and strong internal and external integration.[1] (Details of the variables used in the integration index are provided in the Appendix.)

Figure 10.2 plots the integration index against the three criteria for measuring development performance. In each diagram, high-integration/high-performance companies cluster in the upper right, while low-integration/low-performance companies are grouped in the lower left. Regions are keyed, and high-end specialists are plotted for reference.

For volume producers, the integration index exhibits a relatively strong positive correlation with all three performance measures, particularly total product quality.* The two high-performing volume producers scored exceptionally high in integration, supporting our argument that consistency in integration and short-cycle problem solving is critical to high performance.

Strong regional patterns are also evident in Figure 10.2. On average, Japanese firms tend to be more integrated than their Western counterparts, although there is substantial overlap. These findings seem to be consistent with the notion that the more volatile Japanese market environment has demanded greater effort in internal and external integration (see Chapter 2).

The clustering of Japanese producers in the upper area of the productivity and lead time diagrams is consistent with the historical importance of short model life and product variety in Japan. European and U.S. firms tend to inhabit the lower left portion of these two

---

* Spearman rank order correlation coefficients within the volume producer group are as follows: development productivity = 0.47 (n = 17, almost significant at 5% level); speed of development = 0.62 (n = 17, significant at 1% level); and total product quality = 0.70 (n = 17, significant at 1% level).

Figure 10.2 Integration Index and Development Performance

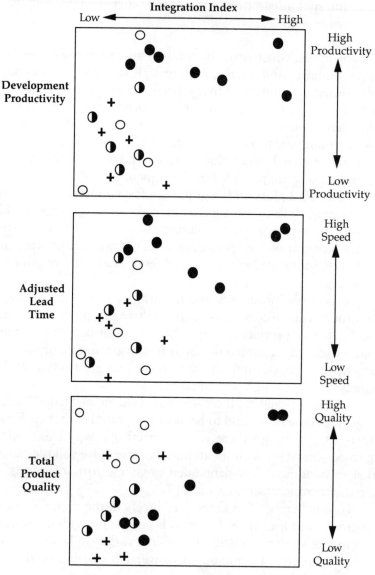

Note: One Japanese company was dropped from the current analysis because the process and organization patterns measured, rather than representing the overall profile of the company, represented a special project in which the company tried to overhaul its traditional product development system.

● Japanese Producer   + U.S. Producer

◑ European Volume Producer   ○ European High-End Specialist diagrams. Within regions, we see no clear correlation between integration consistency and performance in lead time and productivity. In Europe and the United States, where the integration index varies only moderately, other variables (e.g., manufacturing capability and unmeasured differences in design) may be more important in driving the relatively modest differences in adjusted lead time and productivity. Thus, for lead time and productivity, the apparent correlation seems to reflect cross-regional differences in performance and organization, especially the distinctive pattern of the Japanese firms.

Where we do see intraregional correlations is in total product quality; a clearly positive correlation exists particularly among Japanese companies. Part of this effect, as we saw in Chapter 9, is due to differences in external integration across firms. But it appears that other elements of integration are also correlated with total product quality. Differences in consistency—in the pattern of integration in engineering and problem solving across functions and with the market—seem to be at the root of differences in quality performance.

The patterns in Figure 10.2, particularly regional differences in lead time and productivity and the strong link between integration and quality, bear a close resemblance to the patterns we saw in Chapter 9, implying a close link between the role and strength of the product manager and other dimensions of integration. It appears, for example, that firms with heavyweight product managers also have highly capable, integrated engineering organizations. But this is not to suggest that all elements of the integration index affect all dimensions of performance equally. Table 10.2 presents patterns of correlation between our three performance measures and the four elements of the integration index mentioned earlier: power and responsibility of the concept creator (i.e., strength of external integration); power and responsibility of the project coordinator (i.e., strength of internal integration); integrated, overlapping and short-cycle engineering; and internal integration mechanisms other than the product manager.[*]

We found all four aspects of integration to be correlated with total product quality, with external integration being the most strongly connected. Although only integrated engineering is strongly correlated with the three dimensions of performance, it is not a sufficient

---

[*]   Further details of the classification are provided in the Appendix. Variable 17 (product managers who do concept generation), a key variable for groups 1 and 2, was included in both.

Table 10.2 Correlations between Consistency and Performance

Performance / Consistency	Development Productivity	Lead Time	Total Product Quality
Integration Index (overall consistency)	+	+++	+++
Strength of External Integrator	no	+	+++
Strength of Internal Integrator	+	++	++
Integrated Engineering	+++	+++	++
Other Internal Integration Mechanisms	no	no	++

Note: Based on Spearman rank correlation. N = 17 (volume producers only).

+++ Significant at 1% Level

 ++ Significant at 5% Level

  + Significant at 10% Level

no Not Significant at 10% Level

condition for high performance. As we have seen, several Japanese firms that scored high on engineering capability ranked low in quality. Cross-functional coordination within the firm (internal integration and other mechanisms) is strongly correlated with quality, but only moderately with productivity and lead time, implying that creating coherent teams within an organization may be a precondition for, but does not guarantee, advantage over rivals in product development. Producers without cross-functional teams are not likely to succeed, but the existence of a team solves only part of the puzzle.

Once more, our evidence underscores the importance of consistency across different aspects of organization and management. No one element is sufficient for achieving rapid, efficient, high-quality development. Among volume producers, high performance comes from a coherent, consistent combination of strong product managers who integrate both internally and externally; a dense and supple information network; close, working relationships across product and process engineering; and an organizational philosophy and structure that foster integrity in both process and product.

PATTERNS OF HIGH-PERFORMING HIGH-END SPECIALISTS

As we observed in the previous section, high-end specialists appear to have been playing a different game during the 1980s. Although they scored low on the integration index in Figure 10.2, high-end specialists achieved relatively high levels of total product quality. This finding does not discount the importance of consistency and coherence. Effective performance among high-end specialists may simply require a different pattern of consistency. Believing that this should be characterized as something more than "lack of consistency with volume producers," we turned to a different set of organizational variables to establish a pattern for high-end specialists and relate it to total product quality.

In Chapter 3 we noted that high-end specialists responded to the competitive environment of the 1980s with product differentiation through superior performance in established functional criteria and the creation of contemporary designs that preserved stability and consistency of product concepts and customer expectations across models. High product integrity, however indispensable, is not sufficient to effectively distinguish superior high-end models from the better products of volume producers that also feature high product integrity. What is critical for high-end success is high integrity under extreme conditions—total balance and safety at a cruising speed of more than 125 mph, for example. Relatively stable and homogeneous (though demanding) expectations and relative price insensitivity among customers have allowed high-end specialists to spend more time (and more engineering hours) than volume producers in achieving this integrity.

DEVELOPMENT SYSTEMS OF EFFECTIVE
HIGH-END SPECIALISTS

Effective high-end specialists have employed a relatively classical system of product development, with fewer linkages to the market and less intensive communication across functions than we saw among volume producers. The information processing systems of effective high-end specialists combine massive organizational memory and information processing capabilities *within* each stage of product development and simple information flows *across* stages and functions (see Figure 10.3).[*]

The consistency and stability of the product concept across models and over time facilitates the sharing of information stock or knowledge throughout the organizations involved in development. In effect, it creates an engineering tradition, which in turn simplifies the content of information flows across units; a relatively simple signal can convey a complex and subtle meaning because concepts and nuances are already shared by the organizational members prior to communication. The effectiveness of this emphasis on cumulatively shared knowledge presumes that the knowledge does not become obsolete rapidly.

To achieve superior functionality under extreme conditions—a central feature of high-end models—the effective high-end specialist pursues step-by-step optimization and links the steps sequentially. The engineers working within each problem-solving unit tend to be perfectionists. Work on a problem continues until a seemingly perfect solution is reached and approved. The next step begins its cycle only after receiving complete output from the upstream stage.

Long lead times associated with this system derive from (1) the perfectionist approach, which results in many iterations within each problem-solving cycle, and (2) the sequential linkage of the cycles. Superior performance advantage and concept stability may offset any disadvantage associated with the longer lead time. Indeed, the long

---

[*] The effective process model for high-end specialists may be characterized as a classical example proposed by Thompson (1967), in which environmental impacts are buffered by boundary-spanning units (product concept units) and technical core units are linked sequentially. The product-concept unit functions as a stabilizer of the market environment, imposing upon consumers the company's stable definition of the best car. Large back orders function as a buffer at the other end of the process.

Figure 10.3 Product Development System of
High-Performing High-End Specialist

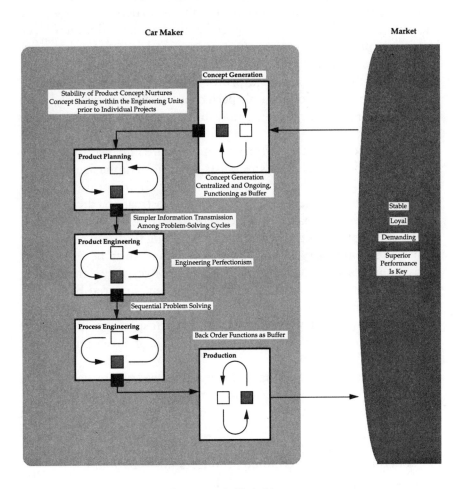

Note: Information flows prior to actions and supplier system are omitted for simplicity.

☐ Alternatives   ■ Evaluation   ■ Final Approval   ➝ Information Flow for Actions

lead time may be turned to a marketing advantage (e.g., "the XYZ coupe is a once-in-a-lifetime product").

Development organizations that employ the kind of information system depicted in Figure 10.3 are likely to emphasize functional specialization. A functional organization facilitates the accumulation of technical expertise through mutual learning and knowledge transfer among subunit members. This process of knowledge accumulation is particularly appropriate to a product line that shares design concepts, themes, philosophy, and standards. Emphasis on depth of knowledge encourages a higher degree of specialization at the individual level. Specialists practice their specialties across models, reinforcing common themes and accumulation of know-how. Among functional subunits, test engineering (e.g., prototype testing), by screening premature outputs and allowing only perfect outcomes to be released from the product engineering stage, may function as a guardian of the engineering tradition.

Because cross-stage information flows are much simpler, effective structures for high-end specialists need not emphasize complex formal organizational mechanisms for internal integration. Batch transmission of complete information from upstream to downstream (i.e., the phased approach) does not require strong integration across stages. Concept sharing and a strong engineering tradition can further reduce the complexity of the information that must be exchanged across subunits. Relatively simple codes can convey very rich meaning when the nuance or connotation they represent is shared by senders and receivers in advance. Even when stronger integration mechanisms (such as a full-time integrator) are adopted, their span of responsibility and authority may be confined to a certain stage of development (e.g., prototype coordinator).

High-end specialists may achieve a high level of internal integrity by virtue of tradition and perfectionism in engineering. Because they are themselves the arbiters of what an outstanding high-end car should be, they may achieve external integrity through the normal course of engineering and testing, without the kind of direct and continuous market contact effective volume producers must maintain.

CONSISTENCY AND TPQ AMONG HIGH-END SPECIALISTS

Total product quality is the principal focus of product development among high-end specialists; hence TPQ is the focus of our study of this segment. We developed for high-end specialists a consistency index similar to the integration index for volume producers using a comparison of six organizational variables across the companies. These variables, based on the hypothetical pattern of effective high-end specialists developed in Figure 10.3, represent relative simplicity of

Figure 10.4 Impact of Consistency of High-End Specialists on TPQ

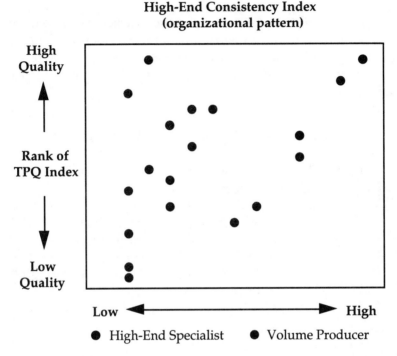

internal and external integration, centralization of concept function, strength of engineering perfectionism, and extent of sequential problem solving. (These variables are discussed in more detail in the Appendix.)

The relationship between consistency and total product quality in the high-end pattern is plotted in Figure 10.4. Although we cannot draw strong conclusions based on a small number of high-end specialists, some significant patterns do emerge:

- High-end specialists as a group tend to show greater consistency than volume producers.
- Among high-end specialists, effective companies have higher degrees of consistency.
- There is no significant correlation between consistency and quality among volume producers.[*]

---

[*]   Spearman rank-order correlation among volume producers in Figure 10.5 (n = 17) is 0.16 and not significant.

The implication is that effective high-end specialists developed a distinctive pattern of organizational structure and process in the 1980s. Firms that achieved superior performance in product quality looked very much like the model sketched earlier. Such companies exhibit a high degree of specialization and perfectionism in engineering; a strong functional orientation; simple, cross-functional patterns of communication; and almost single-minded pursuit of superior functionality.

CONTRASTS AND SIMILARITIES

The decade of the 1980s witnessed two very successful paradigms for product development in the world auto industry. One, applied by a few firms in the mass market, produced cars of outstanding quality rapidly and efficiently. The second, applied by a few firms in the high-end segment of the market, produced cars of outstanding quality that performed at superior levels under extreme conditions. Development that followed the latter paradigm was slower and less efficient than development that followed the former. Table 10.3 compares the strategy and patterns of organization and management that characterize each of these paradigms.

Two things stand out in the table. First, the paradigms, though very different, are coherent and internally consistent. Successful firms, as we have seen, developed patterns of organization and management across many different aspects of concept development, design, and engineering that fit well together and reinforced one another. Second, the paradigms matched the competitive and market environments that faced firms in the respective segments. High-end specialists, enjoying a more stable environment, could afford the long lead times associated with a highly functional approach to development. For volume producers operating in a turbulent and highly competitive market, quick response, high productivity, and total vehicle concept were critical.

Although different competitive pressures gave rise to different patterns for success, we also see similarities between the segments, in product integrity, for example. Effective high-end specialists achieve product integrity through depth of expertise applied to a stable concept

Table 10.3 High-Performing Volume Producers versus High-End Specialists

Strategic Group Dimensions	Consistent Patterns for Volume Producers of the 1980s	Consistent Patterns for High-End Specialists of the 1980s
Performance	high total product quality high development productivity short lead time	high total product quality low productivity accommodated long lead time accommodated

Competitive Strategy	middle- low-priced models
	
	short delivery
	
	tendency to overcapacity
	
	production/profit instability
	
	emphasis on product differentiation by concept:
	
	  1. matching cost and basic performance with rivals
	  2. differentiating by fit of total vehicle concept
		high-priced models
		
		long delivery
		
		tendency to undercapacity
		
		production/profit stability
		
		emphasis on product differentiation by performance:
		
		  1. differentiating by functional superiority under extreme conditions
		  2. stabilizing vehicle concept

Organization and Management	direct and close contact between market and concept creation intensive contact between concept creation, planning, engineering, and manufacturing proactive concept creation and continual concept elaboration integrated problem solving in product-process engineering short-cycle production (application of JIT and TQC) supplier involvement in engineering; intensive communication with suppliers emphasis on internal and external integration consolidation of product manager and concept champion into one role product manager has power heavyweight product manager	centralized control of product concepts for consistency across models massive accumulation of technical expertise and shared engineering tradition perfectionism in engineering phased linking of project stages, each of which perfects output step by step development and production featuring testing and inspection emphasis on functional specialization centralized concept creation units simpler integration mechanisms test engineers have power functional/semifunctional form

within an established engineering tradition. Effective volume producers achieve it through an organizational structure and process that link market imagination to the details of engineering design and integrate components and parts into a coherent whole. However achieved, product integrity is a universal aspect of outstanding performance.

It appears that the success of these patterns is rooted in several common characteristics and similarities: both attracted and satisfied customers in the 1980s; both are characterized by careful balancing of many important details, rather than superiority in a few "critical factors for success"; and for continued strength both depend upon long-term capabilities rather than quick introduction of trendy techniques.

In summary, there is no silver bullet. The key to high-performance development seems to be consistency in the overall pattern, involving a number of variables in different areas rather than a few key variables. No single capability, no one structural characteristic, no particular strategy, no specific process made the difference in the 1980s. Only when a company developed a consistent pattern across many variables in all areas did it achieve superior performance. It appears that to be effective in product development, an organization must do many things well in a consistent way, rather than do a few key things exceptionally well.

NOTE

1. For the concept of consistency index, seen Van de Ven and Drazin (1985) and Venkatraman (1987). The present indicator is at best a rough approximation in that relative importance of each variable included in the index is considered to be equal.

CHAPTER 11

THE DEVELOPMENT FUTURE: RIVALS, TOOLS, AND SOURCES OF ADVANTAGE

Winds of change are blowing through the world auto industry. Toyota, Nissan, and Honda have already launched an assault on the high-performance luxury segment of the market, and such cars from other volume producers are close to introduction. Recently announced acquisitions and joint development arrangements continue trends begun in the 1980s. New technology and vehicle concepts debuting at auto shows around the world are not merely for show; they are serious products with commitments for market introduction. There is a scramble for positioning with the creation of a unified European market in 1992, and recent changes in Eastern Europe may open up new markets and new sources of supply. Supply is on everyone's mind as new plants open up in Europe and America, stimulated largely by the desire of Japanese firms to produce on a global basis.

These and many other developments will have important effects on competition and the role of product development in the years ahead. Moreover, new concepts in management and new information technology may combine to fundamentally alter the practice of development.

Our discussion thus far has focused on management, organization, and performance based on worldwide experience in the 1980s. In this chapter we examine the implications of our findings for possible future developments. We look first at competition between products and the possible growth of rivalry and convergence across competitors. We then discuss potential shifts in the focus of competition to increased performance through advanced components, to the product line as a whole, and to global cooperative networks. Finally, we examine possible changes in the nature of organization and management, with particular emphasis on the impact of new computer technology.

307

RIVALRY AND CONVERGENCE IN
PRODUCT COMPETITION

Globalization of competition, a general trend during the 1980s, will continue in the 1990s. Direct product rivalry on an international scale will further intensify as new models penetrate foreign markets and consumers more frequently consider models from different countries. Even in the Japanese market, where imports had only a minor market share up to the mid 1980s, import sales—mostly European so far—more than quadrupled by the end of the decade and are still growing.

How far such market convergence might go may depend upon the segment. Global convergence of the subcompact and compact segments, for example, is already history. In the U.S. market, the Chevrolet Corsica, Ford Tempo, Honda Accord, Mazda 626, Peugeot 405, and Toyota Camry have become very similar in product characteristics and target customers. U.S. producers may halt independent development of subcompact models, but they will still participate actively in joint development projects with the Japanese (e.g., GM-Isuzu-Suzuki-Toyota, Ford-Mazda, Chrysler-Mitsubishi). The result will be sets of products that sell with little difference worldwide.

The high-end segment, too, has become more international and competitive. Daimler-Benz and BMW, once dominant in the category of high-performance luxury sedan, face new entries from Toyota's Lexus and Nissan's Infiniti. Jaguar, acquired in 1989 by Ford, now has the resources to compete seriously on the continent. General Motors has established a joint venture with Saab, and its Cadillac division is preparing a performance-oriented luxury car—code named Aurora—for possible introduction in the mid 1990s.

The mid-size segment has remained fairly region-specific during the 1980s. We have seen high-volume, low-priced family sedans in the United States (e.g., Taurus and Lumina), chauffeur-driven saloons in Japan (e.g., Crown and Cedric), and quasi-luxury sedans in Europe (e.g., Scorpio, Omega, and R-25). But even this segment might converge in the 1990s. Consumers may compare the Ford Taurus, Audi 100, and Nissan Maxima more directly in the emerging global mid-size segment.

Although some segments may remain highly regional—micromini cars in Japan and large road cruisers in the United States, for example—overall the worldwide market of the 1990s will become more crowded with directly competing models from different regions. Customers will become less loyal to particular makes, and producers will have to be ever more responsive to changes in customer needs.

This, in a sense, is "Japanization" of the global competitive game. Direct product rivalry among many models within each segment has been a hallmark of the Japanese domestic market for decades, affording Japanese auto makers a natural international advantage in playing their favorite game (short lead time and model-change cycles, rapid product proliferation, and high productivity). This advantage will persist well into the 1990s. U.S. and European auto makers will be under continued pressure to reduce the competitive gap and will need a further period of adjustment to reduce lead time, increase productivity, and improve development organization. These pressures are likely to have implications for both volume producers and high-end specialists.

VOLUME PRODUCERS: NARROWING THE GAPS IN LEAD TIME, PRODUCTIVITY, AND TOTAL PRODUCT QUALITY

The Japanese advantage is not likely to last forever. Western volume producers have recognized gaps in product development performance, and many of these companies have launched major efforts to narrow those gaps. The process of closing the gap in product development may be analogous to the process Western producers have been going through since the early 1980s with manufacturing productivity and quality. Sizable gaps in production cost and productivity between Japanese and Western auto makers were first identified around 1980, triggering massive efforts by many U.S. and European producers to narrow the productivity gap.[1] There is evidence that differences had narrowed significantly by the late 1980s, but a gap still remained.[2] We have seen the same trend in manufacturing quality.[3] In product development we are likely to see a similar process of gap recognition and catch-up that will be several years behind the trend in manufacturing performance.

As a result of this adaptation process, gaps in both performance and organization of product development at the individual project level are likely to narrow in the 1990s. Recent data from selected Western companies suggest that the Japanese lead time advantage is already narrowing as some U.S. and European concept-to-market lead times gradually approach the four-year level. Although the Japanese may cut their lead time further, they probably will not, except perhaps in the case of small-volume niche products, pursue drastic reduction of lead time much beyond the three-year level. Some Japanese firms, in fact, are spending more than their normal four-year period to develop high-end models. Moreover, the model-change cycle of some Japanese high-volume products may remain unchanged or get slightly longer. Overall, lead time differences across the regions will narrow during the 1990s.

The productivity gap may persist for a longer time, partly because it is greater than the lead time gap (our data suggest that Japanese projects were nearly twice as productive as Western projects) and partly because engineering productivity is more difficult to measure and is often tracked less carefully than lead time in the auto companies' internal information systems. Moreover, Western volume producers, in concentrating on lead time reduction, have not placed great emphasis on productivity in recent years. But as gaps in lead time narrow, gaps in productivity (which may show up in more frequent model introductions and a wider product line) will stand out in sharp relief, making engineering productivity an increasingly sharp focus of competition. Without productivity improvement, lead time reduction may encounter resource constraints that limit product line variety and/ or fast model renewal. To the extent that lead time drives development productivity (see Chapter 4) and firms pursue lead time reduction through lower specialization and integrated problem solving, faster development may directly enhance productivity to some degree. But a focus on the productivity dimension is clearly called for if U.S. and European companies are to reduce the Japanese advantage.

Much the same may be said of product integrity and total product quality. We have already seen a convergence in conformance quality, as U.S. producers narrowed the manufacturing quality gap in the late 1980s. As noted earlier, differences in functionality—fuel economy, acceleration, ride, and handling—have narrowed, leaving quality of design and total vehicle experience as the critical dimensions of differentiation. These dimensions are likely to define the competitive battleground for the next few years.

European firms stand out in design quality and total vehicle performance, but the gaps are beginning to narrow. In the compact segment, some Japanese models—e.g., the Honda Accord and Mazda 626—have made inroads in the European market. Within the next few years, all major Japanese firms will have fully functional European design studios and engineering groups in place. U.S. firms have already begun to tap their European experience in a much more direct way by transferring key people and key concepts. The Ford Taurus, for example, though designed and engineered in the United States, drew on the company's European experience; designers and engineers with European experience helped to shape the interior and exterior styling and overall character of the vehicle.

This convergence of performance in lead time, productivity, and product quality among volume producers grows out of an intense search for competitive advantage. But convergence does not mean that an individual project or firm cannot achieve competitive advantage; the market will always recognize creativity and outstanding execution. What it does mean is that product advantage will be more difficult to achieve.

HIGH-END SPECIALISTS: IS THE STRATEGY SUSTAINABLE?

During the 1970s and 1980s, European high-end specialists emerged as a distinct strategic group with a premium position in image, performance, and pricing. They played a very different competitive game than volume producers, one in which lead time and engineering productivity were much less important. The name of their game was continuity of design and superior functionality. Were that game and the conditions that have supported it to continue, the high-end specialists would be well positioned for play. But the game is changing. Pressures are being exerted both from within, as competition among the traditional high-end players intensifies, and from without, as volume producers enter the premium market segments. These pressures raise questions about changes within the high-end firms and ultimately about the viability of the high-end strategy.

Already we are seeing signs of future strategic convergence. The Legend and Legend Coupe, for example, introduced by Honda in the 1980s, began to compete with the lower end of the product line of European high-end specialists such as Daimler-Benz and BMW. In

1989, two Japanese volume producers, Nissan and Toyota, introduced high-end models—Infiniti and Lexus, respectively—that may compete seriously in the high-end market with cars such as the Mercedes 300 and BMW 7 series. Although these newcomers have used the same organization—and in some cases the same process—that they use to develop volume products, they have expended more resources and time and have applied testing methods and standards appropriate to high-end markets. Ford, which bought Jaguar, may inject some of its management style and process into its new high-end division.

We are thus likely to see products developed within entirely different contexts competing directly in the high-end market of the 1990s. This will be more than competition between products; it will be competition between two very different strategies. Figure 11.1, a conceptual diagram that compares long-term performance progress of volume producers and high-end specialists in the luxury market, helps to clarify the issue. Assuming that major improvements in performance

Figure 11.1 Catch-Up of Volume Producers in Product Performance

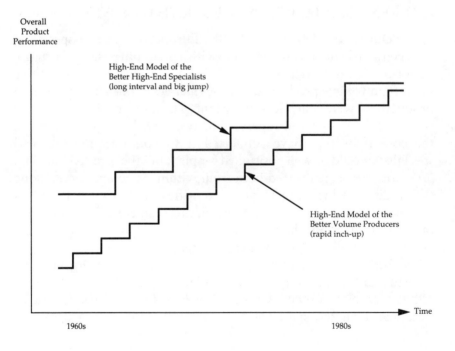

accompany each model renewal, and ignoring minor improvements in between, we see a ladder-like pattern of performance improvement over time. Under these conditions, the long-term pace of functional advancement is determined by two factors: the model-change interval and the performance jump with each model change.

As discussed in Chapter 3, the key to a successful high-end product has been unequivocal superiority in functional performance; such excellence commands a premium price, enhances product image, and nurtures brand loyalty. The traditional organization and process of the high-end specialists—an emphasis on functional specialization and a perfectionist engineering process—have facilitated a great leap upward with every model renewal. Thus the high-end specialists have maintained their technological lead despite a long model-change cycle. The success of this strategy has frustrated some Japanese volume producers, which, each time their tenacious "rapid inch-up" approach has threatened to close the performance gap, have seen the European specialists make a big jump that effectively took them out of range.

Toward the end of the 1980s, a few Japanese firms were closing in on the likes of Daimler-Benz, BMW, and Porsche. Although these specialists will respond with a new generation of models and another jump in performance, competition is now more intense, particularly in the U.S. market, where customers are not as loyal to the traditional high-end brands as their European counterparts.

What will happen next? We can envision at least three scenarios.

Volume Producers Hit a Performance Wall

In the first scenario, volume producers hit a performance wall. Unable to develop real high-end products as long as they stick to their short-cycle approach, their pace of performance catch-up slows. Those that continue to aim at the high-end market have to adapt to the high-end game by altering their organization and process, making them more sequential and perfectionist and prolonging lead time and model-change cycles. Because the structure and process involved are largely incompatible with their existing organizations for creating lower-end products, some may establish separate organizations to produce their high-end models. The high-end specialist strategy thus survives into the 1990s, and this strategic group becomes more crowded and more international in character.

High-End Specialists Change the Development Process

In the second scenario, some volume producers succeed in developing competent high-end models, forcing the incumbent high-end producers to change the way they organize and manage development by adopting many organizational elements of the better volume producers and shortening the model-change cycle to keep pace with the challengers. In the extreme case, the high-end firms abandon the high-end specialist strategy and "descend" into the secular world of the volume producers. We could trace the origin of this trend to the 1970s and 1980s, when high-end specialists first introduced lower-end models (e.g., the Mercedes 190 and Porsche 924/944). Ultimately the specialist strategy disappears during the 1990s as it merges with the volume producer strategy.

High-End Specialists Create a "Super" High-End Segment

In the third scenario, some volume producers are successful, but the high-end specialists adapt by extending their traditional strategy. Instead of changing the development process, they use their expertise to make even bigger jumps in performance, and ascend into the "super" high-end segment. This implies a shift of focus from cars that sell for $30,000 to $70,000 and achieve speeds of 125–135 mph with total control to cars that sell for $60,000 to $100,000 and achieve speeds of 150–170 mph with total control. Thus the high-end specialists might maintain their dominance in a newly established market niche. But this niche may be very small; few people may be willing to pay an extra $30,000 for a performance difference they are unlikely to experience. Though this may be a bridge to the 1990s for small super-car makers such as Ferarri (now a part of Fiat) or Lamborghini, it may not support a company the size of Daimler-Benz, which, in this scenario, might be known in the year 2000 as a diversified giant in electronics and aerospace rather than a major player in the high-end auto business.

The three scenarios are, of course, hypothetical. What we might more realistically expect is some combination of the three—mutual adjustment between the high-end specialists and volume producers. Already high-end specialists are beginning to integrate functions within their organizations and speed development cycles, and volume producers are altering the development approach used for their top-end cars. In fact, the high-end specialists may not need to become as fast as the volume producers. If they can maintain the same performance jump but shorten the cycle somewhat, the high-end specialists may be able to maintain an edge over the volume producers. If the high-end specialists also find it attractive to create the "super" high-end segment for the top end of their model lines, a mixed strategy might emerge; they might shorten lead times and pursue a more integrated engineering approach for low-end models that compete directly with those of volume producers, while striving for extraordinary leaps in performance in their most expensive, exclusive models, thereby preserving their image and enhancing their reputation as builders of superior products. Whichever pattern of adaptation emerges, it is likely that the distinction between volume producers and high-end specialists will not be nearly as sharp in the 1990s as it was in the 1980s.

THE SHIFTING FOCUS OF COMPETITION

Rivalry between individual products, an important feature of competition in the 1980s, is likely to intensify in the 1990s. Projects to develop new models will place great weight on excellence of execution, while competitive pressure will drive a convergence in project performance across the surviving competitors, leading firms to search for competitive advantage in other dimensions of product development. The sources of superior performance in product development in the 1980s—integrated engineering, strong leadership for external and internal integration, skilled supplier network—will continue to be essential, even critical, but they may not be sufficient for competitive advantage.

Figure 11.2 describes four levels of product-related management that help to clarify this notion of shifting competitive focus: technology (component), individual product, companywide product line, and cross-company product line. We speculate that the focus of competition, which during the 1980s resided largely at the single-product level (product integrity, project lead time, project productivity, and so forth), will shift to other levels or to multiple foci as performance gaps at the product level narrow. If this should occur, a balance across these different levels may well be critical.

BALANCING CORPORATE IDENTITY AND INDIVIDUAL PRODUCT RESPONSIVENESS

At the product-line level, we expect customers of the 1990s worldwide to become increasingly conscious of corporate identity. To

Figure 11.2 Hierarchy of Product Development Management

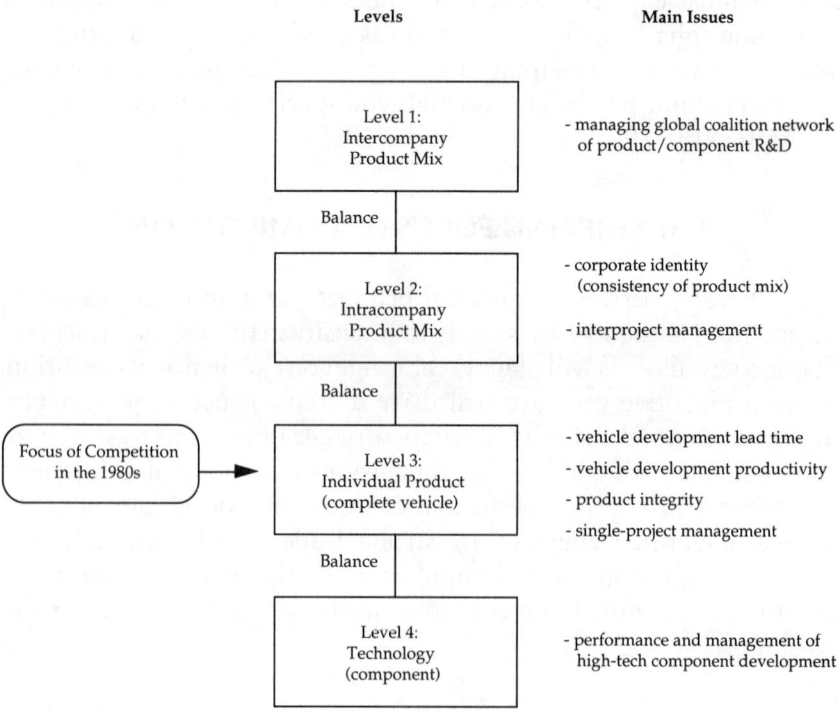

Levels	Main Issues
Level 1: Intercompany Product Mix	- managing global coalition network of product/component R&D
Balance	
Level 2: Intracompany Product Mix	- corporate identity (consistency of product mix) - interproject management
Balance	
Level 3: Individual Product (complete vehicle)	- vehicle development lead time - vehicle development productivity - product integrity - single-project management
Balance	
Level 4: Technology (component)	- performance and management of high-tech component development

Focus of Competition in the 1980s → Level 3: Individual Product (complete vehicle)

the extent that they do, it will become increasingly difficult to compete effectively on the strength of individual products without a distinctive and consistent theme in the product line as a whole. Car producers in the 1990s will have to achieve a subtle balance between corporate identity in the entire product line and responsiveness and variety in individual products.

Corporate identity as discussed here is something more than the superficial commonality of emblems, body silhouettes, front grilles, or common images conveyed in advertising. It is expressed at a deeper level of product character, in common themes, in how details of function and form in hardware are orchestrated across a company's products. It is thus more than marketing or cosmetic tricks of ornamentation, and it involves the entire development process and organization.

Figure 11.3 uses a concept clustering map like those presented in Chapter 3 to illustrate the emerging competitive game. Companies are arrayed across the horizontal axis and product segments across the

Figure 11.3 Concept Cluster Map: Emerging Cluster in the Global Market

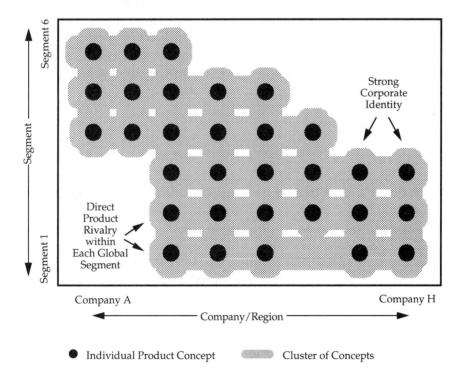

vertical axis. Each product concept is thus part of a company and a market segment. Connections between product concepts indicate the clustering of concepts in the market. Vertical clustering indicates a strong company identity in which individual products share conceptual themes. Horizontal clustering indicates a strong segment concept and direct product rivalry. The map captures the emerging context for automotive competition in the 1990s, in which concepts cluster on a global basis around both companies and segments. In that environment, firms need to balance conceptual commonality across all products in the product line against conceptual distinction in a segment.

Balancing the two axes relies on deliberate interproject coordination. In this, firms can err in both directions. In overemphasizing commonality, they might sacrifice product differentiation. For example, General Motors' so-called "C-body" family (which consists of Cadillac, Buick, and Oldsmobile versions) shared a silhouette that featured an upright rear window. When a similar silhouette showed up in much lower-priced GM models (e.g., the "A-cars" from Oldsmobile, Chevrolet, Buick, and Pontiac), U.S. consumers generally perceived it as absence of divisional differentiation rather than presence of corporate identity. This hurt Cadillac particularly. Customers asked, "Why should I buy a Cadillac when it looks just like an Olds?" Mazda's product line in the mid 1980s represented the opposite case of insufficient corporate identity. Mazda's individual products enjoyed a strong reputation for engineering content and product integrity,[*] but except for a vague European orientation, they lacked a consistent theme across models.

A comparison of Figures 3.1 and 11.3 suggests that the new competitive challenge of balancing overall product line with individual products might have different implications for producers in different regions. For European firms the main challenge is to strengthen individual project performance while retaining traditional strengths in corporate identity. Indeed, we might think of the increasing emphasis on corporate identity as "Europeanization" of the world market, inasmuch as European customers historically have emphasized corporate identity at a deep level. European firms must work to maintain this initial advantage while making individual product development more

---

[*]   The popularity of Mazda models in the technically demanding German market supports this view.

responsive to a diverse and changing market. This will require stronger management of individual projects.

The challenge is quite different for Japanese companies. Because of their experience in a domestic market with strong product rivalry, Japanese firms enjoy a natural advantage in fast and efficient development—critical capabilities for playing the new global game. Historically Japanese auto makers have concentrated on dealing with competitive challenges at the product level and paid less attention to pursuing common themes across product lines. They have been supported by Japanese domestic customers, who, being conditioned to a fragmented pattern of product concepts, have been more or less insensitive to corporate identity. Some Japanese firms began to strengthen their corporate identity in the mid 1980s, but most still lag European firms in this respect. With market expectations for consistent product lines, one task for Japanese car makers will be to improve interproject coordination without sacrificing responsiveness and variety in individual projects. This is no less difficult a task than that which faces European firms.

U.S. producers must make significant efforts on both fronts. At the single-product level, they must make development faster and more efficient and improve product integrity by strengthening external integration in the development organization. At the product-line level, they may have to alter their traditional piecemeal approach to corporate (or divisional) identity, which relies heavily on commonality of components and particular styling elements. In the face of growing consumer demand for product-line consistency at deeper levels of the product, U.S. producers may have to shift to a more holistic approach to corporate identity—realizing a common conceptual theme across models by orchestrating components, layout, and styling.

Success in the 1990s will increasingly depend upon management of the entire product line. Producers that focus on project management to the exclusion of thematic and conceptual integrity across models will be at considerable risk.

BALANCING TECHNOLOGY DEVELOPMENT AND PRODUCT DEVELOPMENT

One of the themes of competition in the 1980s was balance and integrity in total vehicle performance. Innovation in component technology (e.g., multivalve engines) played a role but was successful only when integrated with other components and the overall vehicle concept. We may see component technology grow in importance in the 1990s, creating a need to balance shorter lead time for vehicle development against longer lead time for developing new technology—all while preserving product integrity.

Figure 11.4 summarizes the problem. The top half of the figure suggests that the increasing volatility of competitive environments in the 1990s will demand further reduction in vehicle development lead time, while continued rapid progress in technologies not only in

Figure 11.4 Technology Development versus Product Development

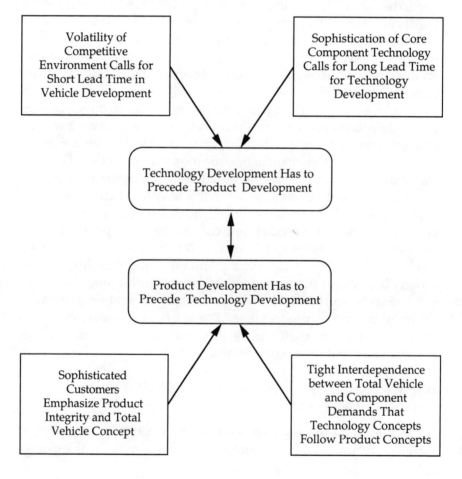

electronics and new materials, but also in new configurations of mechanical components such as engines and suspensions—will make technology development time-consuming (often five to seven years or longer). We may thus see component development lead times in excess of vehicle lead times, particularly in Japan, where vehicle lead time is already short.

One common solution to the problem of lead time differentials is advanced engineering, whereby components with high technological requirements—such as engines, transmissions, and suspensions—are developed in advance and placed in a "refrigerator" to be picked out by vehicle development engineers and modified as needed for a new vehicle. This effectively decouples technology development and product development.

Such decoupling, however, runs the risk that newly "refrigerated" technologies will be used without much consideration for fit between product concept and technology concept. This kind of "technology push" approach might be effective in a market in which consumers demand new technologies regardless of fit with total vehicle concept. In the past, for example, enthusiasm for new technologies among Japanese consumers, particularly young buyers, virtually guaranteed a boost in sales to a company that injected a dose of "first technology in its class" into a model.

But both products and markets are changing. In the bottom half of Figure 11.4, we see increasing consumer sensitivity to product integrity, a trend continuing from the 1980s, and evolution toward technically coherent products with tighter interdependence between components and the total vehicle. Producer response to these forces must be to match technology development to the product concept. In theory this means that vehicle development should precede and drive technology development. This is in conflict with the need for short vehicle lead time, because sophisticated component technologies take longer to develop than the vehicle.

A recent example underscores the growing importance of vehicle-component matching. Honda and Mazda first commercialized four-wheel steering (4WS) technology in the Japanese domestic market in 1987. Although the technological approaches were different (Mazda used electronic control, Honda mechanical), both systems were reasonably sophisticated, economical, and reliable. In the Japanese market of the 1970s, both might have achieved market success. But in the market of the late 1980s, the two systems fared quite differently. Honda's product was quite successful in the domestic market; Mazda's had poor starting sales and was widely regarded as a failure. Some industrial observers were quick to ascribe Mazda's disappointing results to a conceptual mismatch between vehicle and component. Honda had put its 4WS system on the Prelude, a two-door coupe, Mazda on a five-door hatchback. Japanese consumers tended to associate 4WS with a sporty, progressive image, which was consistent with the Prelude concept. The five-door hatchback, a family car, was not perceived as sporty and progressive; hence the message to consumers was confusing.

The 4WS episode illustrates how inadequate the refrigerator or off-the-shelf approach to technology development is in the face of the emerging challenge to car makers: to achieve simultaneously shorter vehicle lead time, sophistication of component technology, product integrity, and a conceptual match between vehicle and components. There are at least three potential alternative approaches to technology development. The first and most conventional approach would be to establish a long-range plan for technology development—a technology cycle plan—and coordinate it with the long-range vehicle, or vehicle cycle, plan.* The technology cycle plan, by emphasizing centralized control of vehicle/component development projects, would guide specific technology development to achieve a product-technology fit despite the lead time gap. The key to this approach is the incorporation of both vehicle and technology concept elements into long-range plans, something conventional cycle planning that emphasizes schedules and resource allocation often does not do effectively.

A second approach, which might be called multigeneration concept development, is to put the current product manager in charge of developing new concepts for the generation after next. Added to the product manager's responsibility for ongoing hardware development for the next-generation model would be responsibility for developing a broad vision or concept for how the model might evolve over at least two generations. In this way, the product manager could lead component technology development while keeping vehicle development cycles short. The product manager might tell the advanced component

---

* Toyota and Nissan each established a unit in charge of technology cycle planning in the mid 1980s.

engineers, "I need such and such component technology for my vehicle. I know it is too late for the next model, but I want this technology to be in the generation coming after that." Thus, though the vehicle model-change cycle may be as short as four years, advanced component engineers would be afforded seven to eight years, enough lead time to develop the most sophisticated technologies.

Multigenerational concept development is a rather decentralized approach relative to technology cycle planning in that each product manager strongly influences long-term product concepts for a particular model series. The challenge in this approach is to balance change and continuity in product concepts. The approach assumes a certain amount of consistency within a product line over generations, yet it must be able to readapt product concepts if the market and technology change in unexpected ways. Preserving basic model themes across generations while flexibly modifying product specifics is likely to be a major challenge in the 1990s.

A third approach is to improve speed and efficiency so that technology development projects can respond to the needs of vehicle development more quickly. This shifts the focus of competition from management of vehicle development to management of component development. Use of advanced CAD-CAM-CAE simulation technology may have a dramatic impact on the improved performance of high-tech component projects. Consider a multilink rear suspension system. This is a very complex technology with many possible variations. In developing its multilink system for its 190 model, Daimler-Benz used CAD-CAE simulation very heavily for the initial screening of basic configurations and geometries. Daimler-Benz engineers reduced the alternatives to eight concepts with 70 variations using the computer and completed final screening with physical prototypes. Nissan apparently relied even more heavily on CAD-CAE simulation to drastically shorten lead time when it developed its version of multilink suspension.[4] New engine development can also profit significantly from CAD-CAE; some engineers estimate that computer simulation can be equivalent to as many as three cycles of prototype construction.[5]

Computer technology is not a panacea. Integration of component engineering units, enlargement of component engineers' task assignments, and reduction of prototype cycles are all critical to reducing development lead times for components. Moreover, in practice the real solution to the problem of matching advanced components and vehicles may be some combination of the three approaches we have outlined here, coupled with a modification of the old refrigerator concept. A firm might, for example, establish both long-range plans for technologies and products and employ multigenerational concept development. Those involved—planners, engineers, and product managers—would work together closely and develop plans jointly. The technology plan, with strong links to product plans and next-generation concepts, would be the basis for advanced development projects. Such a combination of planning and concept development might get projects under way in a timely manner and link them to vehicle concepts, but to address the problem of uncertainty and the need to respond to emerging threats and opportunities, effective component engineering and a modified refrigerator concept would be needed. For components that involve considerable uncertainty, advanced projects would not develop completed components but would rather focus on generating critical know-how in advance of vehicle development, in effect stocking the refrigerator with technical capability.

Technical know-how seldom comes out of the refrigerator as commercial components. Components must be developed, preferably in an integrated manner with the vehicle. Thus when unexpected threats or opportunities occur, it would be important to have the short-cycle, integral development capability to quickly commercialize existing refrigerator know-how.

As components and technologies become more sophisticated, overall management of technology and component development may become a focus of competition. Solving the vehicle-component development dilemma is a tall order. The combination of joint, concept-oriented planning; management of technical know-how; and effective component engineering may help, provided the company possesses the requisite skill in planning, strong cross-functional communication, excellence in engineering, and thoughtful management of knowledge. Firms searching for competitive advantage in the 1990s may well find it in the ability to solve this dilemma.

MANAGING THE GLOBAL COALITION NETWORK IN PRODUCT DEVELOPMENT

The global network, which places significant demands on internal engineering and manufacturing resources and relies on multiple centers of expertise across the major developed (and some developing) countries, is also likely to become a focus of competition in the 1990s. Building cooperative relationships with competitors is one way to meet demands for new products. The challenge to car makers that attempt to exploit a network of cooperative relationships is to maintain the integrity of their internal product mix and individual products while taking advantage of joint product/component development with other companies. This involves balancing conflicting requirements of internally and jointly developed products.

Developments in the 1980s have established a context for the emergence of network management as an important focus of competition in the 1990s.[6] As global competition intensified during the 1980s, major producers, to compensate for weaknesses in particular models or technologies, sought interfirm coalitions in limited product or component areas. Some mergers and acquisitions involving smaller players did occur (e.g., Fiat with Alfa Romeo and Ford with Jaguar), but the predominant trend was this somewhat looser coupling between independent companies involved in joint development and OEM supply of complete vehicles, engines, and transmissions, and joint production and other technical or sales tie-ups. What emerged was a worldwide network in which companies competed and cooperated simultaneously (see Figure 11.5).

The loose web of coalitions that today covers the entire industry is quite different from what some industry analysts in the early 1980s were predicting—that only eight or ten giant car companies would survive the decade. Smaller car companies have survived by participating in the network and exchanging technical or managerial resources, and no major company has been able to avoid becoming a player in the network. Companies maintain their independence by limiting ties to certain areas and sharing with multiple companies. During the 1980s, for example, Renault jointly produced automatic transmissions with VW, diesel engines with Fiat, and gasoline engines with Peugeot and Volvo; the company also cross-licensed some components with British-Leyland, signed a joint research agreement with five other European makers, and acquired a minority share of American Motors and then Volvo.* Chrysler, during the same period, acquired engines from VW and Mitsubishi as well as complete vehicles from Mitsubishi and

---

*   Some of these partnerships and tie-ups are already defunct.

Figure 11.5 Global Network of Automobile Producers in the Late 1980s

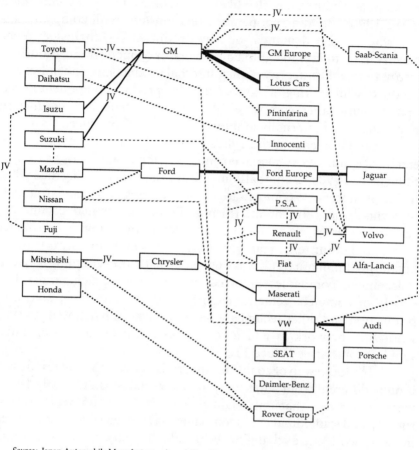

Source: Japan Automobile Manufacturers Association data, various newspapers, and so forth.

━━━ Majority Capital Participation ─── Minority Capital Participation
····· Non-Capital Tie-Ups   JV   Joint Venture

Maserati. Ford jointly developed the Probe and Escort with Mazda and a minivan with Nissan. GM has business ties (joint ventures or equity holdings) with Toyota, Isuzu, Suzuki, Volvo, Pininfarina, and Saab and owns a majority interest in Lotus Cars. Virtually all major players in the world industry are involved in the global network of cooperation, exchanging drawings, tools, components, and complete vehicles at different levels and with different companies.

This global network structure has major implications for the management of product development, namely, the need to balance coherence of internal product lines (corporate identity) and product integrity with the advantage of product and component sharing across companies. For example, developing a car with other companies may save development cost and expand sales opportunity but may introduce product characteristics that are incompatible with the company's corporate identity. A mosaic product mix can destroy the coherence of a company's image and confuse customers. Similarly, jointly developed components might damage the integrity of the models that use them. In the age of global networking, to be part of the network is not enough to guarantee competitive success, because every player is more or less involved in it. The real question is whether a company can establish coalition ties that reduce costs and improve product content without sacrificing corporate identity.

Among the examples of effective development coalitions was "Project Four," in which four European producers—Fiat, Lancia, Alfa Romeo, and Saab—jointly developed mid-size models that shared floor panels and other components yet retained distinctive identities and were received in the market as differentiated products. Another example is the Ford Probe, jointly developed by Ford and Mazda for the U.S. market. Ford engineers, working with their Mazda counterparts, used the chassis and body inner structure of the Mazda 626, a model with a relatively strong reputation in handling, and developed a new exterior and interior design and new suspension setting. The result was superior Mazda functionality in a highly successful sport coupe with a distinctive Ford flavor.

Not all development coalitions have proved successful. GM, for example, has struggled to achieve a coherent line-up of products from its global network. A joint venture with Toyota (NUMMI), captive imports from Isuzu and Suzuki, and a German-engineered model (Opel Kadett) imported from Daewoo of Korea failed to yield a coherent product line in the company's subcompact segment. The character of the models was obscure and, in failing to generate a strong image of new GM subcompacts, this "identity crisis" may have contributed to the erosion of GM's market share during the 1980s. The recent creation of the Geo distribution channel to handle smaller cars developed with foreign partners may help GM instill consistency and coherence into its subcompact line-up.

These experiences suggest that network-related competitive advantage in the 1990s will derive not from being part of a network, nor even from how much a firm uses its network, but rather from how well the network is managed. It is relatively easy to establish ties with other companies, but it is hard to make those ties work well, and harder still to make them work well without destroying corporate identity and product integrity. Because it is hard, firms that succeed are likely to secure an advantage in development.

The challenge is to create and manage an effective coalition of global partners. This requires not only the kinds of skills in structuring and nurturing relationships that are important in any kind of cross-firm venture, but also the ability to manage complex groups that cut across countries and cultures. Managing joint development projects is part of the general problem firms face in creating an efficient global R&D network. It seems clear that the ability to manage an international coalition will be influenced by the quality and degree of integration in a firm's international operations, and vice versa. Firms that have established multinational capabilities and learned to use them in the development of new products (e.g., U.S. and Japanese engineering groups working on a new model) are likely to have developed a set of experiences and skills that will prove useful in joint development with international partners. Firms that are good at managing a network of international resources (whether internal operations or external partners) may have an advantage in a market that is global, differentiated, and intensely competitive.

NEW DEVELOPMENTS IN ORGANIZATION AND MANAGEMENT

As the product development game is played out in the 1990s, competition is likely to drive convergence in organizational structures and processes, at least among volume producers. Under continuing pressure to speed development cycles, Western companies will further integrate their engineering, marketing, and manufacturing organizations and problem-solving processes, and more U.S. and European producers will adopt middle- or heavyweight product manager systems. Integrated problem solving, simultaneous engineering, intensive communication, broader task assignments, and cultures that promote mutual trust and teamwork—trends already evident in the late 1980s—will become the rule rather than the exception.

Other forces currently at work are likely to affect the management of product development throughout the industry. The shifting focus of competition will require new approaches to managing portfolios of development projects and new connections between applied science and product development. Moreover, changes in computer technology, to the extent that they transform the nature of design and engineering, will have implications for the management and organization—as well as the skills—of designers and engineers.

MANAGING THE FRONT END OF DEVELOPMENT

Greater competitive emphasis on technology, management of the product line, and international coalitions will focus attention on what we have called the front end of the development process—the set of activities in research, advanced engineering, technology, and product planning that lay the foundation for a given development project. It is here, at the front end, that the critical linkages between technology development and product concepts that are so important in matching components and total vehicles are established, that conceptual themes that impart a distinctive character to the product line are determined, and that strategies for linking cooperative efforts with international partners to internal projects are devised.

All of the automobile companies we studied have already developed long-term product plans that establish the timing of new model introductions and the required engineering capacity and investment. But competition in the 1990s is likely to require something more. We have noted the importance of a technology plan that examines explicitly the timing of introduction for new concepts in components. For such a plan to be effective, its implications for advanced engineering and research must be thought through in detailed projects in those areas. This presumes much closer relationships and greater interaction between research and advanced engineering than is seen in current practice.

Product planning, as well as development, may be affected by the new competitive pressures. Here the principal challenge will be to bring conceptual themes into the longer-term product cycle plans. Instead of only timing and capacity, such plans would address the evolution of product concepts so that the timing plan becomes the concept plan. At this stage of development, product planners would not take the product concept to the level of detail and completion expected from a product manager. Instead the purpose would be to lay out broad themes for the product, including a profile of the target customer, identification of the target market segment, and changes in the character of the product. Thus the firm would address changes in concept for a given model at the same time it deals with conceptual and thematic relationships across models. Subsequently, product managers would take the product and technology plans as input in developing a detailed and specific product concept.

A longer-term planning process with conceptual content lays the foundation for pursuing individual projects while managing across projects to achieve coherence in the product line. To the extent that it clarifies the role specific projects ought to play in the product line and delineates areas of distinction and differentiation to be sought, such an approach may make a firm more effective in managing the product line and in choosing partners and structuring relationships in its global network.

Adding a technology cycle plan and a conceptual dimension to longer-term product plans may create a framework for developing new components and new products, but it is only meaningful if the framework is linked to the firm's marketing, manufacturing, and engineering strategies, and to specific development projects. When longer-term product planning activities are not linked (or only loosely linked) to decisions about manufacturing or marketing capabilities, new products, even though they may have been in the long-term product cycle plan for some time, are likely to be initiated on the basis of inaccurate assumptions about downstream capabilities and without the necessary support of key functional groups and a shared understanding of their role and mission.

What is needed is a *process* that integrates and links the functional strategies of the firm to choices about new products. Such processes have been described elsewhere. Their essential features include a common language for sharing functional plans; a set of procedures for surfacing and reconciling conflicts; frequent, intense communication across functional boundaries; a staged decision process for new products that is grounded in facts about functional capabilities; and close involvement of senior management.[7] We have found such processes to be relatively rare in practice. But in an environment in which product line character and image are important, where developing complex technologies and matching them with the right product concept is critical, and in which pressures for cost and quality are intense, such an integrative process at the front end of development is likely to be a distinct advantage.

THE IMPACT OF COMPUTER-AIDED SYSTEMS

Computers have played an important role in automobile product development for many years without transforming the development process in any fundamental way. But a transformation may be in the offing. Though computer-aided design and computer-aided engineering are likely to continue to be used in traditional ways to reduce lead time and improve productivity (e.g., by speeding up drafting or improving the accuracy of instructions), firms are likely to greatly expand the range of development activities in which computers find extensive application.

Whereas emphasis during the 1970s and 1980s was on digitizing engineering drawings, the focus of computerization in the 1990s is likely to be in adjacent activities such as testing and advanced engineering and styling. For example, sophisticated simulation programs supported by supercomputers may enable precise testing of vehicle dynamics without physical prototypes, saving time and increasing the number of alternatives tested. In addition, realistic styling models generated by advanced computer graphics may supplant early clay models, and computerization of quality management tools (e.g., computerized failure-mode effect analysis) may improve design quality and facilitate interproject transfer of engineering know-how.[8] To the extent that software programs used to computerize individual development steps can be linked to larger computer-integrated manufacturing systems, emphasis will shift to automating the development cycle as a whole. Such a systematic application of computer tools may enable a reduction of lead times to three years or less.

But computerization will not be a sufficient condition for winning the product development game in the 1990s. Acquisition of advanced hardware by one company is likely to be quickly followed by others as the cost of computing power comes down drastically and new commercial software becomes available to all major car producers. Computer technology may dramatically raise the level of product development performance for the industry as a whole, but by itself it is unlikely to create long-term advantage for one group of companies. Competitive advantage will lie not in hardware and commercial software, but in the organizational capability to develop proprietary software and to coherently integrate software, hardware, and "humanware" into an effective system.

Notwithstanding the popular argument that electronic tele-communications media will substitute for face-to-face contact, inter-personal communication will continue to be critical to new product success. Product development is a simulation of the consumption process, and as customer expectations become holistic, subtle, and equivocal, so does the information that needs to be communicated within the development organization. Until advanced computer systems can handle such information effectively, face-to-face contact, involving verbal communication and presentation of physical artifacts, will continue to be essential for sending multifaceted messages. Because the information to be communicated will become more sophisticated and complex even as the fidelity and richness of the models devised to capture it improve, face-to-face communication will continue to supplement computer technology. Consequently, we will see concurrent emphasis on computer technology and face-to-face communication, rather than substitution of one for the other.

What will be different will be the context in which face-to-face communication occurs. Computer systems may facilitate and enhance group interaction and organizational learning as well as automate specific tasks of the individual engineer. High-speed processors with massive amounts of memory and new kinds of software that combine graphics, data bases, and problem-solving methods will afford development groups rapid access to data, drawings, models, and analysis within a consistent framework.

Consider, for example, the design of a door. Today data on customer experience with the door, door manufacturing processes, and modes of failure in the field are organized in incompatible formats and processed in different computer systems managed by different organizations. The result is that critical questions (such as "From a customer experience perspective, what were the three most severe problems with the doors in our last three programs?" and "What design changes were implemented to deal with them?") take lots of time, paper, and meetings to answer. New systems may not only provide the answers to such questions more rapidly, but also, by supplying everyone involved in the design with the same data, enhance the ability to probe the sources of the problems. The problem-solving group will still employ face-to-face communication, but the conversations will be very different. Communication will be faster and occur within a new framework, possibly using new media. The new systems will in effect provide a new "language" that will allow different functional groups with their own "dialects" to develop shared understanding. Moreover, the computer system will store that understanding and use its collective organizational memory for learning and improvement.

For the potential of such systems to be realized, organizations must be structured quite differently. A fragmented organization with parochial philosophies and substantial barriers to communication will frustrate even the most clever and powerful computer system. Hardware and software must be combined with appropriate "humanware"— the organizational structure and processes, philosophies, and skills needed for rapid problem solving, internal integration across functions, and external integration with customers—to create competitive advantage for car producers.

ENGINEERS IN THE 1990s

Symbiotic integration of computer-aided systems and human organizations will have important consequences for individual engineers. Specifically, effective automotive engineers of the future may be characterized by broader responsibility and a combination of "high-tech" and "high-touch" (i.e., human-fitting) skills.

As computer tools reduce the routine workloads of engineers and as pressures for product integrity and customer orientation increase, effective engineers will broaden their scope, becoming component engineers rather than narrow specialists in piece parts. For example, a door-latch engineer may become a door engineer, and a transmission-case engineer may evolve into a transmission engineer. Such broadening of responsibility will involve more than a change of title; it will entail developing a system perspective and the skills to act on it. A component engineer will need to retain depth of understanding in the design of parts while developing an understanding of the component as a whole, including critical interactions among parts.

Engineers of the 1990s may also be required to integrate their skills and responsibility across development steps, as computer-based tools strengthen informational ties between the phases. We may well see the collapse of walls between jobs in conventional engineering organizations with their specialized groups of design engineers, drafters, checkers, prototype technicians, and testers. One engineer, equipped with an advanced CAE workstation, may become responsible for a more complete cycle of development, including functional design, drawing, checking, modeling, simulation, and evaluation. Other computer linkages may enable component engineers to design basic manufacturing systems, blurring the distinction between product engineers and process engineers. Automobile engineering in the 1990s may be more like engineering in the chemical industry, where product and process engineering are much more consolidated.

The future automotive engineer may also combine technical and commercial skills and orientation, becoming an external integrator who links customer expectations to detailed component designs. For example, whereas traditional transmission engineers have focused on numerical specifications and technical computations, the next generation of transmission engineers may also take into account human factors and customer interfaces, including how customers respond to the feel of the shifting and what gear-shift ratio fits the character of the product.

As with product and process engineers, we may see a blurring of the distinction between component engineers (specialists in internal structures) and industrial designers (specialists in user interfaces). As the development process embraces a network of computer and human organization, engineers will have to become architects of the interface between the two worlds. Already test engineers in some Japanese companies are developing new-vehicle evaluation systems that use computer technology to translate subtle human feelings into numerical data. These system allow a test driver to record impressions about handling, stability, ride, noise, body-shell rigidity, and so forth to engineers in real time using a microphone, while numerical data are collected from sensors attached to both driver and vehicle. The data are immediately analyzed by computers and compared with the driver's comments to establish the relationship between the driver's impression and objective vehicle dynamics. The effectiveness of this system depends on both advanced computer systems and the human sensibility of the engineers who live in the customer-computer interface, quickly translating back and forth between the customer's voice and numerical data.

In summary, engineers of the future will need the skills to integrate the customer's voice and component details, design and testing, engineering and manufacturing, computer and human judgment, whole and part, and left brain and right brain. Engineering in the 1990s will not be a cold system dominated by computers or an archaic organization of craftspeople; rather, it will be an intelligent system of advanced electronics, human-fitting technologies, and highly skilled human beings.

NOTES

1. See, for example, Abernathy, Clark, and Kantrow (1983).
2. See, for example, Krafcik (1988).
3. See *The Power Report on Automotive Marketing* 1989.
4. "Kuruma. Koko ga Hai-Teku: Marutirinkusasupenshon," *Nikkei Sangyo Shimbun* ("Automobile. Here is a High Technology: Multilink Suspension," *Japan Economic Journal*), 1 June 1988.
5. "Nissan: Kawaru Enjin Sekkei no Josiki," *Nikkei Mekanikaru* ("Nissan: Common Sense in Engine Design Is Changing," *Japan Mechanics*), 10 May 1982, p. 85.
6. See Fujimoto (1984, Japanese) for details.
7. See, for example, Hayes, Wheelwright, and Clark (1988, Chapter 10).
8. See, for example, Jaikumar (1986) and Behner (1989).

CHAPTER 12
BEYOND THE AUTO INDUSTRY: CONCLUSIONS AND IMPLICATIONS

We set out on our journey through the world auto industry to learn about the sources of superior performance in product development. We thought that delving deeply into a single industry would yield productive insights into the challenges of managing product development in the new industrial competition. We chose the automobile industry because of its technical and commercial scope, its international character, its size and importance, the intriguing nature of automobile companies, and because it is the industry we know best. Our study has taken us to twenty companies in six countries; we have interviewed hundreds of people and collected reams of data; and along the way we have learned much about the process of developing new cars and about what makes some auto companies far more effective than others. But what have we learned that might be of more general value? What is there here of practical significance for the general manager in a very different kind of business?

We believe there are central themes in the auto story that apply generally to firms that must operate in a turbulent, intensely competitive environment. Our confidence in the general nature of these themes grows out of our experience with numerous case studies in other industries, discussions about the auto study with general managers in diverse businesses, and research on the development of many different products. We believe they will prove useful as a framework for action and a direction for change.

We illustrate the application of these themes in several very different companies and industries, using short case histories that underscore their general nature and suggest how they need to be adapted to fit different circumstances. We conclude the chapter with some observations regarding the challenge of implementation and the critical first steps along the path to high-performance product development.

THE CENTRAL THEMES

Creating an outstanding product development organization requires the orchestration of many complex and interrelated details. Because development touches so much of what a company does, changing it—making it faster, more efficient, or more effective—is a daunting task. Creating an outstanding development organization is analogous to creating an outstanding product. Both require orchestration of detail and are complex and intimidating. The auto study has taught us that a strong product concept can provide a thematic framework, a direction that clarifies, simplifies and integrates the many detailed decisions and actions that define and are embodied in the new product. Similarly, for a new development process or organization, a strong overall concept and clear themes can provide the same kind of clarifying, simplifying, integrating framework. In any given company such a framework will have its own local character— that is, idiosyncratic language, emphasis, and detail. Below we examine the important dimensions and discuss the implications of four broad themes that are relevant to such frameworks—the nature of superior performance, integration in the development process, integrating customer and product, and manufacturing for design.

THEME 1: SUPERIOR PERFORMANCE IN TIME, PRODUCTIVITY, AND QUALITY

Our evidence on product development performance has focused on time to market, productivity, and total product quality. In a turbulent environment, firms that prosper pursue excellence in all three. Outstanding firms are faster and more efficient and achieve higher quality than their competitors, suggesting that managers who seek advantage in product development do not have the luxury of focusing only on time or only on design for manufacturability. Indeed, focusing on a single dimension can cause problems in other areas. Firms must recognize that the three dimensions are interrelated and that each plays a particular role in improving overall performance and competitiveness.

Lead time as a driver. Although all three dimensions of performance are critical, lead time seems to exert a particularly powerful leverage effect on overall development performance. It is thus a useful focal point around which to rally the troops in the search for sustained improvement in product development. Lead time plays much the same role in product development as work-in-process inventory plays in the implementation of just-in-time manufacturing. Making pursuit of lead time reduction part of a total program to improve overall performance will lead the firm to seek out the root causes of lack of speed.

The only way to do things faster without adding people or diminishing the quality of the product is to change the basic structure of development—to introduce integrated problem solving, simplify the engineering change process, and improve prototype management. Reducing lead time may initially create a chaotic situation in development, but, if done right, it will set in motion a chain reaction of favorable effects in cross-functional integration, communication, and simultaneous engineering. The cumulative impact of these changes on product development will be far greater than the effect of the lead time reduction by itself.

Productivity—hidden source of variety and responsiveness. Engineering productivity is a hidden competitive weapon. It is hidden in part because measuring and comparing productivity across firms is difficult. Lacking a firm base in measurement, firms may neglect productivity and focus on more easily observable indicators such as lead time. But lead time reduction, by itself, may fail to yield competitive advantage; rapid product renewal and broad product variety are the joint result of short lead time and high engineering productivity.

Firms with highly productive engineering organizations are capable of sustaining more development projects for a given level of resources. Highly productive engineering organizations are a source of fresher, more attractive products and greater product-line variety. Moreover, productivity in the overall development process, including more efficient use of tools and dies, reduces substantially the amount of investment required to sustain a development program. Here too the effect is to allow the firm to sustain a product line-up that is fresher, more tailored to individual customer requirements, and thus more attractive and competitive than the line-ups of its competitors.

Total product quality—the power of product integrity. A product with integrity not only fits together and works coherently as a total system, but it also creates a total experience that matches customer expectations. Product integrity thus emphasizes the product as a whole. To compete on integrity, a firm must develop a deep understanding of its customers and their use of the product. This requires a sensitivity to and appreciation for the subtle and holistic aspects of the product and the customer's evaluation of it.

Component technology and superior functionality are critical in many markets, but with the press of competition and advance of underlying technological knowledge, products with integrity exact a premium in the marketplace. As we have seen in the auto study, there is no substitute for great products. A company can be fast and efficient, but unless it produces great products—and in this environment that means products with integrity—it will not achieve competitive advantage. Moreover, product integrity derives not from a single major success, but rather from consistent performance over time.

THEME 2: INTEGRATION IN THE DEVELOPMENT PROCESS

In a turbulent, competitive environment in which customers are demanding and speed is essential, the underlying source of superior performance is integration. In the development process, integration means linking problem-solving cycles, bringing functional groups into close working relationships, and achieving a meeting of the minds in concept, strategy, and execution. Our evidence suggests that integration reduces lead time and substantially improves productivity in engineering. Firms that want to bring new products to market faster and more efficiently must confront the implications of integration for managerial action. We look at three that seem particularly critical.

Overlapping and communication. Integration, by nature, requires overlapping in time, space, concept, skill, language, methods, attitudes, and philosophy. Overlapping in time (e.g., through changes in timing charts) without improving communication and fostering concept sharing, mutual trust, and a sense of joint responsibility will simply confuse the process and jeopardize morale. Integration is thus more than doing things at the same time or in the same place, though both are critical to success. When products are complex and time is of the essence, people need to work closely together. Truly integrated problem solving and cross-functional integration thus require depth of understanding and a shared commitment to the objectives of the enterprise.

Size and specialization. The size of the team working on a development project has a profound influence on its performance. Too small a team and the work is likely to be burdensome, incomplete, and slow. Too large a team and the work is likely to be burdensome, incomplete, *confusing*, and slow. Experience in the auto industry suggests that engineering organizations are far more likely to be overspecialized than too broad in the focus of expertise, and that the drive for specialization has led firms to create development teams that are far too large. Integration is far easier and far more effective if teams are relatively small and team members' responsibilities are relatively broad. We have found car companies with much less specialization at the individual engineer level to be capable of putting high-quality, high-performance products into the marketplace far faster and with much better productivity than their overspecialized competitors.

Organization. Just as smaller teams are more integrated than larger teams, simple, flatter organizations are more integrated than complex, hierarchical organizations. We found in the auto study numerous examples of large, complex organizations in which upward of 50 people representing many departments and divisions were involved in decisions about the direction and content of a car program. The same phenomenon shows up in the engineering change process, where 15–20 signatures may be required to implement a design change. Too many parochial interests and too many interfaces and organizational boundaries make integration very difficult to achieve. A simpler structure—with many fewer assistant chiefs, deputy assistant directors, and subdepartment supervisors—is far more amenable to the development of common understanding and a common language needed to facilitate integration.

Our evidence suggests that to achieve an integrated development process, managers must bring people together in time, space, concept, and attitude; reduce the size of development teams; broaden individuals' skills; and simplify and flatten the organization. To succeed, such actions require the support of improved communication, greater investment in training, and a willingness to nurture responsibility, trust, and confidence throughout the organization.

THEME 3: INTEGRATING CUSTOMER AND PRODUCT

The hallmark of a great product is integrity. Creating a product that is internally coherent and functions well as a system (and in turn creating an experience that satisfies and even delights customers) requires development organizations that have high integrity, that have not only achieved internal integration, but that have also integrated customer needs and interests into the design and development process in an intimate and consistent way. Used effectively as a simulation—a dress rehearsal of commercial production and customer use—the development process will accurately reflect the needs and expectations of future customers.

In a world in which customer needs and interests are not always articulated and change frequently, integrating customer and product requires that design, production, and the market be viewed as an integral system and organized and managed to link all three activities intimately. The key to product integrity is managerial action that makes the entire development organization customer focused and creates processes that infuse a powerful product concept into the details of design.

Heavyweight product managers. A strong product manager can significantly influence the degree of internal integration a firm achieves in development. A true heavyweight product manager is essential if a firm also desires external integrity. Merging a strong project coordinator and concept champion into a true heavyweight manager appears to be an effective strategy for meeting diverse, uncertain, and inarticulate customer needs. Such heavyweights must be multiskilled and multilingual, and must possess a deep understanding of and appreciation for the customer. This cannot be an appreciation born of reading market research reports; it must derive from direct experience and be informed by an intuitive sense of what future customers' needs are likely to be.

The behavior of effective heavyweight product managers is distinctive. They walk around, intervene in the details of design, encourage, guard, and stimulate; they drive the effort to realize a product that will excite and attract future customers in the details of its design. Status and position have little to do with their effectiveness. Product managers are heavy because the organization empowers them to lead, coordinate, and champion the effort. They must have the skill and ability to do so, but the organizational context must expect and support heavyweight action.

Customer access and orientation. Though heavyweight product managers are critical, product development is not a solo performance. The entire development organization, from the chiefest of chief engineers down to the most junior technician, must become customer oriented. Moreover, because product integrity grows out of attention to nuance and detail, orientation toward and involvement with customers cannot be skin-deep. Putting designers and engineers into direct contact with customers has a powerful motivating influence on their behavior. However valuable systematic market research may be, the evidence suggests that there is no substitute for face-to-face interaction with customers in the marketplace, particularly for those who, like test engineers, play the role of future customers in the development process.

It is sometimes possible to bring customers directly into the development process. But customers may not always be able to articulate latent needs nor to predict in an accurate way how the market will respond to a potential product. Product managers and product planners need to actively interpret latent customer needs; they must be able to envision the future market.

Leadership by concept. Access to customers and the direct involvement of a strong product manager provide individual engineers important direction and guidance in the details of design. But because it is necessarily limited, such interaction is likely to be far more effective if informed and guided by a strong product concept.

A strong product concept evokes in the minds of the designers and engineers a palpable vision of the future product experience. A powerful concept, in relatively few words or phases or metaphors or images, captures a whole complex of customer needs and interests. It crystallizes the inarticulate and makes clear to engineers and designers the complex and subtle trade-offs that pervade the design of a new product.

In effective organizations the heavyweight product manager is the concept champion. The concept, in effect, becomes the vehicle through which the product manager provides substantive, purposeful direction throughout the development process. It is an articulation of the product manager's vision of the product and the customer's experience with it. A product concept—well conceived and translated by the heavyweight product manager into terms that each member of the development team can understand—can be a powerful integrating force.

THEME 4: MANUFACTURING FOR DESIGN

Much has appeared in the public and trade press and academic literature about design for manufacturability. Taking care in design to comprehend the requirements of the manufacturing process can significantly affect subsequent manufacturing costs and quality. Our research suggests that turning the process around (that is, focusing on manufacturing for design) can exert a powerful influence on the development process. Manufacturing for design focuses on those critical activities in which product and production process come together, such as the activities that create the working prototypes that will be used to test the design and the production process and tools and dies that will be used in commercial production. Here we are dealing not with concept but with practice.

Effectively manufacturing prototypes and tools and dies yields advantages in time, quality of problem solving, productivity of engineers and capital resources, and the smoothness with which products move into commercial production. Managing manufacturing for design relies on the infusion of world-class manufacturing concepts and practices into the development process and a rethinking of the roles of prototyping and the manufacture of tools and dies.

Manufacturing principles. Management of product development and management of manufacturing have often been separated both in concept and in practice. Yet outstanding capability in manufacturing can have a significant influence on the development process. We have found many of the principles that characterize outstanding manufacturing organizations to have direct application in the development process. Firms would thus do well to borrow and learn from the experiences of their manufacturing organizations in introducing just-in-time, total quality control, and continuous improvement. In the case of just-in-time, for example, manufacturing firms often discover that less is more, that driving down inventory, reducing work in process, and moving to a more product-focused manufacturing process can lead to significant improvements in productivity, throughput, reliability, and overall performance. The same principles apply to manufacturing for design. Reducing inventory, streamlining operations, and substantially increasing process control in the manufacture of parts, prototypes, tools, and dies can yield corresponding reductions in lead time, engineering changes, and the cost of development.

The role of prototyping. Traditionally treated as a way to test the design of a product, prototyping can be viewed more broadly as a rehearsal of a product's production. This broader view treats prototyping as an integral part of the problem-solving process in development, involving product designers, manufacturing engineers, purchasing and quality assurance personnel, parts suppliers, technicians, and line operators. An effective prototype operation reflects outstanding manufacturing capability, operating efficiently, swiftly, and with representative quality.

Building tools and dies. The manufacture of tools and dies is on the critical path of auto development programs and represents a significant fraction of the total investment in a new product. Consequently, the ability to manufacture tools and dies swiftly and efficiently can have a decisive impact on overall lead time and productivity. Moreover, the close relationship between the design of a product and the design of associated tools and dies makes effective operation of the tool and die manufacturing system critical to the creation of a high-quality product.

It is not a coincidence that the firms in our study that achieved an outstanding level of product development also exhibited superior manufacturing capability. Managers who recognize the power of manufacturing for design and act to develop and implement outstanding capability in prototyping and the manufacture of tools and dies will reap the benefits of faster, more efficient product development.

THE THEMES IN ACTION

The themes that characterize high performance product development in the world auto industry—superior performance in lead time, productivity, and quality; integration in the development process; linking products and customers; and manufacturing for design—also characterize outstanding performance in other industries in which competition is intense, customers are demanding, and time is of the essence. To illustrate the application of these themes to other kinds of businesses and products, we consider short case histories in high-performance disk drives, 35-mm cameras, pocket pagers, microwavable soup, hospital beds, commercial construction, and household appliances.

HIGH-END DISK DRIVES

In 1983, Quantum Corporation, a manufacturer of hard disk drives for minicomputers, founded the Plus Development Corporation to bring to market an expansion board-mounted hard disk drive for the IBM PC.[1] To develop the product, called Hardcard, Quantum managers assembled a development team of hardware and software engineers from Plus, manufacturing engineers from a Japanese company that was to manufacture the product, and representatives from marketing and customer service. Because Hardcard would be sold directly to consumers, Plus management believed the product needed to achieve a level of reliability and manufacturability unprecedented in the history of Quantum. Development thus emphasized integration of product design and process design; design engineers and process engineers worked in the same offices, taught each other their respective languages, and discovered the power that comes from close integration and development. The result was a product that set new standards of reliability in use and new standards of performance in manufacturing. During the first two months of commercial production, Plus achieved its highest manufacturing yields ever.

Although Quantum's traditional business had focused on a very different kind of customer (minicomputer manufacturers), and although technical requirements in the high end of the market in which Quantum competed were much more demanding than in the Hardcard market, Quantum senior managers were so impressed with the impact of the Plus development process that they adopted the integrated development approach for their high-end business. The new approach entailed shifting away from engineering teams to relatively small, multifunctional heavyweight teams led by a heavyweight project manager and charged with development from concept to commercial production. Bringing marketing, manufacturing, manufacturing engineering, and design engineering under the leadership of a strong project manager produced dramatic results for Quantum, which has achieved significant market penetration, substantially reduced its development time, and continued to market functionally excellent products with superior reliability.

THE AUTOFOCUS SLR 35-MM CAMERA

The market for single-lens reflex (SLR) 35-mm cameras was quiet in the late 1970s and early 1980s. The Canon AE1 had been the market leader for almost a decade, but overall sales in the segment were stagnant. Although Canon had developed next-generation products with new technologies (e.g., electronic control, LCD display, and autowinders), none had successfully captured the imagination of customers. What was missing was product integrity.

This situation changed dramatically in 1985 when Minolta, a relatively low-market-share competitor, established market leadership with the introduction of an autofocus SLR camera. Suddenly the market became volatile; a rash of new product introductions led to very short product lives amid rivalry among the major players for market share and product leadership.

Canon faced a difficult choice: develop a me-too product within one year, or develop a well-differentiated product with a completely different concept (lens-in-motor-autofocus versus Minolta's motor-in-body concept), which might take three years based on previous experience.[2] Canon chose to develop a technically distinctive product, but to do so within two years—a major challenge. To meet the challenge, Canon devised a new approach to product development that involved the creation of a coherent project team, strong conceptual leadership from the industrial design group, and integrated engineering involving both product and process design. Though the new camera, called the EOS, used component technologies developed in previous projects, it was distinctive in the way these components were integrated and in the design of the customer interface. Furthermore, Canon brought the new, more integrated, more attractive product to market within the two-year target and regained market leadership.

MICROWAVABLE SOUP

Developing a new soup is quite different from developing a new automobile. Soup has a relatively simple internal structure, and, in its traditional form, the customer interface is well established and relatively straightforward—pour the soup out of the can, add water, and heat. But as Campbell Soup Company discovered in the mid 1980s, developing a *microwavable* soup is a different proposition.[3]

When it set out to develop a new line of microwavable soup products in 1983, Campbell had a large technical and engineering organization built around specialized departments. It appointed a lightweight project manager for microwavable soup to coordinate process development, packaging, soup design, and testing. By 1988, the project had moved from prototype to pilot-line stage, but the process had yet to meet volume or cost objectives, and major issues in product design remained unresolved. Furthermore, the competitive environment had become much more intense. Campbell needed to move quickly to catch competitors who had already put microwavable products on the market.

The problems Campbell faced were rooted in the nature of the new product. A microwavable soup requires different packaging (e.g., plastic, heat-resistant, and sealed containers) and must satisfy a different set of requirements. The new packaging involved not only materials issues, but also strong interaction between package design and the production process. New issues in process development (e.g., new methods of filling and sterilization) took considerable time to resolve and threatened to slow down the entire project.

To resolve the processing problems and bring the product more quickly to market, Campbell appointed a new heavyweight project manager who began to employ overlapping, intensive communication and integrated engineering principles and ideas discussed in this book. He created a multifunctional team with a strong project leader, colocated the team around the production process, and involved suppliers, equipment developers, process engineers, production workers and supervisors, and package engineers in the development effort. The new product manager changed in a fundamental way the nature of the development process. Traditionally, different specialized departments worked independently on different pieces of the process and product. Only when each was satisfied with its respective solution were all the solutions brought together in an integration phase of the program. The functional nature of the program led to substantial delays and redesign efforts as different specialized solutions failed to integrate well.

The new project manager brought the various elements of the project together and began to operate the line in order to determine its system characteristics. Instead of trying to debug each of the system parts separately, the team began to examine the process as a system and focus on more integrated solutions. With a dedicated multifunctional team, strong product leadership, and a development process that emphasized system performance, Campbell experienced substantial improvement in the development of its microwavable product. For Campbell the remaining challenge is to implement the insights and approaches learned from the microwavable experience into its total development system.

THE BANDIT PROJECT—FLEXIBLE AUTOMATION FOR POCKET PAGERS

In 1987, Motorola's pocket pager division launched the Bandit project, which aimed at creating a flexible, automated production process for producing fully customized versions of a line of pocket pagers.[4] The project involved product redesign, software and equipment development, and overall integration carried out by a multifunctional team comprising design and manufacturing engineers, software developers, and suppliers under the direction of a strong project leader. Bringing suppliers onto the team proved to be a major contributor to the project's success.

In addition to pursuing the tight integration of product design and process development that seems to characterize outstanding projects, Motorola adopted a new approach to prototyping. Instead of tying prototyping to the completion of various subcomponents and subactivities within the organization, Motorola introduced periodic prototyping, in which prototype production was set for a specific date each month using available product and process design information. Prototype production thus reflected directly the evolution of the various elements of the product, which served to focus the organization's attention on outstanding issues and made integration (and the issues surrounding integration) clearer and therefore more manageable. Periodic prototyping appeared to be the decisive influence on the speed with which Motorola was able to bring its new automated process into full-scale commercial production.

The Bandit project was a resounding success. The complex process devised by the project team reduced Motorola's time to product redesign from four years to 18 months. Moreover, the line achieved significant improvements in quality, uptime, and reliability. The Bandit project underscores the notion that a truly integrated product (in this case product and process) is a reflection of the organization that creates it.

FAST-TRACK COMMERCIAL CONSTRUCTION

Lehrer McGovern Bovis (LMB), a commercial construction firm, developed a strong reputation for its fast-track construction methods, whereby traditionally sequential stages of design and construction are overlapped.[5] Design is done in phases, with construction commencing as different phases are completed. The contractor begins to dig a hole in the ground and place footings and foundation before the architect has completed the detailed design of the building. Because overlapping in fast-track construction, as in automobile development, relies on very close communication and interaction between designers, client, architects, and subcontractors, a critical element of the firm's approach is the creation of a team consisting of the construction manager (usually a heavyweight), the client, and the architect. LMB also works closely with suppliers, integrating them in a fundamental way into the design and construction process.

LMB's restoration of the Statue of Liberty was perhaps its most famous project. LMB was awarded the job of managing the restoration of the statue after competition with more than 25 firms. The project, to restore the statue before its July 4, 1986 centennial celebration, involved coordinating and managing the activities of some 500 engineers, architects, contractors, and technicians. Time was short and the work—complex and difficult to begin with—was vastly complicated by the location of the statue in the middle of New York Harbor. Despite these challenges, LMB's fast-track approach—specifically its skill in integrating suppliers, designers, engineers, and craftworkers—brought the project to completion on time and under budget. The time pressure, as one manager observed, was intense: "We couldn't reschedule the centennial celebration to August 16."

BSA INDUSTRIES - BELMONT DIVISION

The Belmont Division of BSA Industries has carved out a strong position in the market for acute-care hospital beds.[6] Belmont had been successful throughout the 1970s and 1980s in introducing innovations in safety, comfort, information, and communications capability. By the late 1980s, its products were state-of-the-art, fully integrated care and recovery systems that could be used in patient areas throughout the hospital. Belmont attributed much of its market success to its ability to identify and serve customer needs. In addition to market research capability, the firm cultivates close relationships with administrators and heads of nursing services, and with maintenance and other hospital personnel involved in the selection and management of patient-room furniture and equipment. The result is a deep understanding of the total customer system and the ability to design products that fit that system well. In short, Belmont built its competitive advantage around what we have called product integrity.

As Belmont expanded into other kinds of patient-room equipment and other parts of the hospital beyond acute care, it recognized an opportunity to substantially increase its growth and penetration by improving product development even further. A primary objective was the reduction of development lead time. Although the functional areas (design, engineering, manufacturing, and marketing) had depth of skill and capability, development cycles were long and often involved design changes late in programs. To reduce cycle time and the frequency of late changes, Belmont introduced a new development process organized around heavyweight project teams. The idea was to assemble core teams of people from marketing, design, engineering, and manufacturing under heavyweight project managers. Implementation of this concept required that the functional organizations change their development procedures and processes. Particularly critical was that support groups—such as the model shop, quality assurance testing, and parts suppliers—reduce their own cycle times to avoid becoming bottlenecks in the accelerated development cycle. The effect of these changes was to create a substantially faster, more integrated development process that built upon Belmont's historical strengths in product integrity.

In all these cases, development characteristics responsible for process improvement and market success—product integrity, close working relationships among engineering departments and between engineering and manufacturing, processes that link customers to the details of design, skill in prototyping, and cross-functional teams with heavyweight project leaders—are the same characteristics we have found in the outstanding firms in the world auto industry. Implementation, of course, is different. The fast-track construction teams at LMB are managed differently from the Quantum teams, yet both companies have substantive, heavyweight leadership. The methods and approaches Belmont uses to develop customer insight are different from those Campbell Soup uses to determine how its package design affects customer experience with its microwavable soup products. But where they succeed, both organizations have processes that bring into the development process at a fine level of detail insight into customer use of the product and the total product experience.

IMPLEMENTATION: LAYING THE FOUNDATION

The evidence from the auto study has important implications for the implementation of new approaches to product development. Because a new development process requires new skills, new sequences of activities, new attitudes, and new structures across a wide range of departments and functions within the firm, the focus of implementation must be far-reaching and long term. A detailed discussion of the implementation process is beyond the scope of this book, but we can suggest important actions that need to be taken to lay a foundation for improvements in product development.

Creating more effective product development requires change in both macroscopic structure and microscopic processes. Effective development organizations pay careful attention to both the whole and the parts. A significant top-down change in the organization chart is unlikely to bring about superior performance unless accompanied by changes in details at the working level. Similarly, promoting teamwork and high morale in a small working group will not improve overall development performance without consistency in detailed practice, behavioral patterns, attitudes, organizational structure, skills, and managerial philosophy. There is no single critical factor or magic solution to successful product development. Managers, engineers, marketers, and manufacturers who seek improvement in product development must do many things consistently and simultaneously. Superior development performance relies on consistent long-term efforts by everyone involved in development to bring together and orient toward customer satisfaction and market competitiveness all the important details.

This does not mean that all elements of organization and management must be consistent all the time. Our notion of pattern consistency is dynamic rather than static. For example, we might introduce major changes in one project and make it a model for the rest of the organization, or we might first introduce a significant change in the structure of the development process (e.g., create heavyweight teams) that creates problems in the rest of the organization. Similarly, a unilateral reduction in lead time may create imbalance and tension that may become a motivation for further organizational transformation. A short-term imbalance thus becomes the impetus for achieving long-term consistency in the overall development pattern. Alternatively, a firm may choose to change its overall organization of management carefully and incrementally, making sure to maintain balance at every step. Whether improvement is achieved through a balanced, step-by-step approach or via dynamic imbalance will depend upon the nature of competition, the skill of management, and the structure of the organization. A small company under serious competitive threat may opt for a more drastic approach than a large established company with a long history of strong functional organization.

Whichever approach is taken, successful implementation is a matter of long-term consistency between detailed actions and the overall pattern and direction of the new development process. Creating and ensuring depth of consistency is not something a powerful senior manager can do alone. Indeed, given the complexity of product development and the importance of detail, senior managers may not know everything that is going on in the implementation of a new product development process. Consequently, everyone involved in the development process, from senior managers to the most junior working-level engineer, must share an understanding of the overall pattern of development the organization seeks. Individuals need to understand how their part of the development process fits into the whole, how their actions, attitudes, and skills fit into the overall vision and concept of what the development process should be. Though a powerful senior manager cannot do it all, strong conceptual, substantive leadership is nevertheless crucial. The requisite leadership is neither cheerleading, nor administrating, nor clever slogans. Leadership in the creation of a new development process is rooted in the ability to articulate a powerful, substantive, and compelling vision of the development future.

Our experience in the auto industry leads us to believe that the first steps on the journey to making a new development process a reality must be in the direction of establishing coherent leadership that integrates both the parts and the whole of the product development process. This leadership may be provided by a top manager, a senior executive, a product manager, a chief engineer, a chief designer, or even by lower levels of management, depending on the circumstances of the company and the nature of its markets. It may also be provided by one strong leader or by a collective leadership involving many managers and engineers.

Whatever form leadership takes, it must endow the organization with an evocative, compelling vision of what the development process should be. That vision may reflect the underlying themes that seem to characterize high-performance development, but it must be tuned and tailored to the particular technologies a firm uses, the customers and markets it serves, and its overall strategy for competitive advantage.

A shared understanding of the overall pattern of development, a common vision of the development future, close attention to detail, and coherence and consistency across the full range of activities in development—these will be the hallmarks of the firms that meet the imperatives of the new industrial competition. These firms will apply outstanding manufacturing capability in development as well as in commercial production. They will be close to customers and integrate deep understanding of customer experience with the product into details of design. Their engineering and manufacturing organizations will overlap in time and communicate intensively. Their product managers will be heavyweights, and their development organizations and the products they create will possess integrity. The success of such firms will be measured in the rapid, efficient development of great products.

NOTES

1. For further information, see Plus Development Corporation (A) (687-001) and Plus Development Corporation (B) (688-066).
2. The account here is based on authors' interviews conducted at Canon in 1989.
3. For further information, see Campell Soup Company (690-051).
4. For further information, see Motorola, Inc.: Bandit Pager Project (690-043).
5. For further information, see Lehrer McGovern Bovis, Inc. (687-089).
6. For further information, See BSA Industries—Belmont Division (689-049).

BIBLIOGRAPHY

Abernathy, William J. "Some Issues Concerning the Effectiveness of Parallel Strategies in R&D Projects." *IEEE Transactions on Engineering Management* EM-18, no. 3 (August 1971): 80–89.

———. *The Productivity Dilemma*. Baltimore: Johns Hopkins University Press, 1978.

Abernathy, William J., Kim B. Clark, and Alan M. Kantrow. *Industrial Renaissance*. New York: Basic Books, 1983.

Abernathy, William J., and James M. Utterback. "Patterns of Industrial Innovation." *Technology Review* 80, no. 7 (June–July 1978): 2–9.

Aldrich, Howard, and Diane Herker. "Boundary Spanning Roles and Organization Structure." *Academy of Management Review* (April 1977): 217–230.

Alexander, Christopher. *Notes on the Synthesis of Form*. Cambridge, MA: Harvard University Press, 1964.

Allen, Thomas J. *Managing the Flow of Technology*. Cambridge, MA: MIT Press, 1977.

Allen, Thomas J., and Oscar Hauptman. "The Influence of Communication Technologies on Organizational Structure." *Communication Research* 14, no. 5 (October 1987): 575–578.

Altshuler, Alan, et al. *The Future of the Automobile*. Cambridge, MA: MIT Press, 1984.

"Ampex Corporation: Product Matrix Engineering." Harvard Business School Case #687-002.

"Applied Materials." Harvard Business School Case #688-050.

Armi, C. Edson. *The Art of American Car Design*. University Park, PA: The Pennsylvania State University Press, 1988.

Ashton, James E., and Frank X. Cook, Jr. "Time to Reform Job Shop Manufacturing." *Harvard Business Review* (March–April 1989): 106–111.

Behner, Peter. "New Aspect in FMEA Processing Using Advanced Databases and Its Effects on Design for Assembly." Unpublished Diploma Thesis, Lehrstuhl fur Produktionssystematik, WZL, RWTH Aachen, West Germany, 1989.

"Bendix Automation Group." Harvard Business School Case #684-035.

Bettman, James R. *An Information Processing Theory of Consumer Choice*. Reading, MA: Addison-Wesley, 1979.

Bohn, Roger E., and Ramchandran Jaikumar. "Dynamic Approach: An Alternative Paradigm for Operations Management." Harvard Business School Working Paper, 1986.

"BSA Industries—Belmont Division." Harvard Business School Case #689-049.

Burgelman, Robert A., and Leonard R. Sayles. *Inside Corporate Innovation*. New York: Free Press, 1986.

Burns, Tom, and G. M. Stalker. *The Management of Innovation*. London: Tavistock Publications, 1961.

"Campbell Soup Company." Harvard Business School Case #690-051.

"Ceramics Process Systems Corporation (A)." Harvard Business School Case #687-030.

Chandler, Alfred D., Jr. *Strategy and Structure*. Cambridge, MA: MIT Press, 1962.

"Chaparral Steel (Abridged)." Harvard Business School Case #687-045.

Child, John. "Organizational Structures, Environment and Performance: The Role of Strategic Choice." *Sociology* 6 (1972): 1–22.

Clark, Kim B. "Competition, Technical Diversity, and Radical Innovation in the U.S. Auto Industry." *Research on Technological Innovation, Management and Policy*, vol. 1 (1983): 103–149.

————. "The Interaction of Design Hierarchies and Market Concepts in Technological Evolution." *Research Policy* 14 (1985): 235–251.

————. "Project Scope and Project Performance: The Effect of Parts Strategy and Supplier Involvement on Product Development." *Management Science*, vol. 35, no. 10 (October 1989): 1247–1263.

————. "What Strategy Can Do for Technology." *Harvard Business Review* (November–December 1989): 94–98.

Clark, Kim B., and Takahiro Fujimoto. "Overlapping Problem Solving in Product Development." Harvard Business School Working Paper, 1987. Also in *Managing International Manufacturing*, edited by Kasra Ferdows. Amsterdam: North-Holland, 1989: 127–152.

————. "The European Model of Product Development: Challenge and Opportunity." Presented at the Second International Policy Forum, International Motor Vehicle Program at Massachusetts Institute of Technology, 17 May 1988 (1988a).

————. "Lead Time in Automobile Product Development: Explaining the Japanese Advantage." Harvard Business School Working Paper, 1988 (1988b). Also in *Journal of Engineering and Technology Management* 6 (1989): 25–58.

————. "Shortening Product Development Lead Time: The Case of the Global Automobile Industry." Presented in Professional Program Session, Electronic Show and Convention, Boston, 10–12 May 1988 (1988c).

————. "Product Development and Competitiveness." Paper presented in the International Seminar on Science, Technology, and Economic Growth, OECD, 7 June 1989 (1989a).

————. "Reducing the Time to Market: The Case of the World Auto Industry." *Design Management Journal*, vol. 1, no. 1 (Fall 1989) (1989b): 49–57.

Cusumano, Michael A. *The Japanese Automobile Industry*. Cambridge, MA: Harvard University Press, 1985.

Daft, Richard L., and Norman B. Lengel. "Organizational Information Requirements, Media Richness and Structural Design." *Management Science*, vol. 32, no. 5 (May 1986): 554–571.

Daimler-Benz AG. *Daimler-Benz Museum*. Stuttgart: 1987.

Davis, Stanley M., and Paul R. Lawrence. *Matrix*. Reading, MA: Addison-Wesley, 1977.

Drucker, Peter F. *The Practice of Management*. New York: Perennial Library, 1954.

Dumas, Angela, and Henry Mintzberg. "Managing Design—Designing Management." *Design Management Journal*, vol. 1, no. 1 (Fall 1989): 38–44.

Ealey, Lance A. *Quality by Design: Taguchi Methods® and U.S. Industry*. Dearborn, MI: ASI Press, 1988.

Engel, James F., Roger D. Blackwell, and David T. Kollat. *Consumer Behavior*. Hinsdale, IL: Dryden Press, 1978.

"Everest Computer (A)." Harvard Business School Case #685-085.

Freeman, Christopher. *The Economics of Industrial Innovation*. Cambridge, MA: MIT Press, 1982.

Fujimoto, Takahiro. "A Note on Technology Systems." Presented at International Conference on Business Strategy and Technical Innovation, Japan, March 1983. Abridged Japanese translation in *Gijutsu-Kakushin to Keiei Senryaku* (Technological Innovation and Business Strategy), edited by Moriaki Tsuchiya. Tokyo: Nihon Keizai Shimbun-sha (1986): 141–161.

———. "Organizations For Effective Product Development: The Case of the Global Automobile Industry." Unpublished D.B.A. diss., Harvard Business School, 1989.

Fujimoto, Takahiro, and Antony Sheriff. "Consistent Patterns in Automotive Product Strategy, Product Development, and Manufacturing Performance—Road Map for the 1990s." Presented at the Third International Policy Forum, International Motor Vehicle Program at Massachusetts Institute of Technology, 7–10 May 1989.

Galbraith, Jay R. *Designing Complex Organizations*. Reading, MA: Addison-Wesley, 1973.

———. "Designing the Innovating Organization." *Organizational Dynamics* (Winter 1982): 5–25.

"General Electric Lighting Business Group." Harvard Business School Case #689-038.

Gobeli, David H., and William Rudelius. "Management Innovation: Lessons from the Cardiac-Pacing Industry." *Sloan Management Review* 26, no. 4 (Summer 1985): 29–43.

Hall, Robert W. *Zero Inventories*. Homewood, IL: Dow Jones-Irwin, 1983.

Hayes, Robert H., Steven C. Wheelwright, and Kim B. Clark. *Dynamic Manufacturing*. New York: Free Press, 1988.

Higuchi, Kenji. *Jidosha Zatsugaku Jiten (A Cyclopedia of Miscellaneous Matters on the Automobile)*. Tokyo: Kodansha, 1984.

Hirschman, Elizabeth C., and Morris B. Holbrook. "Hedonic Consumption: Emerging Concepts, Methods and Propositions." *Journal of Marketing* (Summer 1982): 92–101.

Holbrook, Morris B., and Elizabeth C. Hirschman. "The Experiential Aspects of Consumption: Consumer Fantasies, Feelings, and Fun." *Journal of Consumer Research* 9 (September 1982): 132–140.

Ikari, Yoshiro. *Daiichi Sharyo Sekkei-bu (Vehicle Design Department #1)*. Tokyo: Bungei Shunju, 1981.

———. *Nissan Ishiki Daikakumei (Great Cultural Revolution of Nissan)*. Tokyo: Diamond, 1987.

————. *Skyline ni Kaketa Otoko-tachi (The Men Who Bet on Skyline)*. Tokyo: Soryu-sha, 1982 (1982b).

————. *Toyota tai Nissan: Shinsha Kaihatsu no Saizensen (Toyota versus Nissan: The Front Line of New Car Development)*. Tokyo: Diamond, 1985.

Imai, Ken-ichi, Ikujiro Nonaka, and Hirotaka Takeuchi. "Managing the New Product Development Process: How the Japanese Companies Learn and Unlearn." In *The Uneasy Alliance*, edited by Kim B. Clark, Robert H. Hayes, and Christopher Lorenz. Boston: Harvard Business School Press, 1985.

Imai, Masaaki. *Kaizen*. New York: Random House, 1986.

Jaikumar, Ramchandran. "Postindustrial Manufacturing." *Harvard Business Review* (November-December 1986): 69–76.

Johansson, Johny K., and Ikujiro Nonaka. "Market Research the Japanese Way." *Harvard Business Review* (May–June 1987): 16–22.

Juran, Joseph M., and Frank M. Gryna, Jr. *Quality Planning and Analysis*. New York: McGraw-Hill, 1980.

Juran, Joseph M., Frank M. Gryna, Jr., and R. S. Bingham, Jr., eds. *Quality Control Handbook*. New York: McGraw-Hill, 1975.

Kamien, M. I., and N. L. Schwartz. *Market Structure and Innovation*. Cambridge: Cambridge University Press, 1982.

Kanter, Rosabeth M. "When a Thousand Flowers Bloom: Structural, Collective, and Social Conditions for Innovation in Organizations." *Research in Organizational Behavior* 10 (1988): 169–211.

Katz, Ralph, and Thomas J. Allen. "Project Performance and the Locus of Influence in the R&D Matrix." *Academy of Management Journal* 28, no. 1 (1985): 67–87.

Keller, Robert T. "Predictors of the Performance of Project Groups in R&D Organizations." *Academy of Management Journal* 29, no. 4 (1986): 715–726.

Kotler, Phillip. *Marketing Management: Analysis, Planning, Implementation and Control.* 6th ed. Englewood Cliffs, NJ: Prentice Hall, 1988.

Krafcik, John. "Triumph of the Lean Production System" *Sloan Management Review* (Fall 1988): 41–52.

Larson, Erik W., and David H. Gobeli. "Organization for Product Development Projects." *Journal of Product Innovation Management* 5 (1988): 180–190.

Laux, James M. *In First Gear: The French Automobile Industry to 1914.* Liverpool: Liverpool University Press, 1976.

Lawrence, Paul R., and Davis Dyer. *Renewing American Industry.* New York: Free Press, 1983.

Lawrence, Paul R., and Jay W. Lorsch. *Organization and Environment.* Homewood, IL: Richard D. Irwin, 1967 (1967a).

"Lehrer McGovern Bovis, Inc." Harvard Business School Case #687-089.

Levy, Sidney. "Symbols for Sale." *Harvard Business Review* (July–August 1959): 117–124.

Lorenz, Christopher. *The Design Dimension.* Oxford: Basil Blackwell, 1986.

Maidique, Modesto. A., and B. J. Zirger. "A Study of Success and Failure in Product Innovation: The Case of the U.S. Electronics Industry." *IEEE Transactions on Engineering Management* EM-31, no. 4 (1984): 192–203.

———. "The New Product Learning Cycle." *Research Policy* 14 (December 1985): 299–313.

Marquis, Donald G. "The Anatomy of Successful Innovations." In Michael L. Tushman and William L. Moore, eds. *Readings in the Management of Innovation.* Cambridge, MA: Ballinger, 1982: 42–50.

Marquis, Donald G., and D. L. Straight. "Organizational Factors in Project Performance." MIT Sloan School of Management Working Paper, 1965.

Marsh, Peter E., and Peter Collett. *Driving Passion*. Boston: Faber and Faber, 1986.

Matsui, Mikio. *Jidosha Buhin (The Automobile Parts Industry)*. Tokyo: Nihon Keizai Shimbun-sha, 1988.

McDonough, Edward F. III, and Richard P. Leifer. "Effective Control of New Product Projects: The Interaction of Organization Culture and Project Leadership." *Journal of Product Innovation Management* 3 (1986): 149–157.

Miles, Raymond E., and Charles C. Snow. *Organizational Strategy, Structure, and Process*. New York: McGraw-Hill, 1978.

Miles, Robert H. *Macro Organizational Behavior*. Glenview, IL: Scott, Foresman, 1980.

Mintzberg, Henry. *The Structuring of Organizations*. Englewood Cliffs, NJ: Prentice-Hall, 1979.

———. *Mintzberg on Management*. New York: Free Press, 1989.

Mitsubishi Research Institute. *The Relationship between Japanese Auto and Auto Parts Makers*. Tokyo: Mitsubishi Research Institute, 1987.

Monden, Yasuhiro. *Toyota Production System*. Atlanta: Institute of Industrial Engineers, 1983.

Morozumi, Takehiko (Okazaki, Hiroshi, ed.). *BMW*. Tokyo: Shincho-sha, 1983.

Morton, Jack A. *Organizing for Innovation*. New York: McGraw-Hill, 1971.

"Motorola, Inc.: Bandit Pager Project." Harvard Business School Case #690-043.

Myers, Sumner, and Donald G. Marquis. *Successful Industrial Innovations*. Washington, DC: National Science Foundation, 1969.

Nevins, Allan, and Frank E. Hill. *Ford: Expansion and Challenge, 1915–1933*. New York: Charles Scribner's Sons, 1957.

Nishiguchi, Toshihiro. "Competing Systems of Automotive Components Supply." A paper presented at the First International Policy Forum, International Motor Vehicle Program, Massachusetts Institute of Technology, May 1987.

Nissan Motor Co. Ltd. *Jidosha Sangyo Handbook (Automobile Industry Handbook)*. Tokyo: Kinokuniya (Japanese, annual).

Nonaka, Ikujiro. "Creating Organizational Order Out of Chaos: Self-Renewal in Japanese Firms." *California Management Review* 30, no. 3 (Spring 1988, 1988a): 57–73.

Oshima, Taku, and, Shigeki Yamaoka. *Jidosha (The Automobile)*. Tokyo: Nihon Keizai Hyron-sha, 1987.

Perrow, Charles. "A Framework for the Comparative Analysis of Organizations." *American Sociological Review* 2 (1967): 79–105.

Peters, Thomas J., and Robert H. Waterman, Jr. *In Search of Excellence*. New York: Warner Books, 1982.

"Plus Development Corporation (A)." Harvard Business School Case #687-001.

"Plus Development Corporation (B)." Harvard Business School Case #688-066.

Porter, Michael E. *Competitive Strategy*. New York: Free Press, 1980.

———. *Competitive Advantage*. New York: Free Press, 1985.

Roberts, Edward B. "Managing Invention and Innovation." *Research-Technology Management* (January–February 1988): 11–29.

Rosenberg, Nathan. *Inside the Black Box*. Cambridge: Cambridge University Press, 1982.

Rosenbloom, Richard S. "Technological Innovation in Firms and Industries: An Assessment of the State of the Art." In *Technological Innovation*, edited by P. Kelly and M. Kranzberg. San Francisco: San Francisco Press, 1978: 215–230.

———. "Managing Technology for the Longer Term: A Managerial Perspective." In *The Uneasy Alliance*, edited by Kim B. Clark, Robert H. Hayes, and Christopher Lorenz. Boston: Harvard Business School Press, 1985: 297–327.

Rosenbloom, Richard S., and William J. Abernathy. "The Climate for Innovation in Industry." *Research Policy* 11 (1982): 209–225.

Rosenbloom, Richard S., and Michael A. Cusumano. "Technological Pioneering and Competitive Advantage: The Birth of the VCR Industry." *California Management Review* 29, no. 4 (Summer 1987): 51–76.

Rosenbloom, Richard S., and Karen J. Freeze. "Ampex Corporation and Video Innovation." *Research on Technological Innovation, Management and Policy*, vol. 2 (1985).

Rothwell, Roy, et al. "SAPPHO Updated: Project SAPPHO Phase II." *Research Policy* 3, no. 3 (1974): 258–291.

Rubenstein, A. H., A. K. Chakrabarti, R. D. O'Keefe, W. E. Souder, and H. C. Young. "Factors Influencing Innovation Success at the Project Level." *Research Management*, vol. 19, no. 3 (May 1976): 15–20.

Sayles, Leonard R., *Management Behavior*. New York: McGraw-Hill, 1964.

Scherer, Frederic M. "Time-Cost Tradeoffs in Uncertain Empirical Research Projects." *Naval Research Logistics Quarterly* 13 (March 1966): 71–82.

———. *Innovation and Growth*. Cambridge, MA: MIT Press, 1984.

Schonberger, Richard J. *Japanese Manufacturing Techniques*. New York: Free Press, 1982.

Scott, W. Richard. *Organizations: Rational, Natural and Open Systems*. 2d ed. Englewood Cliffs, NJ: Prentice-Hall, 1987.

Shapiro, Benson P. "What the Hell Is 'Market Oriented'?" *Harvard Business Review* (November–December 1988): 119–125.

Sheriff, Antony M. "Product Development in the Automobile Industry: Corporate Strategies and Project Performance." M.S.M. diss., Sloan School of Management, Massachusetts Institute of Technology, May 1988.

Shibata, Masaharu. *Nani ga Nissan Jidosha wo Kaetanoka (What Changed Nissan?)*. Tokyo: PHP, 1988.

Shimokawa, Koichi. *Jidosha Senryaku Kokusaika no Nakade: Kiro ni Tatsu Dealer Keiei (Dealer Management and Internationalization of Automobile Strategy)*. Tokyo: Japan Automobile Dealers Association, 1981.

———. *Jidosha (The Automobile Industry)*. Tokyo: Nihon Keizai Shinbun-sha, 1985.

Simon, Herbert A. *The Science of the Artificial*. Cambridge, MA: MIT Press, 1969.

Sloan, Alfred P., Jr. *My Years with General Motors*. Garden City, NY: Anchor/Doubleday, 1963.

Sobel, Robert. *Car Wars*. New York: McGraw-Hill, 1984.

Soderberg, Leif G. "Facing Up to the Engineering Gap." *The McKinsey Quarterly* (Spring 1989): 2–18.

"Sony Corporation: Workstation Division." Harvard Business School Case #690-031.

Taguchi, Genichi, and Don Clausing. "Robust Quality." *Harvard Business Review* (January–February 1990): 65–75.

Thompson, James D. *Organizations in Action*. New York: McGraw-Hill, 1967.

Tushman, Michael L. "Special Boundary Roles in the Innovation Process." *Administrative Science Quarterly* 22 (December 1977) 587–605.

Tushman, Michael L., and David A. Nadler. "Information Processing as an Integrating Concept in Organizational Design." *Academy of Management Review* 3 (July 1978): 613–624.

Urban, Glen L., John R. Hauser, and Nikhilesh Dholakia. *Essentials of New Product Management.* Englewood Cliffs, NJ: Prentice-Hall, 1987.

Utterback, James M. "Innovation in Industry and Diffusion of Technology." *Science* 183 (February 15, 1974): 658–662.

Van de Ven, Andrew H. "Central Problems in the Management of Innovation." *Management Science* 32, no. 5 (May 1986): 590–607.

Van de Ven, Andrew H., and R. Drazin. "The Concept of Fit in Contingency Theory." *Research in Organizational Behavior* 7 (1985): 333–365.

Venkatraman, N. "The Concept of Fit in Strategy Research: Towards Verbal and Statistical Correspondence." *Academy of Management Best Paper Proceedings,* 1987.

von Hippel, Eric. "The Dominant Role of Users in the Scientific Instrument Innovation Process." *Research Policy* 5 (1976): 212–239.

———. *The Sources of Innovation.* New York: Oxford University Press, 1988.

Waterson, Michael. *Economic Theory of the Industry.* Cambridge: Cambridge University Press, 1984.

Weick, Karl E. *The Social Psychology of Organizing.* 2d ed. Reading, MA: Addison-Wesley, 1979.

White, Lawrence J. *The Automobile Industry Since 1945.* Cambridge, MA: Harvard University Press, 1971.

APPENDIX

DATA COLLECTION

Any study of the product development process faces several difficult problems in data acquisition. As publicly available information does not provide enough evidence on either the performance or the operating characteristics of firms' internal product-development processes, a study of this kind must rely on the collection of field data. Difficulties in field data collection arising from confidentiality of information and differences in technical vocabularies presented us with a major challenge. Given our desire to link product development and international competition in a broad market context, we faced the additional requirement that the research be international and inter-disciplinary, which further complicated the study.

THE SAMPLES

Our study of product development involved the collection of data, primarily between 1985 and 1988, from 29 new car development projects conducted in 20 companies located in all major car-designing regions of the 1980s: the United States (3 companies), Western Europe (9 companies), and Japan (8 companies).[1] These companies accounted for about 70 percent of worldwide car production in 1986. Average annual production was 1.2 million cars, with ten companies producing more than 1 million cars and all producing more than 200,000 cars or car-type vehicles in the same year. Despite their significant production volume, neither newly industrialized countries (e.g., Korea, Taiwan, Brazil, Mexico, and Spain) nor Eastern European nations (e.g., the Soviet Union, Yugoslavia, and Poland) were included as full-scale product development projects were still rare in these areas in the 1980s.[2] Other developing countries and Oceanic nations were also excluded for the same reason, while producers such as Rolls-Royce, Aston Martin, Lamborghini, Maserati, and Avanti were excluded because of their small volume. The small sample size (of projects and organizations) enabled us to do systematic comparative analyses without losing a sense of reality, uniqueness, or dynamism in the individual cases.

All producers in the sample were multiple model manufacturers. Number of basic models (platforms) per producer ranged from 3 to 14, averaging about 7. Retail prices of these models ranged from $5,000 to $15,000 (in 1987) for the sixteen "volume producers" and more than $20,000 for the four high-end specialists.[3] Collectively, they are estimated to have developed about 120 new models from 1982 to 1987, or about 90 percent of new models developed in the three major regions during that period.

The sample projects, 6 in the United States, 11 in Europe, and 12 in Japan covered approximately 20 percent of all new product projects for the period 1982 to 1987.[4] As five years is a relatively short period in terms of product development, and a car's average model life worldwide is more than five years, our sample is effectively drawn from one generation of products and thus represents a cross-section as opposed to a time series.

Sample projects exhibited significant variety, ranging over large and mid-size passenger cars, small passenger cars, small vans, and micromini cars and vans. Retail prices ranged from less than $5,000 to more than $40,000 as of mid 1987. Other areas of project content that exhibited considerable variation included number of body types, ratio of common parts, technical innovativeness, and degree of supplier participation in engineering. In order to be able to use project data as general indicators of product development organizations, we adjusted the original data for these differences to the extent possible.

Another potential problem was a bias of the sample projects in terms of market success or competitiveness. Because it was extremely difficult, for reasons of competitiveness, to persuade companies to disclose project data, we had to be satisfied with the projects they provided as samples. Most, understandably, provided projects that had met with relative market success. In light of this potential bias, it may be appropriate to regard these project as comparisons of "best practices of the period."

SOURCES AND METHODS

Data were primarily of three types: proprietary company information; publicly available information; and opinions of experts from outside the companies.

Proprietary data. Proprietary information was collected by three methods: in-depth interviews, questionnaire surveys, and internal documents. A series of questionnaires was distributed to key project participants for each of the sample projects studied. To make the questions as relevant and sensible as possible, pilot surveys were conducted in selected companies. Interviews, both structured and unstructured, were conducted with managers of R&D units (e.g., head of the R&D group, engineering administration staff, chief engineers of engineering departments) and core participants in sample projects (e.g., project managers, assistant project managers, product planners, product/process engineers). Unstructured interviews were designed to provide a feel for the reality of product development and generate working hypotheses, structured interviews to examine the hypotheses. A format was developed for the latter to make interview data as comparable as possible across organizations. At least two rounds of interviews, each involving from five to twenty interviewees, were conducted for each organization. Internal documentary materials—including organizational charts, product planning documents, engineering schedule data, project accounting reports, materials for internal training and education programs, and internal reports and memoranda—used in the study were verified against the interviews and questionnaires.

Public data. Publicly available documents included both statistical and descriptive information. Data on company financial and business performance were derived primarily from annual reports and periodicals that reported industrial statistics. Statistics on product lines, product histories, and basic product specifications were available through popular car magazines and regional industrial associations. The study relied on *Consumer Reports*, reports by J. D. Power and Associates, and "buyer's guides" published by popular magazines and individual car critics for evaluations of customer satisfaction, marketability, and defects or design quality. Books and articles describing the process and organization of product development in specific companies or for specific products were consulted to supplement our own descriptive data about product development organizations.[5] Specifically, the following publications were used as sources for Tables 3.2, 3.5, Figure 4.5, and Figure 11.5: *Automotive News, Buyers Guide, Car & Driver, Consumer Guide, Driver* (Japanese)*, Japanese Motor Vehicles Guide Book, Jidosha Gijutsu, Katalog der Automobil Revue, The Motor Industry of Japan, Motor Magazine* (Japanese)*, Motor Trend, NAVI* (Japanese)*, Nikkan Jidosha Shimbun, Nikkei Mechanical, Nikkei Sangyo Shimbun, Jidosha Sangyo Handbook, The Power Report on Automotive Marketing, The Wall Street Journal, Ward's Automotive Yearbook, What Car?* (London)*,* and *World Motor Vehicle Data.*

Outside experts. Data on design quality were provided by an expert panel of professional car evaluators (technical editors of car magazines and freelance critics) formed especially for this purpose. Seven professional evaluators (two from the United States, two from Europe, and three from Japan) were asked to rate the quality of product design of recently developed models at each company in terms of such criteria as concept, styling, performance, comfort, value for money, and overall design quality. Their ratings were taken as partial indicators of product development effectiveness.

UNIT OF ANALYSIS

A distinction is warranted between "unit of data collection" and "unit of comparative analysis." Statistical and clinical data were collected at the former level and the collected data aggregated, rearranged, and compared at the latter. These levels, though not the same, largely overlapped.

Unit of data collection. Empirical data were collected at three levels—project, organization, and company—depending upon relevance and availability. "Project" refers to a major new car development project, including both a major model renewal and a completely new model development in which more than half the components are redesigned. Empirical data on lead time and product development productivity and on project content variables that might affect them were collected at the project level. "Organization" refers to a collection of product development subunits (projects and/or functional departments) that are coordinated for the purpose of developing a group of products. As automobile producers normally have only one car development organization, organization is in practice generally synonymous with company as a unit of analysis.[6] There were 22 organizations in our study: 5 U.S., 9 European, and 8 Japanese. The data on organizational patterns and indicators related to total product quality were gathered mainly at the organizational level. "Company," by our definition, includes subsidiary companies that have distinct product lines (e.g., European subsidiaries of U.S. producers). Thus, some companies provided data on more than one project. Data on overall corporate performance, typically derived from annual reports, were collected at this level.

Unit of comparative analysis. The main unit of comparative analysis was either organizational or regional/strategic group. Data collected at the project or company level were either aggregated or allocated to the organizational or regional level for comparative analyses.

Organizational was selected over project level because project performance tends to be affected by random events, short-term phenomena, or other idiosyncratic factors specific to particular projects that might obscure the significance of long-term relations among the organization, environment, and performance. For example, the success or failure of a single project may be affected by the genius of a particular product engineer, personal characteristics of the project leader, the timing and strength of rivals' new products, unexpected changes in oil prices, a fad among young consumers, chance, and so forth. Such circumstances are difficult to duplicate from project to project. Because we were interested in systematic relationships between the long-term performance of product development and longer-term aspects of organizations and environments, we examined organizational patterns and practices shared among the projects launched by each organization. We also analyzed and compared average performance for a series of projects by a particular organization for a given period, with an emphasis on consistency of performance and organization over time and across products.

A "regional/strategic group" is a collection of car-developing organizations that share a strategy and/or a regional origin (i.e., a primary regional market). We identified two competitive strategies (volume producer and high-end specialist) and three regions (the United States, Western Europe, and Japan). Data were compared either by region or across four regional/strategic groups (splitting

European firms into volume producers and high-end specialists), our hypothesis being that organizations that operate in the same environmental segment tend to share certain organizational capabilities and performance levels as a result of long-term adaptation processes.

To the extent that the current study emphasizes both environmental influences and efforts by individual organizations, it compares performance and organizational patterns at the level of both the individual organization and the regional/strategic group.

VARIABLES

Prerequisite to acquiring statistical data was to define relevant terms, understood to mean the same thing to project engineers in different companies. These definitions had to be specific enough to be operational in analysis. Variables were identified in four main categories: product development performance and product line policy (Chapter 4); project content (i.e., product complexity and project scope, Chapter 6); manufacturing capability (Chapter 7); and development organization and process (Chapters 8–10).

PRODUCT DEVELOPMENT PERFORMANCE

Three dimensions of product development performance were measured: engineering hours (development productivity), development lead time, and total product quality (TPQ).

For comparability across projects and organizations, data were adjusted for such project-specific factors as product complexity, innovativeness, project scope, and so forth using engineering methods, statistical methods, or both. Engineering methods used engineers' estimates of adjustment coefficients based on practical experience. We used these estimates to adjust data on hours, for example, for differences in the number of body types. We also developed a formula for project scope adjustment based on ratios of common parts, supplier participation, and parts-specific engineering. Statistical methods replaced engineers' practical experience with statistical estimates of adjustment coefficients using regression models. Dummy variables for regional/strategic groups are included in the models to account for environmental and organizational factors specific to each region or strategy (the Japanese volume-producer group was designated as the base case).

Although both engineering and statistical methods were applied, statistical methods were adopted for the main analysis. Engineering methods were used primarily as reality checks on the statistical estimates.

Engineering hours. As measured in raw form through questionnaires and interviews, engineering hours includes the time not only of engineers, but also of technicians and other administrative personnel who participated directly in the project. It does not include hours of an overhead nature (e.g., the vice president of engineering), hours spent on process engineering and tool manufacturing, hours spent on engine transmission development (except those required to match the engine-transmission to the vehicle), and hours committed by parts suppliers or body manufacturers (except when the entire process of vehicle engineering was subcontracted). Engineering hours are thus essentially hours spent within a project on concept generation, product planning, and product engineering for vehicle (primarily body and chassis) development. Raw data were adjusted as discussed above to arrive at a measure of development productivity; adjusted data thus take into account the role of suppliers as well as differences in product content.

Development lead time. Development lead time (or simply lead time) refers to the time in months between the beginning of a development project and market introduction of the first version of the model.[7] In addition to concept-to-market lead time, schedule data were collected for other development phases, including concept generation, product planning, advanced engineering, product engineering, process engineering, and pilot run. Except for *planning* and *engineering lead time*, such detailed schedule data were not used for further statistical analysis.

Total product quality. Total product quality (TPQ) was captured by multiple indicators representing various aspects of customer satisfaction generated by the product experience, as well as long-term market share improvement. Data collection, conducted between 1985 and 1987, was carried out at the level of organization rather than the project whenever possible to emphasize consistency in the development of a series of products. Several indicators were used to arrive at a TPQ index.

Data on *perceived total quality* were collected from three different sources. Two are indices of actual users' "repurchase intention" (from *Consumer Reports* and J. D. Power and Associates). The ranking is based on the percentage of respondents (U.S. users) who said they would buy the same make again.[8] The unit of analysis in the J. D. Power survey is "make," which generally corresponds to product divisions among car producers. Consequently, U.S. producers with multidivisional structures are represented by more than one rank. The other total quality indicator is based on an expert evaluation constructed from the percentage of models recommended by *Consumer Reports* in 1986, 1987, and 1988.[9] All three indicators were converted to rank variables for subsequent data analysis.

Organizational averages of the number of technical failures per vehicle reported by users as of ninety days after delivery were used to rank organizations in terms of *conformance quality*.[10] Results for two different years (1985 and 1987) were calculated in the interest of checking the stability of the data. Because the unit of analysis is make, American organizations are represented by more than one observation.

An expert panel was employed to measure *design quality*. Each of the seven experts rendered an overall evaluation of each company's models in the most recent generation as of mid 1987.[11] Evaluation criteria were concept, styling, performance, comfort, value for money, and overall evaluation. Definitions of these criteria and the scale by which they were scored are shown in Table 1.[12] Experts were asked to take the target customer's view as much as possible, relative to rival models, at the time of introduction. Scores were designed to be adjusted for price differences across different product segments, as well as for differences in year of introduction.[13] Another overall indicator, with price effects taken out, was estimated using regression analysis.

A *long-term market share* index was developed using domestic unit sales share (in cars) on the assumption that a firm's domestic market position plays a strategically important role in the firm's competitive performance. Alternative indicators showing changes in the share of recent 6-year cumulative sales against a previous 6-year period or the recent 12-year period were also calculated. Six-year cumulative share was regarded as a rough approximation of the share of the car population in one generation, 12-year cumulative share as that of the entire car population.[14] Results of these different indicators generally showed consistency.[15]

Table 1 Evaluation Criteria in the Design Quality Survey

S C A L E	5: Superior to rivals--one of the best in class 4: Better than rivals 3: Average--same as rivals 2: Worse than rivals 1: Inferior to rivals--one of the worst in class
C R I T E R I A	Concept. How well the total product concept fits target customer needs; total balance and consistency in all aspects of the product rather than a specific aspect; overall attractiveness of a vehicle. Styling. Aesthetic aspects of body exterior; ignore "absolute" styling sophistication and evaluate styling relative to rival products in light of target customer needs (thus a score for a minivan can be higher than that for a sports car); ignore fit and finish. Performance. How quickly, smoothly, and safely the car starts, runs, turns, and stops; measures an assessment of overall performance relative to rival products in light of target customer needs and encompasses handling, acceleration, and braking. Comfort. Degree of comfort in driver, navigator, and rear seats, including measures such as ride, noise, vibration, interior aesthetics, roominess, air conditioning, and other ergonomic aspects relative to rival products in light of target customer needs. Value for Money. Overall appraisal, which may include initial cost, resale value, maintenance costs, and operating costs; these factors as a whole may vary in importance for different types of vehicles. Overall. Overall evaluation of a product's design quality.

Source: Instruction for respondents to the design quality survey.

These indicators were used to calculate a *TPQ index*. Based on interviews and other industry experience, we subjectively assigned specific weights to each indicator: 0.3 for perceived total quality; 0.1 for conformance quality; 0.4 for design quality; 0.1 for long-term share improvement. For the first three categories, we assigned 100 points to the top one-third organizations, 50 points to the middle one-third group, and 0 points to the bottom one-third. Disagreements among the indicators were resolved by applying the "democracy" rule. For market share increase, we assigned 100 points for share gain, 50 points for share loss, and 75 points for border cases. The TPQ index was thus the weighted average of the four indicators.

Although the index is a convenient way to summarize evidence, the use of subjective weights raises the possibility of biases in the analysis. It appears to us, however, that the index as reported is a fair summary of the evidence in the multiple indicators. First, indicator weights were corroborated by most of the companies studied by virtue of general agreement with their rankings. Second, the rankings, particularly at the tails of the distribution, were relatively insensitive to application of different weights. As the data in Figure 4.5 illustrate, the top firms are strong in all measures while the bottom firms are uniformly weak. Since our basic interest in the analysis was on relatively broad groupings of firms (i.e., top or bottom one-third), the basic conclusions in the chapters dealing with total product quality (see especially Chapters 9 and 10) are little affected by changes in relative weights. It is important to note that the index is already adjusted for relevant project-specific factors such as price and product categories. Thus, unlike engineering hours and lead time, we do not need any further statistical adjustment for project content variables.

PROJECT CONTENT VARIABLES

Three subgroups of project-specific factors that might affect engineering hours and lead time were identified: product complexity (e.g., price, body types); technological innovativeness; and project scope (e.g., common parts, supplier involvement). Although we examined many indicators in the preliminary analysis stage, we used six indicators for the main analysis reported in the book. These are described in Table 2.

Table 2 Selected Project Content Variables

Product Complexity	Retail Price. Average suggested retail price of the major versions of each model in 1987 U.S. dollars is used as an indicator of product complexity. Prices of models not sold in the U.S. market are estimated by multiplying the relative price ratio of an equivalent global model by the ratio of the U.S. retail price of that model. Number of Body Types. The number of significantly different body variations, in terms of number of doors, side silhouette, and other major features, is used as an indicator of project complexity.
Technological Innovativeness Index	Pioneering Component Index. Project engineers' subjective judgments established innovativeness relative to competing products in five major component areas: body/paint; engine; transmission/transaxle; electric/electronics; steering/brake/suspension. A value of 1 was assigned if the product was pioneering in at least one component area, otherwise 0. Major Body Change Index. Project engineers' subjective judgments established as an indicator of innovativeness the amount of development effort required in four major process-technology areas: final assembly; painting; body welding; stamping. A value of 1 was assigned if the product had a major change in at least one process, otherwise 0.
Project Scope Index	Common Parts Ratio. The fraction of total parts that a model shares in common with other models (both its predecessor and other models still in production) at the level of engineering drawings. Supplier Participation Ratio. The fraction of component developmental workload carried out by parts suppliers was calculated on the basis of the project engineer's estimate of the degree of supplier engineering (in terms of purchasing cost) in three types of parts: supplier proprietary parts (developed 100% by suppliers as standard products); black box parts (developed jointly with car makers doing basic engineering --30%--and suppliers doing detailed engineering--70%); detail-controlled parts (developed 100% by car makers).

PRODUCT-LINE POLICY INDICATORS

Indicators representing each producer's basic product-line policy, including rate of product renewal, rate of model proliferation, and pace of overall product development (see Chapter 3) are taken from Sheriff.[16] The *output index* measures the number of new models a company introduced between 1981 and 1988, scaled to the number of the company's models in 1981. It thus reflects how frequently a company carried out major product development projects during the mid 1980s. This index can be broken down in terms of whether major model development is for replacement of an existing model or expansion of the model mix (model proliferation). The *replacement index* is used to measure the percentage of product a company replaced between 1981 and 1988. It provides a reasonably good proxy for the company's product replacement cycles: the higher the index, the shorter the model renewal cycles. The *expansion index* accounts for new models that contributed to expanding a company's model line. It is assumed that a manufacturer with a high expansion index is able to respond more flexibly to diversification of market needs.

MANUFACTURING CAPABILITY

Two indicators of manufacturing capability were analyzed statistically: prototype lead time and die lead time (Chapters 7 and 8).

Prototype lead time. Lead time to develop the first engineering prototype—the first physical representation of the total vehicle, as opposed to such partial prototypes as clay models, mockups, and mechanical and component prototypes—is divided into (1) the time from the release of the first prototype parts drawing to prototype parts makers (in-house or outside) to the final release of parts drawings, and (2) the time from final release of drawings to completion of the prototype. We call these periods *drawing release lead time and post-release lead time*, respectively. The former may reflect either cross-component differences in parts design speed or differences in prototype parts procurement lead time. A large fraction of the latter is prototype assembly lead time.

Die lead time. Process engineering's development of tools and equipment is measured in terms of the months required to design and fabricate a die set for a major body panel such as a rear fender or quarter panel. Total die lead time is divided into (1) the time from the first release of rough body part drawings to final detailed drawing release, (2) the time from final release of parts drawings to delivery of dies, and (3) the time from die delivery to completion of tryouts. The first phase corresponds roughly to the die planning period (developing process sequence plans, estimating costs, and so forth), the second phase to the die manufacturing period (casting, machining, assembly, finishing). Detailed die design is carried out during the first few months of the second period, often in parallel with casting. Thus, we call the three components of total die lead time *die planning lead time, die manufacturing lead time,* and *tryout lead time.* In this book, we use total die lead time (Chapter 8) and die manufacturing lead time (Chapter 7) for statistical analysis.

ORGANIZATION AND PROCESS

Indices in this category (excepting the simultaneity ratio and number of project participants) are constructed from multiple indicators of organization and process. Table 3 lists 29 qualitative variables (0 or 1) representing organizational aspects of effective volume producers of the 1980s and 6 variables representing organizational aspects of effective high-end specialists of this period. Most of the indices are constructed by adding up affirmative cases for these variables or their subsets. Since each organizational variable represents part of the hypothetical "ideal pattern" for successful product development, aggregated, they make up consistency, or "ideal profile," indices.[17] The ten indices are listed in Table 4.

DATA ANALYSIS

Statistical data analyses were employed to examine the relations among performance, project content, and organization, to calculate adjusted engineering hours and lead time for each project, and to estimate the performance difference after adjustment across regions and strategies. The statistical methods applied here are relatively simple: ordinary least squares regression for project-level data (24 to 29 samples) and Spearman rank order correlation for organization-

Table 3 List of Organizational Variables

1. Variables for Effective Volume Producers

1. Product managers exist
2. Product managers are responsible for wide development stages/areas
3. Project liaison teams or task forces exist
4. Liaison roles exist
5. Project team is composed of people from a broad range of functions
6. Project execution teams exist
7. Product managers maintain direct market contact
8. Concept creators have strong influence over marketing decisions
9. Concepts are created through cross-functional discussion under the leadership of concept creators
10. Concept generation and product planning stages are merged
11. Concept creators perform product planning
12. Concept creators perform layout
13. Simultaneous development of concept and styling
14. Simultaneous development of layout, styling, and engine choice
15. Product managers perform product planning
16. Product managers are responsible for layout
17. Product managers perform concept generation
18. Product managers have significant influence (formally and informally) over product engineering
19. Product managers maintain direct contact with working engineers
20. Liaison persons have strong influence over working engineers
21. Many prototypes are developed and tested
22. Prototypes are built quickly
23. Test engineers cannot veto product designs
24. Early feedback from manufacturing
25. Project teams involve process engineering
26. Product managers have strong influence outside the engineering function
27. Manufacturing cannot veto product designs
28. High degree of overlap between product and process development
29. High perceived effectiveness of product-process communication

2. Variables for Effective High-End Specialists

1. Product managers do not exist or have narrow responsibility
2. Centralized concept creation units
3. Sequential and perfectionistic engineering (reflected in engineering lead time)
4. High degree of goal achievement in product performance
5. Test engineers can veto product designs
6. Emphasis on prototype testing (reflected in number of prototypes)

Table 4 Organization and Process Indices

<table>
<tr>
<td rowspan="2">I
N
D
I
C
E
S</td>
<td>

<u>Overall Integration Index (consistency index for volume producers)</u>. A composite of four subindices (external integration index, internal integration index, integrated engineering index, and other integration mechanisms index) constructed by aggregating affirmative answers to a subset of the 29 organizational variables. The index is a rough approximation of organizational pattern consistency since apparent differences in importance of the 29 variables are not taken into account.

<u>External Integration Index</u>. A subindex of the overall integration index (variables 1, 2, 7, 15–20, and 26 in Table 3) that measures pattern consistency in terms of strong power/influence and wide responsibility of external integrators, typically product concept creators (see Chapter 9).

<u>Internal Integration Index</u>. A subindex of the overall integration index (variables 8–14 and 17 in Table 3) that measures pattern consistency in terms of strong power/influence and wide responsibility of internal integrators, particularly the product manager as full-time project coordinator (see Chapter 9).

<u>Integrated Engineering Index</u>. A third component of the overall integration index (variables 21–24 and 27–29 in Table 3) that represents integrated and short-cycle engineering for both product and process.

<u>Other Integration Mechanisms Index</u>. The final component of the overall integration index (variables 3–6 and 25 in Table 3) that measures the existence of cross-functional coordination mechanisms other than full-time product manager, including cross-functional task forces, project teams, and liaison roles.

<u>Integrated Problem-Solving Index</u>. A combination of the internal integration index and integrated engineering index meant to represent the intensive communication and short-cycle problem solving needed for effective implementation of simultaneous engineering or overlapping problem solving (see Chapter 8).

<u>Organizational Type Index</u>. Rearranges the variables used in the external and internal integration indices (variables 1, 2, 7–20, and 26 in Table 3) so that the 22 sample organizations are placed on an organizational spectrum ranging from functional organization to heavyweight product manager system (see Chapter 9).

<u>High-End Specialist Index</u>. An aggregate of the six variables for effective high-end specialists meant to represent pattern consistency for a successful high-end specialist of the 1980s (e.g., sequential problem solving, functional specialization, perfectionistic engineering).

<u>Simultaneity Ratio</u>. Derived from stage-by-stage schedule data, it measures the degree of overlap in product and process engineering from a timing perspective (see Chapter 8).

<u>Number of Project Participants</u>. A surrogate for the degree of specialization at the individual level; the higher the number (of dedicated project participants, including those who worked for more than one project), the higher the specialization level (see Chapter 9).

</td>
</tr>
</table>

level data (15 to 22 samples). The latter was adopted to avoid the potential problem of small sample size.

BASIC REGRESSION RESULTS: THE EXAMPLE OF ENGINEERING HOURS

Tables 5 to 8 present basic regression models for four performance variables: engineering hours, overall (concept to market) lead time, planning lead time, and engineering lead time. Dummy variables representing regional and strategic groups, and major project content variables, such as price, body types, innovativeness, and project scope, are included in the models. Both linear and logarithmic (log) specifications are presented, the former for estimating the impact of project content on performance in absolute terms, the latter for estimating the impact in relative terms. To simplify interpretation of the results, the same model specifications were applied to the four performance criteria (10 models for each dependent variable). The tables present estimated regression coefficients and standard errors for the independent variables and adjusted R^2 as a summary of each model.

We illustrate the regression analysis for engineering hours (in thousands of hours) in Table 5. Model EH1 shows regional differences for *unadjusted* engineering hours. The Japanese producer group having been selected as the base case, the constant term of model EH1 (i.e., 1.155 million hours) is average unadjusted engineering hours in sample Japanese projects. Regression coefficients for the two dummy variables (i.e., 2.323 million hours and 2.363 million hours) represent differences in U.S.-Japan and Europe-Japan averages, respectively. The sum of the constant term and each regional coefficient (i.e., 3.478 million and 3.518 million hours) thus represents the regional averages of the U.S. and European groups, respectively. The small size of the standard errors implies that regional gaps are statistically significant. Model EH2 examines a similar comparison of unadjusted engineering hours with the Europeans further divided into high-end specialists and volume producers and with similar results.

Correcting the performance averages by project content generally narrows cross-regional differences in engineering hours. Model EH3, for example, adjusts engineering hours by project complexity (price, body types) and innovativeness (pioneering component, body major change). Model EH4 further corrects engineering hour data for

Table 5 Basic Regression Results for Engineering Hours

Independent Variable \ Model	Engineering Hours (000 H)						ln (engineering hours)			
	EH1	EH2	EH3	EH4	EH5	EH6	EH7	EH8	EH9	EH10
Constant	1,155	1,155	-1,329	-7,710	-7,713	-6,779	1.675	2.041	2.565	0.094
U.S. Company	2,323† (724)	2,323† (738)	1,794* (768)	1,075# (575)	1,073# (602)	1,521* (581)	0.678* (0.289)	0.486# (0.250)	1.088† (0.368)	
European Company	2,263† (604)		1,510# (772)	801 (577)		1,302* (556)	0.706* (0.277)	0.531* (0.239)	0.871† (0.276)	
European Volume Producer		2,252† (702)			805 (616)					
High-End Specialist		2,281* (852)			785 (1021)					
Retail Price ($000)			0.050 (0.038)	0.071* (0.028)	0.072# (0.038)	0.050# (0.028)	*0.459* (0.219)	*0.514* (0.185)	*0.397* (0.181)	*0.730†* (0.175)
Number of Body Types			530# (291)	874† (222)	873† (230)	738† (229)	0.329* (0.102)	0.428† (0.091)	0.357† (0.095)	0.509† (0.098)
Innovativeness (pioneering component)			742 (680)	828 (490)	825 (526)		0.292 (0.246)	0.310 (0.206)	0.403# (0.198)	0.459# (0.225)
Innovativeness (major body change)			912 (592)	554 (434)	558 (482)		0.459* (0.214)	0.343# (0.183)	0.292 (0.173)	0.381# (0.197)
Unique Parts Ratio (1 - C)									*1.247†* (0.317)	*1.077†* (0.365)
In-House Component Engineering Ratio (1 - S)									*0.148* (0.489)	*1.241†* (0.404)
Project Scope Index (NH)				9,656† (2,090)	9,655† (2,141)	10,103† (2,202)		*1.857†* (0.582)		
Sample Size	29	29	29	29	29	29	29	29	29	29
Adjusted R-squared	0.38	0.33	0.40	0.69	0.67	0.64	0.59	0.71	0.74	0.64
Degrees of Freedom	26	25	22	21	20	23	22	21	20	22

Note: Standard errors in parentheses. Price coefficients in the lead time regressions have been multiplied by 10^3.
† Statistically significant at 1% level
* Statistically significant at 5% level
# Statistically significant at 10% level
ln Natural log
Italic characters represent natural log transformation of independent variables.

Table 6 Basic Regression Results for Overall Lead Time

Independent Variable \ Dependent Variable / Model	Overall Lead Time (months)						ln (lead time)			
	LT1	LT2	LT3	LT4	LT5	LT6	LT7	LT8	LT9	LT10
Constant	42.6	42.6	36.1	10.6	11.4	13.4	2.87	2.94	3.08	2.10
U.S. Company	19.3† (4.0)	19.3† (3.9)	15.9† (4.4)	13.0† (4.0)	13.6† (4.2)	14.7† (3.8)	0.299† (0.083)	0.260† (0.080)	0.409† (0.122)	
European Company	18.1† (3.4)		14.1† (4.4)	11.3* (4.1)		12.7† (3.6)	0.294† (0.030)	0.258† (0.077)	0.342† (0.092)	
European Volume Producer		15.0† (3.7)			10.4* (4.3)					
High-End Specialist		23.4† (4.5)			15.6* (7.1)					
Retail Price ($000)			0.34 (0.22)	0.42* (0.20)	0.29 (0.27)	0.33# (0.18)	0.091 (0.063)	0.102 (0.060)	0.073 (0.060)	0.204† (0.062)
Number of Body Types			0.07 (1.66)	1.45 (1.57)	1.61 (1.60)	1.00 (1.50)	0.003 (0.030)	0.024 (0.029)	0.006 (0.032)	0.065# (0.034)
Innovativeness (pioneering component)			1.42 (3.88)	1.76 (3.45)	2.56 (3.65)		-0.001 (0.071)	0.003 (0.066)	0.025 (0.066)	0.051 (0.080)
Innovativeness (major body change)			4.97 (3.38)	3.54 (3.05)	2.59 (3.34)		0.100 (0.062)	0.076 (0.059)	0.063 (0.058)	0.094 (0.070)
Unique Parts Ratio (1 - C)									0.271* (0.106)	0.209 (0.129)
In-House Component Engineering Ratio (1 - S)									-0.003 (0.163)	0.411† (0.143)
Project Scope Index (NH)				38.6* (14.7)	38.8* (14.9)	41.5† (14.4)		0.383# (0.187)		
Sample Size	29	29	29	29	29	29	29	29	29	29
Adjusted R-squared	0.56	0.59	0.57	0.66	0.65	0.66	0.59	0.64	0.66	0.47
Degrees of Freedom	26	25	22	21	20	23	22	21	20	22

Note: Standard errors in parentheses. Price coefficients in the lead time regressions have been multiplied by 10^3.
  † Statistically significant at 1% level
  * Statistically significant at 5% level
  # Statistically significant at 10% level
  ln Natural log
Italic characters represent natural log transformation of independent variables.

Table 7 Basic Regression Results for Planning Lead Time

Independent Variable / Model	Planning Lead Time (months)						ln (planning lead time)			
	PT1	PT2	PT3	PT4	PT5	PT6	PT7	PT8	PT9	PT10
Constant	13.6	13.6	9.0	-27.1	-27.0	-24.6	1.77	2.16	2.56	2.10
U.S. Company	9.2*	9.2*	7.9	3.8	3.9	4.4	0.30	0.10	0.56#	
	(3.9)	(4.0)	(4.6)	(3.6)	(3.8)	(3.4)	(0.26)	(0.21)	(0.30)	
European Company	6.2#		3.7	0.3		1.3	0.29	0.10	0.36	
	(3.3)		(4.6)	(3.6)		(3.2)	(0.25)	(0.20)	(0.22)	
European Volume Producer		6.0			-0.5					
		(3.8)			(3.9)					
High-End Specialist		6.7			0.4					
		(4.6)			(6.4)					
Retail Price ($000)			0.13	0.24	0.22	0.24	*0.072*	*0.131*	*0.040*	*0.179*
			(0.23)	(0.18)	(0.24)	(0.16)	*(0.199)*	*(0.152)*	*(0.147)*	*(0.124)*
Number of Body Types			0.78	2.72#	2.75#	2.42#	*0.046*	*0.152#*	*0.104*	*0.169**
			(1.74)	(1.40)	(1.45)	(1.34)	*(0.093)*	*(0.075)*	*(0.077)*	*(0.069)*
Innovativeness (pioneering component)				3.13	3.62	3.75	*0.087*	*0.106*	*0.181*	*0.186*
				(4.07)	(3.08)	(3.30)	*(0.223)*	*(0.170)*	*(0.160)*	*(0.160)*
Innovativeness (major body change)				0.16	-1.87	-2.03	*-0.002*	*-0.126*	*-0.168*	*-0.111*
				(3.54)	(2.73)	(3.03)	*(0.194)*	*(0.151)*	*(0.141)*	*(0.140)*
Unique Parts Ratio (1 - C)									*1.273†*	*1.173†*
									(0.258)	*(0.259)*
In-House Component Engineering Ratio (1 - S)									*0.432*	*0.975†*
									(0.397)	*(0.026)*
Project Scope Index (NH)				54.7†	54.7†	53.0†		*1.978†*		
				(13.1)	(13.5)	(12.8)		*(0.478)*		
Sample Size	29	29	29	29	29	29	29	29	29	29
Adjusted R-squared	0.14	0.11	0.02	0.44	0.41	0.45	-0.05	0.40	0.48	0.44
Degrees of Freedom	26	25	22	21	20	23	22	21	20	22

Note: Standard errors in parentheses. Price coefficients in the lead time regressions have been multiplied by 10^3.
† Statistically significant at 1% level
* Statistically significant at 5% level
# Statistically significant at 10% level
ln Natural log
Italic characters represent natural log transformation of independent variables.

Table 8 Basic Regression Results for Engineering Lead Time

Independent Variable \ Dependent Variable \ Model	Engineering Lead Time (months)						ln (engineering lead time)			
	ET1	ET2	ET3	ET4	ET5	ET6	ET7	ET8	ET9	ET10
Constant	30.8	30.8	23.6	21.9	21.9	25.0	1.86	1.84	1.96	1.06
U.S. Company	9.3* (3.6)	9.3* (3.4)	5.1 (3.4)	4.9 (3.7)	4.9 (3.8)	7.3# (3.8)	0.149 (0.108)	0.158 (0.113)	0.274 (0.179)	
European Company	11.1† (3.0)		7.1# (3.5)	6.9# (3.7)		8.1* (3.7)	0.227* (0.103)	0.235* (0.108)	0.301* (0.134)	
European Volume Producer		8.2* (3.3)				6.9# (3.9)				
High-End Specialist		16.2† (4.0)				6.8 (6.5)				
Retail Price ($000)			0.39* (0.17)	0.39* (0.18)	0.40 (0.24)	0.24 (0.18)	*0.161# (0.082)*	*0.158# (0.084)*	*0.137 (0.088)*	*0.251† (0.77)*
Number Of Body Types			-0.14 (1.31)	-0.05 (1.41)	-0.52 (1.46)	-0.61 (1.51)	-0.000 (0.38)	-0.005 (0.041)	-0.021 (0.046)	0.029 (0.043)
Innovativeness (pioneering component)			0.54 (3.04)	0.57 (3.11)	0.55 (3.34)		-0.040 (0.092)	-0.041 (0.093)	-0.025 (0.096)	0.013 (0.099)
Innovativeness (major body change)			7.33* (2.65)	7.23* (2.75)	7.26* (3.06)		0.237† (0.080)	0.243† (0.083)	0.232* (0.084)	-0.111 (0.140)
Unique Parts Ratio (1 - C)									*0.013 (0.154)*	*-0.180 (0.160)*
In-House Component Engineering Ratio (1 - S)									*-0.209 (0.238)*	*0.087 (0.177)*
Project Scope Index (NH)				2.6 (13.3)	2.6 (13.6)	8.7 (14.5)		*-0.087 (0.264)*		
Sample Size	29	29	29	29	29	29	29	29	29	29
Adjusted R-squared	0.32	0.38	0.49	0.46	0.43	0.34	0.46	0.40	0.42	0.34
Degrees Of Freedom	26	25	22	21	20	23	22	21	20	22

Note: Standard errors in parentheses. Price coefficients in the lead time regressions have been multiplied by 10[3].
† Statistically significant at 1% level
* Statistically significant at 5% level
# Statistically significant at 10% level
ln Natural log
Italic characters represent natural log transformation of independent variables.

project scope. Regression coefficients for project content variables are all positive and those for price, body type, and project scope are statistically significant. Model EH5, which separates European firms into high-end and volume producers, generates very similar results, suggesting that average high-end specialists and average volume producers are not significantly different in terms of development productivity.

Except for innovativeness, our measures of product content are significant and have the expected effects. Because innovation variables are based on engineers' judgments of degree of innovation, it is not surprising that they are not statistically significant. (We experimented with a variety of other specifications of the innovation variables, but found little explanatory power in them.) However, the results suggest that more innovative projects may require more hours—a reasonable expectation—and that there may be important regional differences. The regional dummies have smaller coefficients, with the innovation variables included. We investigated the innovation effect further by running Model EH4 for volume producers only. We found that innovation variables were even less significant and regional effects were not statistically different if innovation variables were excluded. On further examination it became apparent that the effects of the innovation variables in Model EH4 were the result of unusual circumstances (i.e., outlier effects) surrounding two high-end projects. For these reasons, we decided to estimate Model EH6 without the innovation variables. The estimates of adjusted engineering hours used in this book (i.e., our measure of development productivity) were calculated from Model EH6.

Models EH7 to EH10 present log specifications that estimate the impact of project content on engineering hours in relative terms. Coefficients for the price and project scope index represent "elasticity," or increase in engineering hours in percentage when the content variable is increased by 1 percent. These results do not change the qualitative conclusions based on the linear specification in Models 1 through 6.

Models EH9 and EH10 separate the effect of project scope into the unique parts ratio (reverse of common parts) and in-house component engineering ratio (reverse of supplier participation ratio). Model EH9 includes regional dummy variables, Model EH10 excludes them. These results shed light on the regional character of the impact of suppliers. For Model EH9, in which regional effects are taken into account, the supplier variable is small and insignificant. When we drop the regional effects in EH10, the supplier variable is quite strong and significant, implying that the effect of suppliers in our data is a regional phenomenon. In effect, we find that although supplier involvement plays a major role in explaining differences between Japanese firms and their Western competitors, it does not explain variation in performance within regions. Use of off-the-shelf parts, however, has a strong effect with or without the region effects included. Thus, the effect of parts strategy is not a regional phenomenon; it applies both within and across regions.

We proceeded in a similar manner for overall lead time, planning lead time, and engineering lead time. Model specifications are comparable across all tables. For engineering hours and lead time we use Models EH6 and LT6 to estimate "adjusted engineering hours" (our measure of development productivity) and "adjusted lead time" (our measure of the speed of development). In correlation analysis and in scatter diagrams (see Chapters 8–10), we use the residuals from the regressions as our measure of adjusted engineering hours and lead time. (Note that in the scatter diagrams we have added back the coefficients on the regional dummies to the residuals so that the diagrams capture regional effects.) We also use the regressions to estimate hours (or time) required to develop a standard product (see Chapter 4). We do this by entering into the regression model the price, body types, and project scope associated with a standard vehicle, multiplying by the regression coefficients, and adding them together with the constant term and appropriate regional effects (e.g., we use the European dummy for the European projects).

REGRESSION RESULTS FOR TOTAL PRODUCT QUALITY

Unlike hours and lead time, our total product quality index already has been corrected for differences in price class, target market, and overall product complexity by the way we defined the underlying variables. However, further analysis is needed to see if there are regional differences and to determine whether the index is associated with project scope and the amount of innovative effort in the project. We examine these issues in Table 9. The regressions show no statistically significant differences in regional averages of the overall index and

Table 9 Regression Results for Total Product Quality

Independent Variable / Model	Total Product Quality		
	TPQ1	TPQ2	TPQ3
Constant	53.4	-8.1	-9.8
U.S. Company	-17.3 (13.8)	-29.3 (14.4)	-27.2 (13.5)
European Company	2.9 (11.5)	-1.2 (12.4)	-2.3 (11.0)
Innovativeness (pioneering component)		-.32 (12.41)	
Innovativeness (major body change)		9.62 (10.82)	
Project Scope Index (NH)		99.0# (51.3)	110.1* (48.6)
Sample Size	29	29	29
Adjusted R-squared	0.01	0.10	0.14
Degrees of Freedom	26	23	25

Note: Standard errors in parentheses.
† Statistically significant at 1% level
* Statistically significant at 5% level
# Statistically significant at 10% level

little effect of the degree of innovation. We find, however, that project scope has a positive effect. It appears that using more new parts and doing work in-house has a positive effect on product quality.

REGRESSION RESULTS FOR MANUFACTURING CAPABILITY

We next examined whether lead time for manufacturing activities in development affects development performance and regional differences in performance. We tried three indicators, prototype lead time, die manufacturing lead time, and total die lead time, the first two to reflect a project's capability in short-cycle manufacturing, the latter is an indicator of integrated problem solving in engineering. Table 10 presents the result for engineering hours, overall lead time, planning lead time, and engineering lead time.

For each performance measure, we started with the basic regression models for adjustment (EH6, LT6, PT6, and ET6 in Tables 5–8) and added one of three prototype/die variables. The results suggest little connection with engineering hours but a strong impact on lead time. As noted in the text, for example, the coefficient on prototype lead time in Model ET11 suggests that a one-month decrease in prototype time leads to a one-month decrease in engineering lead time.

We also examined the effect of die lead time on process engineering stage length. As discussed in the text, this gives us a chance to see the impact of rapid die manufacturing on the completeness of design at pilot production. Regressions in Table 11 show no statistically significant differences in average stage length, although mean values for European and U.S. firms are a few months above those for Japanese firms. However, when we control for product content, scope, and die lead time, we find that Western firms spend less "effective" time in process engineering, given the complexity of their products and the length of time required to design and build dies.

REGRESSION RESULTS FOR INTEGRATED ENGINEERING PROBLEM SOLVING

Table 12 summarizes regression results for integrated problem solving. We first look at the engineering simultaneity ratio and its impact on engineering lead time. The results show a negative effect of the simultaneity ratio on lead time, particularly when regional effects

Table 10 Regression Results for Manufacturing Capability

Independent Variable \ Dependent Variable / Model	Engineering Hours (000 H)			Overall Lead Time (months)			Planning Lead Time (months)			Engineering Lead Time (months)		
	EH11	EH12	EH13	LT11	LT12	LT13	PT11	PT12	PT13	ET11	ET12	ET13
Constant	-7,464	-6,489	-7,659	2.9	12.2	6.5	-22.5	-17.9	-28.6	12.8	18.3	18.3
U.S. Company	1,020 (801)	1,568 (1,042)	742 (943)	7.3 (4.6)	8.1 (5.8)	7.3 (5.3)	5.2 (4.7)	6.8 (5.4)	-0.4 (5.3)	-1.5 (4.0)	0.9 (4.7)	-0.2 (4.2)
European Company	867 (731)	1,301 (1,258)	292 (1,135)	6.3 (4.2)	6.1 (7.0)	5.0 (6.4)	1.9 (4.3)	3.5 (6.6)	-5.5 (6.3)	0.5 (3.6)	3.9 (5.7)	2.8 (5.0)
Retail Price ($)	0.054# (0.029)	.056 (.034)	.051 (.033)	0.37* (0.16)	0.33 (0.19)	0.24 (0.19)	0.24 (0.17)	0.25 (0.18)	0.26 (0.19)	0.30* (0.14)	0.19 (0.15)	0.05 (0.15)
Number of Body Types	733† (236)	739* (345)	672* (301)	1.02 (1.36)	0.06 (1.92)	0.94 (1.70)	2.17 (1.39)	1.53 (1.80)	1.61 (1.68)	-0.67 (1.18)	0.14 (1.55)	-0.07 (1.34)
Project Scope Index (NH)	10,816† (2,298)	10,556† (2,731)	10,826† (2,533)	51.1† (13.2)	46.5† (15.2)	43.1† (14.3)	54.2† (13.5)	52.0† 14.3	56.4† (14.1)	20.9# (11.5)	13.4 (12.3)	8.4 (11.3)
Prototype Lead Time (months)	58.2 (91.2)			0.93# (0.53)			-0.27 (0.54)			1.05* (0.46)		
Die Manufacturing Lead Time (months)		-25.2 (75.6)			0.44 (0.42)			-0.48 (0.40)			0.64# 0.34	
Total Die Lead Time (months)			52.4 (61.4)			0.58 (0.35)			0.32 (0.34)			0.64* (0.27)
Sample Size	28	24	25	28	24	25	28	24	25	28	24	25
Adjusted R-squared	0.63	0.59	0.63	0.72	0.77	0.73	0.44	0.46	0.46	0.52	0.56	0.59
Degrees of Freedom	21	17	18	21	17	18	21	17	18	21	17	18

Note: Standard errors in parentheses. Price coefficients in the lead time regressions have been multiplied by 10^3
·† Statistically significant at 1% level
* Statistically significant at 5% level
# Statistically significant at 10% level

Table 11 Regional Differences in Process Engineering Stage Length

Independent Variable	Dependent Variable / Model	Process Engineering Stage Length	
		PE1	PE2
Constant		21.6	-0.8
U.S. Company		4.5 (3.8)	-9.6# (4.9)
European Company		5.2 (3.2)	-17.1† (5.9)
Retail Price ($000)			0.50† (0.17)
Number of Body Types			-1.92 (1.57)
Project Scope Index (NH)			25.7# (13.2)
Total Die Lead Time			0.66* (0.32)
Sample Size		29	25
Adjusted R-squared		0.03	0.41
Degrees of Freedom		26	18

Note: Standard errors in parentheses. Price coefficient has been multiplied by 10^3.

† Statistically significant at 1% level
* Statistically significant at 5% level
# Statistically significant at 10% level

Table 12 Basic Regression Results for Integrated Engineering Problem Solving

Independent Variable \ Dependent Variable / Model	Engineering Simultaneity Ratio		Engineering Lead Time (months)		Conformance Quality (1985)		Conformance Quality (1987)		Total Product Quality Index	
	SR1	SR2	ET14	ET15	CQ1	CQ2	CQ3	CQ4	TPQ4	TPQ5
Constant	1.75	1.41	37.9	40.8	19.1	20.6	4.0	17.2	-2.2	25.8
U.S. Company	-0.17 (0.11)	-.23# (0.18)	5.2 (4.0)		1.5 (3.5)		11.4† (3.4)		9.3 (14.5)	
European Company	-0.20* (0.09)	-0.33† (0.11)	5.0 (4.2)		1.0 (3.2)		10.2† (3.1)		28.7* (12.8)	
Retail Price ($000)		0.12* (0.06)	0.35# (0.20)	0.45† (0.15)						
Number of Body Types		0.04 (0.05)	-0.23 (1.50)	0.30 (1.40)						
Project Scope Index (NH)		0.24 (0.45)	10.96 (14.29)	18.5 (13.3)						
Engineering Simultaneity Ratio			-9.18 (6.66)	-13.8* (5.6)						
Index of Integrated Problem Solving					-2.12* (0.77)	-2.32† (0.58)	0.33 (0.76)	-1.4# (0.75)	10.27† (3.23)	6.41* (2.5)
Sample Size	29	29	29	29	23	23	23	23	29	29
Adjusted R-squared	0.10	0.15	0.36	0.36	0.35	0.40	0.43	0.11	0.27	0.16
Degrees of Freedom	26	23	22	24	22	21	19	21	25	27

Note: Standard errors in parentheses. Price coefficients have been multiplied by 10^4 (SR2) or 10^3 (ET14).

  † Statistically significant at 1% level
  * Statistically significant at 5% level
  # Statistically significant at 10% level

are excluded (Model ET15), suggesting that the effect is largely regional in character. The magnitude of the coefficient in ET15 implies that a move from totally sequential engineering (SR=1) to totally simultaneous (SR=2) would reduce engineering lead time by 13.8 months.

Table 12 also presents evidence on the impact of integrated problem solving on product quality. The regressions show a strong effect on the total product-quality index, an effect that is not regional in character (the coefficient is strong with or without the regional dummies). Regressions with conformance quality data as the dependent variable indicate that the level of integrated problem solving is connected to measures of product reliability in the field, although 1987 results suggest that in that year, the effect was weaker and largely a Japanese phenomenon. (Note that the coefficient on the index signifies that a high level of integration is associated with fewer technical problems in the first three months of ownership.)

RANK CORRELATIONS AMONG PERFORMANCE INDICATORS

Table 13 summarizes rank-order correlations among the three performance criteria aggregated at the organization level (sample = 22). No significant correlations are identified between total product quality and the other two performance variables, suggesting that total product quality has to be explained by something else, such as organization and management. As noted in Chapter 4, there is a significant positive correlation between adjusted engineering hours and adjusted lead time.

Table 13 Rank Correlations between Performance Indicators

	Adjusted Development Productivity	Adjusted Speed of Development	Total Product Quality
Adjusted Development Productivity (high = efficient development)	1.00	0.58† (22)	0.07 (22)
Adjusted Speed Of Development (high = fast development)		1.00	-0.03 (22)
Total Product Quality			1.00

Note: Spearman rank correlation coefficients are presented. Sample size in parentheses.
† Significant at 1% level

RANK CORRELATION BETWEEN ORGANIZATIONAL MANAGEMENT AND PERFORMANCE

Results of a series of rank correlation analyses of performance variables and various indicators of organization, process, and management are summarized in Table 14. Data analyzed here are aggregated at the organizational level. Cases may be inclusive or exclusive, depending upon the purpose of analysis, and sample size may vary due to missing or inappropriate values. Engineering hours and lead time are already adjusted for project content, and total product quality is adjusted for project content as defined and measured. The results underscore the close association of patterns of consistency and high performance development for volume producers. In contrast, the patterns for effective high-end specialists show little relationship to performance for volume producers.

Table 14 Rank Correlation between Organization/Management and Performance

Construct	Indicator	Interpretation of Ranking	Adjusted Development Productivity High=Efficient	Adjusted Speed of Development High=Fast	Total Product Quality
Product-Line Policy	Output Index	High = frequent product development per model	0.60† (22)	0.58† (22)	0.20 (22)
	Replacement Index	High = frequent product renewals	0.29 (22)	0.40# (22)	0.28 (22)
	Expansion Index	High = fast product proliferation	0.50* (22)	0.49* (22)	0.08 (22)
Manufacturing Capability	Adjusted Assembly Productivity	High = efficient assembly operation	0.34 (18)	0.42# (18)	-0.21 (18)
Integrated Problem Solving	Adjusted Engineering Simultaneity Ratio	High = high stage overlapping	0.16 (22)	0.57† (22)	-0.06 (22)
	Integrated Problem-Solving Index	High = close connection and fast cycles	0.45* (22)	0.54† (22)	0.22 (22)
Specialization	Adjusted Number of Project Participants	High = high individual specialization	-0.53* (16)	-0.67 (16)	0.05 (16)
Organizational Integration	Organizational Type Index	High = heavyweight product manager	0.45# (17)	0.63† (17)	0.51* (17)
Pattern Consistency for Volume Producer	Overall Integration Index	High= close to ideal profile for volume producer	0.47* (17)	0.62† (17)	0.70† (17)
	External Integration Index	High = strong concept creator/champion	0.24 (17)	0.40# (17)	0.74† (17)
	Internal Integration Index	High = strong product manager as coordinator	0.40# (17)	0.60* (17)	0.51* (17)
	Integrated Engineering Index	High = fast and integrated engineering	0.70† (17)	0.67† (17)	0.61* (17)
	Other Integration Mechanisms Index	High = existence of liaison, team, task force, etc.	-0.08 (17)	-0.21 (17)	0.51* (17)
Pattern Consistency for High-End Specialist	High-End Specialist Index	High = close to ideal profile for high-end specialist	-0.22 (17)	-0.47# (17)	0.16 (17)

Note: Spearman rank order correlation coefficients are presented. Sample size in parentheses. Italic characters signify that only volume producers are included.

† Statistically significant at 1% level
* Statistically significant at 5% level
# Statistically significant at 10% level

NOTES

1. For reasons of confidentiality of data, the names of neither the participating companies nor the sample projects are disclosed.

2. In 1987, countries other than these in North America (the United States and Canada), Western Europe, and Japan manufactured about 5 million cars, or about 15 percent of world production (33 million) in 1986.

3. For a definition of volume producers and high-end specialists, see Chapter 3.

4. There were two exceptions, one European project resulted in a 1980 market introduction, one Japanese project in a 1981 market introduction.

5. For example, histories of specific product development projects have recently become a popular subject of Japanese auto journals.

6. Exceptions were some U.S. producers, in which more than one product division had an independent R&D organization.

7. Development lead time begins with the first concept study meeting or when the participants of a concept study team are appointed. As versions developed by a project are often introduced to markets sequentially by body type or geographic market, introduction of the first version (typically sedans for the domestic market) is generally regarded as the end point for lead time. Although most of the companies studied maintained their schedule records in relation to start of production (SOP), start of sales was chosen as the end point for lead time in accordance with the customer-based view of product development. The present study suggests that volume production typically commences one to three months prior to market introduction.

8. All three total quality indices are based on the evaluations in the U.S. market, hence are subject to bias due to tastes specific to U.S. consumers.

9. Evaluations by *Consumer Reports* are generally known to be based both on design and conformance quality. This indicator is expected to show highly positive correlations with the "repurchase intention" index as the two evaluations share basic survey data.

10. Data were collected from *The Power Report*, news releases, and other publicly available sources.

11. The experts were asked to evaluate 68 individual models in the same manner.

12. In order to minimize potential biases because of the regional origins of the raters, the mean of the regional averages, instead of simple averages of the seven raters, were defined as total averages of the rating for each criterion. That is, the weight assigned to each rater for calculating the total average was one-sixth for U.S. and European raters, and one-ninth for Japanese raters. This seems to be a reasonable summary, as aggregate-unit car production volume by the producers studied was roughly comparable across the regions: 8 million in U.S.-Canada, 8 million in Japan, and 9 million in Western Europe in 1987. The resulting total averages were then converted to rankings for further analyses.

13. The original overall design quality index was intended to take within-segment price differences into account by incorporating "value for money" criteria. The design quality index without the price effect was then estimated using regression analysis. Specifically, the overall evaluation was regressed on the component criteria. Regression coefficients were regarded as weights each rater attached to the criteria and were used to calculate design quality evaluations without the "value for money" component. Averages of the new evaluations were regarded as price-unadjusted indices and converted to ranking for further analyses. Thus, two summary indices of design quality, one adjusted for within-segment price effect and the other unadjusted, were developed. In practice, the adjustments have little effect; the correlation between them is 0.94.

14. Scrappage patterns were assumed to be similar across the products within a given domestic market, hence changes in cumulative market shares could be directly translated into changes in the car population share.

15. The customer-base share index should not be compared across countries as it is based on sales in a specific market. What is important here is whether the customer base share increased or the customer base of the company expanded more rapidly than the overall customer base.

16. See, also, Sheriff (1988) and Fujimoto and Sheriff (1989).

17. See Van de Ven and Drazin (1985) and Venkatraman (1987) for a theoretical discussion of the use of the ideal profile index in studies of organization and strategy.

INDEX